The North Irish Irish Horse in the Great War

The Irishman is innately a good soldier, and,
above all things, loves a horse.

Navy & Army Illustrated, 2 August 1902, on formation of the North of
Ireland Imperial Yeomanry

The North Irish Horse in the Great War

Phillip Tardif

Pen & Sword
MILITARY

First published in Great Britain in 2015 by
Pen & Sword Military
an imprint of
Pen & Sword Books Ltd
47 Church Street
Barnsley
South Yorkshire
S70 2AS

Copyright © Phillip Tardif 2015

ISBN 978 1 47383 375 3

A CIP catalogue record for this book is available from the British
Library

Typeset in Ehrhardt by
Mac Style Ltd, Bridlington, East Yorkshire
Printed and bound in the UK by CPI Group (UK) Ltd,
Croydon, CRO 4YY

Pen & Sword Books Ltd incorporates the imprints of Pen & Sword
Archaeology, Atlas, Aviation, Battleground, Discovery, Family
History, History, Maritime, Military, Naval, Politics, Railways, Select,
Transport, True Crime, and Fiction, Frontline Books, Leo Cooper,
Praetorian Press, Seaforth Publishing and Wharncliffe.

For a complete list of Pen & Sword titles please contact
PEN & SWORD BOOKS LIMITED
47 Church Street, Barnsley, South Yorkshire, S70 2AS, England
E-mail: enquiries@pen-and-sword.co.uk
Website: www.pen-and-sword.co.uk

For my parents
John and Patricia

Contents

Maps, Figures and Illustrations   viii
Acknowledgements   xi
Glossary and Abbreviations   xiii
Introduction   xvi

Chapter 1   1908–1914: Farmers and Farmers' Sons   1

Chapter 2   1914: The Gay Careless Fox-hunters of the North   11

Chapter 3   1915: 'It's a Great Life Out Here'   63

Chapter 4   1916: No Role For Cavalry   97

Chapter 5   1917: Never Yet a Chance of Killing   139

Chapter 6   1918: Overwhelmed by the Hun   185

Chapter 7   1918: Gallant to a Degree   223

Chapter 8   1919 and Beyond: The Promise of a Nation's Gratitude   269

Postscript   282
Appendix I: North Irish Horse Timeline 1908 to 1919   285
Appendix II: Monthly Recruitment: August 1914 to December 1916   296
Appendix III: North Irish Horse Casualties 1914 to 1921   297
Appendix IV: North Irish Horse Awards and Decorations 1914 to 1919   314
Bibliography   323
Index   329

Maps, Figures and Illustrations

Maps

1. Ulster and the north of Ireland, 1914–1919   xxii
2. The retreat from Mons and Battle of the Marne, 1914   12
3. The Western Front, 1915   62
4. The Western Front, January to June 1916   98
5. The Western Front, July to December 1916   118
6. The Western Front, 1917   140
7. Trench raid near Havrincourt, 3–4 November 1917   166
8. The Western Front, 1918 – German Spring Offensives   184
9. German offensive on the Somme, 21 March to 5 April 1918   193
10. Advance to Victory, August to November 1918   222

Figures

1. Outline structure of British Expeditionary Force   xx
2. 1st North Irish Horse Regiment – structure   120
3. 36th (Ulster) Division, September 1917   159
4. North Irish Horse Cyclist Regiment   187
5. 36th (Ulster) Division, February 1918   190

Illustrations

A troop of the North of Ireland Imperial Yeomanry at annual camp at the Curragh, 1905. *(Image courtesy: Jim Crabtree)*

A private of the North of Ireland Imperial Yeomanry, 1902–08. *(Image from a collection by author R.J. Smith)*

Private Charles Delmege Trimble, dismounted review order, c.1908. *(Image from a collection by author R.J. Smith)*

Captain Eustace King-King, review order, c.1910. *(Image from a collection by author R.J. Smith)*

Lieutenant Samuel Barbour 'Barrie' Combe, first officer of the North Irish Horse killed in action, 30 September 1914.

Officers of C Squadron relaxing at Chateau Dhuizy in France, September 1914.

A North Irish Horse troop at Antrim, late 1914. *(Image courtesy: James M. Rankin)*

'A group of members of the North Irish Horse who are preparing for the fray at the show grounds, Londonderry'. *(*Larne Times and Weekly Telegraph, *17 October 1914)*

Private Frank McMahon as a new recruit, late 1914.

Private Jack McGuigan, who enlisted with Frank McMahon and served with him until evacuated with trench fever at the end of 1917. *(Image courtesy: Anne Cosgrove, Newry)*

Brothers Robert, Albert and Alexander Dundee, who enlisted together on 7 September 1914. *(Image courtesy: Mrs Dorothy Harcourt)*

A North Irish Horse private at Ballyshannon, County Donegal.

A North Irish Horse lance corporal.

A mounted North Irish Horse private.

Captain Neil Graham Stewart-Richardson. *(Image courtesy: Brigadier P. Stewart-Richardson OBE and Sir David Ralli Bt.)*

Lieutenant Lancelot Charles Wise, who served in France with D Squadron before transferring to the Indian cavalry. *(Image courtesy: Edinburgh University Library, from University of Edinburgh Roll of Honour 1914–1919)*

A group of North Irish Horsemen, probably at Antrim, 1915. *(Image courtesy: Deputy Keeper of Records, Public Records Office of Northern Ireland (PRONI) – Cat. No. D1977/1)*

Captain Arthur Noel Vernon Hill-Lowe, who went to France as a lieutenant with F Squadron.

Lance Corporal Hamilton Stewart.

Private Ernest George Matthews. *(Image courtesy: Shaun Matthews)*

Signallers of the 1st North Irish Horse Regiment at Pas, on the Somme front, August 1916. *(Image courtesy: PRONI – Cat. No. D1977/2)*

A group of North Irish Horsemen at rest.

Private David Hunter Bond. *(Image courtesy: Mrs Melva White)*

New Zealanders Gilbert Hutton Grigg, Richard Berry Kellock, Harold Plumer Kellock and John Hutton Grigg. *(Image courtesy: Penny Otto and Jill McLaren)*

Second Lieutenant Gilbert Hutton Grigg. *(Image courtesy: Tessa Grigg)*

Temporary grave marker for Private Frederick Thomas Cordwell. *(Image courtesy: Dr John Cordwell)*

Private James Lynn with his family in Randalstown in 1916. *(Image courtesy: Len Kinley)*

Corporal Frank McMahon in Egypt, September 1917.

Private Charles Magill and two other North Irish Horsemen in Egypt, September 1917. *(Image courtesy: Paul Magill)*

Major Holt Waring, who died of wounds on 15 April 1918.

Private James Wilson, gassed on 30 August 1918. *(Image courtesy: Patrick Wilson Gore)*

Second Lieutenant James Bailey Young.

Private Charles Elder, the last North Irish Horseman killed in action, 7 November 1918. *(*Belfast Evening Telegraph, *2 January 1919, image courtesy: Nigel Henderson)*

North Irish Horse signaller at Vignacourt, c. January 1919. *(Louis and Antoinette Thuillier Collection. Courtesy: Kerry Stokes Collection, Perth, Australia, British-19-024)*

North Irish Horse cyclist, possibly wounded, at Vignacourt, c. January 1919. *(Courtesy: Kerry Stokes Collection, British-40-008)*

North Irish Horse cyclist at Vignacourt, c. January 1919. *(Courtesy: Kerry Stokes Collection, British-21-016)*

North Irish Horse cyclists, one a Lewis Gunner, at Vignacourt, c. January 1919. *(Courtesy: Kerry Stokes Collection, British-19-028)*

North Irish Horse cyclists, one with a wound stripe, at Vignacourt, c. January 1919. *(Courtesy: Kerry Stokes Collection, British-19-022)*

North Irish Horse officers at Vignacourt, c. January 1919. (*Courtesy: Kerry Stokes Collection, British-01-021)*

A Squadron football team at Vignacourt, c. January 1919. *(Courtesy:Kerry Stokes Collection, British-05-008)*

A Squadron at Vignacourt, c. January 1919. *(Courtesy: Kerry Stokes Collection, British-04-024)*

Margaret, widow of Major Holt Waring.

Private Thomas Bryson and the 'unknown' North Irish Horseman, Queens Cemetery, Bucquoy, France. *(Image courtesy of Peter Woodger)*

Acknowledgements

The *North Irish Horse in the Great War* began as a search for the story of my grandfather, Frank McMahon ('Cobber' to his Australian family). The more I discovered, the more my interest grew in his regiment and the men with whom he rode, marched and fought.

More people have helped me on this project than I could possibly mention here. Their generosity in sharing their research, time and ideas has been wonderful, and has helped bridge the distance between my home in Australia and the Ireland, France and Belgium of a century ago.

Gerry Chester, a North Irish Horse veteran of the Second World War, together with Doug and Hugh Vaugh, made much material available to me in the beginning, particularly the regimental diaries, which I was able to transcribe and share with others via the Internet. My particular thanks to Nigel Henderson, Nick Metcalfe, Paul Magill and Bracken Anderson, each of whom has helped me on this project and left his mark on it. Patricia Tardif – my mother and Frank McMahon's first child – has shared every step of the journey. Her quiet persistence has unearthed many of the gems that make this work much more than a compilation of official records.

It is the personal stories – the private musings of those who were there – that bring stories such as this to life, and this work would be much the poorer without two of these in particular. Major John Cole, commander of A Squadron, wrote numerous frank and revealing letters to his parents, and I am grateful to the Deputy Keeper of Records, Public Record Office of Northern Ireland, for allowing me to publish extracts here, together with a number of other documents and photographs sourced from there. Another North Irish Horse officer, Lancelot Wise, also wrote numerous letters to his parents, revealing a young man bursting with excitement at the adventure of which he had become a part, and telling much about the day-to-day activities of the regiment. His descendants, Lance and Peter Wise, have been extremely generous in sharing this wonderful and hitherto unknown collection of letters, and allowing me to include them in this narrative.

Sarah Parkes and Stefanie Tardif, my daughters, never failed to encourage me to keep going, and Sarah spent many hours on my behalf in the National Archives at Kew when I'm sure she had much better things to do in London. I thank the staff at Kew for their polite efficiency in helping both Sarah and myself when I was able to visit the Archives. Cathy Hudson and Jeff House were generous enough to read early drafts of this work and offered much by way of helpful commentary. My thanks also to the many expert members of the Great War Forum who helped answer my random and assorted questions on the war. My editor Richard Doherty was a pleasure to work with, as was the team at Pen & Sword.

I am grateful to the many people and organisations who have allowed me to use the images that appear in this work, in particular the Kerry Stokes Foundation for the large.number of wonderful images from the Louis and Antoinette Thuillier Collection.

Finally my thanks to Cobber, for surviving the war and its bitter aftermath in Ireland, and for telling his children something of what he went through. I hope there is not too much in these pages that he would have found cause to dispute, though I know there is much he could have added.

Phillip Tardif

Glossary and Abbreviations

Adjutant	An officer who assists the commanding officer in the details of his command
APM	Assistant Provost Marshal – responsible for enforcing military discipline
ASC	Army Service Corps
AO	Army Order
Bar	Additional award of same medal, usually displayed as a clasp on the ribbon of the first medal
Batman	An officer's servant
Bde	Brigade
BEF	British Expeditionary Force
BET	*Belfast Evening Telegraph*
Blighty	A wound serious enough to have one shipped to hospital in England.
Bn	Battalion
BNL	*Belfast News-Letter*
Bomb	Hand grenade
Cadre	A small number of officers and men comprising the nucleus of a regiment
CB	Confined to barracks
Commission	Appointment as an officer
Coy	Company
CQMS	Company Quartermaster Sergeant
CSM	Company Sergeant Major
CWGC	Commonwealth War Graves Commission
DoW	Died of wounds
Draft	A group of men sent as reinforcements
Enfilade	To direct fire along a trench from the side
Fatigue	A party detailed to work on trench digging or other labour
Flammenwerfer	Flame-thrower

GHQ	General Headquarters
GOC	General Officer Commanding (of a division)
GSW	Literally 'gunshot wound', but a broad term encompassing wounds by shrapnel as well as bullets.
Inniskillings	Royal Inniskilling Fusiliers
Jack Johnson	A type of German artillery shell
IV	Irish Volunteers
KIA	Killed in action
KR/KRR	King's Rules and Regulations
LG	Lewis gun
LG	*London Gazette*
MGC	Machine Gun Corps
MIC	Medal Index Card
MMP	Military Mounted Police
NA	National Archives, Kew, London
NCO	Non-commissioned officer – the rank between private and officer (usually sergeant, lance sergeant, corporal, lance corporal)
NIH	North Irish Horse
OR	Other ranks – all men who were not officers or warrant officers
OTC	Officer Training Corps
Pillbox	A reinforced concrete defensive post
Pineapple	A German ball grenade
PoW	Prisoner of war
PRONI	Public Record Office of Northern Ireland
Quartermaster	An officer responsible for the provision of food, clothing and equipment
RA	Royal Artillery
RAF	Royal Air Force
RAMC	Royal Army Medical Corps
RE	Royal Engineers
Redoubt	A fortified defensive post
RFA	Royal Field Artillery
RFC	Royal Flying Corps
RGA	Royal Garrison Artillery
RIrF	Royal Irish Fusiliers

RIR	Royal Irish Rifles
RIRegt	Royal Irish Regiment
RSM	Regimental Sergeant Major
SAA	Small arms ammunition
Salient	Ground projecting into the area held by the enemy, and therefore subject to fire from the flanks.
Salve	To salvage material left on the battlefield such as guns, wire and grenades
Scheme	A field training exercise
SSM	Squadron Sergeant Major
Sub/Subaltern	A junior officer – lieutenant or second lieutenant.
TMB	Trench Mortar Battery
Trench foot	A condition similar to frostbite, caused by prolonged exposure to cold and damp.
Trench fever	A bacterial infection transmitted by body lice.
Trooper	A cavalry rank equivalent to private. Men serving in the North Irish Horse were often referred to as 'Trooper'. However this was incorrect, as the rank did not apply to the reserve regiments such as the North Irish Horse.
Uhlan	German light cavalry lancer, a term used by British troops to describe any German cavalryman carrying a lance.
Ulster	In this work the term 'Ulster' refers to the most northern of the four Irish provinces, comprising the nine counties – Antrim, Armagh, Cavan, Donegal, Down, Fermanagh, Londonderry, Monaghan, Tyrone – and the city and county boroughs of Belfast and Londonderry.
UVF	Ulster Volunteer Force
WO	War Office
WO	Warrant Officer – a rank between commissioned officer and NCO

Introduction

In his account of the British Army's role in the first months of the Great War, Sir John French, its former Commander-in-Chief, praised 'the fine work done by the Oxfordshire Hussars and the London Scottish' as the first non-regular army units 'to enter the line of battle' in the Great War. He added, by way of a footnote, that 'The North and South Irish Horse went to France much earlier than these troops but were employed as special escort to GHQ.' In other words, these Irish units could not claim the distinction of being the first non-regulars involved in the fighting in the First World War.[1]

That would have been news to the families of North Irish Horsemen Private William Moore of Balteagh, County Londonderry, Private Henry St George Scott of Carndonagh, County Donegal, and Lieutenant Samuel Barbour Combe of Donaghcloney, County Down, whose deaths in September and October of 1914 were so far into the 'line of battle' that their bodies were never recovered. It would also have surprised Private William McLanahan of Garvagh, County Londonderry, who at this time 'accounted for three Uhlans and took two horses single-handed'.[2] The truth is that the North Irish Horse was the first non-regular unit of the British Expeditionary Force actively engaged in fighting in the First World War, their presence in France dating from 19 August, just two weeks after Britain declared war, and their involvement with the enemy dating from just five days later.

The men of the North Irish Horse saw action throughout the war and in almost every theatre, though mostly in France and Belgium. They were rearguard to the British army on the retreat from Mons and advance guard when the Germans were forced back to the Aisne in August and September 1914. They took their turn in the trenches on the la Bassée front, on the Ancre and at Ypres. They were at the Somme on 1 July 1916 as witness to the destruction of the 36th (Ulster) Division, and through that month cleared the battlefield of the massed and mangled bodies of the men who had fallen that day. At Messines and Passchendaele in 1917 they waited in vain for the order to advance through broken German lines. As infantry, they fought with the Ulster Division in the assault on the Hindenburg Line at Cambrai. They were in the lines in front of St Quentin when the Germans threw all they had at them in the offensive of March 1918, fighting a desperate retreat to Amiens. Weeks later at Kemmel they faced another offensive. As infantry and as cyclists they joined the 'Advance to Victory', a three month offensive that broke German resistance and brought the war to an end.

By then the North Irish Horse was barely recognisable from that which had rushed to France in August 1914. When the war began they were a part-time reserve regiment, staunchly Unionist, and the regiment of choice for the wealthy landed gentry, farmers and rural tradesmen of Ireland's north. By the end of 1918 they were very different – professional, urban, more religiously diverse, and with officers and men drawn from as far afield as England, Canada, New Zealand, South Africa and Australia. Most obviously, they had been dismounted and converted to cyclists and infantry, retaining their 'cavalry' title in name only. Many whose service began in the North Irish Horse found themselves transferred elsewhere; they saw action as tank crews, airmen, military police and artillerymen in the European Theatre, the Mediterranean and further afield.

As many as one-in-ten never returned to Ireland. They lie in Belgium, France, England, Egypt and Palestine. Their names are inscribed amongst the ranks of the missing at Pozières, Tyne Cot, Thiepval, Cambrai, le Touret, Loos and Ploegsteert, and on gravestones in more than ninety cemeteries around the world; stones that speak of family grief and faith.

> The glory dies not, and the grief is past.
> He died for us.
> Having served his generation, by the will of God, he fell on sleep.
> In memory of our son who is sadly missed, by his father, mother, brothers and sisters.
> Not dead to those that loved him.
> Death is swallowed up in victory.

This work tells the story of these men, and all those who served with the North Irish Horse in the Great War.

Three issues arose in the writing of this work that are worth touching-on here. First, how to deal with the Irish political question? What emphasis should it be given? One answer would have been to ignore it and focus solely on the military role of the regiment in the war. However, given the role played by the officers and men of the North Irish Horse in the Home Rule question in the lead up to the war and their continuing concern about events at home, it would have been absurd to pretend the issue was not there. The conflict in Ulster was very much a part of the character of the regiment that this book describes. So while its main focus is on the role of the North Irish Horse in the conflict in France and Belgium, it does not lose sight of events at home. It does reflect on (without labouring) the regiment's place in Irish sectarian politics and the attitude of officers and men to developments such as the 1916 rebellion and calls for conscription in Ireland.

The second issue arises from the emphasis on personal stories in this work. Inevitably the documents, both private and official, sometimes shine a light on events and behaviours which are less than praiseworthy. Should this information be included? The decision has not always been easy. To excise information too readily may smack of censorship or prurience. However, while none of the men in this book are alive, their children and grandchildren often are, and hold their memory dear. When faced with a record that shows a North Irish Horseman in a light that may be painful to his family, I posed the question 'Does it add to the narrative?' If not, I have left it out. If, however, there is some value in including the information, I have done so without using the man's name. While it may be worth reporting, for example, that an officer was forced to resign his commission due to alcoholism, there is nothing to be gained by naming him. I hope in this way to have not sanitised the story but also shown respect to the families of the men who served. There may still be instances where the story I have told does not match a family's memory. For any hurt this causes I extend my apologies.

The third issue was one of classification. Who exactly was a North Irish Horseman? The answer is not as simple as it might seem. Clearly the men serving in the five squadrons of the regiment sent to France are included, as are those in the three reserve squadrons at Antrim. The men in the two North Irish Horse regiments formed in France in mid-1916 are also included, though here it gets more complicated, for one squadron of the 2nd North Irish Horse Regiment was the 6th Inniskilling Dragoons (Service Squadron), and they maintained a separate identity while part of the regiment. I have decided to include these men, provided they were with their squadron when it was part of the 2nd North Irish Horse Regiment.

The 1st North Irish Horse Regiment was dismounted and converted to a cyclist regiment in March 1918. As it retained its North Irish Horse title and continued to draw its reinforcements from the regimental reserve at Antrim, it clearly falls within the scope of this work. More problematic was the status of the 9th (North Irish Horse) Battalion, Royal Irish Fusiliers. Technically this was not a North Irish Horse regiment. Originally called the 9th (Service) Battalion, Princess Victoria's (Royal Irish Fusiliers), in September 1917 it absorbed the disbanded 2nd North Irish Horse Regiment, but apart from the change of name it remained part of the same infantry structure and had no links to the North Irish Horse reserve at Antrim. However, because of the large number of North Irish Horsemen who transferred to the battalion (more than 500), I have included it in the narrative. It would have been pointless and artificial to end the story of the men of 2nd North Irish Horse when their regiment was disbanded in 1917, given that so many continued to serve together in a unit that retained the 'North Irish Horse' title. However, in telling the story of this battalion, I have focused on the story of its North Irish Horsemen, rather than the other infantrymen of the battalion who had no prior service with the North Irish Horse as a mounted unit.

During the war many officers and men left the North Irish Horse to serve in other units, either as individuals or in larger groups. For example, at the end of 1916 a hundred North Irish Horsemen transferred to the 1st Royal Irish Rifles, and in the latter years of the war many 'other ranks' of the regiment were commissioned as officers and posted elsewhere. To the extent possible, this work follows their progress with these other regiments.

A note on the structure and organisation of the British Expeditionary Force

For those not familiar with the structure of the British Army, the multitude of terms used in this work such as brigade, squadron, corps and division can be confusing and make the narrative difficult to follow. Nor is it helped by the changes that occurred as the war progressed, and by the use of terms such as 'regiment' both as a generic descriptor for a military unit and as a quite specific type of unit. Set out below is a basic outline of the structure of the British Army in France between 1914 and 1918. Bruce Gudmundsson's *The British Army on the Western Front 1916* is recommended for those who wish to gain a more detailed understanding.

Working from the top, the British Expeditionary Force comprised several *armies*, each commanded by a general. Each army comprised a number of *corps*, commanded by a lieutenant general. Within each corps was a number

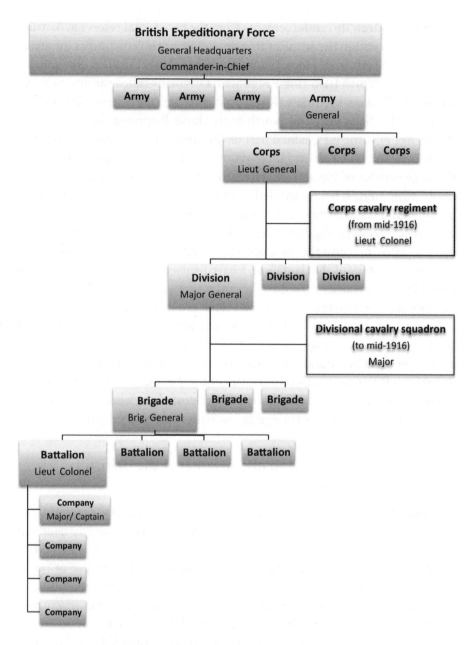

Figure 1: Outline structure of British Expeditionary Force.

of *divisions*, usually three, commanded by a major general. Divisions comprised three infantry *brigades* (commanded by a brigadier general), within which were four *battalions* (three from February 1918), commanded by a lieutenant colonel. The battalion was the key fighting unit in this structure. It was the battalion that the ordinary soldier saw as the unit to which he belonged, and it was the battalion's badge that he wore on his cap. A battalion comprised just over 1,000 men at full-strength. Battalions were divided into four *companies*, which in turn were divided into four *platoons*, each comprising four *sections*.

A number of cavalry divisions also served in the British Expeditionary Force and, like the infantry, each division comprised three brigades. Each brigade comprised three *regiments*, with three *squadrons* to a regiment and four *troops* to a squadron. (Thus the cavalry regiment was roughly equivalent to an infantry battalion, the squadron equivalent to a company, and the troop equivalent to a platoon.) Not all cavalry squadrons formed part of a cavalry division. From the beginning of the war, each infantry division had attached to it a squadron of cavalry to act as its eyes and ears and to assist with communication. This was the role assigned to each squadron of the North Irish Horse. However, in mid-1916 the system of divisional cavalry squadrons was abandoned. Instead, regiments were formed by bringing together three divisional cavalry squadrons. These were assigned to army corps as their corps cavalry regiment. Thus, for example, A, D and E Squadrons of the North Irish Horse left their divisions, combined to form the 1st North Irish Horse Regiment and were attached to VII Corps.

The figure opposite is a simplified representation of the British army structure, showing where the North Irish Horse squadrons and regiments fitted-in to the picture.

Notes

1. French, *1914*, p.294.
2. MacDonagh, *The Irish at the Front*, p.36.

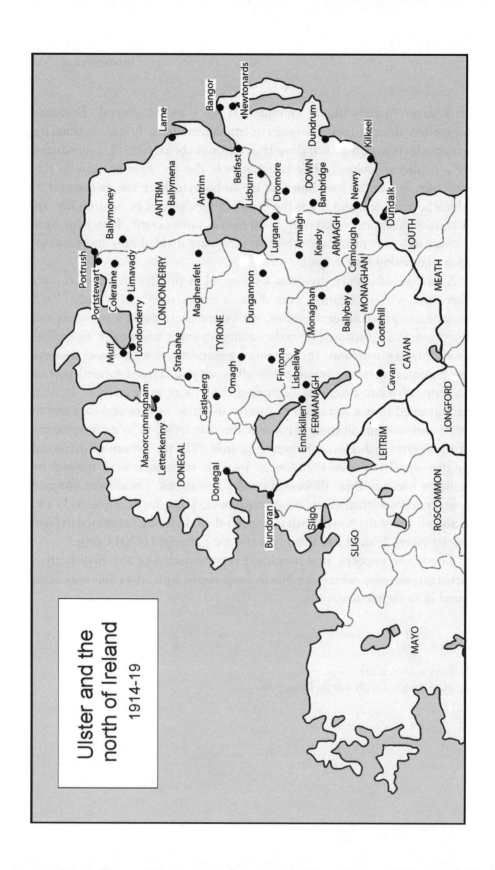

Ulster and the
north of Ireland
1914-19

Chapter One

1908–1914: Farmers and Farmers' Sons

The vast majority ... of the men of the regiment are farmers or farmers' sons owning their own horses, and it is this type of true yeoman that is required to fill the ranks of our Yeomanry and similar corps.[1]

The North Irish Horse was formed on 7 July 1908 at Newbridge near the Curragh in County Kildare. Its immediate ancestry dated from the Boer War, when twelve squadrons of Imperial Yeomanry were raised in Ireland. Between 1900 to 1902 they sailed for South Africa, winning no lasting glory in a war that did the British army little credit.

Following the war's end, the British government decided to form sixteen new yeomanry regiments, including two in Ireland. There was some nervousness about the Irish proposal, yeomanry or volunteer forces not having been maintained there for a long time, 'owing to the unfortunate extent to which political feeling is so often carried in that country'.[2] However such objections were overruled and the two regiments, the North of Ireland Imperial Yeomanry and South of Ireland Imperial Yeomanry, came into being.

These yeomen were very much part-timers. They attended drill parades on one afternoon a week in the spring, followed by three days of rifle practice on an open range, and a two and a half week camp for the regiment every summer. The first camp was held at Blackrock, Dundalk, County Louth. In 1904 they trained at Finner Camp, Bundoran, County Donegal, the following year at the Curragh, County Kildare, then at Ballykinlar Camp, Dundrum, County Down and in 1907 again at the Curragh, where they joined the manoeuvres of the regular army.

In 1908 significant reforms were made to the structure and organisation of Britain's auxiliary forces, the object being to strengthen the ability of the Army to fight a prolonged war. All Britain's yeomanry and volunteer units were converted into a new county-based Territorial Force, comprising infantry battalions and yeomanry (i.e. mounted) regiments. The militias were disbanded and reconstituted as a new Special Reserve of the Regular Army.

This would have meant conversion of the Irish Imperial Yeomanry into Territorial yeomanry units, except that a decision had also been taken that there would be no Territorial units in Ireland. Instead they were disbanded, but replaced with two mounted regiments of the Special Reserve – thus becoming the only mounted reservists.[3] With the new structure came new names – the North Irish Horse and South Irish Horse.

The change came into effect after the annual camp at the Curragh in July 1908. The old regiments were disbanded, photographs were taken to mark the occasion, speeches were made by senior officers praising the men's discipline, and prizes distributed to the winners of various competitions. Volunteers had already been called to join the new regiment, but only about 190 came forward, the shortfall attributed to a greater commitment of time required for training. To balance this, the pay was much improved. Each man would receive £5 a year, plus 1s 2d per day for each of the twenty-four days of annual camp, at which he also received allowances for messing and forage for his horse. His uniform, saddlery and equipment were provided, though he had to bring his own boots.

The North Irish Horse comprised four squadrons, based at Belfast (A Squadron), Londonderry (B Squadron), Enniskillen (C Squadron) and Dundalk (D Squadron). Headquarters was at Skegoneill Avenue, Belfast. Each squadron maintained a peacetime establishment of six officers and 112 men. In the event of war the regiment was required, at forty-eight hours' notice, to provide one squadron for deployment with the British Expeditionary Force, formed as a composite of the four squadrons, plus the necessary specialists (signallers, saddlers, farriers). The men were selected on a rotational basis, so that each had his year 'on call'.

The squadron thus formed would be assigned as mounted troops to an infantry division. This was a more restricted role than that assigned to the regular cavalry, which could operate independently and undertake large-scale offensive operations. Field service regulations detailed the role expected of divisional cavalry squadrons like the North Irish Horse. When the enemy was at a distance they would gather information about their movements and location, and the 'tactical features, resources, and roads of the country' in front of them. They would also fight off enemy attacks and prevent them from gathering information. When the enemy was close, their duty was to 'clear up the tactical situation' through 'offensive action'. When their division was advancing the mounted squadron would form an advance guard to scout ahead of the main body, locate and drive in the enemy scouts, discover the enemy's dispositions, and secure any tactical points. In retreat the mounted troops would form a rear guard, the object being to check or slow the enemy's advance and thus relieve pressure on the main body. They would also be employed on outpost duty – forming 'picquets', 'cossack posts' and 'vedettes' – to give early warning of the approach of an enemy force.[4]

The Horsemen's dress uniform was distinctive, and largely unchanged from that adopted by the North of Ireland Imperial Yeomanry in 1903:

> a bottle green tunic, double-breasted, with white cuffs and collar patches and white piping along the seams, the skirt being outlined in white piping and buttons. Shoulder straps were of chain over white patches. The girdle was of white and green bands. Trousers ... were dark blue with a broad white stripe down the outer seam, fitted very tightly and strapping under the half-wellington boots, which were decorated with swan-neck spurs.[5]

To complete the picture they wore white wrist gloves and a black bowler-style hat, similar to the Italian Bersaglieri, with a broad thick brim and a large plume of green feathers on the left side (earning the sobriquet 'them of the cock's plumes' from their South Irish counterparts). The regiment's badge, an Irish harp surmounted by an Imperial crown above a scroll inscribed 'North Irish Horse' was worn on the collars, with a larger and more ornate version worn at the front of the hat. The service uniform was the standard British Army khaki service-dress tunic, riding breeches and cap, with a simpler version of the North Irish Horse badge worn on the cap, and brass NIH titles on the shoulders.

For weaponry, the horsemen were issued the Short Magazine Lee-Enfield (SMLE) rifle. By 1914 they carried their rounds in nine-pocket leather bandoliers, with the rifle carried in a leather rifle bucket secured to the right side of the mount. Swords were not issued to the men until 1914, when they received the old pattern curved-blade cavalry sword.

From the beginning, members of the North Irish Horse held a position of prestige in the rural communities of Ulster. Despite the initial shortfall in enlistment the numbers were quickly made up, another 200 joining in the first twelve months. The recruitment process was rigorous and selective. 'Before a recruit is finally approved of', wrote regimental Adjutant Edward Mungo Dorman, 'he has to pass a riding test under the supervision of one of the squadron officers or the adjutant. The vast majority, about 90 per cent, of the men of the regiment are farmers or farmers' sons owning their own horses, and it is this type of true yeoman that is required to fill the ranks of our Yeomanry and similar corps … The recruits are men of some substance … Here, then, we have splendid material to work on.'

Despite the regiment's popularity, each year saw the departure of large numbers of men. Enlistment was for four years, after which a man could renew for twelve months each year. Those wishing to leave could do so either by purchasing their discharge or by not renewing the contract when their four years was up. Many others simply failed to turn up – often they had emigrated. Every year saw 100 or more new recruits join the regiment, suggesting an annual turnover of 20–25 per cent.

The main difficulty for the regiment was how to build a cohesive, efficient force from men spread far and wide across Ireland's north, and therefore unable to practise any but the simplest of mounted drills at the regiment's thirty-two drill stations. The annual camp was therefore crucial, as well as being the highlight of the year for the men of the North Irish Horse, who 'regard it as a holiday among their friends, and one which does not cost them anything, and, indeed, puts a little money in their pockets. There is a considerable amount of Scottish blood in the North Irishman.'[6]

From 1909 to 1914 the North Irish Horse held its camps at Ballykinlar Camp, Dundrum Bay, County Down (1909); Magilligan Camp, Bellarena, County Londonderry (1910); Newbridge, the Curragh, County Kildare (1911); Ballykinlar Camp (1912); Finner Camp, Bundoran, County Donegal (1913); and once again at Ballykinlar Camp in 1914. The men brought their own horses, mainly half-breeds and hunters, and a month before camp received their saddlery, which had to be polished to perfection. According to Dorman:

> The annual training … takes place in the early summer, as it is found that at that time the men can most easily get away, and their horses are not then required on the farms …
> The discipline is very good. There is a little difficulty in getting the men to show due respect to their troop sergeants or section leaders, whom they probably call 'Bill' or 'Jim' in private life, but with whom they work wonderfully well at camp. There are very few cases indeed of offences which have to be brought before the commanding officer; in fact, the average is about two per training … There is one offence – viz., drunkenness – for which the only suitable punishment is instant

dismissal from the corps, a punishment which is felt much more by the man than any award of detention, for he has to undergo not only the ridicule of his comrades but also that of his friends when he gets home. Certain minor offences have to be dealt with rather leniently from a Regular soldier's point of view; but, on the whole, there is very little difficulty as regards discipline.[7]

Horsemen Willie Acheson and Charles Trimble described a typical day at camp:

After reveille every morning long slacks were donned and an hour was spent grooming the horse … an officer inspected the job afterwards – rubbing the hair the wrong way for instance, in search of dandruff … As well as brush and curry-comb the men had towels, to wash out the sleep from the horses' eyes! Your name and number were taken if your grooming was considered unsatisfactory.

It was remarkable how quickly the horses came to know the long trumpet note – 'Feeed' – which marked the end of stables. Immediately there was neighing and stamping of feet until they were able to plunge their noses into the nosebags, so that each troop sergeant could report to his officer – 'All fed and feeding, Sir'.

Breakfast, of the bacon and eggs type with unlimited bread and butter, was quickly over and all ranks got back to the lines for a final polish-up of buttons and badges before saddling-up and filing out for parade at 8 a.m., followed by the ride out to the exercise ground or beach for cavalry drill.

Back to camp for about 12 noon, when horses were watered and then well groomed until, before 1 p.m. once again the long 'Feeed' rang out from the trumpet and again noses dived into nosebags.

Dinner consisted chiefly of one main course, generally of roasts one day and stews the next … There were always lashings of potatoes and vegetables.

After dinner, generally nothing to do until 3 p.m. or later and so the general custom was for an hour's lie down.

Afternoon parades were for lectures on general subjects – horse-management and care, map-reading, care of the rifle with aiming and loading practice and so on, specialists like the signallers and scouts having their own separate spheres of interest.

Then, after about an hour, there would be a break until evening 'stables', when again the horses were watered, rubbed down and finally rugged up for the night with the remainder of their day's ration of hay to keep them quietly munching during the evening hours.

There was usually something hot for tea, and then everyone was free until 'Lights Out' at 10.15 p.m. Some rested, others dressed up and paid a visit to the nearest town or village, while some remained in camp. There was always the canteen (nothing stronger than Guinness or Bass) and there were impromptu competitions. Perhaps a little boxing, tent-pegging for the ambitious and so on.[8]

The men also learned how to mount and ride their horses cavalry-fashion.

In those days infantry moved in columns of four and mounted troops in columns of two or four. They formed up in line, numbered '1,2,3,4,1,2,3,4' and got into column by wheeling in twos or fours, right or left. A similar wheel brought them back into line.

A very few hours taught the rudiments of this, and then the separate troops formed into their squadrons and learned to do the same all over again on a larger scale, moving in column of troops, thirty or more abreast, and getting into line, a hundred and twenty or more horses and men abreast, riding six inches from knee to knee, keeping line …

They were taught reconnaissance work, advance, rear and flank guard work, one part of the squadron operating against another. Going into action three men of each section running up to occupy a position while the No. 3 of the Section took all four horses to cover until they were needed for advance or retreat …

Then towards the last week, the four squadrons manoeuvred as a regiment in attack and retreat schemes, banging off much blank cartridge and enjoying it all.[9]

For the officers, the annual camp was as much a part of country life as riding to hounds. These officers were without exception wealthy landowners. A number, such as Robert (Bobby) Jocelyn, Algernon Skeffington and Arthur Maxwell were peers of the realm.[10] Membership of the leading hunts in the north of Ireland was almost a prerequisite. At least six members of the County Down Staghounds were with the North Irish Horse, or would serve with it during the war – Barrie Combe, Holt Waring, Forster Green

Uprichard, Warren Murland, Thomas Hughes and Robert Noel Anderson. Most lived locally, and those who had seen military service were cavalrymen. Habits of command came naturally to them, and their 'intimate association with the country', and consequent 'close touch with the men' won them easy acceptance as leaders from the farmers and farmers' sons who made up the other ranks of the North Irish Horse.[11]

The North Irish Horse and Home Rule

Given the make-up of the North Irish Horse – officered by the landed gentry, manned by Ulster's rural middle-class, and Protestant to the core – it is hardly surprising that they played an active role in the Home Rule crisis of 1912 to 1914. The crisis had been brought on by the introduction of the Third Home Rule Bill in the House of Commons. The intent of the Bill, to grant self-government to Ireland, was passionately opposed by Ulster's Protestant majority. Its political leaders vowed to oppose any form of Home Rule, by force if necessary. In a well-organised show of strength on 28 September 1912 more than 470,000 men and women across Ulster and elsewhere signed a 'Covenant' (for men) and associated 'Declaration' (for women), pledging 'to stand by one another in defending for ourselves and our children our cherished position of equal citizenship in the United Kingdom, and in using all means which may be found necessary to defeat the present conspiracy to set up a Home Rule Parliament in Ireland.'[12]

In January 1913 the Ulster Unionist Council approved the creation of a paramilitary Ulster Volunteer Force (UVF) from the disparate volunteer units then springing up from Orange lodges across Ulster. The following year, in what would be known as the 'Curragh Incident', the British government was forced into a humiliating backdown when it became clear that most army officers in Ireland would resign or face dismissal rather than carry out orders to enforce Home Rule. And in April the UVF armed itself with tens of thousands of rifles and tons of ammunition in an audacious and impressively organised smuggling operation – the most prominent being the Larne gun-running.

Off duty, the men of the North Irish Horse participated in much of this activity. Perhaps the most overt manifestation of the blurred lines between the North Irish Horse and paramilitary Unionism was the formation in 1912 of the Enniskillen Horse. Privately raised by outspoken newspaper editor William Copeland Trimble, the Enniskillen Horse soon became a full unit of the UVF.

They held regular parades with their assorted lances and carbines, in defiance or with the connivance of the authorities, and often supported by regular army officers. A Royal Irish Constabulary report in 1914 claimed that 'with the exception of half a dozen, most are members of the North Irish Horse'.[13] Across Ulster, other UVF mounted units were raised in imitation of the Enniskillen Horse, with off-duty North Irish Horsemen helping fill their ranks.

Many of the North Irish Horse's officers also served as officers in the UVF. Viscount Massereene and Ferrard, for example, commanded the UVF's 3rd Battalion South Antrim Regiment, Lord Farnham led the County Cavan Regiment and Captain Emerson Crawford Herdman the 1st North Tyrone Battalion. Others included Viscount Jocelyn, Captain Holt Waring, and Lieutenants Robert Livsey Yates, Samuel Barbour (Barrie) Combe, John Grant and Ronald Deane Ross. Another UVF officer, Neil Graham Stewart-Richardson, a retired regular Army officer, would join the North Irish Horse on the outbreak of war. A number of these officers were active in landing and spiriting-away the smuggled rifles from the ship *Mountjoy II* at Larne and Bangor. In 1914 Barrie Combe was presented with a gift to which was attached a silver plaque inscribed with the red hand of Ulster, a ship's anchor and crossed rifles, and the text:

A SOUVENIR OF
APRIL 24–25TH
1914
To
S.B.COMBE ESQ.
FROM
DONACLONEY.

S.S."FANNY". S.S."MOUNTJOY".

God helps those who help themselves

When North Irish Horse Captain Holt Waring and his new bride returned to Lurgan from their honeymoon, they were greeted not only by the Waringstown troop of A Squadron of the North Irish Horse, but the men of F Company of the 2nd Battalion West Down Regiment UVF. Waring was commanding officer of both. Addressing the UVF contingent, Waring praised the work of the men who had carried out their duties in the recent arms smuggling episode.

Certainly those opposing home rule were preparing for every contingency, including paramilitary action, and the officers and men of the North Irish Horse played their part in the preparations.

Last peacetime camp

Despite the risk of civil war, or perhaps because of it, the mood at the last peacetime camp for the North Irish Horse in June and July of 1914 was one of excited optimism. The Curragh Incident and the smuggling of arms under the noses of the authorities had, many felt, demonstrated 'that the people of Ulster were a force to be reckoned with … and that they would have something to say if it came to any attempt being made to place them under the heel of a Home Rule Parliament'.[14]

Prominent Ulster industrialists Warren and Howard Murland, driving home after delivering a cargo of ammunition to the UVF companies in County Antrim, made a social call on the officers at the North Irish Horse camp:

> went out on the sand hills and watched the North Irish Horse. Saw Masserene, Farnham, young Maude, Bobby Jocelyn and had a great chat with Holt Waring and Barrie Combe.[15]

A shooting competition, the Enniskillen Cup, was won by Sergeant William Lockhart of Jerrettspass, near Newry, scoring six bull's eyes out of eight shots. Squadron Sergeant Major John Whiteside, a veteran of the Boer War with the Irish Yeomanry, was presented by Colonel Maude with a long service medal and praised as 'a credit to the regiment'.[16] And Lieutenant Barrie Combe wrote a letter from camp full of domestic concerns to his 'Dearest Old Girl':

> I got home safe and sound but found that I was Orderly Officer again this morning, which was rather a bore … I am rather lonely in Camp today as there is no one about, and I miss you all very much, after the nice day we had yesterday.
>   Love to you all, my own darling, and thousands of kisses to the children and your dear old self,
>   Ever your old, Barrie[17]

Within six weeks the officers and men of the North Irish Horse would be putting their training to the test.

Notes

1. Dorman, 'The North Irish Horse', in *The Army Review*, Vol.III, 192, October 1912, p.540.
2. *Navy & Army Illustrated*, 2 August 1902.
3. A third mounted regiment of the Special Reserve, King Edward's Horse, was formed in 1913.
4. War Office, *Field Service Regulations: Part I, Operations*, pp.88–107.
5. Trimble, *Memories of the North Irish Horse*.
6. Dorman, op. cit., pp.540–1.
7. Ibid, pp.541–2.
8. First paragraph and part of the third paragraph, Acheson in Mac Fhionnghaile, *Donegal, Ireland and the First World War*, p.88. The remainder in Trimble, op. cit.
9. Trimble, op. cit.
10. Jocelyn was the 8th Earl of Roden, Skeffington the 12th Viscount Massereene, and Maxwell the 11th Baron Farnham. (Murland, *Departed Warriors*, pp.125–6.)
11. Dorman, op. cit., pp.543–4.
12. Covenant, in *BNL*, 30 Sep1912.
13. Dougan, Quincey, 'When the UVF took to horse power', in *News Letter*, 2 May 2012 (www.newsletter.co.uk).
14. Holt Waring quoted in *Lurgan Mail*, 9 May 1914.
15. Murland, op. cit., p.126.
16. *BNL*, 16 June 1915.
17. Letter dated 29 June 1914, from Combe/Waring collection.

Chapter Two

1914: The Gay Careless Fox-hunters
of the North

*In the little room on the ground floor of the Ulster Club ... big, muscular
horsy men sit and sip and smoke, in the uniform of the North Irish Horse
... Some talk sense, some nonsense, others say nothing at all. But they all
appear to think that those who get through will eat their Christmas dinners
in Berlin! ... They talk of a picnic ... The gay careless fox-hunters of the
north finish their drinks with a clink of glasses and rise to depart to their
horses and ships.*[1]

On 4 August 1914 Britain declared war on Germany. In England,
Scotland, Wales and Ireland, and in every corner of the Empire, the
British military machine swung into action with great efficiency. At
least twenty infantry battalions were based in Ireland, and all mobilised and
converged on the port cities of Dublin, Belfast and Cork.

At North Irish Horse regimental headquarters in Belfast, mobilisation
telegrams were despatched to each officer and man, ordering him to report
to his nearest squadron headquarters. The regiment was required to provide
one squadron for the Expeditionary Force, comprising six officers and 152
men: a major, a captain, four subalterns, a sergeant major, a quartermaster
sergeant, eight sergeants, a farrier sergeant, four shoeing smiths, a saddler,
two trumpeters, eight corporals, three signallers, 104 privates, seven drivers
and twelve batmen. On paper, the North Irish Horse had four squadrons,
fully up to the required peacetime strength of 476. It was therefore decided
that they would furnish not one but two squadrons, with more to be raised
later if needed. The first, A Squadron, was commanded by Major John
Henry Michael Cole. The second, C Squadron, was commanded by Major
Algernon William John Clotworthy Skeffington, Viscount Massereene and
Ferrard. Cole, 38, was the eldest son of the Earl of Enniskillen, of Florence
Court, County Fermanagh. Educated at Eton, he began his military career
in the 3rd Royal Inniskilling Fusiliers before joining the 7th (Queen's Own)

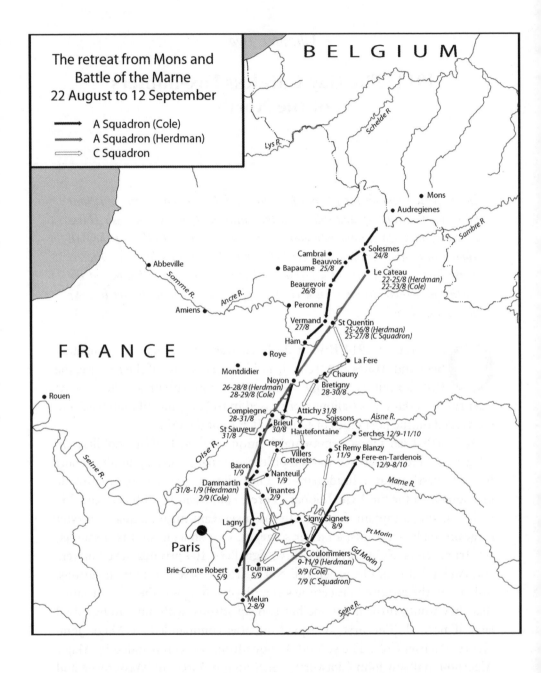

The retreat from Mons and
Battle of the Marne
22 August to 12 September

→ A Squadron (Cole)
→ A Squadron (Herdman)
⇨ C Squadron

BELGIUM

Schelde R.

Lys R.

Mons

Audregienes

Sambre R.

Abbeville

Somme R.

Ancre R.

Cambrai
Beauvois
Bapaume 25/8
Beaurevoir
26/8
Peronne

Solesmes
24/8
Le Cateau
22-25/8 (Herdman)
22-23/8 (Cole)

Amiens

Vermand
27/8
Ham

St Quentin
25-26/8 (Herdman)
25-27/8 (C Squadron)

FRANCE

Roye

La Fere

Montdidier
Noyon
26-28/8 (Herdman)
28-29/8 (Cole)

Chauny
Bretigny
28-30/8

Rouen

Compiegne
28-31/8
St Sauveur
31/8

Attichy 31/8
Soissons
Brieul   Hautefontaine
30/8
Crepy

Aisne R.

Serches 12/9-11/10

St Remy Blanzy
11/9   Fere-en-Tardenois
12/9-8/10

Oise R.

Villers
Cotterets

Seine R.

Baron
1/9
Dammartin
31/8-1/9 (Herdman)
2/9 (Cole)

Nanteuil
1/9
Vinantes
2/9

Marne R.

Lagny

Signy Signets
8/9

Pt Morin

Paris

Coulommiers
9-11/9 (Herdman)
9/9 (Cole)
7/9 (C Squadron)

Gd Morin

Brie-Comte Robert
5/9

Tournan
5/9

Melun
2-8/9

Seine R.

Hussars. He had served with the Hussars in the Boer War. Massereene, 40, was the eldest son of Clotworthy John Skeffington, 11th Viscount Massereene. He too had served in the Boer War, with the 17th Lancers. Wounded at Dewetsdorp, he was awarded the Distinguished Service Order and twice Mentioned in Despatches.

The men of the North Irish Horse said their farewells to friends and families and reported for duty. One, Private Hugh Bennett, was not so lucky. Bennett, a section leader of the Dungannon battalion of the UVF, had been in Castlecaulfield paying farewell visits before joining his regiment. While cycling home an unidentified man fired on him with a revolver, wounding him twice. He would later recover and rejoin the regiment but, due to a re-emergence of childhood epileptic seizures, was discharged as medically unfit.

Others found an easier path to mobilisation. Willie Acheson, for example,

had just got back from the 1914 camp and still had his harness at home when war-alert was announced. All went to the barracks in Enniskillen … Apart from an odd parade and routine duties they hadn't much to do; after five o'clock tea he could cycle home and be in the barracks again by 10 p.m. After about ten days of this Lord Enniskillen addressed them: 'Good news men. I have been in communication with the War Office and we've been ordered to entrain tomorrow at 7 a.m. for France. All ranks are confined to barracks'.[2]

Willie Acheson was attached to A Squadron, which had begun entraining at Belfast for the Curragh on Thursday 6 August. Here the men drew their equipment, resumed training, and tried to contain their excitement. Meanwhile in Belfast the officers and senior NCOs at regimental headquarters, now located in a vacant furniture repository in Great George's Street, worked hard to bring together the numbers for the second squadron. It didn't take long. The Horsemen continued to answer their mobilisation notices, and the books were opened for new recruits on Saturday 8 August. Some of the recruits were far from typical. Many of Ulster's well-to-do were so keen to be 'in it' that they volunteered to serve as privates rather than wait for a commission. They included James Kenneth MacGregor Greer, the son of a prominent Ballymoney solicitor, who was studying law at Dublin's Trinity College, and 27-year-old 'gentleman' Leslie Ernest McNeill of Stranocum, County Antrim. Richard Annesley West, a member of an old County Fermanagh family and a veteran of the Boer War, knew that his appointment as an officer would come through soon, but, it seemed, not soon enough for him to sail with C Squadron. According to Squadron Sergeant Major Trimble:

as the time for the departure of the squadron came near, [Mr West] wired the War Office asking that his commission be confirmed. There was not any reply to that nor to a further telegram, so he sent yet one more wire, this time 'reply paid'. The answer came, that he must wait his turn.

Mr West would not wait. Late one night, a day or two before the Squadron left Belfast, he came into the makeshift orderly room in Great George's Street and awakened the author of this article, who was sleeping on a stretcher on the floor.

'Fill in an attestation form for me,' he directed and added forcibly that he was not going to wait for the War Office gazetting but would go to France as a trooper. The Form was filled in and Mr West took it away and shortly afterwards brought it back, duly signed by Lord Massereene.

'Private' West was immediately given command of a troop, allowed to wear an officer's uniform (though without any badges of rank), and lived in the Officers' Mess. His commission came through in September.

As A and C Squadrons awaited orders, the regular Army regiments that had been based in Ireland sailed for France. Joining them was one North Irish Horseman, Sergeant Walter James McCartney, who would thus become the first man of the regiment to land in France.

Mac ... was quartered in the furniture store in Great George's Street in Belfast at the time a part of the Expeditionary Force was embarking there, when a message was received asking if the NIH had anyone who understood wireless – then quite in its infancy. The Horse rose to the occasion: they had McCartney, who had learned something about wireless with the Ulster Volunteer Force. It did not matter where he learned it. What did matter was that here was a man who could replace a sick operator on a transport due to leave that night for France. And so off Mac went, to return a week or two later full of stories of the landing of the BEF.[3]

On 16 August A Squadron received its much awaited embarkation orders. It had been a frustrating wait, watching the regulars go on ahead of them, but at last the squadron rode to the docks, to an enthusiastic send-off from the citizens of Dublin.

Embarking the men on the SS *Architect* was a simple task, but the job of loading the horses was one for experts. These were a mixed lot, but generally of good quality. Not surprisingly the officers had brought their own, and usually more than one. For the most part the men were given their horses from the remount depot. Government agents were then scouring the country for horses to buy for the various arms of the service. At least some of the men, however, were able to bring their own.

On 17 August the *Architect* sailed from Dublin's North Wall quay. It was just thirteen days since war had been declared, and eight since the British Expeditionary Force had begun landing at le Havre and Boulogne in France. On board were the six officers commanding A Squadron – Major Cole, Captain Emerson Crawford Herdman, Lieutenants Robert Soame Jocelyn, David Alfred William Ker and Ronald Deane Ross, and Second Lieutenant Thomas William Gillilan Johnson Hughes – and 166 other ranks, plus a small number of Army Service Corps men. Also on board was B Squadron of the South Irish Horse. The journey to France was uneventful, the men kept busy with the trials of 'looking after a strange horse which had become extremely nervous in his floating stable'. And while Arthur McMahon and Willie Acheson would later speak disparagingly of the comforts of the 'tramp steamer' or 'coal-boat', most were too excited by the thrill of adventure to notice.[4] The *Architect* docked at le Havre on 19 August.

C Squadron wasn't far behind. On 20 August 159 men of the squadron sailed from Belfast, followed the next day by another nineteen.[5] One who missed the boat was 23-year-old William Martin from Castleblayney, County Monaghan. Martin was discovered absent on 18 August. Two months later he turned himself in and was court martialled for desertion and losing his kit. He escaped with the relatively mild sentence of thirty-five days detention and loss of pay.

For the officers, this was the beginning of a grand adventure. A fellow officer, Frank Crozier, later described an encounter on the eve of C Squadron's departure:

In the little room on the ground floor of the Ulster Club – that holy of holies – big, muscular, horsy men sit and sip and smoke, in the uniform of the North Irish Horse. Their blood is up and they are proud. Why not? Are they not to accompany the British Expeditionary Force to France? They are not regular soldiers – though many of them have been – yet they are chosen, on account of merit, to accompany the greatest, hardest, best trained, most gentlemanly little army the world has ever seen, on the greatest adventure the world has ever known. Truly they have reason to be proud! Some talk sense, some nonsense, others say nothing at all. But they all appear to think that those who get through will eat their Christmas dinners in Berlin! A few have had experience of war, though none of them knows anything of modern combat. They talk of a picnic …

The gay careless fox-hunters of the north finish their drinks with a clink of glasses and rise to depart to their horses and ships, and as they do so a waiter hands me a letter on a salver … All eyes are on me, for the cover is oblong in shape and official in character. There is silence. I read, put the letter in my pocket, and lean back in my chair.

'Coming with us?' asks one sportsman.

'No,' I reply, 'not yet. I am to join the Royal Irish Fusiliers in Dublin, and raise a company.'

This announcement is received with a roar of laughter by the departing horse soldiers as they leave the room.

'Hope your company will be well trained, Cro,' says one, Stuart by name, 'by the time we get back! You'll have to hurry up!'[6]

Among the exclusive band of nineteen who sailed on 21 August were C Squadron's six officers: Major Viscount Massereene and Ferrard, Captain Eustace King-King, and Lieutenants Neil Graham Stewart-Richardson, John Vanner Gilligan, John Grant and Samuel Barbour (Barrie) Combe. (Ironically, Barrie Combe's brother-in-law Ruric Waring had only just written to Combe's wife 'What are Barry & Holt doing. I hope they have not been fools enough to go to Belgium.'[7] 'Belgium' was exactly where Combe was headed, and Ruric's brother Holt would follow within months.) The others included four last-minute 'gentlemen recruits' destined for rapid promotion – Privates West, Greer and McNeill (mentioned earlier), and Lance Sergeant Worship Booker. One of these, presumably Greer or McNeill, had so little military experience that he 'had to be shown how to load a rifle while on the troop ship'.[8]

C Squadron arrived at le Havre on 22 August, the men full of enthusiasm for the task at hand. Private Tom Savage for example wrote home from the transport of the new chums he had met, and boasted 'I'll be able to "swank French" when I come back'.

With A and C Squadrons now in France, the North Irish Horse had twelve officers and 339 men on active service. It is worth pausing the narrative to look at who these men were. Five of the officers had been with the regiment when it was formed at Newbridge in July 1908 – Cole, Massereene, Herdman, Ker and Ross. But of the other ranks, only nine were 1908 originals, plus another five who had joined later that year – Squadron Sergeant Majors William Moore and John Whiteside; Sergeants John Adams, Robert Alexander Wylie, Hugh Ashcroft and William Christopher Bracken; Lance Sergeant George Hicks; Corporals Samuel Wylie and James Boyd; and Privates James McArow, John Gillespie, George Nesbitt, John Henderson and Donald Wallace.

Most of the men, some 296, were pre-war recruits. The service records of forty-eight of them have been located. These include much about each man's background – his place of birth, age, address, religion and occupation, for example, and give a clear picture of the make-up of the two squadrons that sailed for France in August 1914.

Of the pre-war recruits, all but four were born in the counties of Ulster, the exceptions being Squadron Sergeant Major Thomas Barns, from Berkshire, David Service from Renfrew, Scotland, James Dickson from Rossinver, County Leitrim, and Andrew Lindsay from Drumcliffe, County Sligo. More than half hailed from the western counties of Fermanagh and Donegal, while Armagh, Cavan, Down, Londonderry, Monaghan, Tyrone and Antrim were represented in smaller numbers. They were very much country boys, all but eight being farmers. Of the others, Robert Averell was a groom, Thomas Barns a professional soldier, George Ewart a joiner, James Wray a carpenter, William Livingstone a grocer, Gordon Richardson a compositor, Thomas Seawright a butcher and Robert Sterling a journalist. Their ages ranged between 17 and 39, averaging 24, the youngest being Francis Colquhoun, just 17, from Manorcunningham. Eighteen gave their religion as Presbyterian, sixteen Church of England, ten Church of Ireland, three Methodist and one Wesleyan. (The enlistment form did not give Church of Ireland as an option, relying on the recruit to strike out 'England' and replace it with 'Ireland', as many did.)

The forty-three men in A and C Squadrons who had enlisted after the war began were quite different from the pre-war enlistees. The fifteen service records located reveal them as typically older, from Belfast, many with previous military experience (often with the North of Ireland Imperial Yeomanry), and rather than being farmers, having a mix of urban-based occupations. Some, a small number, were upper-middle class professionals and businessmen who would ordinarily expect a commission rather than service in the ranks, such as Norman ffolliott Darling, son of a Lurgan medical practitioner, John McKinstry, a Belfast factory manager, James Dowling, a Belfast timber merchant, and Robert Hutchinson Andrews, a civil engineer from Banbridge. Eleven of the forty-three wartime enlistees in A and C Squadrons would become officers. The ex-soldiers included William James McFerran of Crumlin, Belfast, a veteran of the Boer War, and Jack Wright, a well-known local footballer who had served with the Royal Irish Rifles in South Africa. Edward Menice of Shankill, Belfast, heavily tattooed on both arms, was just 24 but had already served with the Royal Irish Rifles, as had Philip Holland, a 25-year-old labourer and plater's helper from Cable Street in Belfast.

Only two of the wartime enlistees sailed with A Squadron, not surprising given that squadron's early departure. William Moisley and James Goggin must have had particular skills needed by A Squadron, for they had enlisted just a week before the squadron sailed. The other wartime recruits sailed with C Squadron, a quarter of its number. This gave it a quite different character from A Squadron – still mostly rural, but leavened with a mix of blue collar urban workers, older ex-soldiers, professionals, businessmen and young gentlemen.

The port of le Havre was the main entry point to France for the British Expeditionary Force, and by the time the North Irish Horse squadrons landed there, most of the regulars had already left for the front. Close to forty regiments had been through the port, converging on Field Marshal Sir John French's General Headquarters at le Cateau in northern France. Having disembarked, the squadrons of the North and South Irish Horse proceeded to one of the many camps in the district – A Squadron to No.1 Camp at nearby Sainte-Adresse – on the way enjoying a warm welcome from the French civilians. 'We were treated with the greatest kindness by the French people,' wrote Private Robert Watson, 'being given wines and fruits in abundance. Needless to say, the few days we spent here gave us a very good impression of our French Allies.'[9]

News soon arrived of the role each squadron would play – A Squadron would be General Headquarters' cavalry, and C Squadron cavalry to the 5th Division. On Friday 21 August A Squadron marched to the railway station and boarded trains, as Horseman James Elliott recalled,

> cattle-trucks whose pace was so slow that a soldier could jump off, do a message, and jump on again. Though the army wasn't fussy about accommodation for its privates there was no despondency: as the trains moved out the men were all mooing and baahing![10]

A Squadron detrained at Busigny, and a short ride brought them to le Cateau. Here they reported for duty and were detailed as escort to the Commander in Chief, Field Marshal French. The atmosphere at GHQ was busy, and newcomers struggled to find out what was happening. Travis Hampson, an officer in the Field Ambulance, found

> a complete absence of news, at least we couldn't get hold of any, but much rushing about in motor cars by the staff and motor bike despatch riders ... The only troops in the town are the First Battalion Cameron Highlanders acting as GHQ guard, and the North Irish Horse, ... with other oddments, REs, ASC and ourselves.[11]

By 22 August the BEF was fanned out to the north of le Cateau, searching for the German force that they knew was advancing towards them through Belgium. They had no idea that it was the main tactical thrust of the German offensive. Sir John French, the British Commander in Chief, was unsure whether to advance, consolidate or withdraw, even as news came through that the French Fifth Army on his right had begun to fall back. Reports of masses of German infantry and large concentrations of cavalry were dismissed as 'somewhat exaggerated'.[12] It is hardly surprising then that when the German First Army fell on the BEF at Mons and west to Condé on the morning of 23 August, the British were not as well prepared as they might have been. The battle continued for most of the day, but the dozen British battalions, heavily outnumbered, finally gave way, having sustained 1,600 casualties and inflicting at least as many. The 'retreat from Mons' had begun.

Thus was the pattern set for the next fortnight; desperate rearguard actions as units took turn to cover each other's withdrawal and buy time by slowing the advance; seeking to keep touch to avoid gaps in the lines between units of the BEF and with the French on either side, avoiding encirclement, saving the guns, marching, and the cavalry everywhere, seeking out the enemy, fighting on horse and dismounted, passing messages, and protecting the rear.

As the army pulled back from Mons, a fresh division, the 4th, was arriving at le Cateau. In the rush to join the fighting they had left behind their divisional cavalry, so GHQ ordered two troops of the North Irish Horse under Major Cole to assist them. The other two troops under Captain Herdman remained as escort to the Commander in Chief.

Having detrained at le Cateau on 24 August, two battalions of the 4th Division marched north to Briastre and towards Solesmes, with Cole's North Irish Horse troops as advance guard. It seems that at least some of the North Irish Horsemen scouted much further north on this day, getting mixed up in a cavalry charge by the 9th Lancers and 4th (Royal Irish) Dragoon Guards at Audregnies. According to Private Hiram Robinson of Brookeborough, 'A troop of the regiment … got lost … [and] when they were retiring Humphrey Boyd (Maguiresbridge) and a few of them were left behind and they joined the 9th Lancers, and were in the thick of the Lancers' charge.'[13] The charge itself was brave but futile. Attacking enemy positions but with no clear objective, they were cut to pieces. A Squadron saw more action this day, according to Private William Morton of Lurgan:

we were doing a flanking movement. When we came in contact with a patrol of the enemy we dismounted, and, taking up a position, opened a rapid fire. We succeeded in bringing down about fifty of them, and the remainder, who galloped round a wood, were finished by some infantry on our left. Immediately then the German big guns and Maxims began to play on us, and again we had to retire through a village which was in flames[14]

It has been claimed that the first North Irish Horseman to account for an enemy fighter was Farrier Sergeant Ernest Gilliland, an event that most likely occurred during this action. Gilliland, a 31-year-old from Drumar, County Monaghan, was a veteran of the regiment, having enlisted in March 1909. The eighty or so men of these two troops of the North Irish Horse had just become the first non-regulars in the British army to see action in the war.

Early next morning Cole's half squadron returned to le Cateau, where they covered the arrival of the remainder of the 4th Division and escorted them to Solesmes. By then GHQ and the rest of A Squadron had decamped south to St Quentin.

The 4th Division held their positions near Solesmes all day. It was crucial that it did, for it was through this village that the main roads from the north, north-east and north-west passed and therefore, was the main line of the retreat from Mons. The day was stifling hot as the tired and hungry troops made their way south to positions around le Cateau. About 5.00pm a thunderstorm broke, soaking them through. Late in the evening the 4th Division pulled out of Solesmes, marching in heavy rain to Fontaine-au-Pire, where they took up a defensive line from that village to Wambaix. The troops of the North Irish Horse accompanied them and reported to 4th Division headquarters for further instruction. They were sent to assist two companies of the 2nd Inniskilling Fusiliers in an advance post at Bévillers to the north of the Cambrai–le Cateau road. Lacking cavalry 'eyes', the division was desperately short of intelligence about the German positions, and the Inniskillings had already been surprised by a troop of enemy horses and a motor convoy, which they were able to see off with rapid fire. At 3.00am the Horsemen were sent to Longsart, just north of Haucourt, where it seems they came under the command of the 3rd Division.

Lieutenant General Smith-Dorrien, in command of II Corps around le Cateau, faced a dilemma that night. He had been ordered by Sir John French to continue the withdrawal in order to maintain touch with I Corps and the retreating French forces. It soon became clear to him, however, that the Germans were so close and his troops so exhausted that he must stand and fight. Only then, with luck, could he hope to resume the march south. In a hasty exchange of letters French relented, though uncomfortable with the decision. With Allenby's Cavalry Division and Snow's 4th Division falling under his command, Smith-Dorrien prepared to fight.

The next morning found Cole's two troops of A Squadron in the vicinity of Beauvois, waiting for the German assault in what would be known as the Battle of le Cateau. At dawn on 26 August the German artillery opened up along the eight-mile British front. The morning was dominated by heavy artillery fire from both sides, with the German infantry attempting to advance after noon. Fighting against overwhelming numbers, the British held their own, though losing some ground and gradually being outflanked. By late afternoon Smith-Dorrien ordered the retreat, which the Germans did not pursue with any vigour. Losses had been high on both sides. What role the men of the North Irish Horse played on this day is unknown, but it is likely they fought with the infantrymen of the 3rd Division at Caudry, dismounted and using their rifles to good effect. A Squadron's Private Kyle of Tyrone later told the Belfast News-Letter about the fighting he saw and what he heard from others on that day:

> Two troops of the North Irish Horse, numbering 56, ... were engaged assisting to stem the onward rush of the Germans ... All day long the battle raged, but although the Germans were vastly superior in numbers they were repulsed every time, and towards evening, when pursuing a company of flying Germans, Trooper Kyle got an arm broken and was taken to hospital.[15]

Private William Morton's account below also appears to describe the fighting at le Cateau, although the location of the regiments he names may be problematic:

> I shall never forget the day we had the bayonet charge with the Inniskillings. My troop, under Lieutenant Hughes, took up a position on the railway line. The enemy was about 500 yards away, when suddenly their artillery opened fire and we had to retire in the open under a heavy shell fire. I shall never forget the sound of the bursting of their 'Jack Johnsons', as the Highlanders call them. When we took up another position with the Gordons and Inniskillings we made our rifles tell on the advancing German infantry. It was horrible to see the heaps of dead and dying, both men and horses.[16]

II Corps had broken off the fight and resumed its retreat by 5.00pm, Cole's North Irish Horse assisting as rearguard to the 3rd Division. One Horseman had been left behind at Le Cateau. Private Andrew Smith of County Tyrone was picked up by the Germans and made a prisoner. Accounts of the march vary greatly. '[I] lost the whole of the Division,' wrote Lieutenant Brereton of the Royal Field Artillery, 'got blocked by cavalry on the road, wandered all round the place, lost our way sometimes, and half the battery at others. A perfectly miserable night. I was dead beat ...'[17] Count Gleichen, commanding the 5th Division's 15 Brigade, thought it "a regular nightmare",[18] while Lieutenant Pennycuick of the 5th Division thought it was like a crowd coming away from a football match, but not one that felt its team had been defeated.[19] Nonetheless, the men were tired, soaked and hungry.

By around midnight Cole's North Irish Horsemen, with the 3rd Division, reached Beaurevoir, having come via Elincourt and Malincourt.

> Everywhere, when the order to halt was given, the men dropped down on the road, and were asleep almost before they reached the ground. The only precautions possible at the late hour were to push small picquets out a few hundred yards on each side of the road. Officers of the cavalry and artillery, themselves half dead with fatigue, had to rouse their men from a semi-comatose state to water and feed the horses, then to rouse them once more to take the nose-bags off, taking care lest they should fall asleep in the very act. And all this had to be done in inky darkness under drizzling rain.[20]

It may have been this night that the men of A Squadron fought a short action, as later described by Private McArow:

> [At] night they were pegging down their horses in garden, preparatory to retiring for the night's rest in some hay lofts, when suddenly bullets whistled overhead. Lord Cole, who was in command, shouted to Lieutenant Hughes: 'Get your men out, Hughes.' The men readily responded, and fixed bayonets. They advanced through a field of vegetables in the direction from which the sound of firing came, and then heard the cheers of the 2nd Inniskillings and Cameron Highlanders as they charged the enemy. Lord Cole ordered the charge, and the North Irish Horsemen answered with cheers, and rushed forward along with the infantry. The Germans did not wait, but took to their heels. The Horse then retired that night a further ten miles, escorted by the two foot battalions, and thus gained a short respite from the pursuing Germans.[21]

Meanwhile, Lieutenant General Smith-Dorrien, arriving at St Quentin on the evening of the 26th, found that GHQ had already left for the safety of Noyon farther to the south. With them had gone the Cameron Highlanders and their escort, and the other half of the North Irish Horse's A Squadron. As one eyewitness ruefully observed, 'GHQ took "some watching" in those days. If one turned around it was likely to disappear to the southward.'[22]

What of Massereene's C Squadron? They had arrived at le Havre on the night of Saturday 22 August and on Sunday moved to a camp about two miles out of town. After a couple of days they entrained for St Quentin, arriving at about 3.00pm on Tuesday 25 August. It seems that their departure was rushed, for according to Private Harry Newell they left their kitbags behind at le Havre. 'I could only take with me what I stood in and what I managed to roll up in my great-coat.'[23] At St Quentin C Squadron spent two days billeted in a slaughterhouse while its officers tried to obtain clear orders. They had been told to join the 5th Division, and on 27 August the remnants of this and other divisions began pouring into St Quentin on their long march south from le Cateau. Here these units were told to march south west for Ollezy, four miles east of Ham. For C Squadron, all was confusion. They could get no orders from headquarters, so at midnight 'Massereene decided to trek backward too, so we left St Quentin's at midnight and went to La Fer[e] arriving there 5 AM after a miserable night march in pouring rain.'[24]

Unfortunately this was not the path taken by the 5th Division. La Fère, on the Oise river, was the most easterly point of the BEF's line, and through it was marching much of Haig's I Corps. C Squadron was lost, and no doubt Haig's men sent them on their way.

We left Major Cole's two troops of A Squadron on the night of 26 August catching a fitful sleep at Beaurevoir. Orders were received that their division would now head for Ham, many miles to the south. Passing through the village of Nauroy the Horsemen met a battalion of the Hampshire Regiment resting up after the previous day's retreat and warned them that German cavalry units were close behind. Soon after the Hampshires pulled back as the enemy began shelling the village.[25] Vermand was reached by late afternoon, where the men finally received a meal and were allowed a few hours' rest. The march to Ham was then resumed, with little trouble encountered from the pursuing Germans. The men of the North Irish Horse brought up the rear. No rest greeted the troops at Ham, for orders had been issued that II Corps had to be clear of it by daylight on the 28th and march another ten miles to Noyon. They reached the vicinity, at nearby Crisolles and Genvry, by day's end. Here the Horsemen rejoined the 4th Division and next day marched out to camp at Sempigny, where they were allowed a day's rest and no doubt reflected on what they had been through. 'It was terrible to see the poor refugees in that awful retreat,' wrote Private William Morton.

Our food was very scarce; for days we lived on a few biscuits, but the French were very good, and gave us lots of fruit and wine. Want of sleep and marching at night also came hard on us. We lost our transport, which was shelled to pieces, so there was no way of bringing provisions along.[26]

Not far to the south at Compiègne the rest of A Squadron was in more comfortable circumstances at French's new headquarters in 'a very fine old palace'[27]. Orders had been issued by GHQ that BEF transport wagons should leave behind ammunition and all unnecessary impedimenta so that exhausted and wounded men could be carried. GHQ, however, had managed to preserve some of its own necessities during the withdrawal. When Travis Hampson of the Field Ambulance caught up with them at Noyon or Compiègne, he was invited to the mess of the North Irish Horse, where Lieutenant Jocelyn gave him a prized bottle of whiskey. 'They ran a decent mess,' Hampson observed days later when he gratefully opened the bottle.

Most of the BEF managed to get some well-needed rest on 29 August, while Sir John French and the commander of the French forces, General Joffre, conferred at Compiègne. The BEF now sat between two French armies – Lanrezac's Fifth on the right and General Maunoury's Sixth on the left. Joffre was keen to see the British forces stay in position, but the British commander wanted to take them further back, so a further withdrawal was ordered that night. There was no let-up the following day as the march south continued in hot, dry weather that taxed the men's endurance. Fortunately the German forces did not press the retreating army, but they were getting closer.

While A Squadron was at Compiègne with GHQ it sustained the regiment's first fatality of the war, though an unlikely one for the North Irish Horse, the man not being Irish, a cavalryman or a Protestant. Driver Matthew Callanan was a member of the Army Service Corps, but was attached to A Squadron of the North Irish Horse soon after he was mobilised in Dublin, his role most likely being to help manage the squadron's baggage train. A Roman Catholic born at Knightsbridge, London in 1878, he was relatively old for war service, but had prior military experience, having served three years with the ASC at Aldershot a decade before the war. Perhaps Callanan had Irish connections, because by August 1914 he was living in Dublin. When the call went out for all reservists to mobilise, Callanan went to the nearest

ASC depot and joined 19 Company. Three days later he was attached to A Squadron of the North Irish Horse and in a week was sailing with them for France.

Exactly how he died isn't known, except that it resulted from a broken spine sustained in an accident at Compiègne on or about 30 August. His comrades passed his body and personal effects to the care of GHQ's Field Ambulance. He was quickly buried, his personal effects were no doubt left behind, and the location of his grave forgotten. His name is now inscribed on the la Ferté-sous-Jouarre Memorial, Seine-et-Marne.[28]

The night of 31 August found the BEF strung out in a line west-east from Verberie (4th Division) to Crépy-en-Valois (5th Division), Villers-Cotterêts (3rd Division), Laversine (2nd Division) and Missy (1st Division), the latter two divisions well north of the rest. Cole's two troops of A Squadron had marched with the 4th Division from Noyon south to Breuil on the north-eastern edge of the Forêt de Compiègne, then made a tricky march west through the forest to Verberie.

GHQ, with Herdman's two troops of A Squadron, had withdrawn to Dammartin. That evening, anxious to avoid a further clash with the Germans, French ordered that the retreat continue. The Germans were now pressing hard and some severe actions would be fought before the day was out. Camped at Néry, close to the 4th Division's line of march, was 1 Cavalry Brigade and L Battery of the Royal Horse Artillery. This group was surprised in the early morning mist by a large German cavalry force under Lieutenant General von Garnier, which had occupied the high ground to the east of Néry. After a brave defence by the British, the German cavalry was driven from the field. It was a small victory in the overall scheme of things, but Néry was the BEF's first of the war.

To the east, C Squadron had moved as quickly as it could to find the 5th Division. At 10.00am on 28 August they rode from la Fère south-westward along the Oise river to Chauny, then to Brétigny, where they bivouacked for two days. They found the 5th Division nearby, around Pontoise, the division having marched south from St Quentin and through Noyon. They resumed the retreat on the afternoon of 30 August, marching south to Attichy on the Aisne. The weather was terribly hot, trying for horses and men alike. In the haste of retreat the squadron lost its transport wagons, and Barrie Combe was sent off with an orderly to find them. As soon as he returned he was sent to deliver a load of gun cotton to a group of Royal Engineers five miles distant, presumably engaged in bridge-blowing on the Aisne. By the time Combe got back to Attichy he found that C Squadron had moved off to Hautefontaine. However, Combe found little time to rest there, as the squadron was on the move again. They rode nine miles south through the forest to Villers-Cotterêts, west to Vauciennes and then to Crépy-en-Valois, before turning south to Nanteuil, which they reached in the evening of 1 September. Here they were able to steal a night's rest.

During the ride from Villers-Cotterêts to Nanteuil C Squadron had become mixed up in the rearguard action around Crépy-en-Valois. At dawn on 1 September German forces had attacked the 5th Division's outpost lines to the north of Crépy and by 10.00am mounted an infantry assault. Brigadier General Gleichen's 15 Brigade was in action north of divisional headquarters at Crépy.

Cavalry was reported everywhere, but it was difficult to know which was English and which German. The latter's patrols were fairly bold, and single horsemen got close up to us ...

The two battalions working up north-west from Duvy had just extended and were moving carefully across country, when I received word that a large force of the enemy's cavalry was moving on to my left rear. I did not like this, and pushed out another battalion (Norfolks) to guard my flank. But we need not have been worried, for shortly afterwards it appeared that the 'hostile' cavalry was the North Irish Horse, turned up from goodness knows where.[29]

It wasn't the only case of mistaken identity for C Squadron this day, despatch rider Frederick Watson reporting another scare when a hostile party of 'Uhlans' turned out to be North Irish Horsemen.

On another occasion, Lieutenant West of C Squadron and Major Allason of the Bedfordshire Regiment were out scouting.

They had just been falling back at a walk with the information they had gathered, when they heard a clatter of hoofs behind them, and beheld a German cavalry officer and his man trying to gallop past them – not to attack them – apparently bolting from some of our own cavalry. Allason, who was in front, stuck spurs into his horse and galloped after the officer and shot his horse, bringing the German down, the latter also being put out of action. Then they bound up the German's wound and took all his papers from him, which proved to be very useful, giving the location of the German cavalry and other troops. Meanwhile the officer's servant stood by, with his mouth open, doing nothing. As they couldn't carry the officer off, they left them both there and came on.[30]

The rearguard action that day did its job, with the 5th Division away by noon and the Germans not heavily in pursuit. During the fighting, two men of C Squadron were captured by German cavalry – Private Stewart Harris Moir, a 17-year-old from Belfast, and Trumpeter William James McFerran, an old Irish Yeomanry soldier who had served in the Boer War. The two were soon freed when their Uhlan captors were in turn forced to surrender by a party of the Suffolks. Another man, Farrier Sergeant Alexander Kennedy, was captured around this time, probably having been left behind at St Quentin. Kennedy of Tullyheron, County Down, was aged 22 and a four-year veteran of the regiment. It was not until the following February that his parents received news that he was alive and well, and not until January 1919 that he returned home from captivity. C Squadron's Private Wingfield Espey nearly met the same fate when he and other men of the squadron were ordered to assist a machine-gun and observation post sited on top of a hill.

> The Uhlans could be seen advancing in swarms, and Espey's party signalled by means of the field telephone to the British artillery. They soon found the range, and for the first time in his life Espey saw both horses and men being literally blown into the air. The Uhlans rapidly retreated, but the shell fire followed them accurately and inflicted heavy losses. So interested were Espey and a companion in the scene that they did not observe the departure of their officer and the other men. They were unable to overtake them, and had given themselves up for lost, as the Germans were rapidly approaching in the rear, when a British staff officer overtook them and on finding that Espey had not got a map of the country, directed him to go through a wood which was in front. On entering the wood Espey found that it was intersected with cross roads every hundred yards or so, but taking his direction from the sun he and his companion fortunately debouched on a road filled with retiring British troops.[31]

It was another two days before they found their squadron.

By the end of 1 September the British line stretched west-east from Baron to la Ferté Milon. That night GHQ moved out of Dammartin in an atmosphere of panic after a large body of German cavalry was spotted nearby. This was von Garnier's 4th Cavalry Division, forced south after the fight at Néry. The last thing the battered German cavalry wanted was trouble, but GHQ wasn't to know this, and 'sped on through the night as though all the German devils were on our trail'. [32]

Nearby was a squadron of aeroplanes belonging to the Royal Flying Corps. The infant force had been doing valuable reconnaissance work for the army, spotting the movements and location of the German forces well before traditional methods could have done so. A troop of GHQ's North Irish Horse and some French Territorials were left behind to guard the machines until they could take off at dawn. 'The Aerodrome was in a field by some cross-roads,' wrote RFC officer Maurice Baring. 'Troops were disposed so as to defend it ... Some of the North Irish Horse kept on champing up and down this road all night and disturbing us. One of them kept on treading on me. Uhlans were supposed to be about three miles off.'[33]

Given the closeness of the German forces, French had ordered that the BEF continue its southerly march without rest through the night. This was just as well, for the German First Army orders that night were to attack and encircle them. The British slipped away just in time.

The night of 2 September found the BEF in an ever-shortening line from Meaux north-west to Dammartin, with GHQ having moved well back to Melun on the Seine. Cole's two troops of A Squadron were still working as rearguard to the 4th Division and camped at Dammartin. C Squadron was at Vinantes, near the village of Montge, having helped 15 Brigade as rearguard for the 5th Division on its march from Nanteuil.

Every day brought the BEF closer to Paris, and while the pace of the march began to slow, and the Germans had ceased to pursue them, confusion amongst the men grew. At Lagny that day Mildred Aulich, an American-born resident of France, met a party of men from the North Irish Horse in a comic encounter that gives some idea of the men's mood.

Just before the train ran into Lagny – our first stop – I was surprised to see British soldiers washing their horses in the river, so I was not surprised to find the station full of men in khaki. They were sleeping on the benches along the wall, and standing about, in groups. As to many of the French on the train this was their first sight of the men in khaki, and as there were Scotch there in their kilts, there was a good deal of excitement. The train made a long stop in the effort to put more people into the already overcrowded coaches. I leaned forward, wishing to get some news, and the funny thing was that I could not think how to speak to those boys in English. You may think that an affectation. It wasn't. Finally I desperately sang out:–

'Hulloa, boys.'

You should have seen them dash for the window. I suppose that their native tongue sounded good to them so far from home.

'Where did you come from?' I asked.

'From up yonder – a place called la Fere,' one of them replied.

'What regiment?' I asked.

'Anyone else here speak English?' he questioned, running his eyes along the faces thrust out of the windows.

I told him no one did.

'Well,' he said, 'we are all that is left of the North Irish Horse and a regiment of Scotch Borderers.'

'What are you doing here?'

'Retreating – and waiting for orders. How far are we from Paris?'

I told him about seventeen miles. He sighed, and remarked that he thought they were nearer, and as the train started I had the idea in the back of my head that these boys actually expected to retreat inside the fortifications. *La! la!*[34]

GHQ and Herdman's North Irish Horse troops remained at Melun on 3, 4 and 5 September. On 3 September the BEF withdrew over the Marne and the bridges were blown; Cole's two troops of A Squadron fell back with the 4th Division to Lagny. C Squadron with the 5th Division crossed the Marne at Trilbardou, then marched to Bouleurs and nearby Montpichet. Barrie Combe and his troop were kept busy:

I was sent out as right flank guard to the Division and chased three German Uhlans killing one and taking his horse. We then marched to Boulears. I was again delaid from squadron to act as an escort to a company of R.E. who were blowing up bridges & I got that job done at 5 P.M. and followed up squadron to where they had been ordered to go to, but their orders had been altered and I missed them. I spent night in a clean pigsty and moved next morning 3 A.M. and rejoined squadron.

Friday 4 September saw little pressure from the Germans, who had crossed the Marne but turned east towards what they saw as the last hurdle to complete victory, the French Fifth Army. The men enjoyed a welcome rest before a further march south – their last – to a line roughly east-west through Tournan. Cole's A Squadron troops with the 4th Division did rear-guard work to Jossigny and C Squadron for the 5th Division to the vicinity of Tournan. According to Combe:

> spent first slack day for many days, and washed and shaved and generally cleaned up … However got orders at 8 P.M to march to Tournant, and marched all night. I took bad with cramps and had to be slung in a wagon – was awful bad. Next day spent at a Chateau of Tournan where we licked our sores and I recovered.[35]

The great retreat was over. In just thirteen days the BEF had conducted a fighting retreat covering as much as 200 miles. They had lost 15,000 men killed, wounded or missing and a large number of guns. But in the face of vastly superior numbers, their triumph was that they were still intact. A and C Squadrons of the North Irish Horse had played their part and survived with only one fatality, a small number of wounded and injured, and two captured, Cole's two troops of A Squadron having seen the most action.

Somehow Barrie Combe found time to get off the shortest of letters to his wife Mary:

> Dearest Old Girl
> All well
> Love to kids and yourself.
> Barrie[36]

Around this time one of C Squadron's troops, under Lieutenant Grant, were detached as escort to II Corps' commander, Smith-Dorrien.

Joffre was now ready to hit the Germans hard in the flank they had exposed by turning to the east. The BEF, sitting between the two French armies, was part of his plan, but first many units had to retrace their steps, having spent 5 September withdrawing further. The move to the offensive was a wonderful tonic for the British troops.

> We awoke early to a gorgeous day. We were actually going to advance. The news put us in marvellous good temper … The Staff was almost giggling, and a battalion … that we saw pass, was absolutely shouting with joy. You would have thought we had just gained a famous victory.[37]

Through 6 September the BEF marched in a roughly north-easterly direction towards the Grand Morin. For the North Irish Horse this meant a reversal of their role. Now they were acting as advance guard – scouting, flushing out and chasing the German cavalry. For indeed the Germans were withdrawing. Cole's A Squadron troops advanced ahead of the 4th Division to Magny-le-Hongre, and C Squadron through the Forêt de Crecy to Mortcerf, where the inhabitants were happy to ply their liberators with fruit to refresh them on what was another sweltering hot day.[38] During the afternoon C Squadron engaged in a brief but successful clash with German cavalry at Dammartin-sur-Tigeaux, as related by despatch rider Watson:

> Later in the afternoon I was sent off to find the North Irish Horse. I discovered them four miles away in the first flush of victory. They had had a bit of a scrap with Uhlans, and were proudly displaying to an admiring brigade that was marching past a small but select collection of horses, lances, and saddles.[39]

According to Corporal Fred Lindsay:

> Trooper McClennaghan, of Garvagh, accounted for three Uhlans and took two horses single-handed; and two others and myself, firing simultaneously at an escaping Uhlan, brought both horse and rider down at 900 yards' distance. Sitting on the roadside later eating biscuits and bully beef with the rest of us Viscount Massereene complimented us, saying, 'Boys, you have done a good day's work. If we only had an opportunity like this every day!'[40]

Combe wrote that 'we had a scrap with Uhlans & knocked blazes out of them. They fled in all directions NIH pursuing gallantly – I took another horse but had to shoot it.'[41]

Around this time two men of C Squadron were wounded, and were lucky to escape with their lives:

a corporal named James White, from Lisbellaw, Co. Fermanagh … and a trooper, also named White (from County Monaghan) were out on a reconnoitring patrol one afternoon, when they were fired on by a party of Germans secreted in the fringe of a small plantation. Both men were wounded and Trooper White's horse was shot dead. Although suffering great agony, and whilst still under fire, Corporal White succeeded in getting his comrade up behind him on his own horse, and both got away from further danger.[42]

On 7 and 8 September the BEF crossed the Grand Morin and sweep north, across the Petit Morin and towards the Marne itself. Lord Cole's A Squadron troops continued their work as advance guard for the 4th Division, reaching Signy-Signets on the 8th. C Squadron advanced with the 5th Division, still attached to Gleichen's 15 Brigade. On 7 September they reached Coulommiers and next day advanced in the heat across open fields to the Petit Morin. Massereene's C Squadron, working as advance guard with a party of the 5th Lancers, had a 'thrilling encounter' as they reached the Petit Morin. In a letter home Private Robert Sterling wrote:

they almost pinned us and a crowd of the Lancers at a small village, and we had to gallop out of it as hard as we could along a road bordered with trees. The bullets were cutting the leaves of the trees all around us, and several of our horses were hit. A chap who was in front of me had his horse shot dead under him, but he succeeded in catching a horse belonging to a Lancer who was killed, and on it he got clear. When we got off the road into the open fields they got the big guns to play upon us, and the shells tore up the earth all around. However, we got safely to cover; but it was a terrible experience and one I never wish to have again. It was a miracle we did not lose a lot of men.

On another occasion during the advance men of C Squadron clashed with a party of German cavalry, chasing them out of a town and killing and capturing a number. 'We had our Cossack posts put out near a small deserted village," wrote Private Sterling,

"whilst the remainder of the troop, with our officer (Captain Richardson) were in a yard in the village feeding our horses. Whilst there the sentry informed us that he had seen a German looking round the corner at the bottom of the village street. It was not long until we had the saddles tightened up, and out we dashed in the direction the German had been seen. When we got round the corner we saw seven or eight Germans galloping away as fast as they could. We gave hot chase, firing after them, but as it is impossible to take aim sitting on a galloping horse, we only succeeded in killing one of them. The others had too much of a start, and scattered in different directions. There were six of us, and had they turned on us with their lances they might have done damage.[43]

Such clashes were common during the British advance. Many began with a surprise encounter around the corner of a village street. Lieutenant West was leading a patrol when,

on rounding a corner in a village, was confronted by a similar patrol of Uhlans, trotting confidently towards the same corner. Mr West did not hesitate. With a shout, he charged straight at the Germans, his troop clattering round the corner after him. Taken by surprise, the Germans, not knowing how many more were coming, wheeled and galloped for safety, the Irish Horsemen after them. The Uhlan's officer turned into a field and Mr West followed and chased him round the field, the two exchanging shots and the German was killed. One or two prisoners were taken with several of the Uhlan steel lances ... In such a scrap with the Germans, Mr West lost his regulation pattern cap, which he replaced with a rather battered slouch hat, turned up on the left; on a puggaree there was fastened an other ranks' cap badge with the crown broken off.[44]

Another 'round the corner' encounter was witnessed by John Lucy of the Royal Irish Rifles:

One day while the Battalion was in the van during the advance to the Marne one of our forward sections watched with interest while a cavalry screen composed of North Irish Horse reconnoitred the village. The infantry section on high ground could see the village plainly, and all the approaches to it, but the cavalry operating on low ground ahead had no such advantage.

The leading point of the British cavalry patrol rode on well ahead of his comrades towards the crossroads in the centre of the village, and at the same moment our infantry were delighted to see a German Uhlan riding similarly towards the same crossroads along the road running into it at right angles from a flank. No verbal warning could be given by the observers. They were too fascinated to think of firing their rifles. German and Irishman met precisely at the crossroads, and each wheeled a rearing horse and galloped away from each other as hard as they could pelt.[45]

Versions of such encounters soon appeared in the Irish press, reading as if from the pages of a *Boys' Own* adventure. 'I was attached to the Field Artillery for two weeks,' wrote A Squadron's Private Robert Watson.

During this period we took a field gun and also a Maxim gun after a very hot time, and we further succeeded in capturing a large German transport wagon heavily laden with mutton, which we very much appreciated. A few days later I managed to get back to Mr Ross's troop in time to take part in a very lively encounter the North Irish had with the enemy, under Lieutenant Ross. Unfortunately I lost my horse, and had to run three miles holding on to the stirrup of Mr Ross's saddle. This was the toughest job I ever experienced.[46]

Most contact was with parties of German cavalry. Corporal Fred Lindsay of C Squadron described an occasion in which

Trooper Ellison … of Belfast, rode by mistake into a Uhlan camp, but happily for him the night was so dark that he had discovered his mistake before he was recognised, and was almost clear of the camp again before the Uhlans were aware that he was not one of themselves. Just as he came to the high wire fence surrounding the camp one of the Uhlans struck a match to light his pipe, and Ellison stood revealed. Putting spurs to his horse, he attempted to jump the fence, but his mount baulked and threw him over its head into a drain on the outside. Amid a hail of bullets Ellison managed to run along the drain and escape in safety to the high road.[47]

In general the British and Irish cavalrymen took a dim view of the fighting skills and courage of their opponents. Stewart-Richardson wrote to a friend that 'They run like scalded cats when they see you, and are always in close formation as if they were frightened to separate.'[48] Lance Sergeant Richard

Irwin described the Germans as 'a great pack of cowards, one man could chase a dozen of them; in fact I have seen one Lancer capture ten Germans without firing a shot, so you see they are a poor lot when out from cover.'[49] Robert Sterling wrote: 'it is characteristic of the Uhlans to run when fired upon; they are the greatest cowards I have ever come across.'[50] This from Barrie Combe: 'Their artillery is magnificent but infantry & cavalry worth very little. Their much vaunted Uhlans even the NIH hunted like sheep.'[51]

On 9 September the British forces crossed the Marne, but their advance north was considerably slowed by well positioned and determined German artillery and infantry. The weather, which had continued hot and dry, finally broke in the evening with showers that soaked the many men sleeping in the open. On this day Cole's two troops of A Squadron left the 4th Division and re-joined their fellows at GHQ – the squadron had been split since le Cateau. GHQ had by now moved up to Coulommiers on the Grand Morin.

For three days the French and British forces pursued the retiring German flank across the ground between the Marne and the Aisne. C Squadron again found itself close to the action as the 5th Division pushed on to the Aisne. On Friday 11 September Gleichen's 15 Brigade marched to Chouy in cool weather that turned to rain in the afternoon. Not finding Chouy to his liking he pushed on to St-Rémy-Blanzy, where

> [we evacuated] some cavalry and [made] them move on to some farms a bit ahead – including Massereene and his North Irish Horse, who, I fear, were not much pleased at having to turn out of their comfortable barns.[52]

It wasn't only accommodation that was proving difficult for the men of the North Irish Horse. During the retreat 'all the luxuries the people possessed they showered on us', wrote Harry Newell, but it was a different matter advancing over ground too recently occupied by the invaders. 'As we follow up the Germans and sometimes thousands of our own troops, you can guess how impossible it is to get anything to buy. Our fellows all have plenty of money, yet cannot buy matches.'[53]

On 12 September the BEF reached the banks of the Aisne. In dreary, pouring rain, C Squadron with the 5th Division found billets around Ciry, Serches and Nampteuil, and watched the activities of the Germans on the steep hills on the other side of the river. A Squadron, having marched with GHQ across the Marne to la Ferme Paris near Marigny-en-Orxois on 11

September, now moved to Fère-en-Tardenois, fourteen miles south of the Aisne – 'quite a tiny little place, about the size of Strabane,' according to Captain Herdman.[54] Here they found themselves comfortable billets in what would be their home for almost a month.

The British and French commanders were unsure whether the Germans would stand and fight at the Aisne or continue their retreat. Prospects for further success appeared good, and orders were issued to cross the river and continue the advance. However the Germans had done a good job destroying the Aisne's bridges, and the river's north bank, with steep spurs running down close to the water's edge, made it an ideal defensive position. By the end of the day only tenuous footholds had been gained at several crossing points, particularly by I Corps on the right. In the centre of the British line II Corps had crossed with great difficulty at Vailly and Missy. Between the two the bridge to Condé, at the foot of the steep Chivres spur, was untouched, but likely to be so well covered by enemy machine guns and snipers that it was thought to be a trap and was left alone.

Late that night Captain Herdman of A Squadron settled down and wrote to his wife, referring to the difficulties of getting food and the heavy rains, which made marching difficult, and that motors bringing supplies to the front were coming through night and day:

For the last forty-eight hours there has been constant cannonading ten miles north. The Germans have got a strong position there – the last, they say, they can take in France. Our guns never cease. It is hard to believe they are slaughtering each other so close. We have got comfortable billets here, but we had not much time to enjoy them, as after dinner we got an order to go out this morning early in search of Uhlans who had been cut off and were hiding in the woods. We got up at 2.30 o'clock, and left at four. After searching the woods all day I got back at five. We were sent the wrong way, and only heard at 2.30 p.m. where the Uhlans were. We arrived at the place about three, and then found that the Highlanders had taken them all. There were about sixty of them, a great proportion being officers. They were quite glad to surrender to the British, but would not to the French. They were all starving ... The country is a sad sight to see – some corn cut, some not, and I am afraid it will never be brought in ... We had quite a 'bend' to-night – bacon, boiled eggs, with potatoes and butter, and two bottles of 'fiz,' which Cole (Lord) had bought. We found about six German motor lorries abandoned yesterday (which is a good sign), and also another huge one with a trailer, which our A.S.C. officer, with a beaming countenance, was driving at about two miles an hour.[55]

Writing a more heartfelt letter at this time was Fanny Colquhoun, a mother concerned for her boy:

Would you kindly give me information as to Frank Colquhoun's whereabouts. I think his number is 590. I have had no word from him since he landed in France & I am most anxious about him, being his mother. Would you kindly give me all possible information at once & oblige,
F. M. Colquhoun.[56]

Her worry is easy to understand, for although Frank had been with the North Irish Horse for more than three years, he was still only 17 years old. While the lad had been too busy to write, he was safe with his squadron at Fère-en-Tardenois.

No breakthrough was made by the BEF on 14 or 15 September as the Germans stood their ground. The fighting began to take on all the characteristics that would mark the remainder of the war – dominance of artillery and machine guns over attacking forces, high casualties for small gains, and lengthening and deepening trenches along relatively static lines. The bridge at Condé, still intact, remained a no man's land, carefully watched by both sides lest the other rush it. 'Just on our side of the bridge,' wrote despatch rider Watson, 'was a car containing two dead officers. No one could reach them. There they sat until we left, ghastly sentinels, and for all I know they sit there still.'[57]

Not all were aware of the dangers of this place. On 15 September three men of C Squadron, Sergeant George Hicks, Private Harry Scott and Private William Moore approached it on patrol. Coming across the car, they were about to dismount to investigate when a machine gun opened on them, killing Scott and Moore and bringing down Hicks's horse. Hicks grabbed Moore's horse and galloped away at full speed. These were the regiment's second and third fatalities of the war. Private Henry St George Layard Scott of Carrowreagh, County Donegal, was aged 27. He had been a sergeant in the North Irish Horse and re-enlisted at Londonderry as soon as war broke out. Private William Moore, from Balteagh, County Londonderry, had enlisted at Limavady in 1910. The bodies of Scott and Moore were never recovered.[58] Along with the fatalities, more were wounded, including Privates Timothy Sproule, John Sands and William Kilpatrick. Kilpatrick had his horse shot from under him. The unfortunate beast fell on him and he lay there for some time until he could be freed.

As the front line consolidated into a bloody infantry slog the cavalry, including the men of the North Irish Horse, had more time on their hands and were able to see to duties neglected in recent weeks. Letters were written home to anxious loved ones, ill-discipline was punished, and the sick found medical help. Donegal man Lance Corporal James Wray lost his stripe for neglecting his duty while on guard. Edward Menice committed an offence at II Corps headquarters and received fourteen days' Field Punishment No.1 with loss of twenty-eight days' pay. Field Punishment No.1 was a severe one, designed to humiliate as much as inflict pain. For two hours a day the soldier was secured to a fixed object, often a cart, wagon wheel or tree. When not undergoing this punishment he was confined or put to hard labour. Sick parade found a number of men whose bodies had not coped well with the weeks in the open. The most common complaints were influenza and rheumatism. Joseph Moore, for example, a 20-year-old farmer from Limavady, County Londonderry, had a severe cough and was sent home. Four months later he was invalided out with bronchitis and suspected tuberculosis.

On 15 September Lieutenant West wrote an up-beat letter to his wife:

Very fit and well – better than I have been for years; the life suits me. Generally up at 3 a.m.; trek and fight sometimes all day, and often don't get into camp till 8 or 9 at night … This is a beautiful country. We were sleeping out, but the rain came about a week ago, and now we doss in châteaux or farms. Very few of the men go sick; very healthy country. Big fight going on at present. There is much less hardship than in South Africa – in fact, so far, none.[59]

Captain Herdman wrote:

I took the squadron out to exercise this morning, but had hardly got there when I received an order to come back at once and go Uhlan-hunting. But we might just as well look for a needle in a bundle of straw. They are in enormous woods, which it would take a brigade of cavalry to search. We spent all day interviewing villagers and searching

deserted farm-houses. What a mess the Germans have made of them
– nearly everything smashed, and furniture, cupboards, and bedding
scattered all over the houses! In one village the streets were covered
with broken and bent German lances and all sorts of their stuff. The
French cavalry had attacked them there and routed them.[60]

Lieutenant Stewart-Richardson wrote to a friend in Australia, where he had
once served as Aide de Camp to the Governor General:

Here we are in the land of frogs and honey, and ladies; but there are
plenty of frogs, no honey, and no women. We have had a hell of a time
the last three weeks or a month, and have had to run like hell with
400,000 Germans against only 70,000 British ...

The shellfire is absolute Hades ... I've been here all day with my
troop, and we've been shelled since daylight with lyddite, and have to
keep moving the horses every now and then. The average at the moment
is about a shell every minute, but all are going over us by about 100
yards, so one does not mind so much; but it's a nerve-racking business,
I can tell you. I am relieved at 8 to-night, and go back about three miles
to my quarters; but the devils have started shelling at night all along the
ridge, so it's warm work getting home, even in the dark.[61]

... and to a friend in Ireland:

We are now in the middle of the biggest fight of the lot. This is the fifth
day of it, and it is getting what I call a little stale. If I was managing
director I should be inclined to take off a piece.[62]

A week later Lieutenant West wrote home, telling something of what his
squadron had been through and how it was now placed:

From my own experience, I had far rougher times in South Africa
than in this show. They feed the troops splendidly; but, of course, the
chances of being knocked out are greater here than in Africa on account
of their artillery, which is very good – very smart at coming into action
and picking up ranges. We are living in great comfort in a château which
overlooks part of the ground on which the present great battle of the
Aisne is being fought.

There is at present no work for cavalry to do, it being principally long range artillery fire and some infantry attacks, so our horses are getting rested and the sore backs healing up. I have turned the stables of the château into sick-lines, and have all the sick horses there. There is any amount for them to eat, as this is, probably, the greatest agricultural country in the world.[63]

Barrie Combe, comfortably ensconced in a gentleman's shooting box at Chateau Dhuizy near Serches, wrote at length to his wife:

We have been under fire constantly. I have lost one man shot & 6 horses, & four or five men sick and one man missing.

The shell firing is very terrifying but not very effective. I think shrapnel is the worst as it burst over such a large area. My troop had a gallop across open over ½ a mile with shrapnel bursting all round.

One day I went down with an orderly to examine a bridge and a large shell burst just beside me. I galloped back over a plane [sic] pursued by 6 shells bursting just beside & behind me – very frightened at times – rather amusing afterwards. Now one does not care a damn for shells. We never interrupt our conversation when one bursts near one.

We are in a splendid little house here, and have had a good weeks rest.

I shall have great stories to tell you. I have seen some awful sights, but one becomes inured to such things – one thinks of nothing but one's self and one's own troop …

My trophies of war were two complete saddles, with sword and carbine & a lance, but I had to leave them. However I have kept one sword which I hope to bring home.

We are all very well. Some of the other troops of the Squadron have lost 5 or 6 men.[64]

And on the following day:

Since arriving here we have had a most luxurious time of it and Alec West, Stewart Richardson & I are living in a rich French man's shooting box. The people themselves have fled and have left everything all standing. It happens to be one of the few places the Germans have missed on their way and it is absolutely untouched. Massereene and the other two officers[65] are living at a farm beside us, but are not anything like as comfortable.

There is a place called Ciry where each troop of the Squadron have to take turns in guarding and generally it is a very hot little corner as some times during the day the Germans light a few shells on to it. Last time I was down we were very nearly caught. However the last few days things have been very quiet there, and it has not lived up to its reputation.

It is very sad to see the havock made in the country by the passage of so many troops over it. First the Germans passed over it going out and then coming back, finally we ourselves following them up. However we have been able to live very well by dint of buying bread, milk and eggs & butter to eke out our ordinary rations.

We are getting very fat during the last few days – we got a bit fine drawn during our first three weeks. This squadron ... has seen more service than any of the other Ir. Horse Squadrons and indeed has seen quite as much as the average regular corps ...

Greer [&] McNeil, the two gentlemen recruits who you saw at the Northern Counties Hotel have proved a great success. They are two of the best men I have got. Also I have a son of Dr Darling in my Troop and a young Coey – all good men.[66]

At the same time Stewart-Richardson wrote to an Irish friend:

Just a line to tell you we are well and cheery, and enjoying life as much as we can ... The French are getting around well on the left and right, and we have repulsed every attack night and day, and all prisoners taken are fed up, so things, I think, look rosy. So far as we can see, the next stand will be on the Meuse.[67]

By month's end Stewart-Richardson was no closer to the Meuse, but just as chipper:

Here we are hard at it, and very well. We've given the dirty Allemanders hell. To-day I've been out on patrol and observation, and the blighters are running. At least, I saw a lot of their transport moving back. I hear we've caught old von Kluck, the general, to-day; but I don't get back till late, so can't say if true or not yet. We are thoroughly enjoying ourselves, in a way.[68]

On 29 September Lieutenant Combe wrote to his wife:

Dearest Old Darling,

You do not know how I prize your dear letters. I read them over and over again, and read extracts to the other officers until they must think me a terrible bore. As a matter of fact they do not, as anything that savours of home is very welcome. For instance my Troop asked for the loan of the photos you sent me (including yours) and passed them round from hand to hand ...

Things are much the same as usual. I was up at 3 a.m. this morning, and my Troop is doing this same old observation job, which is either very exciting or very slow. However the Engineers have spoilt the job by building bomb-proof shelters for us, and when we are shelled we retire into them, instead of fleeing wildly as we have always done up to the present, to cover. We take it in turns to do this job ...

I must close now so with the very best love to the dear old boys, and tons to yourself.

Ever your loving old Barrie[69]

This was Barrie Combe's last letter, for on 30 September the bridge at Condé claimed him as its third North Irish Horse victim.

On that day, Combe and his troop were taking their turn at the observation post overlooking the enemy lines on the Aisne. Soon after midday he was ordered to ascertain whether the Germans had evacuated Condé village, which sat on the far side of the bridge, in the shadow of Condé Fort. Combe set out with one man, Private Darling, telling his sergeant that no search party should be sent if they did not return. Passing through the line of picquets, they rode to within 200 yards of the bridge. Combe left Darling and their two horses under cover and proceeded on foot. After a couple of hours Darling became concerned and went in search of his officer. He made his way to the bridge and hunted up and down the riverbank but finding no trace, returned to the outpost. When the news reached the squadron, Privates McIlwaine and Greer volunteered to find the missing officer. One report suggests that as they approach Condé 'they were fired at from the upstairs room of one of the houses. Bullets then came fast and furious, and recognising the futility of their search, they reluctantly rode back and rejoined their company.'[70]

For some time Combe's fate was unknown, but hopes were held that he had been captured. Massereene wrote to Combe's wife:

> I am more sorry than I can say at the loss which I and my squadron have sustained at the disappearance of your husband, who is a most capable officer in every way, and greatly liked by every one.
>
> I cannot help thinking that your husband has been captured and is now on his way to Berlin.[71]

Months later, however, news of his fate came via a German officer, Ottakar Vollert, who wrote through neutral channels:

> Will you drop a few lines to Mrs Combe, widow of the lieutenant in the North Irish Horse, who was shot by us when approaching our position most bravely. We buried him near the Castle of Conde, and have made a nice cross with the words 'Pro Patria' and name. He was a brave soldier. War is most terrible, and it seems that there is no end of it. Let us hope that it will ultimately clear the atmosphere.[72]

The location of Barrie Combe's grave was soon forgotten and he is now commemorated on the le Touret Memorial.

The Ypres front

With the stalemate along the Aisne continuing into October, both sides now looked north in an attempt to regain the initiative by outflanking the other. British, French and German forces moved day by day through the Somme, Arras, Armentières, la Bassée, and Ypres regions, countering each other's attacks all the way, until the line inevitably reached the sea at Nieuport

On 8 October A Squadron of the North Irish Horse entrained with GHQ for Abbeville on the French coast. On 12 October they were joined by C Squadron. Here it was announced that C Squadron officers Massereene and West had been Mentioned in Despatches. Nor did the other ranks miss out on the honours. Privates Frank Colquhoun of Manorcunningham, County Donegal, and James McArow from Tamlaght, County Fermanagh, both of A Squadron, were awarded the Médaille Militaire, a French award roughly equivalent to the Distinguished Conduct Medal. This time, no doubt,

Colquhoun did write home to his mother, for soon after the *Belfast Evening Telegraph* carried his picture and the news of his award,

> granted for valuable service in scouting, and presented personally by General French. Private Colquhoun, who is eighteen years of age, left for the front with the First Division under Lord Cole. He is a brother of Constable Andrew Colquhoun, of Musgrave Street Barracks, Belfast, a well-known athlete.

On Tuesday 13 October GHQ moved again, this time to St Omer, an industrial and commercial town in northern France. In the south of this sector, Smith-Dorrien's II Corps had moved into a line running north from Givenchy, linking up with the French Tenth Army to their right. Beginning on 11 October they began to push forward, but after some success the attack ground to a halt. To the north of II Corps Allenby's two cavalry divisions and III Infantry Corps pushed east against thin German defences. On 14 October III Corps took Bailleul and linked up with the French cavalry corps. The Cavalry Corps occupied a line from Neuve-Église to Wulverghem and Messines to Wytschaete. With the British 7th Infantry Division, the 3rd Cavalry Division, French Territorial divisions and a Naval brigade to the north and then the remnants of the Belgian Army on the Yser from Dixmude to the sea, a continuous Allied line had been completed. Further advances were made until 18 October, including the capture of Armentières, and a large salient was pushed out east around Ypres.

After arriving at St Omer with GHQ, the North Irish Horse had played some role in the advance, though details are sketchy. It is conceivable that they may have been briefly at Allenby's disposal in the initial phase where Mont Noir and Kemmel were secured, as suggested in the recollections of A Squadron's Willie Acheson, although the information is too general to allow more than guesswork:

> The first big charge they took part in was at Kemmel Hill using swords. They became hemmed in by Germans. A comrade, Dan Wallace, never called Lord Enniskillen (John Cole) anything but John. 'You may blow the whistle, John, 'cause we're cornered here.' Blow it he had to, and all retreated.[73]

On 17 October A Squadron came under the orders of the Assistant Provost Marshal and marched to Hazebrouck. The next day they marched to Bailleul, detailed for police duties and road control. For a week they manned the roads between Estaires and Messines, ensuring smooth movement to the front of troops, guns, ammunition and supplies for the 1st Cavalry Division and the 4th and 6th Infantry Divisions of III Corps. It was no easy task. The roads were not made for such heavy traffic; accidents and breakdowns were frequent; and the constant movement of British and French units across each other's paths, the flow to the rear of wounded men, and the occasional motor vehicle carrying senior officers demanding urgent passage, required considerable skill, patience and diplomacy – not to mention a certain stubborn courage and alertness for German 'spies'. One of the squadron's traffic control posts was at St Jans Cappel:

> One afternoon a staff officer, resplendent in red tabs, rode up, dismounted and began to question the sentry about the numbers and units of troops which had passed that day. Immediately suspicious, the sentry said 'You had better ask the corporal.'
> Out came Corporal W____, and immediately asked to see the Officer's credentials – some proof of his identity. But he had none, he had omitted to bring the papers with him, and promptly was told that he would have to stay there until someone came to identify him. The officer fumed and protested, but the corporal was unimpressed – the officer would have to remain under guard until he had been identified, nor was there anyone to spare to send for that identification. At length a passing despatch-rider was stopped and brought a note to the officer's unit, and soon someone came out and identified him.[74]

On 24 October A Squadron marched out of the line and returned to St Omer and GHQ duties.

C Squadron's movements in this period are less clear. Private Sterling wrote on 15 October, 'we are having a comparatively easy and comfortable time doing General's mounted escort.'[75] It seems the squadron's four troops remained scattered. Grant's probably remained attached to Smith-Dorrien's headquarters, and Lieutenant Gilligan's may have remained with its division. One at least was based at Bailleul.

British optimism that the enemy's flank could still be turned was broken on 19 October when the Germans launched a massive attack along the Ypres front in a bid to break the Allied lines and seize the Channel ports. Intense fighting continued through October and much of November, frequently in heavy rain that turned the trenches into a quagmire of mud and made the pavé roads behind them slippery and dangerous for any sort of traffic. It was touch and go at times, some territory was conceded, and the Ypres salient dangerously narrowed, but the line held. After five weeks the German attacks petered out. The cost was enormous. From 14 October to the end of November the BEF lost some 58,000 men, the French almost as many, and the Germans 130,000.

The North Irish Horse, however, came through relatively unscathed. A Squadron remained at St Omer on GHQ troop duties. This would have included travelling with French on his frequent visits forward to advance headquarters at Bailleul, and to corps and divisional headquarters at Kemmel, Hooge and other places close to the fighting. But despite these excursions to the front, life for those at St Omer was a world away from that of the ordinary soldier in the fighting zone.

The regiment's last fatality of the year occurred with the death in England of 23-year-old Corporal Edmond Buchanan. Buchanan, from Rathdonnel, County Donegal, had been a UVF drill instructor and section leader. Evacuated to an English hospital on 15 October, he died there eight days later. Other casualties were sustained in this period, though none fatal. Lieutenant Stewart-Richardson became ill and was sent to London for treatment, then home to Antrim. Lieutenant Jocelyn became ill at the end of November and departed for home. William Livingstone and James Buchanan of A Squadron were hospitalised and send home suffering from severe rheumatism. Corporal William Hall was sent home with bronchitis. In early December Private Robert Kinnear sustained a bullet wound to his left foot and was admitted to the military hospital at Boulogne, before being shipped home to Glarryford, near Ballymena. At the end of December Private Stewart Harris Moir was sent to hospital in England, where it was discovered that he was under-age. He was sent home and discharged. He would later join the Royal Air Force.

The relative idleness imposed on the two squadrons of the North Irish Horse by the light duties as headquarters cavalry brought some ill-discipline amongst the horsemen. The official response was usually proportionate. Sergeant William Bracken was severely reprimanded when found guilty of neglecting his duty, Private John Henderson was given seven days' Field Punishment No.2 for creating a disturbance in the barracks, and Lance Sergeant James Coburn severely reprimanded for allowing a disturbance in his troop billet. However, at other times the punishment was severe. Trumpeter William McFerran, found guilty of drunkenness, not only lost his trumpeter's patch, but was sentenced to 120 days' imprisonment with hard labour. Corporal John Kerr faced a court martial for leaving his post without leave. He was demoted and given ninety days' Field Punishment No.1. Private George Ewart received eighty-four days' Field Punishment No.1 for being drunk while on outpost duty.

At the beginning of December His Majesty King George V visited the BEF in France and Belgium. Troops of the North Irish Horse were assigned as his escort, with two men from C Squadron, Sergeant Hugh Ashcroft of Coagh and Sergeant John Mountford of Ballymena, assigned as the King's orderlies. When he departed the King presented Ashcroft and Mountford each with a pipe as a souvenir of his visit.

Through November and December, heavy rain fell, alternating with deep frosts and snow, making conditions almost impossible for troops in the battle zone. In their billets behind the lines, the men of the North Irish Horse found life more comfortable. C Squadron's Robert Sterling, now a corporal, wrote home:

We are having a fairly easy time now, and have not much dangerous work to do. The weather, however, is very severe. We have had a heavy fall of snow, accompanied by frost, and the ground is white and hard. Exercise with our horses is pleasant and exhilarating these mornings, especially when we have some good cross-country runs over ditches and hedges. It is just like hunting on a frosty day at home. I have not seen a German – except prisoners – for quite a long time, and I don't care if I never see any more. We got enough after we came out here to do us for the remainder of our lives.[76]

As Christmas approached, those who could took leave to visit family and friends at home. One who was lucky enough to receive a Christmas leave pass was Sergeant Hugh Ashcroft, who regaled his father and friends at Carryhill, Coagh, with exciting tales from the front and showed off the pipe given him by the King. Another who skipped over the Channel was Massereene. Many of his fellow officers, particularly those in the infantry, weren't so lucky, as Lieutenant Colonel George Brenton Laurie, commanding the 1st Royal Irish Rifles, ruefully pointed out in a letter to his wife.

I wish I could run across and see you, but it will be hard for me to get a fortnight just now like your cousin Massereene. You see, he is Cavalry, and attached to the Staff Headquarters of the Division[77]

For those left in France, Christmas was relatively peaceful. The men of the North Irish Horse were showered with Christmas gifts, season's greetings, cakes and other foods by friends, relatives, businesses and private charities. Perhaps the gift most valued by the men was the Princess Mary Christmas tin. Funded by public subscription, this was a small brass box, well-made, with a decorated lid featuring the 17-year-old daughter of the King and Queen, and assorted military and imperial images. It typically contained a pipe, an ounce of tobacco and packet of cigarettes in a distinctive yellow monogrammed wrapper, a tinder cigarette lighter, a Christmas card from the Princess and a photograph. More than 350,000 were distributed to men in the Army and Navy by Christmas. The contents were eagerly consumed and many troops posted the tin home as a keepsake.

In their letters home the North Irish Horsemen showed their pride in the role they had played fighting alongside the professional soldiers of the BEF, and also in their political origins. 'We are proud of our little regiment of NIH, which has made a name for itself,' wrote William Morton, 'as well as being the first regiment, other than regulars, to go into action.' Sergeant Richard Irwin wrote to his brother that 'The North Irish Horse have by no means disgraced Ulster; on the contrary, they have won a name for themselves. Although it is not all sunshine out here, we are ever ready and willing to brave the elements for King and country, and, if spared to return home, to do the same for Ulster.' Private Frank Kidd of Fintona told his mother that 'The troops on the march called us "Carson's Horse", and we always said we were,' while earlier, Hiram Robinson had written proudly about the 'gay little regiment ... I think it is doing its part in this war anyway, and men of other regiments, talking to us, ask us if we're all Carson's men, and we're not ashamed to tell them we are.'[78]

The view from Ulster

While A and C Squadrons had been helping hold back the German army in France and Belgium, a different sort of contest had been underway in Ireland. From the beginning the War Office had been keen to secure as many recruits as it could for Kitchener's 'New Armies' and it was clear that the men of the UVF, already partially trained and well-disciplined, could provide thousands of new soldiers. However, the Unionist leadership was torn. They were ready for a fight, but not this one, and feared what might happen at home if their carefully prepared force was handed over to the British and sent to France, with the Home Rule question postponed. As naval officer Ruric Waring wrote:

> I confess for my own part I rather agree with the UVF who have been kept on the strain for 2 years & now if they want them to go the matter should be at least settled. At the end of the war all these people will have no sympathy & probably send their army to shoot down any that are left by the Germans.[79]

However, following negotiations with the War Office, Unionist leader Edward Carson agreed to throw his support behind the recruiting drive, having won a guarantee that if he could find enough recruits – as many as 16,000 – they could serve together in a single Ulster division. This meant that UVF regiments could join the British Army and maintain their pre-war identity, and that their officers might become army officers. They could even wear a distinctive cap-badge, an oval disc in bronze showing the Red Hand of Ulster (although this decision was later reversed). The Ulster Unionist Council readily agreed, and recruitment for the new 36th (Ulster) Division commenced on 4 September.

The Irish Volunteers (IV) – the Nationalist paramilitary force raised in response to the rise of the UVF – was another potentially rich source of manpower. On 18 September the Nationalists' long-dreamed of Home Rule became law, though with two important caveats – deferral for the duration of the war, and unspecified special provisions for Ulster. Their leaders now called for the creation of an 'Irish Brigade' so that men of the IV could be drafted together into the British Army. The newly announced 16th (Irish) Division, though not created specifically for that purpose, was quickly adopted by the Nationalists as 'their' division (though it also included an Ulster Brigade).

In the highly-charged political atmosphere of Ulster, recruitment now became a competition to prove which side of the sectarian divide was the more committed to fighting and winning the war, with claim and counter-claim printed in Irish newspapers, depending on their editorial bias. The impact on wartime recruiting has been much debated. One recent study concluded that:

the political influence exerted, at least in the 16th (Irish) and 36th (Ulster) Divisions, appears to have been mostly malign. This saddled both divisions with some incompetent officers from the pre-war paramilitary organisations, and threatened many of the regular army's tried and trusted methods of maintaining morale, most notably the regimental system [and] meant that both were painfully slow at recruiting to establishment.[80]

While rival political leaders like Carson and Craig, and Devlin and Redmond traversed the country to drum up recruits from the ranks of their supporters, some well-to-do civic leaders had also taken it on themselves to raise a military unit. For them, this was a matter of prestige, as well as one that brought the promise of officer rank. On 3 October, for example, recruitment commenced at Enniskillen for a squadron of cavalry for the Ulster Division, to be known as the 6th Inniskilling Dragoons (Service Squadron). This was at the initiative of William Copeland Trimble, the town's newspaper publisher, who had earlier led the formation of the UVF's Enniskillen Horse.[81]

Trimble's difficulty was that he was competing with the recruiters of the North Irish Horse, which was already forming a third squadron for France. Despite Trimble's enthusiasm, volunteers for the Inniskilling Dragoons came in slowly at first, with fewer than forty men joining in the first week. Many of the UVF mounted troops had already joined the North Irish Horse, been called up as reservists, or enlisted with infantry battalions. It was not until 7 November that Trimble's numbers had reached 150, and recruiting was formally closed in December. (A request for permission to raise a second squadron was refused.)

This was a problem faced on a bigger scale by Carson in seeking recruits for the Ulster Division. Many men of the UVF had already joined other regiments. On 19 September, for example, the *Irish Times*, noting that 400 members of the Londonderry regiment of the UVF had joined the Ulster Division, explained that 'a large number of members of the Ulster Volunteer Force from the Maiden City have joined the North Irish Horse and Scottish and English regiments'. Similarly, reporting on a recruiting visit by Carson to Ballymena, the paper noted that 'about 40 reservists who were members of the Volunteer Force had previously rejoined [their army unit] … and a number of the mounted troop had also enlisted in the North Irish Horse'.[82]

The North Irish Horse, being an established regiment, had been able to get off to a flying start and pick the best men available. Trimble felt the competition keenly. For him, the reward he sought was a commission in the army; he didn't see his sixty-two years as a barrier. The authorities had a different view, and in January 1915 Trimble wrote a desperate letter to Carson.

> The matter is simple. Major Craig telegraphed to me to call at head-quarters. I went, & then & there I was asked to raise a squadron of Horse for the Ulster Division, & Brig. General Hickman promised military rank. I said I would do it.
>
> His Grace of Abercorn (whom we all admire) had been here twice or three times to obtain recruits for the North Irish Horse, & had not got one recruit. I raised the full squadron of the Inniskilling Dragoons, (6th service squadron) which with the approval of head-quarters I so named.
>
> I expected that the military rank would have come to me within a few days to ease my path & facilitate the work, but, as it did not come I was in a unique position, of being while a layman in sole command of the barracks, & administrator of & commander of the squadron ...
>
> Personally, I do not think about military rank, although since I wrote the Historical Records of the Inniskillings in 1874 I have been closely identified with military life & movements. But when a Nationalist is made a captain for bringing 52 men to the Irish Brigade at Fermoy, my own men of the Volunteer Enniskillen Horse feel hurt at their commander being ignored, & as one of them said – 'If you were the 33rd cousin of a Lord, sir, you would have been appointed long ago.' And another said – 'If our own people treat you that way, what may we expect?'[83]

If Carson did try to assist Trimble, he was unsuccessful, although a silver war badge was issued to him in August 1916.

From the beginning the North Irish Horse had operated with real efficiency. Added to the regimental headquarters at Skegoneill Avenue in Belfast was a more capacious base in a vacant furniture repository in Great George's Street. This worked well for the task of mobilising and seeing off A and C Squadrons, but a more permanent site was needed for training, exercises, stabling, recruitment and administration. While the showgrounds at the Brandywell, Londonderry, became a temporary training base, the Antrim showgrounds were soon offered up and the regiment began moving in at the end of August.

Tented at first, huts were soon erected and electricity was provided from a near-by saw mill. The grandstand was sheeted in and became the quarter-master's store ... The Deer Park at Antrim became the training ground and soon columns of men and horses, many of each being recruits, were to be seen each morning filing out from the Depot to the Park.[84]

The North Irish Horse had no trouble attracting recruits. By the time the first two squadrons had sailed for France, another sixty men had enlisted, most of these making up the numbers in C Squadron. The recruitment process was a relatively simple one. On arrival, the men were given a form to record personal details such as their name, place of birth, age, trade, marital status, and any previous military service. They signed on for the duration of the war, and made their oath of allegiance. Further particulars were then taken, including the man's religion and physical description. A medical officer checked whether the man was physically fit to serve. Men desperate to enlist went to great efforts to conceal physical defects, and many regular army veterans no doubt had their disabilities overlooked. At the same time, medical checks weeded out men already in the regiment who couldn't make the grade for overseas service.

Others at home who were unable to join were nonetheless keen to show they were doing their bit. Wealthy businessmen made large contributions to 'regimental comforts' funds, and weren't shy about advertising the fact. Well-to-do ladies threw themselves into fundraising to send cakes, cigarettes, socks and wagonloads of every sort of comfort to the boys at the front. Aileen Farnham and Emily Maude, the wives of senior officers of the regiment, began an appeal for public contributions to fund a North Irish Horse motor ambulance.

On 13 October two unlikely recruits walked into the recruiting room at the Antrim Showground – Francis McMahon and Jack McGuigan of Newry. What made them unusual was not their age, their fitness or their experience; it was the fact that they were Roman Catholics. It is true that they were not the first of their faith to join. Maurice Edward Cotter had enlisted on 9 August, but his was simply a continuation of his pre-war occupation – valet to Richard Griffith Oliver Bramston-Newman at his Cork Estate, Newberry Manor. Bramston-Newman was a captain in the North Irish Horse and wished Cotter to continue in his service as his batman. Another Roman Catholic, 39-year-old John Crawford, had joined in September. No doubt it was his years of experience in the Royal Inniskilling Fusiliers in India and in the Boer War that persuaded the recruiting sergeant to take him on. It would have been the same story for 42-year-old Drumcree man John Donaldson, a Boer War veteran and experienced army cook with the Royal Irish Fusiliers.

Jack McGuigan and Frank McMahon had no military experience, nor had they worked in service to the landed gentry. Like every man, woman and child living in Ulster, they understood the sectarian divide that ran through the land. However, it seems that the men's love of horses and the undoubted glamour of serving in a cavalry regiment overcame any fears they may have had. Years later McMahon recalled the path that brought him to the North Irish Horse. 'Previous to the war, to enlist was only for corner boys and ne'r do-wells. But now it was "the proper thing to do" ... At that time I was indentured to a firm of wholesale and retail, milling and shipping merchants, a job which I hated.' Frank's pal Jack suggested that they 'run away to Belfast and enlist in a cavalry regiment. The next morning we got a train to Belfast and proceeded to enlist. We wanted to enlist in the Inniskilling Dragoons but they had closed recruiting and advised we try the North Irish Horse.'[85]

The decision to try the Inniskilling Dragoons was either brave or foolish. Advertisements seeking volunteers for the new squadron explicitly sought UVF members, so it is not surprising that the recruiting sergeant told them to go elsewhere. Certainly the 'recruiting closed' excuse was not true, as fewer than half the places had been filled when McMahon and McGuigan turned up in early October. Undeterred, they travelled to Antrim to try their luck with the North Irish Horse. It seems that the extent to which politics overrode the need for recruits varied from unit to unit. Squadron Sergeant Major Scammell at the regiment's recruiting office signed their papers,

we enlisted, were sworn in and received our day's pay of 1/- each.[86] The next day we were issued with a rifle, sword, saddle, blankets and other equipment and were each given a horse; our day was occupied with drawing equipment and all other gear. The next morning Reveille at 5.30am, beds made up, floors swept and then fall in at 6am for physical jerks, dismissed at 6.15am to stables, where one man was detailed to ride one horse and lead 3 for exercise and watering, the remainder of the troop cleaned out the stables, then the exercise party returned at 6.30am and each man started grooming his horse ... The Sergeant kept warning you to be 'careful of that horse, he cost £40, you can get a soldier for a shilling'.[87]

McMahon's mother Catherine was horrified when she heard what he had done, and made him swear that he would never be tattooed – branding him for life as a Unionist sympathiser. Tattooing was a common practice for servicemen, and in Ulster it often sent a political message. North Irish Horseman James Allen, for example, had 'King William III 1690' tattooed prominently across his chest.

By mid-October the North Irish Horse had all the men they needed, and soon after the books were closed to all but a small number with useful trades or professions and the odd special case. Those chosen by the North Irish Horse were the pick of the bunch, there having been no shortage of applicants, and the officers of the regiment had no hesitation in throwing out any who did not meet expectations. Thus, for example, when Lieutenant Colonel Maude found one recruit constantly in trouble – absent from evening stables, drunk, thieving, breaking out of camp, absent from watch-setting, asleep at his post whilst a stable sentry – he simply applied to have him discharged,

> owing to the excellent class of recruits now being trained at Antrim it is not considered to be of benefit to these men, or in the interest of the service that he should be retained ... Numbers of excellent men are daily presenting themselves for enlistment so that his services could be replaced with benefit to the service.[88]

The men who made up this 'excellent class of recruits' were very different from the young farmers and farm labourers who had joined the regiment before the war. Leaving aside the forty-three wartime recruits by then serving with A and C Squadrons in France, 367 others enlisted from 4 August to 31 December 1914. They now heavily outnumbered the pre-war recruits left behind at Antrim and Londonderry, who probably numbered no more than 150, and some of these were soon discharged as unfit, unhealthy or too old.

Surviving service files show that these men were older than the pre-war recruits – their average age was 27 years, ranging from 14 to 44, with four men aged 40 or over. Perhaps the youngest to enlist was 14-year-old James Craig from Ballymena. On 4 September he turned up at the Ballymena recruiting office, claiming to be 18 years and 349 days old. Standing 5 feet 4 inches, blue eyed, fair haired, weighing 10 stone and with a chest measurement of 33 inches, he passed as fit and was taken on. But James's time in the army would not be happy. Based in Antrim through 1915, he was twice punished for being absent without leave. In France he was given five days' Field Punishment No.1 for ill-treating a horse and later another fourteen days for disobeying orders and insubordination. By then it seems young Craig had had enough. After a week of the punishment he reported his true age, and was sent back to England while enquiries were made to confirm it. He was discharged on 25 September 1916 and his record marked 'indifferent'. Soon after, however, Craig re-enlisted, this time with the Royal Inniskilling Fusiliers.

At the other end of the scale was 44-year-old coachman Joseph Humphries from Lanarkshire, Scotland, who had already served thirteen years with the Royal Scots Greys, and Stuart Harrison, a 41-year-old commercial traveller from Dromore, County Down. Both were Boer War veterans. However, among all the North Irish Horsemen at Antrim, none could match the age of pre-war enlistee Farrier Quartermaster Sergeant James Mooney. As Charles Trimble recalled, while he and an officer were checking the enlistment paperwork in 1915, Mooney happened to enter the room:

> 'What is that first medal ribbon you are wearing?' Mooney was asked, and he replied – 'The Zulu War, Major.' 'But here is your attestation form and it states that your age is 34. That war was fought before you were born,' Mooney was told.[89]

In fact Mooney was 56 years old. He had indeed served in the Zulu War in 1879, having joined the Lancers the year before. He later served in East India and in South Africa before being discharged as medically unfit in 1902. In 1911 he joined the North Irish Horse, claimed he was 29, and omitted mention of his previous service. It is hard to believe that the recruiters didn't know he was much older than he claimed. He quickly rose to his former rank of Farrier Quartermaster Sergeant, but his age kept him home-based through the war.

The occupations of the wartime recruits varied widely, and were a world away from the rural background of the earlier North Irish Horsemen. Only a small number were farmers or had equine-related occupations – grooms, coachmen and horse dealers for example. There was a large number of the skilled urban working-class – engineers, a fitter, a painter, a riveter, a mechanic, a french polisher, an iron turner, a tramwayman, a machineman, a plater, a brakesman, a motorman and a carter. There were also carpenters, an auctioneer, a photographer, a hairdresser, a tenter, a bleacher and a baker. The clerical, retail and professional classes were also well-represented, and many from this group would later become officers. Others included medical students, a musician, mill manager, journalist and picture theatre manager. It is clear from the above that there were significantly more city and town-dwellers amongst these recruits, with many born in Belfast. Most were from the eastern counties of Antrim, Down and Armagh.

More than a third had previous service in the regular Army, many in the Boer War and others in India. Despite their age, their fighting experience would have made them attractive recruits. However, age also made them more vulnerable to illness and less able to withstand the rigours of a hard campaign. By the end of the war only a small proportion of these men were still in service overseas.

Also interesting was the disciplinary record of the wartime recruits. Compared to the earlier North Irish Horsemen, these men would prove a much harder group to control, particularly the former soldiers. Not many would see out their time with a clean record, and even those of the professional class who were destined to become officers were not immune from running foul of the authorities.

One thing that the majority of wartime recruits did have in common with their predecessors was their religion. More than half were of the Church of England or Ireland, and more than a third Presbyterians. But even here there was a difference, if only small. As many as one-in-fifteen were Roman Catholics, and one, Bernard (Bert) Weiner, a travelling photographer from Dublin, was a Russian Jew.

Among the 1914 wartime enlistees were, of course, a number of brothers. Three who joined the North Irish Horse were Alexander, Robert and Albert Dundee. Aged 26, 22 and 19 respectively, they had grown up in Ballylinney, County Antrim, part of a family of at least eight brothers and one sister. Their older brother was serving in South Africa, while their younger brother, 16-year-old Charles, had overstated his age and enlisted in the Royal Irish Rifles. Brothers Hubert, Randal and David McManus from Dungannon, County Tyrone, were also quick to join up. David and Hubert joined the North Irish Horse at Antrim on 5 October, while Randal joined the 6th Inniskilling Dragoons (Service Squadron) a few weeks later. Not all brothers were able to join together, of course. Londonderry man William Warke's two younger brothers were not old enough when he enlisted with the regiment on 7 September, but both joined as soon as they could – Jasper with the Royal Inniskilling Fusiliers and Samuel with the Royal Irish Rifles.

In December another contingent of North Irish Horsemen, D Squadron, departed for overseas. The ladies of the town sent them off with a pleasant entertainment at Antrim's Protestant Hall, with tea and speeches, a concert by the Massereene Silver Band, and dancing until midnight. D Squadron sailed for England, where they joined their division, the 51st Highland, and found billets in Cople, near Bedford. Soon after this the squadron training at Londonderry showgrounds under Lord Farnham left by special train for Antrim. They numbered three officers and 103 men, and were given 'a hearty send-off' by a large number of their friends.[90]

At the same time a draft of eighteen men under the command of Second Lieutenant Arthur Charles Nugent of Rostrevor left Ireland for France. This was the first reinforcement draft sent to A and C Squadrons, and perhaps their number gives an indication of the casualties sustained in the first months of the war. All but one were wartime enlistees.[91]

By Christmas, around 410 men had joined the North Irish Horse since the war began. If needed, they could have had many more. To fill the places left by the departure of D Squadron and the reinforcement draft, recruitment was re-opened at Antrim on 19 December, and at Skegoneill Avenue nine days later.

Notes

1. Crozier, *A Brass Hat in No Man's Land*, pp.16–17.
2. Mac Fhionnghaile, op. cit., p.89.
3. Trimble, op. cit. Ironically, despite being the first North Irish Horseman in France, Sergeant McCartney's short stay there meant he did not qualify for the 1914 Star. It appears that another man arrived in France before the main contingents of A and C Squadrons – records show Private James Rodgers as having embarked for France on 16 August, a day before A Squadron's departure.
4. Mac Fhionnghaile, op. cit., pp.21, 89.
5. It is not clear whether they did in fact sail on separate vessels, but the 159 are shown on the medal rolls as embarking on 20 August, and the remainder on 21 August.
6. Crozier, op. cit., pp.16–18. 'Stuart' is probably Lieutenant Neil Graham Stewart-Richardson.
7. Letter dated 15 August 1914, from Combe/Waring collection. Ruric Waring was lost at sea on 15 October 1914 when his ship *HMS Hawke* was sunk by a German U-boat.
8. Trimble, op. cit.

9. *BET*, (?) January 1915.

10. Private James Alexander Elliott, in Mac Fhionnghaile, op. cit., p.21

11. Davies (ed.), *A Medical Officer's Diary and Narrative of the First World War.*

12. *Official History of the Great War: Military Operations, France and Belgium, 1914, Vol. I*, p.514.

13. *BNL*, 13 November 1914.

14. *BNL*, 29 December 1914.

15. *BNL*, 19 September 1914.

16. *BNL*, 29 December 1914.

17. Holmes, *Riding the Retreat*, p.196.

18. Gleichen, *The Doings of the 15th Infantry Brigade*, pp.57–8.

19. Holmes, op. cit., p.196.

20. *Official History of the Great War, 1914, Vol. I*, p.199.

21. *BNL*, 6 November 1914.

22. Coleman, *From Mons to Ypres with French*, p.63.

23. *BNL*, 12 October 1914.

24. Lieutenant Combe, letter to his wife, 23 September 1914, from Combe/Waring collection.

25. Private diary of Lieutenant Colonel Hicks in NA Kew, WO 95/1495/1.

26. *BNL*, 29 December 1914.

27. Davies, op. cit.

28. After the war Callanan's medals went unclaimed. His only next of kin, his younger brother John, could not be located and the medals were scrapped.

29. Gleichen, op. cit., pp.78–9.

30. Ibid., pp.80–1.

31. *BNL*, 15 June 1915. No date given in Espey's account, but the timing given here seems a reasonable assumption.

32. Coleman, op. cit., pp.82–3.

33. Baring, *R.F.C. H.Q. 1914–1918*, pp.32–3.

34. Aldrich, *A Hilltop on the Marne*, pp.91–3.

35. Letter dated 23 September 1914, from Combe/Waring collection.

36. Letter dated 4 September 1914, from Combe/Waring collection.

37. Watson, *Adventures of a Despatch Rider, p.77.*

38. Gleichen, op. cit., p.87. Watson, op. cit., *p.78.*

39. Watson, op. cit., *p.79.*

40. MacDonagh, op. cit., p.36. 'Trooper McClennaghan' would be Private William McLanahan.

41. Letter dated 23 September 1914, from Combe/Waring collection.

42. Letter from Private Sterling dated 15 October 1914, in Mary Combe press clipping file, Combe/Waring collection. The date of this incident is not certain.

43. Letter from Private Sterling dated 15 October 1914, in Mary Combe press clipping file, Combe/Waring collection.

44. Trimble, op. cit.

45. Lucy, *There's a Devil in the Drum*, p.200.

46. *BET*, (?) January 1915.
47. *BET*, (?) 1915.
48. *BNL*, 9 October 1914.
49. Elliott, Leslie & Stevenson, *The Story of a Banner*, p.14.
50. Letter from Private Sterling dated 15 October 1914, in Mary Combe press clipping file, Combe/Waring collection.
51. Letter dated 23 September 1914, from Combe/Waring collection.
52. Gleichen, op. cit., p.108.
53. *BNL*, 12 October 1914.
54. *Irish Times*, 3 October 1914.
55. *BNL*, 28 September 1914, and *Irish Times*, 3 October 1914.
56. NA, Kew, WO 364.
57. Watson, op. cit., p.110.
58. Scott was initially listed as missing and the date of his death is incorrectly recorded as 8 October 1914.
59. *Irish Times*, 1 October 1914.
60. *BNL*, 28 September 1914.
61. Letter dated 16 September 1914 published in *The Register*, Adelaide, and *The Argus*, Melbourne, 18 November 1914.
62. *BNL*, 9 October 1914.
63. *Irish Times*, 10 October 1914.
64. Letter dated 23 September 1914, from Combe/Waring collection.
65. Lieutenant John Vanner Gilligan and Captain Eustace King-King.
66. Letter dated 24 September 1914, from Combe/Waring collection.
67. *BNL*, 9 October 1914.
68. Letter dated 29 September 1914 published in *The Register*, Adelaide, 18 November 1914.
69. Letter dated 29 September 1914, from Combe/Waring collection.
70. From article dated 11 May 1915, possibly *Lurgan Mail*, in Mary Combe press clipping file, Combe/Waring collection.
71. Letter dated 1 October 1914, from Combe/Waring collection.
72. Dublin Law Reports, undated, in Mary Combe press clipping file, Combe/Waring collection. Vollert was subsequently killed near Soissons.
73. Mac Fhionnghaile, op. cit., p.92. Private Donald Wallace was a long-serving Horseman and probably an employee of Cole, as his address was Florence Park, Cole's estate.
74. Trimble, op. cit.
75. Letter from Private Sterling dated 15 October 1914, in Mary Combe press clipping file, Combe/Waring collection.
76. *BNL*, 30 November 1914.
77. Vere-Laurie (ed.), *Letters of Lt-Col George Brenton Laurie*.
78. *BNL*, 29 December (Morton), 16 October (Irwin), 17 December (Kidd), 13 November 1914 (Robinson).
79. Letter to his sister Esther dated 6 September 1914, from Combe/Waring collection.
80. Bowman, *The Irish Regiments in the Great War*, pp.90–1.

81. *Irish Times*, 2 October 1914. William Copeland Trimble was the uncle of North Irish Horseman Charles Trimble who is quoted several times in this and the previous chapter.
82. *Irish Times*, 19 September and 2 October 1914.
83. Letter dated 20 January 1915, PRONI, D1507/A/11/5.
84. Trimble, op. cit.
85. McMahon, *Round the World on a Bob a Day*. McMahon wrote much of this story in the third person. I have changed this to first person for ease of reading.
86. In fact cavalrymen drew 8s 2d per week on enlistment (1s 2d per day), infantrymen 7s per week.
87. McMahon, op. cit.
88. Letter dated 20 November 1914, James Hogg service file, NA, Kew, WO 364.
89. Trimble, op. cit.
90. *Irish Times*, 15 December 1914.
91. One man had gone out prior to this – Squadron Sergeant Major Trimble had embarked for France at the beginning of November, but was home again six weeks later.

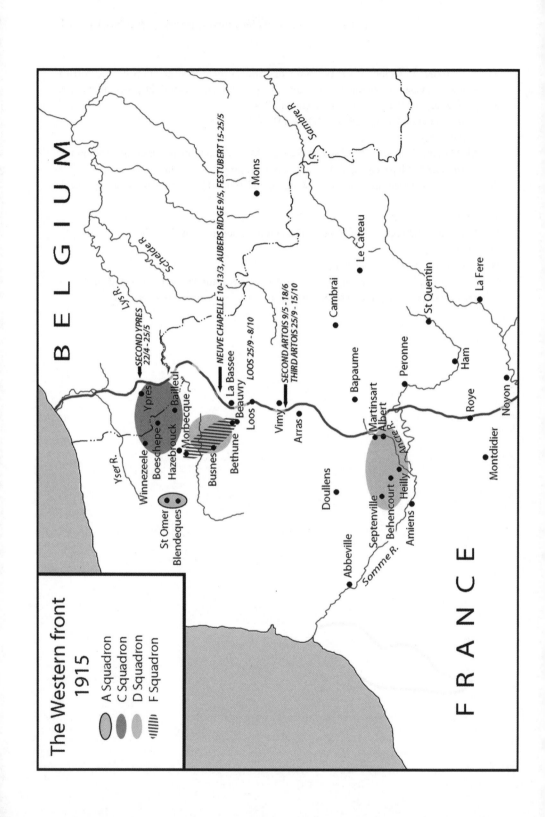

The Western front
1915

A Squadron
C Squadron
D Squadron
F Squadron

BELGIUM

FRANCE

Mons

Le Cateau

La Fere

St Quentin

Cambrai

Ham

Bapaume

Peronne

Roye

Noyon

Montdidier

Sambre R.

Schelde R.

Lys R.

Yser R.

Somme R.

Ancre R.

SECOND YPRES
22/4 - 25/5

NEUVE CHAPELLE 10-13/3, AUBERS RIDGE 9/5, FESTUBERT 15-25/5

LOOS 25/9 - 8/10

SECOND ARTOIS 9/5 - 18/6
THIRD ARTOIS 25/9 - 15/10

Ypres
Boeschepe
Bailleul
Hazebrouck
Morbecque
Winnezeele
Busnes
Beauvry
Bethune
La Bassee
Loos
Vimy
Arras
Martinsart
Albert
Heilly
Behencourt
Septenville
Amiens
Doullens
Abbeville

St Omer
Blendeques

Chapter Three

1915: 'It's a Great Life Out Here'

*I think we are doing pretty well so far ... Am awfully fit and terribly
sunburnt! It's a great life out here.*[1]

For the British, 1915 would be a year of bitter disappointment. Hopes
that the lines of trenches running through France and Belgium
to the sea would be a temporary phenomenon were not realised.
Awaking from the torpor imposed by a freezing winter, the British sought
a breakthrough at Neuve Chapelle in March. They made some ground but
were quickly halted, at the cost of 12,000 casualties. In April and May the
Germans made a sustained assault on the Ypres salient. Amid appalling losses
the line bent but did not break, and what was left of Ypres remained in Allied
hands. French and British attacks on Aubers Ridge and Festubert achieved
little, and a joint assault from September to October at Champagne, Loos
and Artois resulted in terrible casualties for little gain.

For the North Irish Horse, 1915 was a year of enforced idleness. This
was not a year for cavalry fighting. Two new squadrons joined A and C
Squadrons in France, plus more than 140 other ranks and officers sent as
reinforcements. Some of the men had a blooding in the trenches, but for
most their time was spent in billets behind the lines on the Ypres–la Bassée
front and on the Somme, with occasional fatigues, patrols and road control
work.

Recruitment and training in Ireland

From time to time through 1915 the North Irish Horse opened their books
for new recruits at Antrim and Skegoneill Avenue in Belfast. They had little
trouble finding volunteers. In January around sixty-five men joined. In April
it was agreed that the regiment raise another squadron, the subsequent
rush to enlist yielding 145 recruits. In November some 240 signed on, the
largest monthly intake in the regiment's short history. At other times, places
were found for around twenty to thirty recruits a month, bringing total
recruitment for the year to 680.

Throughout 1915 the authorities did all they could to keep up the numbers, with regular recruiting rallies, marches and calls through the newspapers for men to do their patriotic duty. The *Belfast News-Letter*, for example, spoke of 'a fine opportunity for young men to join a smart mounted corps', that 'the men joining have every prospect of being sent to France in a short period', and that 'training is done at Antrim Show Grounds, where comfortable accommodation is provided'.[2]

Based on an analysis of the ninety-eight surviving service records, the 680 recruits of 1915 constituted a group quite distinct from those who had rushed to join in the first months of the war, and from the pre-war recruits. Gone were the ageing veterans; only a few had prior military service. These included 33-year-old John Percy Ward, who had been an RFA reservist before working as valet to Robert Jocelyn at his Tullymore Park estate in County Down. When he reported for duty on the outbreak of war the RFA ruled him unfit for service. Undeterred, Ward must have had his employer pull some strings, for he joined the North Irish Horse and immediately applied for a transfer. This time the RFA accepted him.

The 1915 recruits were younger than their predecessors, with an average age just under 22 years. Only seven were aged over thirty, the oldest being 37-year-old groom James Lynn from Drumall. At the other end of the scale, young lads were still lying about their age to join early. Victor Ronaldson, for example, a shop assistant from Cootehill, was still a few days shy of his eighteenth birthday, but convinced Recruiting Sergeant Meredith that he was nineteen when he joined in November. Seventeen-year-old Wallace Linton, from Castlewellan, County Down, stated his age as nineteen. A year and a half later, with six months of active service in France under his belt, he applied for a commission. Probably fearing that his youth would count against him, he bumped his age up again, to twenty-two. He was accepted and by 1918 he was back in France as a Second Lieutenant with the Royal Irish Rifles.

The great majority of the 1915 recruits were Protestants – more than half Presbyterians and a third Church of England or Church of Ireland. One-in-twenty were Roman Catholics. They hailed from all over Ireland, though with a heavy preponderance from Antrim and Belfast. Down and Londonderry were the only other counties providing any significant numbers. Some came from farther afield. Frederick Scanlon for example was from Bagenalstown, County Carlow, and Frederick Earnshaw from Drumcondra, County Dublin.

The 1915 recruits varied most markedly from their predecessors in their occupational backgrounds. Rather than the farmers mobilized in August 1914, or the industrial blue-collar veterans who joined in the first few months of the war, this group was for the most part white-collar, from the commercial or retail sectors. Among the office workers and government employees was a large number of clerks from the banks, insurance and law firms, school teachers, a postal official and a library assistant. Retail workers were equally as numerous, and included a large number of shop assistants, a stationer, grocers' assistants, commercial travellers, a draper's assistant, a hotel waiter and a clothing salesman. Among the trades were linen apprentices, a carpenter, a painter, a paper-cutter, a printer, an upholsterer, a dental mechanic and a watchmaker. Industrial workers and drivers made up only a small share of the recruits, mainly from the tram and rail sector, and only around one-tenth were from the more traditional North Irish Horse rural stock.

The recruits also included the occasional local celebrity, such as Irish international footballer Harry Mercer. He joined Irish Rugby international William Stewart Smyth, and Lurgan Rangers' footballer William McMurray, who had enlisted in the regiment the previous year.

Throughout 1915, Deer Park and the showgrounds at Antrim echoed to the commands and shouts of exasperation of NCOs trying to turn civilians into cavalrymen. 'After breakfast the recruits were fallen in for riding school,' wrote Frank McMahon.

> The recruits with their horses formed a large ring in the centre of which stood the riding master; he was a Sergeant with a ram-rod back, a Kaiser William moustache and a fog-horn voice. He taught you the proper way to mount your horse; when you got mounted he gave the order 'Walk March'; after a short time he yelled 'Trot'. The horses were all cavalry trained and on the command 'HALT' from the Sergeant, they all stopped dead, with the result most of the recruits fell over the horses' heads. The Sergeant would then threaten those men who had fallen off with disciplinary action, viz 'Dismounting without an order'.[3]

As time passed and their riding skills improved the recruits also learnt the rudiments of formation riding, reconnaissance work, advance, rear and flank guard fighting. Not all men made it through training. Illness and physical defects, including poor sight, flat feet and the ever-present bronchitis and tuberculosis, saw a number of men discharged. William Henry Moore had been working as a gold miner in South Africa ever since the Boer War, where his service had earned him two medals and five clasps. By 1913 he had contracted miner's phthisis, a lung disease, and lost his job. On the outbreak of war he returned to Ireland and 'felt so much better that he enlisted in the NIH but he had not joined a week before he found he had overestimated his abilities'. Unable to exert himself without becoming breathless and weak, he was kept on as hut orderly until discharged in May.[4]

There were also regular dismissals of men found to be boys when their parents or apprentice-masters claimed them. Linen apprentice Samuel Barrett was accepted as a 19-year-old until his mother wrote with evidence that he was only sixteen. Stanley Bower of Belfast, who had enlisted with his workmate Robert Patterson, was dismissed after just twelve days, the commanding officer at Antrim receiving a heartfelt plea from his invalid father, and another from his apprentice-master:

> With reference to two boys, who we understand applied for enlisting, in your command, we beg respectfully to ask that these two boys be returned, as they are our apprentices and under age, the boy Stanley Bower being born in August 1897, and the boy Robert Patterson born in February 1898, both these boys have gone without the consent of their parents, who have been here with us and want them returned home at once.
>
> We beg to point out that 50% of our men and boys, have joined the colours, and in no case do we object although many of them were our apprentices, but as these two boys are so young, and we have been so much inconvenienced and at such serious loss through want of workers, we are sure that you will recognise our justification and readily exceed [sic] to our request.
>
> We beg to remain,
Your Obedient Servants,
John McLean & sons
[Engineers and Elevator Builders][5]

For the recruits in training, hard lessons had to be learned in military discipline, not easy for those of a rebellious spirit and used to civilian ways, nor for the old soldiers easily able to weigh up the risks and benefits of breaking the rules. There were the usual minor offences – refusing orders, irregular conduct, being absent without leave, creating a disturbance and drunkenness. One man, a 32-year-old ex-soldier from Shankill, was so often in trouble that he was dismissed and his character marked as 'Bad', with the comment on his file 'This man has not misconducted himself with a view to discharge. He is incorrigible.' It was often the 'indifferent charactered ex-soldiers' who proved the most troublesome, as Major Strettell of the 6th Inniskilling Dragoons observed at the time.[6]

Frank McMahon was one who found the transition to military life difficult, but adapted soon enough:

At the beginning ... I had quite a few brushes with the Authorities, but after a few weeks I settled down and began to enjoy the soldiering; the life wasn't bad, you could get a pint of Guinness for 1½d and cigarettes 5 for 1d at the Canteen, you had quite a few good friends and there was always a sing-song in the Canteen from 5.30 pm to 10 pm.

For McMahon and his pal Jack McGuigan military discipline wasn't all they had to adapt to. As the only Catholics in their troop they were obvious targets, but it also had its benefits:

Sunday was a good day for us, we had no Church parade, but for the others they hated it. Church parade was all spit and polish, burnished sword scabbard, burnished spurs and a spotless turnout and a lynx eyed inspection by the Sergeant and then after him by the troop officer. The boys used to rouse and say 'the next bloody war, I'll be a tyke'.

It wasn't long before the recruits of 1914 started to look more like soldiers:

We continued attending the riding school until the final passing-out test; you got the order 'Cross your stirrups over your saddle, fold your arms' and ride your horse over a 4' jump. If you passed the test you were then posted to a troop as a trooper. You were also trained in sword and rifle drill. If you passed your firing test with the rifle you got an extra 6d per day as a marksman.[7]

First to leave for overseas in 1915 was a draft of thirty-two men under Second Lieutenant James Robert Armstrong. They sailed in January. Three more drafts would follow by mid-year – eighteen men in February under

Quartermaster and Lieutenant John Edward Pittaway, nineteen at the end of April under Second Lieutenant Walter Ashley Montgomery, and twenty-one at the beginning of June. One who was none too pleased with the departure of the January draft was Second Lieutenant Lancelot Charles Wise, who wrote to his mother from Antrim:

> Well the senior sub in my sqdn is going to the front on Monday with a draft of 40 men out of the sqdn. Isn't it rotten for us. We now start again & teach 40 recruits & get on the other fellows as well. It puts us back quite a month. We are fed up.[8]

Wise was a young English gentleman whose uncle had commanded a cavalry regiment in the Indian Army. He had joined the King Edward's Horse regiment as soon as the war began (writing to his parents 'Got in passed medical sworn in join tonight ... Isn't it *topping*.') However, he was never going to stay long in the ranks – educated at Temple Grove School, Charterhouse and Edinburgh University, his father a wealthy land agent, by the end of 1914 the 20-year-old had his commission and was posted to the North Irish Horse at Antrim. On 30 January he wrote at length to his father:

> We are now getting along quite swimmingly! Of course I told you a sub & a draft went out from my sqdn. 40 of them. It was a big hole in the sqdn. & we have had to start all over again. Troop drill every morning to teach them drill. None or very few of the recruits had ever ridden before. We are not up to strength yet. I have now got both my horses fit which is a great relief. One is a real topper but has had a pinched back. Fortunately I have got a rattling groom. He has been a groom for years on end I believe. We are getting swords served out next week ... I have got a jolly fine lot of men (or rather boys) in my troop. Mostly the clerk & mechanic sort of class. They really ride fairly well. Their horses are awful screws! We have rather an amusing time in the evening about twice a week doing battles on paper with the Colonel, using 1″ maps. He is a ripper & a very good Colonel![9]

As mid-year approached at Antrim, the two squadrons in training were pronounced ready by the drill sergeants and riding masters at Antrim. E Squadron was ordered to join the 34th Division as its cavalry squadron. They sailed for England and travelled to Longbridge Deverill, a village close to the military training grounds on Salisbury Plain. F Squadron also departed mid-year, their farewell marked with a concert in the dining room of the regiment's headquarters at Antrim organised by the YMCA. Once in England they were billeted at Hemel Hempstead before travelling to Salisbury Plain and joining the 33rd Division.

On the Ypres front – the first six months of 1915

In France, Major Cole's A Squadron spent 1915 as it had ended 1914, as mounted guard and escort to Sir John French at GHQ, St Omer. They also had to take their turn in the trenches. According to Private Henry McCullagh, 'We had a fine time on General French's bodyguard: but we are now moved into the trenches, knee-deep in mud and water. We don't mind the storm or cold weather now, and we are as hardy as wild ducks.'[10]

As the year dragged on with no end to the war in sight and little work for cavalry, the men of A Squadron probably grew bored and frustrated. Clashes with civilians and other disciplinary breaches occurred, such as this from Private Willie Acheson:

Here and there were taps for watering the horses but some areas had none; if a Frenchman saw you taking water from his pump it was: 'No touch'. Once, on such an occasion, Willie had his bucket half-full: he emptied it on the cranky farmer and trotted off before his number could be taken.[11]

Where the men were caught, they found that discipline 'in the field' had not relaxed. Thus Sergeant James Coburn was reduced to corporal for drunkenness. One lance corporal received twenty-eight days' Field Punishment No.1 and lost his stripe for 'committing a nuisance in the barrack room'. James Allen got five days' Field Punishment No.1 for 'irregular conduct' and on the same day Lance Corporal Fred Cunningham lost his lance stripe for neglect of duty whilst in charge of the guard. Robert Kinnear received seven days' Field Punishment No.2 for leaving his horse ungroomed.[12]

Major Cole passed the time with the business and sporting affairs of home. Letters to his parents show that his concerns lay as much with these matters as it did with the war.

Dear Mammie

No news to give you. We are in a very good camp & leading a very healthy life … It is a great thing that the Russians have had another go. It will buck up the others. People seem very sanguine at present. The next 4 months will be very interesting. Irene writes every day from F[lorence] Court and gives me all the news. Things seem fairly well there. I paid Leslie £700 the other day. The old man is over £400 in arrears with the payments he is supposed to make to me. I don't suppose I shall ever see it.

Dear Father

So glad your dogs have done well. I hope Eskimo will retrieve his character this season … I have just heard from Bracken that the setter bitch I sent home from here has arrived & has also obligingly come in season. I am putting her to a good red dog he knows of … [She] followed me home one day when I was out riding. She seemed to have a good nose as he [sic] found several lots of partridges. There are swarms of them here but we are not allowed to shoot … I have been selling cows at very good prices lately. They are up about £4 a head.[13]

Casualties in A Squadron remained light. Early in the year they lost two men, Private William Irwin of Garvary, Enniskillen and Corporal David William Ritchie from Kilrea, County Londonderry, though neither as a result of enemy action. Both died in France and are buried at St Omer. Another A Squadron casualty was Private Albert Milton Boyle, a 27-year-old farmer from Drumcree. Boyle had served in France with the squadron from the beginning, but while at St Omer he contracted tuberculosis. He was shipped home in July and was soon discharged. He died in October 1916.

For the first months of the year C Squadron continued as corps headquarters cavalry, apparently based at Bailleul. Life was fairly quiet, 'never so bored in my life,' according to Richard Annesley West, 'a bloody existence' but the horsemen found enough to entertain them, with hunts over the sodden waterlogged farmland (stopped when 'the French squealed about it'), and other activities as described by an officer of a cyclist unit:

Bailleul was never quite dull. In the spring Territorial Divisions began to arrive, and [we] used to saunter up and down the Square and criticise with a veteran air … From the Square [we] would saunter into the

dirty and smoky *Faucon* or the expensive *Allies Tea Rooms* for a drink
… Later a cinema was provided, while the North Irish Horse, finding
life dull after their old freebooting days, started again the fine old sport
of cock-fighting.[14]

Sport and gambling were a way of life for the Horsemen, as Corporal
Sterling wrote in a letter home:

The fellows out here are as eager to know all that is going on in the
sporting world as if there was no such thing as a war on at all, and
football and racing results are looked up with keen interest when the
papers come in. Some of us are having a franc or two on the Lincoln,
and what we want to know is not when the war will be over, but what
will win!

Irishmen of all persuasions found St Patrick's Day a good excuse for a
celebration:

Yesterday we celebrated St Patrick's Day in an enthusiastic manner.
We have a lot of the Leinsters and Irish Rifles here at present, and the
little trefoil plant was much in evidence, stuck jauntily in the 'bhoys'
caps. It was quite amusing to see several Belgian and French soldiers
sporting it as well. At night we had an excellent concert, at which songs
of the Green Isle were the chief items on the bill. A Belgian soldier
also favoured us with a couple of tunes with characteristic vivacity, and
although we did not quite understand what it was all about, we enjoyed
his singing immensely.[15]

For the men of C Squadron the early months of 1915 were also punctuated
with various disciplinary breaches, together with illnesses both minor and
debilitating. Willie McFerran's eventful war continued with another offence,
earning him ten days' Field Punishment No. 2. Harry Newell of Dungannon
and William Craig of Belfast were sent to military hospitals in France, while
Corporal William Jackson of Loughgall was evacuated to an English hospital
after he injured his leg.

Five of those who had distinguished themselves in the recent fighting
were Mentioned in Despatches by the Commander in Chief – Massereene,
Corporal Jack Wright and Private Richard McIlwaine on 14 January, and

Squadron Sergeant Majors William Sewell and Worship Booker on 31 May. McIlwaine, from Lurgan, had already been invalided home and would be discharged a few months later. Sewell and Booker had enlisted together in the first week of the war. Sewell, a 44-year-old Boer War veteran from London's East End, had been working in the Belfast Corporation Surveyor's Department and spent his spare time as a member of the Belfast Philharmonic Society orchestra.

C Squadron's life of relative ease ended in April when it was ordered to replace A Squadron of the 15th Hussars as divisional cavalry to the 3rd Division. The

Men of C Squadron in France, early 1915 (*Belfast Evening Telegraph*, March 1915).

squadron moved north to the Hussars' old billets at la Manche, near Mont Noir. The men took their turn in the trenches near St Eloi, Lieutenant West commenting dryly 'it's no game for a long man as you must keep your head down'. April and the months following also brought changes to the squadron's command. Massereene left for home on sick leave. (He was then posted to Egypt.) Captain Eustace King-King transferred to D Squadron. Lieutenant West left for a captaincy in the North Somerset Yeomanry. Command of C Squadron passed to Major Holt Waring, late of D Squadron. The squadron's new role meant more casualties. In April Corporal Fred Lindsay received a severe bullet wound to his leg. Private Willie Roulston of Ramelton, County Donegal, was hit by a piece of shrapnel in the chest. A dutiful son, he wrote to his mother to let her know that he was wounded, but not to worry as he was safe in an English hospital. Of course she did worry, and hearing nothing more, wrote to the authorities for news:

> Sir
>
> I received a postcard from my son Private William Roulston 1158 third army corps North Irish Horse, saying that he had been admitted in to hospital wounded, & I would be greatly obliged if you could find out for me his conditions, & what hospital he is in, as I am anxious to hear about him & to know how he is …
>
> Yours respectfully
Mary Roulston[16]

Willie would recover and see the war out in France, by then serving in the Tank Corps. In May Private Edward McKernon was wounded in the knee, the damage severe enough to keep him out of active service for the duration. Another, Private George Harper of Corcreevy, Fivemiletown, died in England of spinal meningitis. He had enlisted in January 1914 and been in France with C Squadron since the beginning. After he fell ill he was sent to the hospital at Netley, Hampshire, where he died, aged twenty-one.

These casualties were but little compared to what was occurring all around the Ypres salient. From 22 April to 25 May the Germans launched a ferocious assault on the French and British lines in an attempt to break through and once again threaten the Channel ports. The salient presented a poor defensive position for the Allies. The Germans were better positioned, more numerous and better armed, and initially they had the advantage of surprise, with large gains made in the wake of the first gas attacks in the battles of Gravenstafel Ridge and St Julien. By the end of April the salient had become so compressed that British forces holding the line out to Zonnebeke and Polygon Ridge found themselves under artillery fire from three sides. A vital but risky withdrawal was ordered to a line just three miles east of Ypres. Although the Germans made further but smaller gains in the Battle of Bellewaarde Ridge, and the outcome was touch and go at times, the line held, and by the end of May the fighting came to an end. British losses in this battle amounted to almost 60,000 killed, wounded and missing. One of these was former North Irish Horseman Lance Corporal William Graham, killed near St Julien while serving in the Canadian infantry.

Meanwhile, time had passed slowly for the men of D Squadron. Since December they had been training at Cople, near Bedford in England. Second Lieutenant Lancelot Wise had joined them here from Antrim. He wrote to his mother:

> I have had to leave my old sqdn & old troop & come here *without horses* which is rather a jar! However, it is much closer to home *& also* France as they are a trained sqdn …
>
> We are billeted in a big house at 6/- a day and no extras which is *much* cheaper. Kirkpatrick has got a car which we all use *whenever* we like to go *anywhere* so we are very lucky.[17]

This is followed by another on 9 April. Rumours were starting to circulate about departure for France:

> We have tremendous news!! I really think by the time you get this we shall have moved 'elsewhere'. I'm sure we shall unless anything out of the way happens. The general has told us so! At any rate we shall have a month in France to settle down in. All the divisions going out lately have had some time to settle down in. Divisional Cavalry don't go in the trenches I believe. (I'm not in the least sorry either!)
>
> … Frightful excitement here, as every day sometime or another, an enormous car rushes out from the general & hurls our sqdn leader into a conference. I have been getting up some rugby football here to amuse the men. They *are* bored as they have been here since Dec 10th & when they left Antrim they thought they were going *straight* to the front.[18]

For three old soldiers, Cople was as near as they would get to the war. Private Samuel Cosgrove, a 39-year-old barber from Shankill, had served twelve years with the Royal Irish Rifles in India and in the Boer War. While at Cople he was 'exposed to all kinds of weather going from his billet to where the horses were kept'. Complaining of shortness of breath, dizziness and black spots in front of his eyes, he was returned to base at Antrim and then discharged in July 1915. Perhaps desperate to provide for his wife Agnes and their eight children, he re-enlisted in 1916 with the Royal Engineers, this time stating that he was a riveter with the shipbuilders Harland & Wolff (but omitting to mention his service with the North Irish Horse). By February 1917 they too discovered his disability and he was again discharged. He died at home on 10 December 1917 and was accorded a military funeral. Frank Brewer had previously served with the York and Lancaster Regiment. He was forty-seven, but claimed to be twenty-nine when he enlisted with his 16-year-old son Cecil in April 1913. Born in Madras, India (recorded as a 'half caste' on his file), he was a musician by trade. His son Cecil was already serving in France with C Squadron when Frank arrived at Cople. It wasn't long, however, before the NCOs of the squadron worked-out that he was badly short-sighted. '[He] is quite unable … at any distance to see the Bull's Eye on a target, even when aided by glasses.'[19] Brewer was sent home and discharged from the service. His son survived the war (though wounded). John Henry Douglas had served two and a half years with the North of Ireland Imperial Yeomanry. His disciplinary record had not been good at Antrim or Cople, but matters weren't helped when a report came through that his wife had lost her 'separation allowance' on the strength of a police report about her behaviour. Further offences saw Douglas shipped back to Antrim, where things didn't improve. After three long absences without leave he was discharged. Another to miss the boat for France was Squadron Sergeant Major Trimble. He had been with D Squadron since returning from France the previous December. In April he was involved in a motor-vehicle accident near Bedford, sustaining a compound fracture of his right knee. It would be another year before he made it to the front.

Rumours of movement continued to circulate through April, and finally Lancelot Wise was able to write to his Aunt Henrietta:

Really & *honestly* we are off on Thursday, Friday or Saturday. The whole squadron have got *everything* new including saddlery. I got a topping new officer's saddle today. I have also got two pretty good horses. One very sporting polo pony pitch black with an odd white nose on it!

... I've *never* worked so hard in my life. The farm was nothing. Brain &
physical labour from 5 AM to at least 11.30 PM. Mostly getting new kit &
marking it & parades & inspections. Today we were on parade *dis*mounted
marching & being inspected from 9 – 1 PM. Then mounted from 2.30 to
6.15 & then tea. We were also on the range from 6–8.30 AM![20]

On 30 April 1915 D Squadron, under the command of Major The Hon
Arthur Hamilton-Russell, moved to Southampton and from there to France.
Half the men of the squadron, all the horses and three officers – Hamilton-
Russell, and Second Lieutenants James Cunningham Gordon Kirkpatrick
and Warren Murland – sailed on the *Anglo-Canadian* on the afternoon of 1
May. The remainder of the squadron, with Major Holt Waring, and Second
Lieutenants John Valentine Adair and Lancelot Wise, sailed at much the
same time on board the *Empress Queen*. The squadron numbered six officers,
141 NCOs and men, and 158 riding and draught horses.

Soon D Squadron was at Busnes in the la Bassée front, and from here
Second Lieutenant Wise wrote a typically frank letter to his father:

Well we had a pretty awful journey here. We always entrained &
detrained in coal yards in the middle of the night in pouring rain!! Tres
agreeable n'est ce pas! Imagine 150 saddles all numbered rather mixed
in a coal yard at 1 AM in pouring rain! It really was pretty bad. Well
we got here at last 5 AM & had to look round the village for our billets
which were written on doors because the man who was supposed to
show us which they were spent the night in the ditch as his car upset!!

Horses are pretty fit but very tired and stiff. The men are very dreamy
at present. We shall soon wake them up! It is very hot here and a lot of
thunder about. Horses in an orchard. I am in a *bed* with *clean sheets* in
a jolly wee house by myself. Quite a decent family. Yest[erday] was the
major's birthday so we had an enormous dinner with champagne, white
wine, W & S & liqueur brandy & cigars. Some dinner![21]

At St Omer, news of the arrival of D Squadron gave Major Cole cause for
satisfaction, though in it he saw proof that the south of Ireland was not
pulling its weight:

Another N. Irish Squadron has just come out with Highland Division.
This makes 3 out here whereas the South have only one. Of all the
shitinest etc etc.[22]

This comment was accurate but unfair, as three more squadrons of the South Irish Horse were in England as divisional cavalry to the 16th (Irish), 32nd and 21st Divisions. They could hardly be blamed for decisions about when their divisions would go to France. During the war six South Irish Horse squadrons saw service in France, compared to five of the North Irish Horse.

D Squadron's division, the 51st (Highland), was the last of the first-line Territorials to go to France. Initially they were held as general reserve and were able to observe the attacks on Aubers Ridge and Festubert. D Squadron remained with them, marching to Pradelles. Lancelot Wise reported to his mother:

We have moved up country now about 12 miles or so ... I got a very dirty smelly room in a still dirtier farmyard! ... Fleas first night but alright afterwards! ... One of our other squadrons is close here. Three officers rode over here to lunch today. Great sport they were too! Most amusing fellows all of them.

... Two officers from the other squadron were in the trenches last night. They were the ones over today and were very interesting about it. They went out into them voluntarily. They got leave with 'instruction' as their excuse. Rather sporting, weren't they.[23]

From 19 May the 51st (Highland) Division moved into the lines in front of Festubert. D Squadron marched to la Gorgue and then to a farm north of the la Bassée Canal, half a mile north of Hinges. The weather, fine and warm with occasional showers, meant that the horses could be kept in open fields, while the men slept in barns, and the officers in farmhouses. Second Lieutenant Wise wrote again to his mother:

We bathe in the canal here every day which is topping. One comes out dirtier than one goes in I believe!! Well we really are fed up losing Holt Waring. He really was a *topper*. About the soundest polo player & horse coper in Ireland.

... There are a lot of Canadians here. They are a priceless lot ... About 200 Canadian horses are passing now. Singing ragtime lustily & rotting each other the whole time. Rotten horses. I am going into a big town close by this afternoon for the mess. I believe I can get most things there ...

Am awfully fit and terribly sunburnt! It's a great life out here.[24]

The first two weeks of June were spent at comfortable new billets in nearby Carvin. The brilliant weather continued and the men of D Squadron made the most of it:

> We are having *gorgeous* weather. Very nearly as hot as Rhodesia. We now get up at 5.0 & have a very light breakfast at 6.0 (feed horses and stables in between). Then we parade at 6.30 AM & go out on something or other. Anything the troop officer likes. Then we come in at 9.30 AM. Stables again. Then a great BRUNCH at 11.30 AM. Nothing till 3 PM when we or somebody else lectures. At 4.15 there is tea. Stables 5.30. Dinner for us at 8.0 PM. It's not a bad day really is it? Early to bed, early to rise, etc. Well I'm fearfully fit and very brown! Quite khaki by now!! ... Everybody is very cheerful ... Many thanks for the socks ... Must fly as Sergt has come to say a horse is lame![25]

Meanwhile plans were made for an assault by IV Corps towards Violaines. No breakthrough was planned or expected, just a supportive action to help the French who were attacking to the south at Artois. Nevertheless, two troops of D Squadron moved to le Touret on 14 June to guard the expected German prisoners. Over three days all assaults were repelled with heavy losses, the 51st Highland losing over 1,600 men. D Squadron waited in vain for the German prisoners. Further moves then took place to various billets on the northern sector of the la Bassée front; first from Carvin to la Pannerie, then to Estaires, la Gorgue and Neuf Berquin. Lancelot Wise again:

> Here we are moved again to within 300 yds of our old billets! Perfectly beastly place. My room is so small you could hardly lie flat in it. We are having a good bit of rain or we should be sleeping out ... We are moving again tomorrow I believe but where we don't know. The horses are *very* fit. I've never seen such a fat lot which is what you want at this time of the year ...
>
> All is very quiet on the front now. Our fellows have earned a good rest.[26]

On 25 June a severe thunderstorm broke the dry spell and more rain followed. The month concluded with the departure of Captain King-King. It was a popular move. 'Our Capt has gone thank heavens!' wrote Lancelot Wise. 'Doctor did it for us!!! We had a fizz supper the day he left!!'[27] The ageing officer left for base to attend a medical board. Suffering from 'debility', he was eventually evacuated to England, his active service over.

The war drags on

As the year wore on, Major Cole's letters home grew increasingly pessimistic. News in May of the Battles of Aubers Ridge and Second Artois drew a gloomy but essentially accurate assessment:

> You will have seen by the papers that the French have done well on our right. Whereas *we* did very little good. It was the biggest show of the whole war. The French had ½ million men engaged & we 300,000. It was hoped that a really big thing might have been done but the swine were waiting for us & we could not get through their wire & machine guns. I do not believe we shall ever get them moving. If the war ever ends we shall still be here.

Soon after he shared with his father a growing frustration at the impact of the war on life at home:

> So they have stopped racing after all ... I am afraid it will be a great bore for you ... What are you going to do in Ireland?? This infernal war will ruin everything. I don't expect there will be any hunting this winter.

In letter after letter his news from the front was either bad, or held out no hope for a break in the deadlock:

> I think the war will be long because I am convinced that it is impossible for either side to make any advance on this flank. I don't believe that all these extra shells will have any effect when they eventually arrive. Neuve Chapelle was a partial success entirely owing to its being a surprise.
>
> ... No war news here except that fresh troops continue to arrive every day. It is a real armageddon as it looks as if the whole of Europe & perhaps America will be involved before it is over. I wonder if the end of the world is coming too.

Occasionally Cole speculated, colourfully but without much hope, on whether there might be better prospects of victory in other theatres:

I wonder what will happen in Servia. If we only could send a big enough force to bore through & relieve the force at Gallipoli it would be a great thing. If only we can do it quickly before the Servians are utterly rodgered. I begin to think the decisive battles will be fought in that direction & not here.

There was also room for gossip from the front about acquaintances, servants, horses and the weather:

I have started breaking in some Australian remounts. 3 of them are a bit awkward as they have been spoilt by some one else allready [sic].
    … I may see Freda on Sunday as I am going to Le Touquet on a joy ride … I am very well & pig fat. Moisley is invaluable as a cook & servant & in controlling the other servants. I would like to send you a photo of our villa but no photos are allowed.
    … I hear the King is coming out here shortly, I suppose to give me a decoration!!

Thoughts of home, work neglected on the Florence Court estate and the peacetime pursuits of a country gentleman were never far from his mind, and Major Cole's letters made clear where he would prefer to be.

Dear Father
    … I am very glad you were able to give a good account of the Children & other livestock on the place. Apparently Crowly has done really well. He is also economical & has saved of a respectable balance. According to Irene he is quite happy there & interested in his work, not like the last shit I had who wanted to be off playing lawn tennis. If I can run to it I will stand him a bathroom (at?) rear when I get back.

Dear Mammie
    … You will be amused to hear that my man caught the parson's sister driving in the garden. Luckily he is at daggers drawn with the parson & ran her out … It only shows that one must *live* in one's place to keep things right.[28]

Cole's A Squadron continued through the year on guard and escort duty to the Commander in Chief. Its casualties remained negligible, although one of its former comrades was less lucky. Private Robert Herron of Tully, Ballymena, who had only recently transferred to the Military Mounted Police, dislocated a shoulder blade, broke a leg and was wounded above his knee-cap when a bomb exploded under his horse and he was thrown off, the horse falling on top of him.

When C Squadron had gone to France in August 1914 it seems that no one had told its gentlemen officers that Field Service Regulations required each unit to keep a daily 'war diary'. During the second half of 1915 Captain Grant, the officer in charge of C Squadron's paperwork, realised his omission. The diary for October was forwarded to the Deputy Assistant Adjutant General. This sparked a terse note, 'The diaries for July, Aug & Sep are awaited', and a confession from Captain Grant in response, 'Regret in Error no diaries were kept for July, August and September.' Nothing was said about the earlier months, and there the matter rested.[29]

In October C Squadron was still working as divisional cavalry to the 3rd Division and was based in Sanctuary Wood, just south of the Menin Road. The front line ran along the edge of the wood and had been bitterly fought over. Fighting here in July and August had been notable for the first use by the Germans of the *Flammenwerfer* (liquid fire), and the first use by the British of steel helmets. C Squadron played a subsidiary role, including as prisoner escort, as this exchange between a British and a German officer shows:

Our troops not far from here, at Hooge, were told to straighten out a salient of the German lines that run towards our trenches. We succeeded beyond our expectations, and made over 200 prisoners ... I came across a batch of them – two officers and 120 men ... The officer in charge of the German machine guns was one of the prisoners ... [He argued that] Germany could continue the war indefinitely, and that we could not increase our numbers because the Irish refused to enlist and to fight. In vain I told him that we had several first-rate Irish regiments in our own division who are a brave as lions. The officer hesitated to believe me. At last I told him, 'You don't understand the irony of your present position. Do you know what troops are escorting you? It is the Loyal North Irish Horse, the very men who you foolishly thought would prevent the Expeditionary Force from landing in France by causing a civil war.' This stopped further slander of our brave Irish boys, whether north or south of Ireland.[30]

On 25 September the British Army mounted a full-scale assault on the Loos front. It was the first time Kitchener's New Army troops had been used, and the first time the British had used poison gas. Despite being handicapped by a shortage of artillery, the need to attack over open ground, inexperienced troops, and wind which blew the gas back on the attacking troops, significant gains were made on the first day. However, the Germans' ability to counter-attack with fresh reserves and the British commander's insistence on holding back reinforcements lost the momentum and much of the captured ground. By the time a halt was called in mid-October the BEF had lost more than 60,000 men for no appreciable gain.

While none of the North Irish Horse squadrons were actively involved in the battle, they lost a former comrade on the first day of the fighting. Robert Hutchinson Andrews, son of a County Down farming family, was one of the first to enlist in the North Irish Horse when war was declared. His family must have had some influence, because despite his having had no previous military experience, he was allowed to join C Squadron when it sailed for France on 20 August, just ten days after he had enlisted. Commissioned as a second lieutenant in August 1915, Andrews was posted to the 1st Royal Irish Rifles, joining the regiment as it prepared to make a small-scale attack on the German trenches at Bois Grenier. The purpose was to pin down enemy reserves while the main attack took place at Loos that day, 25 September. But not a lot went according to plan, and Andrews was killed when a German shell ignited a load of smoke candles brought forward for use in the attack.[31]

For Andrews' former comrades in C Squadron, there was little cavalry work to do as the Battle of Loos continued through September and October, and the squadron took its turn in the Sanctuary Wood trenches. Every five days a party of forty NCOs and men, led alternately by Lieutenant Grant and Captain Ross, assembled in the late afternoon and made their way forward. Here they relieved their pals and continued the work of repairing trenches, constructing defence works and mounting wire.

The remainder of October and most of November were spent well behind the lines to the west of Ypres, firstly near Winnezeele and then Hardifort. The time at the front had taken its toll on some. On 24 November the *Belfast News-Letter* reported that Private Harry Newell was in hospital at Cassel 'suffering from the effects of recent trying experiences'. By December the paper reported he was home as a result of 'illness contracted in France'. Newell, of Dungannon, County Tyrone, had been out since August 1914. He had two brothers serving in France, one with the 6th Inniskilling Dragoons (Service Squadron), and another with the Royal Engineers. Whatever the cause of his illness, Newell recovered and returned to his regiment in the new year. At the end of November C Squadron moved east to Boeschepe.

During the second half of 1915, D Squadron was also having a taste of trench life in France and Belgium. For days at a time through July working parties of up to 100 men marched out of Neuf Berquin to the support trenches east of Laventie, in front of the German-held town of Fromelles. Here they worked on trench repairs and digging trenches to carry a subterranean telephone wire from advanced divisional headquarters to brigade headquarters. They didn't enjoy it much, according to Brevet Major Gore-Browne of the London Regiment:

> Stationed in trenches in front of Rue de Tillelay, Laventie. I have command of a squadron of North Irish Horse under Major Hamilton Russel, a nice person. They are awfully sick at the class of warfare we are waging at present. I haven't a notion of what they expected – a sort of orgie [sic] of shooting and stabbing I suppose – but I tell them they can have as much adventure as they like if they choose to send out patrols at night in front of our barbed wire.[32]

Lancelot Wise's letters through the month showed the frustration and boredom felt by the North Irish Horsemen, but also how they managed to amuse themselves behind the lines and on their trips to the front.

> My Dear old Dad
> ... It is so funny, *everybody* except you & mother write to me out here & talk about the *war*! So *dull*!! You are so fed up with hearing it & of it & seeing it all day & night it's a bit tiresome when you get a 'war' mail instead of a *home* one ... We take in here too all the English papers like the Tatt[l]er etc which *don't* publish war news or photos. They are worth their weight in gold. Cousin Charlotte has just sent me 200 cigarettes. Real gooduns which *she* smokes.[33]

My Dearest Mother

... I think we are in here for the winter (I mean M.F *m*uddy *F*landers). Rather damp but otherwise quiet [sic] alright. The crops here are the best I have *ever* seen *anywhere*. Every field is cultivated to within 1,200 yds of the firing trenches & some sheltered fields even closer. The women do all the work & little boys. It is extraordinary the *children* work. It's *quite* natural & not put on extra. They are a very happy crowd & every one says 'Bon jour' whenever you pass them. Even in your billet if you enter 6 times in half an hour they say it. When you go into any room or house here you always do a sort of salute & say 'Bon jour' as a sort of salute to the household. *Then* you [are] as welcome as if you lived there. We found a piano at _____ yest. & several of us sang and played for an hour. Our interpreter is top hole & sings & plays odd French songs, some love songs & others comic till you simply roll off your chair laughing at him. He is an exceptional interpreter & a *royalist*. Otherwise he would be pretty high in the French army I fancy. The water is bad here so the mess all drinks 'Vichy' a good spring water bottled at 5d a bottle. Then for dinner we have Perrier & Whiskey!! The light red wines are *very* good but I don't care for the white. The red is 10d a bottle. No news to tell you. ½ the sqdn are digging in reserve trenches a mile or so behind the line. Two junior officers are left![34]

... We have been doing 'working parties' on reserve trenches lately. I went out in charge of 50 men and waited at a rendezvous behind the firing line (about 800 yds) for some RE to show us what to do. We had to be there at 11 PM. I got there alright but the RE never turned up *at all*. I came home at 1 AM *very* bored & arrived in at 4 AM!! Of course between 11 PM & 1 AM the men slept in a barn I found but *I* had to rush round to try & find the RE. Eventually I got to the support trenches & used a telephone there. Nobody knew where the RE were. They got lost! We got an apology next morning. No news here at all. We had a service this morning & sang 'fight the good fight' & one or two other good hymns.[35]

... Again we have been digging! I took a party up today. When we got there I was strolling about talking to some fellows I knew who were making experiments with barbed wire ... Suddenly there was an awful noise behind us about 50 yds away. We all looked round & thought we were being shelled! However it was only a fellow who had let off an unexploded German big bomb!! It gave us an awful start.[36]

... I am just waiting for Harry's car to arrive to drive up 20 miles or so to see him & play polo. It is a very stormy day so he *may* not send it but I hope he does. Some of our fellows are learning to bomb throw. It's a very exciting job even practising it. You get the bomb in your hand, then you light a fuse which burns for five seconds & then explodes the bomb! You hold it in your hand for *3* seconds & then throw! Quite a novelty to our fellows, who look upon them as glorified fireworks!! I went out with my troop & practised them in taking verbal messages. It's quite extraordinary how stupid some are about it. When they've gone a mile they have forgotten half & [after] 2 miles you get nothing! Of course there are only about 2 or 3 like that so I *always* send them. One fellow will take one any length you like!![37]

... We had great sport this morning at a digging party. The Boshes [sic] were shelling a battery some distance away from us. Two of us made bets (1d) as to where the shells were going, all bets to be made while the shells were in the air. Nearest man got the 1d!![38]

On 19 July he wrote to his sister Christabel:

Well *no* Hun in sight yet thank goodness. We haven't even shot into the air in the hopes that one was hiding there! However he has condescended to shoot *near* us! Terrible! He hasn't even shot or gassed anyone of us. The whole squadron are here still! They are now using us for digging parties every day or night. Beastly dull. We've only been shelled 3 times since we started and they were about 200 or 300 yds away & perfectly harmless. The great difficulty was to prevent men running out to pick up bits of shell.[39]

At last news came of a change in scenery for the squadron, much to the relief of Lieutenant Wise:

We are moving on Sat but I can't say where. I hope it will be a better place than this. It's *very* dull here. All flat country. Every bit is the same wherever you go. There isn't even a *rise* in sight. They had great polo here yest evening. Our major is awfully good & has 2 topping ponies he trained himself.[40]

Under pressure from the French, the British had agreed to take over more of the line, first the whole of the Ypres salient, and then a second sector, south of the French Tenth Army – a fifteen-mile stretch of the Somme uplands from Curlu Somme to Hébuterne. This fell to the newly-formed Third Army under General Sir Charles Monro. D Squadron's division was one of those ordered to join this new army, and in the last days of July began the move to its new home. D Squadron entrained at Berguette Station and after a day's travel moved into their new billets at Heilly, on the banks of the Ancre river close to its junction with the Somme.

All units were required to assist in the handover of the trenches from the French troops. D Squadron was attached to the 1st/8th Battalion Argyll & Sutherland Highlanders. In the evening of 29 July, sixty men under Major Hamilton-Russell and Second Lieutenants Kirkpatrick and Adair followed the river north through Albert to the village of Martinsart. To the east was Aveluy Wood, and beyond that the valley of the Ancre and the front line. The following evening they marched through the wood, across the river, through the ruins of Authuille and into the trenches, which they took over from the 116th French Regiment. Lancelot Wise was one of the few left behind:

My Dearest Mother

Here we are at last at our new place. Topping country & very good billets. I've got a bed as good as England!! ½ the sqdn is in the trenches & there are only 2 officers left here & 30 men to look after 153 horses. A rotten job!! I'd much rather be up in the ditch with the rest.[41]

The next day he wrote again:

The squadron had no casualties going into the trenches last night. The Germans couldn't think who was there. The only reply our fellows gave was that they were better than Huns!! I have got a new horse. A really 1st class Irish hunter. It was Lord Massereene's 1st charger. He has gone home & I got it in a roundabout way. Jolly lucky. I have now got four good horses & I wouldn't change them for anything. They must be worth quite a lot! ... Major Russell has just turned up from the trenches (7 miles). He says they had a great time.[42]

Major Hamilton-Russell agreed that Wise could take his place in the trenches, and a few days later he penned a quick note to his father:

Trenches

Dear Dad

... We are in the beastly ditches. This is my first day up. I arrived about 1 hour ago. Having walked 2 miles I arrived at a topping dug out ... There are several Scotch fellows in another D.O. next to us. We are attached to a Scotch Battn & form a platoon. 2 officers. We have 60 of our men here. They are lovely trenches & very safe.[43]

D Squadron remained in the trenches at Authille until the evening of 13 August. They had had only one casualty, the squadron cook George McGivern, who was hit in the shoulder by a dropping bullet while in a reserve trench.

For the rest of August and through September, October and November the squadron became familiar with the new front, with regular working parties of fifty men and an officer sent to build and repair the trench system around Albert and Aveluy. The work wasn't too taxing, this being a quiet sector and the weather fine and warm until the first snow fell in mid-November. There were some casualties. Private Andrew Moss was reported wounded in November and Lance Corporal William Cleland was 'invalided from the trenches' to hospital in Belfast.[44] Meanwhile Lancelot Wise and his fellow officers found plenty of time for sport.

My Dearest Mother

... We are starting games of polo next week when the Major gets back. He is away on leave for a week. I have just heard from him telling me where to send his horses to. We are having great races here one day. A horse of mine (charger) against another charger of Kirkpatrick's. I think you might call both racers, as what else they would be good for I don't know. Adair is riding mine as he made the bet provided *I* agreed, so of course I did. It's over a mile course for £2-10s. Also a few side bets!!! Then we are going to race a few troopers. 4 of my troop (owners up) against 4 of Kirkpatrick's. This is to be one race. They go about 1,000 yds including a turn round a hay stack. It will be amusing as they are the worst riders on the fastest horses as it happens. Of course they will go miles beyond the haystack before they will think of turning round & racing back!! We've got a new officer here. Goodness knows *why*! He's a 2nd Lieut aged 42. Sound in wind & limb. No hair!!!! Perhaps they will send a younger fellow to HQ as I believe they are one short there ... I am just off to practise polo. You see I have never played before & everybody else has a *bit* so I practise every available minute.

Must fly as the ponies are waiting.

Fondest love to all

Your loving son

Lancelot

P.S. I enclose flowers I picked between the trenches I forgot to send before.[45]

The 42-year-old bald subaltern referred to by Wise was Thomas Peter Davis Sherston. Sherston was bursar of Wellington College, Berkshire, a prestigious school established to educate the sons of deceased military officers. He had no military experience, but was well-connected enough to have the authorities waive the age limit for new officers.

More frequent than the trips to the front, the race days and the polo were the daily woodcutting parties sent to supply timber for the trenches and for the squadron billets at Béhencourt. This was to be their home for the rest of the year, and while sleeping in barns with the horse lines in open fields was fine for a mobile squadron in mild weather, something more permanent was now required. The men were therefore put to work preparing the camp for winter. With the wood supplied by the timber cutters they built winter stables in the village, comfortable winter quarters for the men, a bathhouse, covered latrines, and a washhouse. They also repaired barns, made beds, and established a canteen and institute in the village. To further occupy their time, training was organised and a weekly concert, 'which ought to be great fun if we could only beef it up & get fresh things,' mused Lancelot Wise.[46]

In October a new draft arrived of one sergeant, a corporal and seventeen other ranks, bringing the squadron up to strength. Lancelot Wise was pleased with the quality of the men. 'They are a splendid lot & *very* well trained too. Among them I got a very good sergeant who was a Corp in the 12th Lancers for some time.'[47]

On 4 November F Squadron was ordered to prepare for the move to France. Twelve days later the squadron – five officers and around 125 men

– sailed from Southampton on the *Western Miller*, arriving at le Havre on 17 November.

In command was Major Richard Griffith Oliver Bramston-Newman, who had recently taken over from Lord Farnham. Farnham had been appointed to headquarters staff of the Ulster Division. Thirty-nine-year-old Bramston-Newman had served as an officer in the 7th Dragoon Guards before joining the North Irish Horse in 1909. The squadron's junior officers were Arthur Noel Vernon Hill-Lowe, Thomas Henry Mowbray Leader, George Waller Vesey and James Robert Dennistoun. Twenty-three year-old Hill-Lowe, born at Stoke Damerel, Devon, had served in the Malay States Volunteer Rifles and King Edward's Horse before being commissioned and posted to the North Irish Horse. Vesey, thirty-three, was the second son of George Lendrum DL, of Corkhill, Kilskeery, County Tyrone. Leader, thirty, from Cork, had worked as a rancher in Canada before returning home to enlist. His brother, a captain in the Connaught Rangers, had been killed at le Grande Fayt in the first month of the war. Dennistoun was an adventurer in the traditional British Empire style. Born at Peel Forest in New Zealand's South Island, he had spent much of his youth exploring and mountaineering, being the first to climb several peaks of the snow-capped southern alps of New Zealand. In 1910 he joined Captain Scott's ill-fated Antarctic expedition, for which he was awarded the King's Antarctic Medal and a Royal Geographical Society Medal. At the beginning of 1915 he travelled to England, where he applied for a commission in the North Irish Horse. The regiment's Lieutenant Colonel Maude supported his application, although at thirty-two he considered him 'a little over age'.

F Squadron was only lightly leavened with pre-war Horsemen, most of these being NCOs such as Hugh Wilkinson, Richard Knox and John Frederick Craig. More than half the men had enlisted in 1915. The squadron was an admixture of men from all social classes and occupations. Some had travelled across the world to enlist. 'We had various talent amongst us,' recalled Frank McMahon, 'University students, 2 Australians, 1 chap from the Canadian North West Mounted police, boilermakers, farm labourers, grocers, you mention it and we had them.'[48]

Once disembarked at le Havre, F Squadron moved by train and horseback to Morbecque, a small town two miles south of Hazebrouck, and soon after marched south to billets in the village of le Cornet Bourdois. Another move occurred on 30 November, this time a little farther east to the village of le Cauroy, close to Béthune, where the infantrymen of their division were taking turns in the trenches. A week of reconnaissance patrols, inspections and other routine duties followed, often in heavy rain, and a lecture was given in 'trench discipline'.[49]

France and Belgium weren't the only destinations for men of the North Irish Horse in 1915. Around the middle of the year volunteers were sought for the Mediterranean theatre. There, British and French forces were defending Egypt and the Suez from the Turkish threat across the Sinai desert, and were bogged down on the Gallipoli Peninsula at Cape Helles and at Anzac Cove. A new attempt would soon be made to force the issue with landings at Suvla Bay, north of the Anzac positions.

About two dozen Horsemen were selected. They embarked for Egypt, attached to headquarters of the 54th (East Anglian) Division as Military Mounted Police. This division was diverted to Gallipoli, where it landed at Suvla Bay on 10 and 11 August. Exactly what role the North Irish Horsemen played there is not known, but one report refers to two of them, Lance Corporals Robert Corry and Thomas Wilton, taking part 'in the famous charge, when the heights were carried'. This may have been the attack on Scimitar Hill on 21 August.[50]

The Suvla operation quickly became another expensive failure. By the end of the year the campaign at Gallipoli was abandoned and the Allied toeholds on the peninsula were evacuated in December and January. The men of the North Irish Horse had remained at Suvla since the landing and left in December. Arriving at Egypt, a number, including Wilton and Corry, transferred to the Military Mounted Police and remained there for the duration of the war. Some others, it appears, had arrived at Alexandria in August 1915 and went on to serve in various elements of the Egyptian campaign. A small number found their way back home. One, Private John Boston of Ballyhenry, was evacuated from Gallipoli to Alexandria and then to England, suffering from jaundice. Once recovered, he joined the North Irish Horse in France, where he was later twice wounded.

Christmas

As the second Christmas of the war approached, A Squadron remained on duty near St Omer. The thoughts of their commanding officer remained firmly focused on home:

Dear Father

We have been on the move a good deal lately so I have not had much time to write ... I wish I could get home to my farm like the two boys are ... I hope to get home on leave Dec 16 & stay over Xmas.[51]

C Squadron remained at Boeschepe. There were occasional duties as road control and frontier police, and days spent labouring at Godewaersvelde and Hazebrouck railway stations loading timber and bricks for the division. On Sunday 19 December the Germans launched a gas attack on the Ypres front, using phosgene for the first time. However, the British and French forces had learned of the planned attack and all troops were on alert. Even as far back as Boeschepe, C Squadron was on stand-by to move at a moment's notice. The gas attack failed to have the desired effect and was not followed up with any serious moves by the infantry, as C Squadron commander Holt Waring wrote in a letter home:

The Hun ... threw a lot of stuff about as you say but did very little harm, and the way his gas attack was defeated was grand. It did a lot of good as everyone now has complete confidence in the gas helmets which proved themselves perfect. Of course you have to get them on pretty quick.[52]

The next day Waring led a working party of fifty NCOs and men to the trenches near The Bluff, a British-held spoil hill next to the Ypres-Comines Canal. Here they spread wire in front of a fire-trench located in a crater north of the canal bank, as related by North Irish Horseman Henry Ernest Craig:

As is usually the case, when a bombardment is on, the high explosive shells directed at the front line trenches demolish the barb wire entanglements, and it falls to our lot to have to repair same ... It is rather a difficult and ticklish job. It must be done under cover of darkness, and when dusk has fallen we quietly climb over the parapet and start to work. As the German trenches are often within 30 yards distance, the order is, 'No talking or unnecessary noise'. Watch is kept from both sides of 'No Man's Land,' by aid of star shells, and when one goes up each man must 'freeze,' as to move means tempting Providence. We have done quite a lot of this sort of work, and have come out of it very luckily.[53]

Christmas Day itself was full of cheer. According to Corporal Sterling,

we had an excellent time, and we enjoyed ourselves immensely. C Squadron is very fortunate in having as its commanding officer a well-known Ulsterman – Major Holt Waring, of Waringstown – and no officer was ever more beloved by his men than he. With characteristic thoughtfulness and kindness he and the other officers of the squadron arranged that we should have a real jolly Christmas, and no effort was spared to the accomplishment of that end. While dinner was in progress Major Waring looked in to see that the boys were enjoying themselves, and he was greeted with vociferous cheers. His health was drunk with all heartiness, and he responded in a neat speech, expressing the hope that that would be the last Christmas they would have to spend amid the mud and misery of Flanders.[54]

Miles to the south on the Somme front, D Squadron's December had featured daily wood-cutting parties, schemes, drill and musketry training. The weather was wet for the most part, reducing the days on which outdoor exercises could be held. D Squadron's Christmas was a happy affair for men and officers alike, according to Lancelot Wise in a letter to his mother:

I gave my troop … an enormous feed … They got the stuff themselves & had as follows. Huge plate of Roast beef, tongue, ham, galantine potatoes, peas & onions, pickles, chutney & sauces, fruit salads & custard & prunes, an enormous barrel of beer & a cigar each! They said they'd never had such a cheery evening since they joined. They had it in a large room with tables, benches, plates etc all hired. I went & saw them start. They afterwards had a sing song.[55]

On Boxing Day D Squadron left Béhencourt, their division being withdrawn from the line for rest in a back area. Few would have been happy to leave the village's comforts, mostly built with their own hands, but at least they were leaving them to fellow Irishmen – S Squadron of the South Irish Horse, freshly arrived in France. However, the new billets at Septenville, four mile to the north, were a disappointment, according to Lieutenant Wise:

The officers are very comfortable & men in large barns but my horses are mostly out, which is rotten … It is such a funny place *here*. It is a

Frenchman's shooting box for partridges, such odd little rooms & *very* bad & little furniture. I am trying to get my horses in a Dutch barn & hope it will come off alright.[56]

On 12 December F Squadron had marched from le Cauroy to a new camp at Cantrainne. Here they found the billets reasonably comfortable, and were able to get most of the horses under cover. The remainder of the month was spent improving the billets and carrying out routine duties. A scheme was held with the division's cyclists, and officers and NCOs were sent to the cavalry school at Busnes. Heavy rain and flooding continued through much of the month. Private Frank MacDonald wrote to friends in Belfast, 'Am in the best of form, but "awfu' coul".' Jack McGuigan found himself in trouble, not for the first time, being absent from roll call, and received ten days' Field Punishment No.2.

On Christmas Day the squadron attended Church Parade, followed by 'a very good dinner with plum pudding, and … a concert in the barn loft in the evening at which all our officers were present', according to Private Fred McCormick.[57] F Squadron left Cantrainne for yet another camp on 30 December. This time it was Beauvry, east of Béthune, which had just been vacated by a squadron of the South Irish Horse. This would be their home for the next four months.

The year had not been unkind to the North Irish Horse. Four squadrons were now in France or Belgium with another on the way, and the regimental reserve was well-established at Antrim. If there had been little glory, there had also been relatively few casualties from enemy action, accident or illness.

Other losses thinning the ranks were purely voluntary, as men applied for and were granted commissions, either being promoted 'in the field' or sent for training as officer cadets. In most cases men commissioned from the ranks were posted to a regiment other than their own. During 1915, thirteen men of the North Irish Horse became officers, joining the six commissioned in 1914. Those from 1914 were mostly men of high social standing who had joined as privates simply to be 'in it' from the start, and couldn't wait for the paperwork for their commissions to go through. West, Greer and McNeill have already been mentioned. The others were Frederick Skillen, Edwin Sinton and Ernest George Matthews. Skillen, the eldest son of a linen factory manager, was commissioned in November 1914 and posted as transport officer in the King's Liverpool Regiment. Sinton, aged thirty-one, was a picture theatre manager from Belfast. He had already served in the South African War and the Camel Corps in East Africa, and was quickly commissioned to the Royal Field Artillery. Matthews from Bangor had been assistant mill manager at William Ewart & Sons of Belfast. He was commissioned and posted to the newly formed 6th Inniskilling Dragoons (Service Squadron).

Of the thirteen who rose from the ranks in 1915, three were commissioned in the field in late July and remained with the regiment. They were Norman ffolliott Darling, James Arthur Coey and Worship Booker – all three had been in France with C Squadron from the beginning. Darling had enlisted just four days after the war began, and would serve in the regiment throughout the war. Coey would later transfer to the Royal Irish Rifles and finish the war as a captain. Booker, a farmer and watchmaker from Crossakeil, County Meath, was easy to spot as a North Irish Horse veteran, bearing a tattoo of the regimental badge on his arm. He had joined the North of Ireland Imperial Yeomanry in 1904 and transferred to the North Irish Horse on its creation in 1908. In 1912 he had left Ireland and joined the 48th Highlanders of Canada, before re-enlisting in the North Irish Horse when the war began. Just before his commission came through he severely fractured his leg and was sent home to recover. He wouldn't get to re-join the regiment in the field until the war was almost over.

The other ten men commissioned in 1915 followed the more traditional path to command – posted to a new regiment, usually after a short period of officer training. Robert Hutchinson Andrews we have already met as a casualty of the fighting at Bois Grenier. Thomas Victor Joyce of Londonderry, who had served in France from December 1914, was posted to the Highland Light Infantry. Alexander Frederick Traill, a horse dealer from Bushmills, whose grandfather had served with the 11th Hussars at Waterloo, was posted to the Royal Field Artillery. James Randal Beresford Cramsie joined the Army Service Corps, Robert Arthur Arland MacReady the Leinster Regiment, and Walter Alexander Edmenson the Royal Field Artillery. Robert Campbell Russell was posted to the North Staffordshire Regiment and in 1916 left for the Mesopotamian theatre. William Shields, a schoolmaster from Mountpottinger, Belfast, was posted to the Manchester Regiment in 1915, and was later attached to No.45 Squadron, Royal Flying Corps. James Acheson MacLean of Coleraine, County Londonderry, went to France in November 1915 with the Royal Field Artillery. Johnston Shaw Kirker Hunter also joined the Royal Field Artillery and was sent to France in March 1916. Half of these officers would not survive the war.

Notes

1. Lieutenant Lancelot Wise, letter to his mother, 21 May 1915.
2. *BNL,* 19 December 1914, 15 April 1915.
3. McMahon, op. cit.
4. NA, Kew, WO 364.
5. Ibid.
6. Ibid.
7. McMahon, op. cit.
8. Letter dated 14 January 1915.
9. Letter dated 30 January 1915.
10. *BNL,* 6 February 1915.
11. Mac Fhionnghaile, op. cit., pp.91–2. The date of this incident is an educated guess.
12. NA, Kew, WO 363, WO 364.
13. PRONI, D/1702/12/50/14 and D/1702/12/50/18.
14. Watson, 'Tales of a Gaspipe Officer', in *Blackwood's Magazine*, January 1916, pp.76–7. Lieut West quotes from letter dated 18 May 1915, National Army Museum (Accession No. 1961-11-146).
15. Sterling, letter dated 18 March 1915.
16. NA, Kew, WO 363.
17. Letter dated 2 April 1915.
18. Letter dated 9 April 1915.
19. NA, Kew, WO 364.
20. Letter dated 27 April 1915.
21. Letter dated 6 May 1915.
22. PRONI, D/1702/12/50/24.
23. Letter dated 18 May 1915. This would be a reference to C Squadron.
24. Letter dated 21 May 1915.
25. Letter dated 9 June 1915.
26. Letter postmarked 26 June 1915.
27. Letter dated 3 July 1915.
28. PRONI, D/1702/12/50. Private William H Moisley (No.968). Freda was Cole's sister.
29. NA, Kew, WO 95/1399.
30. Letter to the Governor of NSW from his brother, in *The Examiner,* Launceston, 13 August 1915.
31. Taylor, *The* 1st *Royal Irish Rifles in the Great War*, pp.58–64, 207.
32. Letter dated 9 August 1915 in Hodges, Paul, '"They don't like it up 'em!": Bayonet Fetishization in the British Army during the First World War', in *Journal of War and Culture Studies*, Vol.1 No.2, 2008, p.135.
33. Letter dated 3 July 1915.
34. Letter dated 3 July 1915.
35. Letter dated 11 July 1915.
36. Letter dated 16 July 1915.
37. Letter dated 17 July 1915.
38. Letter dated 20 July 1915.

39. Letter dated 19 July 1915.
40. Letter dated 22 July 1915.
41. Letter dated 30 July 1915.
42. Letter dated 31 July 1915.
43. Letter dated 3 August 1915.
44. *Irish Times*, 13 November 1915 (Moss). *BNL*, 29 December 1915 (Cleland).
45. Letter dated 10 September 1915.
46. Letter dated 14 October 1915.
47. Letter dated 14 October 1915.
48. McMahon, op. cit.
49. NA, Kew, WO 95/2413.
50. *BET*, 2 March 1916.
51. PRONI, D/1702/12/50/1.
52. Waring, letter to his sister dated 27 December 1915, from Combe/Waring collection.
53. *Central Presbyterian Association Magazine*, February 1916 in *Eddies Extracts* website.
54. *BNL*, 4 January 1916.
55. Letter dated 26 December 1915.
56. Letter dated 26 December 1915.
57. *BNL*, 3 January 1916.

Chapter Four

1916: No Role For Cavalry

... in Static Trench warfare there was no role for Cavalry, except as trench holders as infantry.[1]

The view from Antrim

Throughout 1916 the reserve squadrons at Antrim were kept busy with training, sports and fatigues. One day might find them escorting 900 American mules from the Belfast docks to a holding depot at the other side of town, another entertaining convalescent soldiers with a cricket match at the Muckamore ground, or another raising funds for Christmas boxes for the front with concerts by the 'North Irish Horse Glee Party'.

Occasional small drafts were sent to France, but no more full squadrons were required. Antrim was also the first port of call for newly commissioned officers posted to the North Irish Horse. Here they remained for six months or so before being sent to a squadron in France or Belgium. In the first half of the year these men were an interesting mix of well-educated sons of the Empire who had put their careers on hold or thrown in their businesses and returned home to seek a commission. Few had previous military experience, but nonetheless were considered 'the right sort' to become officers. They included Ernest Philip Beresford, an Irish-born Jamaican planter, Leslie Ion Stuart, a Canadian-born Australian sheep farmer, Arthur Penrhyn Noyce, a Scot returned from South Africa, William Bates Smyth, an Irish mill owner, Herbert Gavin Elliot and Stewart Bruce Macduff Bremner, tea merchants from Shanghai, and John Paul Glyn, an English lawyer. All were posted to France in July and August. Others replaced them through the year, more frequently from officer training establishments in England or Ireland, and waited their turn for France.

Recruitment to the regiment slowed considerably in 1916. Fewer than 290 new men joined, compared to 690 in the previous year. By August the numbers at Antrim had fallen so far below establishment that an active

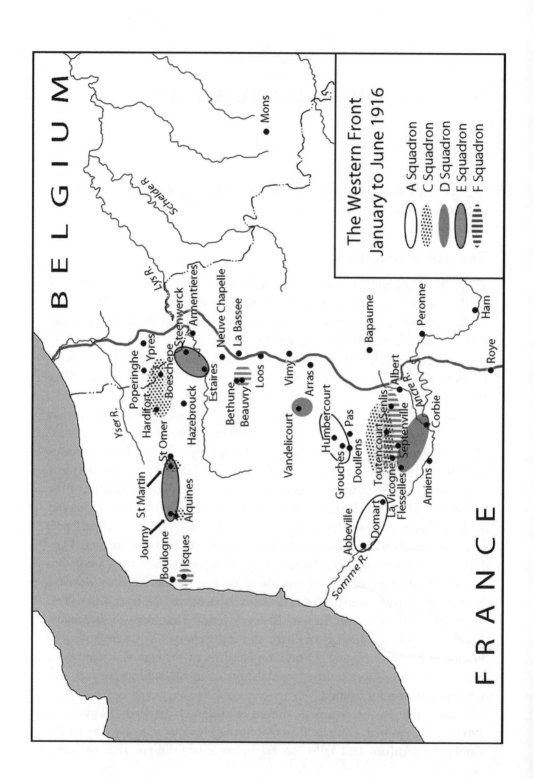

The Western Front
January to June 1916

A Squadron
C Squadron
D Squadron
E Squadron
F Squadron

BELGIUM

FRANCE

Mons

Schelder R.

Lys R.

Yser R.

Poperinghe
Ypres
Boeschepe
Hardifort
St Omer
Hazebrouck
Steenwerck
Armentieres
Neuve Chapelle
Estaires
La Bassee
Bethune
Beauvry
Loos
Vimy
Arras
Vandelicourt
Humbercourt
Pas
Grouches
Doullens
Bapaume
Albert
Senlis
Toutencourt
La Vicogne
Flesselles
Septenville
Corbie
Ancre R.
Peronne
Ham
Roye
Amiens
Abbeville
Domart
Somme R.
Boulogne
Isques
Alquines
St Martin
Journy

recruiting campaign was begun, with newspaper advertisements placed
through to December. The campaign fell short of expectations, with just
over a hundred joining before year's end.

NORTH IRISH HORSE
RECRUITS WANTED 19 years of age and over. Cavalry
rates of pay and Separation or
Dependents' Allowances. Apply personally to Head-Quarters, North Irish
Horse, Skegoniel Avenue, between the hours of 10-0 a.m. and 8-0 p.m., or
by letter to ADJUTANT, North Irish Horse, Show Grounds, Antrim.

Belfast News-Letter, 6 December 1916.

The 1916 recruits were similar to those seen throughout 1915, though it
seems more were found unsuitable to serve. The thirty-seven service records
that survive show more than a third of the men born in County Antrim, with
most of the rest spread across the other northern counties. More, however,
came from the south of Ireland. One, Thomas Robert Gorrie, was from
Oban in Scotland, though he enlisted in Paris. Two fifths were Presbyterians,
almost a third Church of Ireland or Church of England, and a sixth Roman
Catholics. The recruits' occupational background included a preponderance
of urban blue-collar trades and retail workers – including an engine fireman,
mechanic, machinist, van-man, engine cleaner, fitter's helper, steel plate
ricker, grocer, house painter and decorator, cashier, clothing salesman,
lithographic artist and linen trade apprentice. Perhaps a quarter had more
of a rural or at least an equine trade – including farmers, a farm labourer,
a saddler, boot and harness repairer, and a horse trainer. There were fewer
of the 'professional' class, those most likely to become officers, than there
had been in the past. Exceptions included Samuel McCullough Linden,
a theology student at Dublin's Trinity College and civil engineer Francis
McFarland.

Most of the 1916 recruits were very young – the average age was twenty-
one and a half, and half were not yet twenty. The exception was 46-year-
old weighmaster Hamilton Stewart. A veteran of the Boer War with the
Royal Scots Greys, Stewart lived in Belfast with his wife of twenty-one
years, Annie, and their seven children. Fearing rejection when he presented
himself to enlist, he claimed he was just thirty-eight, and made no mention
of his military experience. Another 1916 recruit was the Scottish footballer
William McStay. Signed from Larkhall Thistle in 1912, McStay spent his

first few seasons on loan at Ayr United before joining Celtic. He served out the war in the North Irish Horse reserves at Antrim, where he played as a loan signing for both Distillery and Belfast Celtic.

Less than half of the 1916 recruits would serve overseas. A significant number were found unfit for service, either because of their youth, or physical or mental illness. William McFarland was found to be deaf and therefore 'useless as a soldier', although he had somehow concealed the fact when he was initially examined. John St Claire Clarke, a school teacher, was a first-class shot when he enlisted, but later, following exposure to cold and snow, his vision deteriorated so badly that he was pensioned off. One recruit, from Coleraine, was rarely out of trouble. After a few months the authorities had had enough and he was discharged due to 'deficient intelligence' and the fact that he was under age. His papers recorded that he was 'so mentally unstable as to be absolutely unfit from a military standpoint. Very hazy ideas of right & wrong. Would never become an efficient soldier & might become violent & dangerous at any time. Punishment of no avail.'

Being under age was the most common reason for an early discharge. Vincent Joseph Hamill was fifteen – he lasted less than a month before he was found out and sent on his way. David Bond was only sixteen when he travelled from his home at Drumskinny, County Fermanagh, to join the Royal Inniskilling Fusiliers at Enniskillen. Ten days later his mother came to claim him. Undeterred, he tried again, this time with the North Irish Horse, who were happy to take him.

France and Belgium

In January 1916 A Squadron lost its position of prestige at GHQ when it was ordered to join the 55th (West Lancashire) Division as its cavalry squadron. On 3 January the squadron left Blendecques, entraining for Limeux, a village just south of Abbeville near the mouth of the Somme river. Divisional headquarters was at nearby Hallencourt. A month later they moved to new billets at Humbercourt, north-east of Doullens.

The billets at Humbercourt were well behind the lines, and there is no record that the squadron ventured into harm's way or took a turn on trench fatigues. Major Cole continued to record only scant details in the squadron's war diary, listing the activities over these months simply as 'Squadron training' and 'Divisional Cavalry duties'.[2] However, his letters home give a deeper insight into their activities. What gave him most pleasure was the opportunity to once again play the country gentleman, with the men happily resuming their roles as farmers, estate workers and tradesmen.

We are very lucky to have got this little village all to ourselves. Very good quarters for man and beast ... Another F[lorence] Court man has arrived out here, the son of Balley the blacksmith. A good smith is invaluable here.

... I am amusing myself building sheds for sheltering horses & men. I have just finished a stable for 30 horses, a lean to against a wall with thatched roof, and am in process of building a saddle room and a rear. Also a wooden Guard room with tin roof. I sally off to the forest & cut what trees I want. I have several skilled carpenters & thatchers so am thoroughly at home.

When spring came Cole set his men to work on the local farms:

[Working on the farms] helps at this busy time of year. They are all very short of men and horses. My men look upon a day's farming as a holiday & appear to enjoy it as much as I do.

Not that all the men met with Cole's approval.

Tell old Daly that his protégé Stevenson is not much good. After soaking for some time he got caught drunk & was tried by Court Martial. He is away on detachment at present but when he returns I will read him a lecture.

There were occasional highlights to the daily routine:

I went to a horse show of the Indian Cav[alry] Div[ision] yesterday. The jumping was very good. I was judging at one of the fences. A French officer won the principal open jumping event which will I hope promote the Entente Cordiale.

... and plenty of time to keep the horses in good fettle (and look on with a critical eye at others who did not):

I don't see anybody else's horses & harness look half as well as mine (bar Sells). It is really awful how some of these units such as engineers etc. look after them. Owing to Teetotal ignorance on the part of the officers several lots have been found only feeding them once a day, & as for the shoeing it is awful.

... but mostly there were simply the mundane realities of static warfare:

We have had a lot of snow & frost & and now the thaw has come the roads are beyond description. I had often read of bad roads in warfare but had no idea what it really meant.

Cole often reflected on the state of the war, and not in a way that would have passed the censors' eyes if his men had written the same way, for mostly he was fed up with the war and pessimistic as to the outcome. On 21 February the Germans had begun a massive assault on the fortress city of Verdun. The attack would continue almost unabated throughout the year. In spite of enormous losses the French defenders held on. The fighting at Verdun and the stalemate elsewhere convinced Cole that the war would not be over soon.

... I have given up guessing at the date of the War ending long ago, but am convinced it will not be ended for any *military* reason.
    ... The central powers seem to be on the crest of the wave again. How wonderfully strong they have shown themselves to be!!

One bright spot was the announcement that Cole was to be honoured with a Companion of the Most Distinguished Order of Saint Michael and Saint George (CMG). Naturally though his greatest concern remained the minutiae of family affairs and the management of his estate.

Father certainly was very deaf when I saw him last. I sincerely hope the treatment may do him good. He is much upset at present by William having joined the Cheshire Yeomanry ... Leslie writes to say the war is getting on his nerves to such an extent he can't sleep.
    ... The new parson is as bad as Knox at borrowing things without leave. I have now told my man to forbid him or anyone else to take anything. Irish people are really hopeless.[3]

A Squadron's first fatality for the year took place on 27 April with the death from spotted fever of Private James McArow. McArow was a North Irish Horse original, having joined on its creation at Newbridge on 6 July 1908. He had been with A Squadron in France since 1914, when he had been awarded the French Médaille Militaire. Major Cole wrote home that he was 'a general favourite with officers and men, and his loss will be deeply felt by all'.[4]

Meanwhile C Squadron had remained in the Ypres sector throughout the first months of 1916, still attached to the 3rd Division. January was spent at Boeschepe. On 2 January a party of two officers and sixty men marched to The Bluff to work on improvements to the sector's defences. Here they sustained some casualties, including Private William Rooney, the second time he had been hit. He was shipped home to hospital and a year later discharged as 'no longer fit for service'.

On 5 February the squadron marched to billets in St Martin-au-Laert, just outside St Omer, for a month's rest and training. In March they returned with the division to the front, taking new billets at Boeschepe. Each evening working parties of forty or more were sent forward to dig trenches at Voormezeele, returning just before dawn cold, tired and mud-caked. At the end of the month they were sent to assist the division's 9 Brigade in the attack at St Eloi. This was a 600-yard-wide salient penetrating into the British lines, dominated by a 30-foot-high artificial bank of earth known as 'The Mound'. The night before the attack, three troops under Major Holt Waring marched through snow and sleet from Boeschepe to Dickebusch, their role being to escort any prisoners taken. At 4.15 am six mines were blown under the German lines and the attack commenced. It was largely a success, and numerous enemy troops were captured for the C Squadron escort. Fighting continued here well into April. C Squadron was sent forward into the captured ground to clear the communication trenches and battlefield. This meant trench digging and repairs, salvaging abandoned equipment and removing the remains of British and German casualties to the rear for a decent burial.

On 10 April the squadron was relieved and marched to Alquines, a town halfway between St Omer and the coastal town of Boulogne. Here they spent a fortnight training with the 2nd Cavalry Division, before returning to Belgium, this time at Westoutre, near Boeschepe. During the next week, a sergeant and twelve men went forward to take over observation duties from the Yorkshire Hussars, Captain Uprichard's troop rode to Bailleul to act as mounted troops for the 24th Division, Captain Henry took eighteen men to V Corps Headquarters for duty, and Lieutenant Leader took a working party to Kemmel for construction of defence works.

In May orders came that C Squadron would leave its division and move south to join the concentration on the Somme front for the great push that summer. After three days ride they reached new billets at Val-de-Maison, a small village just north of Rubempré. Although nominally attached to the 49th (West Riding) Division, most of C Squadron's work was in connection with the 36th (Ulster) Division, preparing for its role on the first day of the Somme offensive. Captain Uprichard, Lieutenant Leader and fifteen NCOs took a four-day tour of the observation posts of the division's artillery brigades, followed by a similar party under Captain Henry. Two working parties were sent to help the division at Martinsart, just behind the Aveluy Wood and close to the front line where the division would soon be in action. The connection with the Ulster Division continued through June, with the squadron moving closer to the action at Hedauville Wood, and then to nearby Forceville. From here working parties were sent to build defences and bury communication cables, and the squadron joined in divisional manoeuvres.

D Squadron had spent January at Septenville while their division remained in reserve. Lancelot Wise's thoughts turned frequently to home, leave and his long-running efforts to win a transfer to the Indian Army:

> I have been over to the 3rd Skinner's Horse & stayed a night. I'm *still keener* now than before (if possible). They are a very nice lot of fellows & splendidly mounted. They are supposed to be one of the best mounted cavalry regiments ... The Colonel is going to apply for me if I can get into the Corps which will be very decent for me ... I got 3 new men to my troop today. Jolly good ones I should say ... One of our officers saw a wild boar the other day. Huge excitement!! It is the one thing you may hunt I believe.[5]
>
> ... My leave is now Friday week which is very cheery. I am going to Pen & may go on to Knox's if Harry is on leave too. He may be, which would be great sport. I also might see Chas ... When will you all be coming back? I think the Huns will be smashed this summer alright & then I do so hope you will all be back for a beano after the war!!! ... We are all in a shooting lodge which is rather like a lot of hen boxes! ... I am just going to have my bath. I've got a jolly good one made of rubber. I get hot water from a cottage & pay 2d a night for it.[6]

On 8 February the squadron moved south to Corbie, at the junction of the Ancre and the Somme, the men billeted in three sheds and the horses in the open on the muddy bend of a stream. Lancelot Wise went on leave and returned full of happy tales from a whirlwind of social engagements:

We did have such fun. Harry was on leave from France & Chas on leave just going to the front ... Chas then went & Harry & I stayed on and hunted some hired horses from Reigate. Jolly good they were too ... Then on Thurs. we got more horses & went with a drag over 4½ miles & had great sport ... Then Harry went on Sat & I saw him off & went back to Reigate just in time to hunt ... on Sun[day] Hermon Saunders (lives with Gracie) turned up at 2.30 & said, Come to tea at Brighton. I said Righto & off we went. We started at 3 & got back at 6, having tea in Brighton. He's got a ripping car & very fast. Harry & Chas were both looking very fit & well. Pen seems much better but doesn't *do* anything.[7]

On 21 February the Germans had begun their great offensive against Verdun. The hard-pressed French soon asked the British to take over another part of their line. This was the Arras sector, which separated the British forces on the Ypres-la Bassée front from those on the Somme. The British agreed, and one of the five divisions ordered to move there was the 51st (Highland) Division, assigned to take over a section to the north of Arras, from Neuville-St-Vast to Roclincourt. D Squadron, of course, went with them. On 15 March they reached Vandelicourt and the following evening a party of fifty men was sent to the trenches under Lieutenants Kirkpatrick and Murland. Here they found 'a great deal of work to be done in the trenches to render them more secure & bullet proof, the trenches being much confused by the continuous fighting that had taken place on previous occasions when held by the French. The dug-outs were deep & good but insufficient in number.'[8] After nearly a week they were relieved, having sustained just one casualty, Private Nathaniel Harvey, who was struck in the face and eye by a rifle grenade fragment.

This sector was a quiet one, with the Germans heavily occupied at Verdun and the British too stretched to do more than consolidate what they held. For the remainder of March and all of April, D Squadron was engaged in training exercises with other cavalry squadrons, machine-gun companies and cyclists. Men were sent for instruction in the use of gas masks, learned how to use the Hotchkiss machine gun and were sent on road control and military police duties. On 13 April, officers and NCOs attended 'an unsuccessful demonstration of liquid fire (Flammenwerfer)'.[9]

At the beginning of March Lancelot Wise fell ill with diphtheria and was sent to recover at an isolation hospital at Bléville, le Havre. During months of enforced idleness he wrote cheerful letters to his family:

> Very cheery & dying to get up. I've been here a few days & of course as you know by cable have got a *very slight touch* of Diphtheria. Such a bore as I loose [sic] my squadron for a bit. It's a very comfy place & they look after one very well & good food.
>
> ... I've just had a long talk with the matron who is awfully nice. She has a piano & when I'm up she has given me the use of her own room & piano. There is another fellow here who plays beautifully & she has lent it to the two of us. She is Irish and so is keen on the NIH!!! The men in the ward are a very amusing lot ... There is a French Canadian who practically looks after me & I keep him in cigarettes. He's a jolly good fellow. Then there's an old Irishman who is priceless. I sometimes write letters to his wife Biddy for him. He dances jigs to the gramophone & is very amusing. Then there's a Corp in the Irish Guards who is rather seedy still. Then there's a fellow who has lost his voice & who talks in a whisper as much as everyone else put together.[10]

Lieutenant Wise was granted three months' home leave to continue his recovery. If his letters are anything to go by he spent a very happy time visiting and staying with family and friends – playing tennis, boating on the Thames, country excursions on his new motor bike, picnics on the river, garden parties on the lawn, polo with the Reigate Remounts, and trips to London to see musical comedies and eat oysters and drink 'fizz' at the Carlton.

Wise was soon passed as fit and sent to the North Irish Horse reserve at Antrim. Here the daily routine for an officer was

> mostly work & then golf. I played all today after 1 o'clock ... I am in a Major Herdman's squadron now. He is a topper & the greatest fun imaginable. He very nearly leaves everything to me! Rather good practice for me!! We had a great field day on Friday. I was in command of one side & we won easily."[11]

In early 1917 his long-awaited transfer came through and he sailed for India to join the 3rd Lancers (Skinner's Horse). Sadly, though, the young officer fell ill again and died on 2 May 1917. He is buried in Rawalpindi War Cemetery, Pakistan.

The last North Irish Horse squadron to leave England was E Squadron, attached to the 34th Division. After many months training on Salisbury Plain, orders finally came in December 1915 that the division was to sail for Egypt. Tropical kit was issued and the men prepared to leave. However, the day after Christmas the order was cancelled. Warm clothing replaced sun helmets and shorts, and the men were told to prepare for France. E Squadron left camp at Longbridge Deverill on 11 January. That evening they sailed for France on board the SS *Rossetti*.

The squadron was led by Captain Ian Archibald Finlay, its other officers being Lieutenant Richard Arthur Grove Annesley, and Second Lieutenants Norman ffolliott Darling, John Hutton Grigg and Gilbert Hutton Grigg. Finlay had already seen active service in the Boer War as an officer in the Scots Greys. When the war began he successfully sought appointment as a major in the Scottish Horse, a yeomanry regiment. Desperate to join the fighting, when his regiment was held back he sought and won a captaincy in the North Irish Horse. Lieutenant Annesley was a farmer from Castletownrocks, County Cork. Second Lieutenant Darling had served with C Squadron in France throughout 1914 and in 1915 was commissioned 'in the field' and returned home to join E Squadron.

John and Gilbert Grigg were twin brothers, born at Ashburton in New Zealand, the sons of a wealthy grazier. Although twins, the two men were easily distinguishable, as Gilbert had suffered an accident years before which left his nose looking like that of a prize fighter. When the war began they were studying at Cambridge. The two young gentlemen, with their cousins Harold Plumer Kellock and Richard Berry Kellock, joined the ranks as privates, signing on with the Royal North Devon Hussars. Richard Kellock was only seventeen, but his height and solid build convinced the recruiting sergeant that he was the eighteen years nine months that he pretended. In July 1915 the Griggs transferred to the Inns of Court Officer Training Corps, nominating the North Irish Horse as their preferred regiment. Within a month they were officers and posted to E Squadron as it prepared for France. The Kellock brothers followed them into officer training, also applying to join the North Irish Horse. By January 1916 they too were officers and by mid-year had rejoined their cousins in the regiment in France. The four New Zealanders would prove almost inseparable throughout the war.

Dawn of 12 January found the officers and men of E Squadron disembarked and journeyed to Ebblinghem, a town in the Ypres sector midway between St Omer and Hazebrouck. Within weeks their division had moved into the lines at Bois Grenier, south of Armentières. E Squadron was billeted at nearby Estaires, and then Steenwerck.

The following months were nothing if not frustrating for Captain Finlay, as his squadron was broken up time and again to do various odd jobs for the division – road control, guarding the Bac St Maur Bridge at Armentières, salvage work at Erquinghem, fatigues at the Sailly brickworks, and sniping and machine-gunnery courses. By 21 February, according to Finlay, the squadron had only '2 available men to water & feed 143 Horses at midday'. With more fatigues and guard duties over the coming week, 'the Squadron from a military point of view as an "effective unit" now practically ceases to exist. 23 NCOs & men & 3 officers could be put into the firing line! in a sudden emergency.'[12]

March and the first weeks of April were little different for E Squadron. Cavalry training was impossible, due to the absence of men and horses. When advanced guard to the division was practised, Finlay was only just able to scrape together enough men. However, on 11 April all the squadron's dispersed groups were reunited. The 34th Division was coming out of the lines and E Squadron marched out with them. Following days of intensive training (sword and rifle drill, musketry and range practice, physical and bayonet exercises, saluting and setting-up drill, riding drill, despatch relay system, study of ground and map reading, scouting and 'protection at halt'), they left the 34th Division for good, riding west to Journy for training with the 2nd Cavalry Division.

F Squadron had begun the year at Beauvry on the la Bassée front. This was a mining region and its landscape was dotted with pitheads and slagheaps. The whole stretch of the line in front of la Bassée had a reputation as a dangerous one, with regular tunnelling and blowing of mines under the opposing trenches, trench raids, heavy bursts of artillery fire and sniping.

F Squadron quickly settled into the winter routine, with ordinary duties occasionally interrupted by musketry training, and troop and squadron drills. The winter must have been hard on the horses they had brought from Ireland, for, from January to March, 136 remounts arrived for the squadron.

The first stint in the trenches took place in January at Cambrin. The time passed without any incident worth reporting in the squadron diary, and no casualties were sustained.

During February the squadron was occupied with training, reconnaissance, troop drills and lectures. Twice a sergeant and six men were sent to the trenches on 'special reconnaissance' and over four days, forty men and two officers made up a working party to carry wire to the second-line trenches. On one of these forays to the front Frank McMahon was

"hit on the head with a piece of shrapnel ... but on account of the shortage of men, a Sergeant just cut the hair around the wound with a jack knife, poured some iodine from a field dressing and declared me fit. About a fortnight after I was again in the trenches and was again slightly wounded in the arm with a piece of shrapnel and again the same treatment.[13]

At the end of the month twelve men were detached for traffic duty under the Assistant Provost Marshal. One of the men assigned to the task was a troublesome fellow named O'Sullivan. According to McMahon:

[O'Sullivan] had been a solicitor in Shanghai; he got 14 days imprisonment in England for 'Ill-treating one of His Majesty's chargers', viz. galloping his horse on a hard road. On his discharge from prison he reckoned that was the end of his soldiering. He bought a copy of KRR ... and studied it. When he would be up on a charge, he would quote KRRs section so and so in his defence and the charge would invariably be dismissed. He was a real headache to the Sgt Major, so when there was a request from GHQ for a mounted traffic man, the Sergt Major promptly detailed O'Sullivan for the job. His job was to keep the roads clear for infantry going up the line. One day in Béthune ... a battalion of infantry were going up the line, a French civilian in a cart wanted to break into the column. O'Sullivan tried to stop him, but the French man persisted, so O'Sullivan drew his sword and nearly severed the Frenchman's ear. He was charged with insulting a civilian, [but] he got out of it, saying he was 'carrying out his orders'. Shortly after this incident, he was riding through Béthune where a large number of brass of all regiments were stationed, including the General Commanding the Cavalry Division. O'Sullivan saluted the General's Aide-de-Camp, but the Aide-de-Camp didn't bother acknowledging his salute, so O'Sullivan charged him with 'not acknowledging a soldier's salute' and the Aide was reprimanded. Very soon after this incident O'Sullivan was returned to his unit, much to the horror of the Sgt Major. Apparently by pulling [of] strings by the CO, O'Sullivan was transferred to England. We never knew what happened to him after that.[14]

During March when the squadron went forward on trench fatigue they wore for the first time the now familiar 'Brodie' steel helmet. Until then, the only protection they had had from shot and shrapnel were their cloth service caps. The helmets were taken with some curiosity, but gratefully nonetheless, though former Horseman Lieutenant James MacLean, of Bushmills, thought it 'a clumsy sort of headgear and most uncomfortable, especially in hot weather'.[15]

The passing of winter meant the men of F Squadron could enjoy a wash, with fortnightly bathing parades at Béthune's Écoles des Jeunes Filles. Cavalry duties were not neglected, with field days, reconnaissance, squadron drills, horse and kit inspections, and sword drills regularly reported in the squadron diary. Gas masks, then known as 'smoke helmets', were also inspected. The soldiers had mixed feelings about the masks – necessary but uncomfortable. A Squadron's Major Cole thought them 'very good *if* in perfect order and intelligently used. You can't think how difficult this is.'[16]

With April came change, with three weeks training at Isques, near the coast and not far from Boulogne. This was in preparation for the coming Somme offensive, and it was to there that F Squadron next marched – to billets at Vert Galand, a farm on the road running north from Talmas to Doullens. Here they were assigned to a new division – the 49th (West Riding) Division. It was but a short association, and on 20 May they moved to Senlis, just four miles from the front-line town of Albert, to join the 32nd Division. For the next four weeks F Squadron sent parties forward on trench-digging fatigues around Aveluy and made other preparations for the coming offensive. Lieutenant Hill-Lowe and Sergeant Brunsdon established an observation post in the trenches, two Hotchkiss machine guns were received, and NCOs were instructed as guides.

During the first half of 1916, the steady trickle of disciplinary breaches in the North Irish Horse squadrons continued, although they remained a relatively well-behaved group. In May Samuel Doak of D Squadron was given twenty-eight days' Field Punishment No.1 for an unspecified offence. A veteran of the Boer War, this was by no means his first offence, and would not be his last. James Patterson of the same squadron lost five days' pay for his fifth offence, neglecting to obey an order, and another five days' pay soon after for insolence to an NCO. In April, A Squadron's Robert Kinnear received seven days' Field Punishment No.1 for being absent from the evening's roll call. F Squadron's Jack McGuigan added to his long list of offences with nine days' Field Punishment No.2 and loss of fifteen days' pay for being absent from roll call.

Casualties in the squadrons due to illness, accident or enemy action were also relatively low. On 11 May Lance Corporal Robert Hull of E Squadron was grazing his horses on the roadside in the village of Grouches when one of the horses bolted, kicking him on the head. He was sent home seriously ill with a fractured skull. Private John Alexander of D Squadron accidentally broke his leg on the eve of the Somme offensive. He was sent to hospital in England then invalided home, too disabled for further service. At least one man was sent home and discharged after contracting 'tertiary syphilis', a not uncommon occurrence in the medical records, but rarely referred to elsewhere.

Another cause of loss to the ranks was closed at this time with the passage of legislation stopping the practice of men leaving 'time expired'. While men signing on after 4 August 1914 did so 'for the duration', those who had enlisted in peacetime served for a fixed period of time – four years for those in the North Irish Horse, extendable by twelve months at a time once the original four years was up. In the event of war, twelve months was automatically added to each man's remaining period of service. After that time, his original contract held. Unlike 'duration' men, they became 'time expired', and could choose to leave the army.

From the beginning of August 1915, therefore, some men in the BEF, those whose time had expired, decided that they had had enough of the war and went home. In the months that followed the flow increased. These were pre-war soldiers – regulars – and their loss was sorely missed. The government moved quickly to close off this potentially damaging leakage, first by inducement and then by compulsion. On 20 February 1916 under Army Order 86 they introduced a generous bounty of £15 for soldiers who re-engaged for the duration when their time was up. This was a strong inducement, the equivalent of six months' pay for a North Irish Horseman.

A few months later legislation was passed – the Military Service Act, 1916 (Session 2) – and published as Army Order 202 of 8 June 1916, stating simply that 'no soldier of the Regular Army or Territorial Force will be allowed during the continuance of the present war to be discharged on completion of the period of engagement'. The only exception were men aged forty-one or over at the time their engagement ended. Furthermore, men already time expired and discharged could now be subject to recall (although this did not apply to Ireland). The £15 bounty was retained and made retrospective – extended to men who had already elected to stay when they had become time expired. Each man was allowed a month's leave on re-engagement.

Together these actions stemmed the leakage of time-expired men from the service, but for almost a year – from August 1915 to June 1916 – men had been allowed to go. An examination of how many took the opportunity can therefore provide some idea of the men's enthusiasm to continue in the service once the war had lost its early glamour.

The first North Irish Horseman to leave the regiment 'time expired' was Private Gordon Richardson. The 23-year-old compositor from Lurgan, County Armagh, had been in France with A Squadron since the beginning. He had signed on for four years on 20 August 1910, and with the twelve-month extension of his term on the outbreak of war, he became 'time expired' on 19 August 1915. Perhaps thanking his good fortune, he packed his kit, said goodbye to his pals, and left for home. What they thought of his decision can only be guessed at. Were they resentful, jealous or indifferent? Did they see it as betrayal or good fortune? Was it the equivalent of a 'blighty' wound – an honourable exit from the war, or something shameful?

The pressure on men like Richardson to re-sign as their time approached must have been enormous. To leave the camaraderie of the squadron could not have been easy, especially for those, the majority, who had been together through the fighting of 1914. The life was not always easy, and boredom was a constant companion, but the pay was good, food and lodgings provided, and for the North Irish Horse, casualties to this point had been negligible. Added to this was the risk of conscription. If introduced, a 'time expired' man would be swept up like all the others, and given no choice as to his regiment or where he might be sent. To the Irish serviceman viewing events in 1915, it must have seemed only a matter of time before universal conscription would apply. Speculation about when this would be was rife. As early as November 1914 General Hickman had warned, at a recruiting rally in Enniskillen, that 'if the men don't come ... the Government will take them'.[17] To this was added a sense, at least in the ranks of Ulster Unionists, that Ireland's Catholics were not doing their bit. As early as May 1915 A Squadron's Major Cole wrote to his father:

I suppose we shall have some sort of conscription soon. There will be great play dragging the papists off the mountains. All my men are looking forward to the papists being made to join.[18]

Not that he was above a little self-interest when it came to conscription:

I am in terror of losing my agent at F[lorence] Court which is *sure* to happen if conscription is brought in in Ireland.[19]

Compulsory registration for British residents was introduced through the Derby Scheme in late 1915, with full conscription through the Military Service Act early in 1916 (applying to unmarried men aged eighteen to forty-one, apart from those employed in reserved professions). Four months later the Act was extended, removing the marital status exemption. But Cole's hopes of 'dragging the papists off the mountains' would go unfulfilled, as none of this applied to Ireland. In January 1916 Cole wrote that the news conscription would not cover Ireland had infuriated his men, once again on sectarian lines:

Our men are all frantic that compulsion has not been applied to Ireland & say they would like to be at the sea[r]ching of the mountains for the papists.[20]

Despite such incentives to re-sign – the camaraderie, the patriotism, and the fear that conscription would drag back to the war any who left – a surprisingly large number of North Irish Horsemen found the call of home a greater attraction. From August 1915, when the first man's time was up, to 8 June 1916, when time expired discharges were ended, almost 100 Horsemen who had seen overseas service had the opportunity to return to civilian life. Thirty-six of them, well over a third, chose to leave. Fourteen of these were originals from Major Cole's A Squadron, sixteen from Massereene's C Squadron, five from the January and February 1915 reinforcements and one from D Squadron.

Why the number was so large can only be guessed at, but suggests that the initial enthusiasm for the war had cooled. Perhaps the fact that most were farmers, and felt guilt at the neglect of their land, played a part. Brothers were also enlisting, and a time expired discharge would keep at least one fit young man on the farm. Perhaps they were encouraged (or at least not discouraged) by their officers, who understood the demands of the farm and knew that there was no shortage of men eager to replace them. There is no indication on their service records that the officers thought less of these men because of their decision – all had their conduct marked as 'good' or 'very good'. Nor does age seem to have been a factor – the age profile of those who left, averaging twenty-six to twenty-seven years, seems little different from those who stayed. Perhaps some had been ill or wounded and were recovering at home, the prospect of leaving loved ones and returning to France after they had already 'done their little bit' holding little attraction. Private William Copeland of Newry, for example, sent home sick in June 1915, probably had no intention of returning. When his sick furlough ended he disappeared until his period of service was up. Only then did he surrender himself, facing only a loss of pay for the days he was away.

It seems likely that those who quit did so because they saw no end to a war they had thought would be over by Christmas 1914, and counted themselves lucky that they could get out of it with some honour. There is no evidence that they faced any bad feeling from their pals, perhaps each man being left to decide as his conscience guided. Thus, for example, the two men awarded the Médaille Militaire for gallantry during the fighting of August 1914 went their separate ways. Francis Colquhoun left the service and James McArow elected to stay (a decision that cost him his life).

For most, the decision to leave when their time was up was final. Few seemed to have had any regrets, with records suggesting that only one re-enlisted later. But at least one who went home did feel the need to explain himself. Private John Henderson of Brookeborough, County Fermanagh, had been with the North Irish Horse since November 1908, and had served in France with A Squadron since the beginning. When his time came up in November 1915 he elected to leave. At this time the social pressure on men at home in civilian clothes was enormous. In September 1916 the Government announced that it would provide a 'Silver War Badge' to military personnel who were discharged as a result of 'age, or physical infirmity arising from wounds or sickness caused by military service', in part to protect those who were 'honourably' out of uniform.[21] Henderson, perhaps subjected to accusations of cowardice, wrote to the authorities seeking a badge:

Kindly pardon the liberty I take by writing you. But ... I feel entitled to one of the Silver Badges which I would so much like to have as a souvenier [sic] of this sad war. I have served 7 years and 76 days in the North Irish Horse, 1 year and 76 days in France from the outbreak of War. But to my regret when my time had expired had to cease serving owing to the death of my only Brother and no help at Home but a disabled Father 73 years of age.[22]

Henderson's request was refused, as eligibility for the badge did not extend to time expired men.

The 1916 Rebellion

On 30 April, D Squadron's diary noted that 'The Sinn Fein rebellion started in Dublin on the 24.4.16 is still continuing'.[23] It was the only mention of the fighting in any of the North Irish Horse diaries, but the news from Dublin must have worried officers and men alike. In 1914 the biggest fear of Carson's men when the call came to enlist was that Ireland would be left to the nationalists while the UVF men were busy overseas.

The news from Dublin must have confirmed their worst fears. How the ordinary North Irish Horseman in France felt can only be guessed at. No doubt there was concern, anger and threats of retribution, but the records are largely silent. Major Cole's first thoughts were for the welfare of his family. On 30 April he wrote to his father:

I hope to goodness this finds you fit & at large. I read that it was reported that members of Kildare Street Club had been seized by the rebels on the way back from Fairyhouse & kept as hostages. I have sent word to Irene to find out & until I hear shall be very uneasy. The idea of you languishing in a papist guardroom is too awful.[24]

Later he learned that his father was safe, and wrote to both his parents in typically frank terms:

Dear Mammie.
    ... What do you think of the Sein Feiners. Birrell ought to be hung beside Casement for his neglect of duty & incompetence. I hear they have sent Sir John Maxwell & a large force to control the rebels which

is of course what the Germans want. Anyhow it will I think make Home Rule more impossible than ever.[25]

Dear Father.

... Thank goodness you were not in Ireland. I was very uneasy till I heard from Irene. It is a pity Redmond's lot did not join in with the Sein Feiners as we could then have made a job of the lot.[26]

Beginning on 24 April, the rebellion was over in a week, save for the execution of its leaders in May. The focus of the fighting was in Dublin. In the north, while nationalist volunteers mobilised here and there, nothing much came of it. Substantial numbers gathered at Coalisland and Dungannon, and the County Inspector of the Royal Irish Constabulary in Tyrone later claimed there was a rebel plan to capture the police barracks and the post office at Beragh and then march on Omagh, where they would seize further administrative and military buildings, cut telegraph wires and blow up bridges. The volunteers, however, quietly dispersed.

No matter how unlikely in truth, the possibility of a rebellion in the north was taken seriously, and stretched the resources of Ireland's under-armed reserve regiments, including the North Irish Horse in Antrim.

a squadron was sent out to 'show the flag' in East Tyrone, and marched round Lough Neagh as far as Dungannon; then another squadron was ordered to make a similar march through the Antrim Glens. This left very few men in camp, but worse than this, there were only about two dozen rifles ... Then there were rumours that an attack had been planned on the police barracks at Toome, and a party was sent there at the request of the police.[27]

The regiment's efforts to 'show the flag' did help convince some nationalists that military action had little chance of success. Irish Volunteer James Tomney, for example, recalled going to Dr Patrick McCartan's house in Carrickmore, County Tyrone:

Dr McCartan told me that things looked bad. The military were in the area. Omagh was garrisoned by the North Irish Horse, and Carrickmore was only ten miles from Omagh. He said that he was not in favour of doing anything further, that military action under the circumstances in County Tyrone would be madness, and that I was to take my men home.[28]

At least some North Irish Horsemen found their services called on to help suppress the rebellion. In Dublin the British authorities had fought back with whatever military resources were readily at hand. According to Trimble:

> One recruit of a few weeks standing who had been on leave in Dublin at the time of the rising arrived back at Antrim many days overdue, but his pass had attached to it a certificate to the effect that he had proved himself an excellent soldier when a Dublin barracks to which he had made his way, was attacked. There was no CB for him, but congratulations.[29]

One of the formations rushed from England to quell the rebellion was the 59th (2nd North Midland) Division. In August 1915 a sixth squadron of the North Irish Horse (B Squadron) had been assigned as divisional cavalry to the 59th, then training in England, but in this they were unlucky. The 59th had been designated as a reserve to the 46th (North Midland) Division and wasn't going anywhere in a hurry – at least not until they were ordered to Dublin. Here the division was heavily involved in the fighting. It is not clear what role the North Irish Horse squadron played, or in fact when and where they reached Ireland. However, by May they had left their division and were back in Antrim. (Here they were re-named F Squadron. In France, F Squadron was re-named B Squadron.)

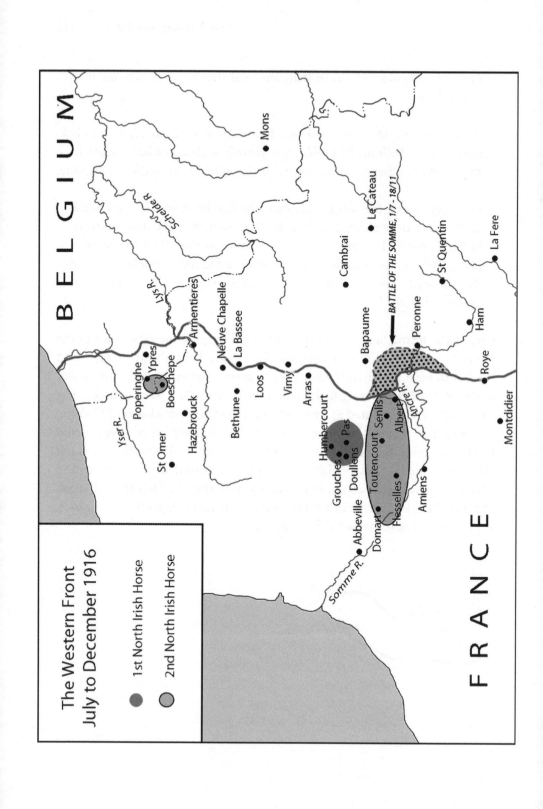

The Western Front
July to December 1916

1st North Irish Horse

2nd North Irish Horse

BELGIUM

FRANCE

Mons

Schelde R.

Le Cateau

Cambrai

La Fere

St Quentin

Ham

Bapaume

Peronne

BATTLE OF THE SOMME, 1/7 - 18/11

Roye

Montdidier

Armentieres

Lys R.

Neuve Chapelle

La Bassee

Ypres

Poperinghe

Boeschepe

Hazebrouck

St Omer

Yser R.

Bethune

Loos

Vimy

Arras

Humbercourt

Pas

Grouches

Doullens

Toutencourt

Senlis

Albert

Ancre R.

Flesselles

Amiens

Abbeville

Domart

Somme R.

The Somme and beyond

May 1916 brought big organisational change for the BEF's divisional cavalry squadrons. These squadrons had originally been provided to each division as a small mobile force for reconnaissance, protective and escort duties. However, the advent of static trench warfare had removed the ability of divisions to act and move independently. It followed that divisional cavalry squadrons had become redundant.

Orders were therefore issued that these squadrons would merge into corps cavalry regiments under the direct control of the corps commander. Each regiment would comprise three squadrons, each with six officers, 134 other ranks, 132 horses, eleven transport vehicles and four bicycles. This meant a reduction of nineteen men in each squadron. Each regiment would be commanded by a lieutenant colonel, assisted by a headquarters of thirty-nine officers and men. The new structure therefore meant a larger command, logistics and administrative structure sitting over fewer front-line cavalrymen.

A, D and E Squadrons of the North Irish Horse came together on 10 May to form the 1st North Irish Horse Regiment. The regiment was attached to VII Corps. Headquarters was established at Grouches just north-east of Doullens. B and C Squadrons were joined by the 6th Inniskilling Dragoons (Service Squadron) on 21 June to form the 2nd North Irish Horse Regiment. They were attached to X Corps and established their headquarters at Toutencourt, nine miles west of Albert. The three reserve squadrons based at Antrim, F, G and H, were consolidated as a reserve regiment under the command of Lieutenant Colonel Maude. Majors Herdman, Crabbe and Stewart-Richardson commanded F, G and H Squadrons respectively.

The 1st North Irish Horse Regiment came under the command of A Squadron's John Cole, who had got wind of the change at the beginning of May and immediately saw in it a prospect for promotion. Cole got his wish, but not everything came up to expectations:

Now that we are a larger formation I have had to get an interpreter. He is most obliging but such an ass. To the simplest question about something about his own country invariably 'I do not know'. Such a bore as an intelligent man would have been so interesting & made such a change in the conversation.[30]

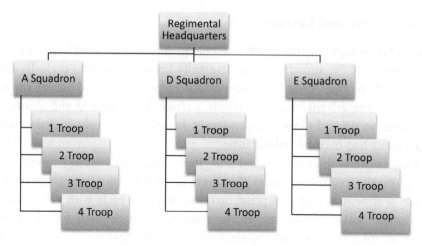

Figure 2: 1st North Irish Horse Regiment – structure.

The 1st North Irish Horse Regiment's role was to serve the Army's VII Corps, which comprised the 37th, 46th (North Midland) and 56th (1st London) Divisions. In truth, little changed from earlier arrangements, as by mid-June each squadron was assigned to a division of the corps on 'provost' duties – that is, as mounted military police and traffic control. With the preparation for the offensive at the end of the month, traffic control became all-important, with thousands of soldiers and their equipment, supplies, artillery, bombs and every other accoutrement of war moving east as quickly and quietly as possible, mostly during the night to avoid enemy observation. On 23 June the regiment moved from Grouches to nearby Pas, some seven miles behind the front.

The first fatality for the new regiment took place on this day, when 19 year-old Private William James Finlay was killed in an artillery barrage while he worked on a trench digging fatigue near Gommecourt. Born in Malta to William James and Maria Concetta Finlay, his was a large family, with at least six sisters and four brothers. Finlay was living in Belfast's Glenallen Street when the war began, and he enlisted as soon as he was old enough. He had only been in France a few months. Soon after his death Private Samuel Gordon wrote a letter of comfort to one of Finlay's sisters:

Dear Miss Finlay,

    I received your letter & parcel which was very nice indeed, the only thing I am sorry at, is that poor Willie was gone, and he was not here to enjoy the contents of same himself. It came rather sudden when your brother was killed, it all happened in a few minutes: I was with him myself and there never could have been a chance of him escaping in the position he was in, in fact I am surprised there was not more of us killed, it was a very rough day in the firing line, and we were on a working party, when we were started a short time the shell came that was the cause of poor Willie's death, he only lasted [...] after he got it, up to the time he died he kept saying, God bless me. I don't think I can't say any more at present. Thank you for your nice parcel and letter, and I hope to be able to see you & have a talk. I could then explain things better. I am yours very truly.

S.L. Gordon[31]

The 2nd North Irish Horse Regiment did not come together until 21 June. Headquarters was established at Toutencourt, though the new commanding officer would not arrive from England for a fortnight. On this day C Squadron marched in from nearby Forceville. Two troops of B (formerly F) Squadron had arrived two days earlier, while the other two troops remained at Senlis on an exercise with the 32nd Division. The new regiment's third squadron, the 6th Inniskilling Dragoons (Service Squadron), rode in from Puchvillers.

Since Christmas 1915 the Inniskillings had been moving around the back areas of the Somme front in support of their division, the 36th Ulster. Their mood as they rode into Toutencourt was most likely both sullen and defiant. Despite the fact that they were joining a squadron that had seen active service since August 1914, and another that had also seen front-line service, and despite the fact that the North Irish Horsemen were for the most part their compatriots in the pre-war UVF, the Inniskillings resented being made to join units below them on the Army List. Their agitation must have found a sympathetic ear, as they were allowed to maintain their separate squadron identity, even though still a part of the 2nd North Irish Horse Regiment.[32] Nevertheless, Frank McMahon and Jack McGuigan may have seen no small irony in the fact that the squadron they had not been allowed to join in 1914 was now being made to join them.

The 2nd North Irish Horse Regiment had been assigned to X Corps, which comprised the 32nd, 36th (Ulster) and 49th (West Riding) Divisions. After coming together at Toutencourt, it seems they found little direction without a commanding officer, and quickly went their own way again, helping preparations for the coming battle. C Squadron stayed at Toutencourt, carrying out routine duties for the rest of the month. The two troops from B Squadron at Tountencourt soon rejoined the others at Senlis, the men kept busy with trench digging. The Inniskillings returned to Forceville to help the 36th (Ulster) Division.

Rumours of preparations for the Somme battle had circulated for months. For the men of the two North Irish Horse regiments it must have seemed that the entire British army was now concentrated in that small part of the front line during May and June of 1916. '[The] guns were moving up day and night,' Frank McMahon later recalled, 'the Artillery were packed wheel to wheel, Cavalry and infantry were there in thousands.'[33]

The attack had been planned to commence on 29 June following weeks of heavy bombardment which would destroy the German trenches and clear the wire, but unseasonably bad weather caused a postponement until the morning of 1 July. The British attack took place along a twenty-five mile front, from Serre to Montauban, with five divisions of the French Sixth Army attacking to the south astride the Somme river itself. Five corps of the BEF were involved in the initial attack – VIII, X, III, XV and XIII.

The 1st North Irish Horse Regiment's corps, VII Corps, also had a role, a major diversionary attack to the north, their object being to pinch out the Gommecourt salient and draw German fire away from the main assault. No breakthrough was expected here, and therefore there was no cavalry role for the North Irish Horsemen. Instead the 1st Regiment took over an internment camp at Pas, built to hold the expected masses of enemy prisoners. Most likely the regiment took on other provost duties – traffic control and picking up stragglers behind the front line.

To ensure that the diversion at Gommecourt was as effective as possible, the British had gone to great pains to ensure that the Germans knew they were coming, making obvious preparations for the attack. In this they succeeded. The enemy was ready and, on 1 July, when the 56th (London) and 46th (North Midland) Divisions attacked, they were repelled with heavy losses. Behind the lines at Pas the 1st North Irish Horse Regiment waited in vain for the masses of captured Germans.

The 2nd North Irish Horse, too, had no cavalry role on the first day of the battle. Its corps, X Corps, was to attack from Authuille Wood to the marshy ground where the Ancre river crossed into enemy territory. The 32nd Division on the right was to capture the Leipzig Salient and the heavily fortified Thiepval Spur. The 36th (Ulster) Division was to push forward from the Thiepval Wood to beyond St Pierre Divion and the Schwaben Redoubt. The attack by the 32nd Division was a bloody failure. However, the 36th (Ulster) Division achieved remarkable initial success, taking the Schwaben Redoubt and pushing on into the second main German trench system. But failure of the attacks on either side left them facing overwhelming artillery, rifle and machine-gun fire and waves of counter-attack, with little prospect that reinforcements could come up in any numbers. By day's end the hard won ground had been surrendered. It would not be taken again for three months.

How the 2nd North Irish Horse was employed on this day is unknown – no diary was kept for 1 to 3 July – but it is likely that the men were used in the same way as those of the X Corps Cyclists, also based at Toutencourt. Its diary shows them engaged on divisional work such as conducting prisoners, manning control posts and straggler posts, and carrying Stokes mortar ammunition to the front line.

By any measure 1 July was a disaster for the BEF. The only real success had been on the right flank, with the capture of Montauban and Mametz and an advance of one mile along a front of three and a half miles. Farther to the right, the French had achieved more, reaching practically all of their first-day objectives. Total British casualties for the day were 57,470, including 19,240 killed. It was the bloodiest day in British military history. More than 2,000 men of the 36th (Ulster) Division died that day, 2,700 were wounded and 165 taken prisoner. At dusk on 2 July the shattered division was withdrawn from the line.

While not actively employed in the fighting on that fateful day, it would be wrong to think that the battle had no impact on the men of the North Irish Horse. Many had brothers, fathers, sons or cousins serving in the infantry battalions of the 36th (Ulster) Division, and many, therefore, had losses to grieve, although news would only drift in over coming days. Private Thomas Wright of Coleraine, for example, lost his older brother John, who had been serving in the 10th Inniskilling Fusiliers. His body was lying somewhere on the ground won and surrendered that day.

Despite the meagre gains, the fighting on the Somme didn't end on 1 July. It ground on through that summer and well into autumn. Little is known of the activities of the 1st North Irish Horse during this time. Lord Cole's typically sparse entry for that momentous July read simply: 'Pas. Corps Cavalry duties'. The entry was the same for August. On 4 September the regiment marched out to Coullemont, four miles to the north. A week later they moved to new billets at nearby Humbercourt. This would be their home for the next seven months. 'Corps Cavalry duties' were the order of the day through autumn and winter, with occasional squadron, regimental and corps training exercises.

Throughout this period, occasional drafts of reinforcements arrived for the regiment from Antrim. They included George Moorhead Shannon, a corporation clerk, and William Brown, a library assistant, both from Belfast, Robert Evans, a shop assistant from Dunmurry, John Forbes, a clerk from Ahoghill, William Cooke, a cinema operator from Dundalk and James Magill, a railway labourer from Ballymena.

Much more is known of the activities of the 2nd North Irish Horse Regiment in the days following 1 July. Initially, C Squadron remained at Toutencourt, while B Squadron and the Inniskillings spent the time in the villages and crowded roads behind Aveluy Wood, where the 36th (Ulster) Division had its headquarters. On 3 July Private Alexander Watt became the new regiment's first casualty. Nineteen-year-old Watt, one of sixteen children, had been in France with the Inniskilling Dragoons (Service Squadron) since October 1915. His twin brother George had joined the North Irish Horse and soon after their older brother William had been severely wounded while serving with the Canadian Mounted Rifles. How Watt died is unknown, but may have resulted from the heavy German shelling of British positions. Frank McMahon recalled that 'the Germans' artillery ranged in on us, by nightfall we had suffered badly in killed and wounded horses and men'.[34] At this time Second Lieutenant Ernest Matthews was twice buried in his dugout as a result of German bombardment, and others in the regiment were reported wounded.

On 4 July regimental headquarters arrived at Toutencourt from England with the new commanding officer, Colonel Walter Goring, and his second-in-command, Major Valentine George Whitla. Goring was aged fifty-two and Whitla fifty-three. Both had already seen much military service, including in the Boer War in the 3rd (King's Own) Hussars. At Toutencourt they met their squadron commanders, Majors Bramston-Newman (B Squadron), Waring (C Squadron) and Chamberlayne (6th Inniskilling Dragoons).

The next day two troops of the Inniskilling squadron were ordered to Aveluy Wood to salvage lost or abandoned equipment. Job done, the men 'had just started to saddle up when a heavy bombardment of high explosive, shrapnel & machine guns was concentrated on the Wood', according to the regiment's war diary.

> The intensity of the fire necessitated Lt Seymour giving orders for the men to take shelter in some old dugouts & trenches close by. The bombardment lasted for ¾ of an hour & then slackened but did not entirely stop. Up to now one horse was killed & four wounded. The men were then ordered to saddle up & lead their horses thro' [the] Wood out on to the road and were waiting for the others to join up when the bombardment opened much heavier than previously, especially on that part of the road where the men were waiting. Lt Seymour moved off up the road leaving 2/Lt Matthews & Sergt McIlroy to round up the stragglers in the wood, as by this time horses were very restive and almost unmanageable. Lt Seymour with his party had reached about 1 mile along the road & turned down a lane leaving the horses in charge of Sergt Quinn. Almost immediately a heavy fire was brought to bear on the horses and Sergt Quinn was wounded. The horses stampeded in every direction, some back to Aveluy Wood. Eventually Lt Seymour was able to round up most of the party & got to Senlis. Lieut Matthews & Sergt McIlroy remained behind. Our losses numbered 16 horses killed or wounded and 2 missing. 2/Lt Matthews was wounded severely in the knee from high explosive and Pte Downes, Nicholl, Gourley wounded (hosp) and [six others] slightly wounded.[35]

Lieutenant Matthews was shipped home, the wound to his knee and impact of being twice buried alive ending his cavalry service.

On 9 July the regiment came under orders of the 32nd Division and was told to 'stand to for the purpose of burying the dead'. None of the men of the North Irish Horse could have anticipated what they would face over the next fortnight. The battle lines had moved forward, desperate yard by desperate yard, leaving thousands of corpses, guns, and bombs littering the ground. Much of it was still under heavy shellfire, but someone had to clean up the mess, at night, and in all weather. Each body had to be searched for identity discs and personal effects. The memory of it all, of corpses blown out of the ground as soon as they were buried, haunted Frank McMahon for the rest of his life.

In the evening of 9 July the Inniskilling squadron marched to the area held by 97 Brigade, but no guide turned up and tools were hard to find, so they were ordered back to camp. B and C Squadrons proceeded to the 14 Brigade area, where they worked through the night under shellfire, returning to camp by 6.30 am. Next evening they returned to the old battlefield, this time to la Boisselle. This had once been a small village, to the north-east of Albert, standing on a spur between Sausage Valley to the south and Mash Valley to the north. Across Mash Valley was the village of Ovillers. The attack on la Boisselle on 1 July had largely failed and resulted in awful casualties for the 34th Division. It was not until 4 July that it was captured. By 10 July the battleline had moved on a little, but Ovillers was still in enemy hands, so the work of clearing the battlefield had to be done at night, while making way for infantrymen moving forward and casualties retiring, and under constant shellfire. Two men were wounded – Privates James Ramsey and Thomas Williamson.

Men of the Rifle Brigade had already been working here on the same task. 'There was a terrific smell,' according to one.

It was so awful it nearly poisoned you. A smell of rotten flesh. The old German front line was covered with bodies – they were seven and eight deep and they had all gone black. The smell! These people had been laying since the First of July. Wicked it was![36]

Private James Elliott was one of the North Irish Horsemen assigned to the task:

The rows of dead in places looked like as if they had been left behind by a reaper and binder. Night was the usual time for burying them; some who had been jammed in trenches or craters were levered out with crowbars or the like, but if this proved impossible the corpse might be cut off at the legs and the trunk then interred in, say, a shell-crater.[37]

In the evening of 11 July the awful task continued for the North Irish Horsemen, with forty-one British and fifty-five German bodies collected and buried amid intermittent shelling. On the following night a party of seventy-five men was sent to the same area, while another party of sixty was sent to Crucifix Corner.

A British attack was made at 11.30 and the men came under heavy fire from German artillery ... Shelter was taken wherever it could be found. The party then continued work which was finished at 2.30. No casualties occurred. Camp was reached at 3 AM.

The attack made that night on Ovillers by X Corps won considerable ground, but the shattered remnants of the village would not finally be taken until 17 July. Meanwhile the North Irish Horse continued their work close behind the fighting.

[13 July] Parties of same strength were sent to the points as per yesterday's events ... On arrival at points where guides were met they were told owing to an attack to be made by the Corps that they would only be blocking up the available passages for troops moving up. A return was made to Camp which was reached at 11.30 pm.

[14 July] 34 British were buried, very few affects found. Only 14 shovels were available for this work, a very creditable performance. 1,600 sand bags were taken up to first line. The Crucifix Corner party buried 62 bodies and collected one waggon load of salvage which was dumped at Ovilliers Post.

By now the Germans had been pushed back far enough to allow some of the work to be done in daylight.

[15 July] 2.0 p.m. Two parties left for same areas, 30 & 60 strong. The Albert-Pozieres Road party buried 28 British and 1 German and collected 25 rifles & some equipment which was taken to Salvage Dump. The Crucifix Corner party buried 83 bodies, all British.[38]

The weather, fine until now, turned wet. The work on the old battlefield continued, though some were sent to the railway station at Contay to unload stones for roadwork and other engineering works. Tuesday 18 July brought more light rain. A party of thirty-six moved up to scour the ruins of la Boisselle for bodies and salvage. Through the day they worked over the shell holes, ruined trenches and dugouts in the land between the Albert-Poziéres Road and Albert-Contalmaison Road. They found and buried thirty-three British and seven Germans, together with much equipment – steel helmets, rifles and Mills hand-grenades. By now the task had become better regulated, with the men moving across the ground grid-reference by grid-reference.

On 19 July they worked their way along a communication trench running across Mash Valley from la Boisselle into Ovillers la Boisselle. Ninety-nine bodies were recovered, along with 300 rifles and numerous grenades. Seeing the state of the men and understanding what they were going through, the commanding officer ordered them a special issue of rum.

On Thursday 20 July they completed clearing the ground east of la Boisselle and south-east of Ovillers. There was some shelling, during which Captain Uprichard was wounded. Seventeen British casualties and three Germans were buried, and 197 rifles and a quantity of equipment salved. The evening fatigue buried seventy-six British casualties found south and west of Ovillers. On 21 July the day party buried one British soldier and salved 160 rifles and a considerable number of bombs, small arms ammunition and equipment. The Inniskilling squadron took its turn at night salvage, burying three officers, forty-eight other ranks and two Germans.

On 22 July, another fine day, the Inniskillings were sent as stone fatigue party to Martinsart. Two troops of C Squadron reported at Bouzincourt for duty with the 48th (South Midland) Division. B Squadron took its turn clearing the battlefield.

> The German Artillery was pretty active, No.1582 Pte T. Wright getting wounded very early in the proceedings. A quantity of ammunition, rifles & other equipment was salved. The officer commanding this party reported that there two dug outs were full of ammunition etc etc & had apparently been forgotten since the 1st July.[39]

Private Thomas Wright was evacuated to a hospital at Étaples but died six days later. The twenty-two-year-old, one of ten children, was from Pullans, a townland on the road between Coleraine and Ballymoney. In May 1915 he had left his job at the Ballyrashane Creamery Company and travelled to Antrim, where he enlisted with the North Irish Horse. His brother John was one of the many lost on 1 July.

That was the last the regiment would see of the Somme battlefield. On Sunday news came that X Corps would move into reserve. On Tuesday 25 July B Squadron and the Inniskillings left Senlis for the six-hour ride to Domart. C Squadron followed some days later. The front line had by now advanced along the Albert-Pozières Road to the town Pozières itself, an objective of 1 July which the 1st Australian Division was only now entering, assisted by the 48th (South Midland) Division. The Battle of the Somme would continue until November, but for the men of the North Irish Horse, the danger was over.

While the regiment waited for C Squadron to rejoin them at Domart, arrangements were made for a parade and mounted drill at Château de la Haye. What followed was a rather comic event for observers, though acutely embarrassing for the officers of B Squadron. While the Inniskilling squadron followed the drill book, B Squadron 'did troop drill under some different arrangement'.[40] Clearly there were shortcomings in the training regime being followed for North Irish Horse recruits at Antrim. Work began immediately to teach them the correct drill.

The next five days at Domart passed quietly, with parades and inspections – the corps commander inspected the camp, the veterinary officer the horses, and the NCOs the arms. On 2 August the regiment began moving camp to Flesselles, ten miles distant. The condition of the place didn't impress the regimental commander:

> The Camping grounds taken over by me here were left in a very dirty condition, manure etc. being left behind; this entails extra fatigues on the troops marching in. There is sufficient water here for horses, but it is of bad quality from stagnant ponds.[41]

At Flesselles, Edward Menice found himself in serious trouble again, this time for being drunk when on duty as night picquet. The court martial gave him three months' Field Punishment No.1 and loss of pay.

August saw many new arrivals to the regiment. Six signallers arrived from Rouen on 4 August and fifty-five NCOs and men six days later. None of the reinforcements for the 6th Inniskilling Dragoons (Service Squadron) came from their reserve in Enniskillen, much to the annoyance of the redoubtable Copeland Trimble. He complained to the War Office, but was told that due to a problem with paperwork the authorities were not aware of the reserve squadron's existence! Instead, their reinforcements had been sent from the 2nd Reserve Cavalry Regiment.

There was change among the officers too. Major Holt Waring, who had commanded C Squadron since 1915, transferred to the Royal Irish Rifles. Seven new officers, all second lieutenants, arrived from the Reserve Cavalry depot at the Curragh – Thomas Humphrey Hesketh, Joseph Auber, Clarence Donovan Kirkbride, Frederick Joseph Whalen, William Henry Hutchinson, Herbert Shelton Dean and Bernard Hancock. The new officers were from all parts of the United Kingdom. Auber was a jeweller from Burton-on-Trent who had served as a sergeant in the North Staffordshire Regiment. Whalen, from Woodford, Essex, had joined the Surrey Yeomanry as a private and served in France throughout 1915 before being commissioned. Hutchinson was Irish, but had lived in South Africa for some years and was on leave from that country's 1st Imperial Light Horse. Hesketh was from Cardiff, Dean from Kettering in Northamptonshire, and Kirkbride from Penrith, Cumberland.

For much of August and September the regiment was split into various mounted and dismounted working parties, including fatigues at the Contay ammunition dump, filling in old trenches south of Flesselles and north and east of the Vignacourt-Amiens railway, and road control work on the Amiens-Albert road. Training also continued, with practice at flank and convoy protection, advance and flank guard, working with a motor machine-gun battery, and reconnaissance. Officers and NCOs also spent time on target practice with their revolvers and the Hotchkiss machine-gun sections perfected their skills.

On 9 September a good many of the regiment rode to Contay for a race meeting. The big interest was a race called 'The New Derby', for Captain Henry of B Squadron had a horse entered and had chosen one of their best horsemen to ride it. Second Lieutenant Richard Reginald Smart was Australian-born, a self-described 'gentleman' who had ridden horses all his life. Smart was a good choice, almost. He had the race won when he made a mistake and 'rode the wrong course'. No doubt, a good many of the officers and men lost wagers on the strength of Smart's mistake. Later that month a more commonplace sporting contest was held, with a football match between teams from the North Irish Horse and a Motor Machine Gun battery – the score was 1–1. The only other organised leisure activity in September was the bathing parade, with every man having use of the town baths.

On 19 October orders came that the regiment would soon move, this time to the Ypres front. The prospect of a winter in the freezing mud of Flanders would hardly have been welcome news. The march north began within days and, on 1 November, the regiment reached its destination at Thorè Farm, near the Belgian town of Poperinghe. Here billets for the men were found to be 'very bad', and even headquarters consisted of just two wooden huts.

The next fortnight was mostly wet. Sixty men were sent on road control work for various divisions, and every night 120 others were loaded into buses and driven forward to dig trenches. On 8 November 228 men had the pleasure of a bath at Poperinghe. This town, crucially located on the march east to Ypres, had become a military metropolis, and its baths were built to process hundreds of men at a time.

There were three huge vats in the brewery and between them there were planks. The first vat was full of hot, dirty, soapy water. The next one had hot water, not quite so dirty. The last one had cold water, fairly clean. You started at one end and you stripped off. You tied your khaki uniform up in a bundle and tied your boots to it and your cap. Your underclothes were taken away to the fumigator ... You went up and there were ropes across the vat, so you pulled yourself across on the rope to the other side, climbed out on to the next plank into the next vat, jumped in there, washed the worst of the dirt off, and then into the last vat. When you got out at the other end, you picked up a towel, wiped down and [found] ... your own bundle, with your hat and identity disc attached to it. Then you were issued with underclothes. If you were lucky you got some that nearly fitted you [42]

In mid–November the regiment moved again, this time the short distance south to Boeschepe, about a mile from the Belgian border. This would be their home for the next six months. Every day (apart from Sunday) a party of 120 men went forward for trench digging. Occasionally they came under shellfire, but no casualties were recorded. The training regime was less intensive than it had been at Flesselles, although the signallers were kept busy. The men's leisure activities were well organised, with a recreation room, canteen and access on Sunday to the divisional baths.

As Christmas approached the weather turned colder, with days of heavy snow, frost, rain, cold and damp, but Christmas Day dawned fine for the horsemen at Boeschepe. A new draft of twenty men and two officers arrived in time to join the celebrations.

Despite the carnage around them, the North Irish Horse had again survived the year relatively unscathed, Privates McArow, Finlay, Wright and Watt being the only fatalities. Five former comrades had also died during the year – Private Milton Boyle, who had died at home on 27 October, a victim of tuberculosis, Lieutenant James Robert Dennistoun, Lieutenant James Kenneth MacGregor Greer, Second Lieutenant Johnston Shaw Kirker Hunter and Private John McClelland Cromie Darragh.

Private Darragh had been living in Canada when the war began, but by late 1914 was home to join the Inniskilling Dragoons (Service Squadron) with his brother Matthew. He had been in France with his squadron since October 1915 and at some stage, probably after the squadron had joined the 2nd North Irish Horse, transferred to the Inniskillings' parent regiment, then part of the Mhow Brigade of the 1st Indian Cavalry Division. The cause of his death, on Christmas Eve, is unclear.

Second Lieutenant Hunter was the son of Dromore barrister Robert John Hunter. He had enlisted in the North Irish Horse in the first months of the war before transferring to the 36th (Ulster) Division's artillery. He had not been long in France when he applied to train as an observation officer in the Royal Flying Corps. However, preparations for the Somme offensive meant that such plans were cancelled. Hunter was serving with his battery when he was killed near Béthune on 30 June.

Lieutenant Dennistoun, the New Zealander who had served in Scott's expedition to the Antarctic, had left F Squadron in June 1916 and been attached to the newly-arrived No.23 Squadron, Royal Flying Corps. The squadron was then flying two-seater 'pusher' biplanes – FE2bs – from an aerodrome at Izel-lès-Hameau, west of Arras. One other at the squadron was Dennistoun's cousin, Pilot Officer Herbie Russell. The two men were permitted to fly together, and after one or two practice flights took off with four other machines on a bombing mission east of Arras. Engine trouble soon forced them back to base, but the squadron commander ordered that they take another aircraft and complete the mission. Russell later wrote:

> When the machine was wheeled out I noticed it had no bomb–racks or bomb sights fitted ... I pointed this out to the C.O. He replied, 'Never mind, let Dennistoun take them up in his arms and throw them over when you think you are about right; you've had enough experience by now to tell, more or less!'[43]

The lone aviators took off and dropped their bombs, 'surprisingly close to the target' according to Russell, but on the way back, over the town of Biache-St-Vaast, they were attacked by three Fokker Eindeckers. Dennistoun took three bullets in the stomach and the plane caught fire. Despite being shot through the lung, and suffering severe burns from the flaming aircraft, Russell managed a crash landing, almost making it across the lines. Both men survived, though badly wounded, and were taken prisoner. According to a letter from Dennistoun's father:

They were taken to a Bavarian Hospital – we think near Douai where they were very kindly treated by Doctors, nurses and orderlies. On 27th June, the nurse Lili Eidam wrote a very kind note to Mrs Dennistoun. On the 29th June she again wrote saying they hoped to pull my son through … My son also wrote … very cheery and hopeful … I have little doubt that had they been able to leave him in this hospital he would have pulled through. However on the 3rd August, they sent them off on a 36 hour railway journey the first 19 hours on very rough wooden stretchers, no blankets, and no food, then they were moved into a comfortable bed and train – mattresses and good soup and black bread, then one hour head and tail in a rough furniture van – and then they reached the camp at Ohrdruf in Thuriugia. For 2½ days they never dressed his terrible wounds.

… they arrived on the 6th August and my son wrote on that day – full of pluck. On the 9th August they had a third operation – from which he recovered – but at 5 minutes past noon he died peacefully.[44]

Lieutenant Dennistoun was buried in the cemetery of the Ohrdruf prisoners' camp.

The fifth former North Irish Horseman to lose his life, Lieutenant Greer, was one of the 'young gentlemen' who went to France with C Squadron in August 1914. Commissioned in the 3rd (Prince of Wales) Dragoon Guards in December 1914, in early March 1915 he had had a close call when 'a bullet from the enemy struck the peak of his cap, passed through his hair, and pierced the back of his cap without injuring him in any way'. He and his friend Leslie Ernest McNeill resolved to keep the damaged cap as a memento. Two months later, while serving with the Irish Guards, he sustained shrapnel wounds to his right hand, left thigh, left shoulder and both elbows at the Battle of Festubert, an action that earned him a Military Cross. On 15 September 1916 on the first day of the Battle of Flers-Courcelette he was fatally wounded. 'It was his splendid fearlessness which gained him his wound,' recalled a fellow officer.

We were trying to get a Lewis gun on a German machine gun, which was playing on the trench we had captured. Two having jammed, J.K., as we always called him, seeing another some way down the trench, set off to fetch it. As the trench was crowded and impossible to get along, he simply sprang up on the parapet and walked along the top. Here he was shot by a sniper.[45]

Greer was evacuated to No.2 Red Cross Hospital at Rouen, suffering from a head wound and fractured skull. He died on 3 October, aged thirty-one.

Two other former North Irish Horsemen who saw action in these months were officers Alexander Traill and James Acheson MacLean, both in the Royal Field Artillery. Traill was awarded a Military Cross for conspicuous gallantry during an enemy bombardment which had set an ammunition dump on fire. MacLean, too, won an MC after he 'attempted to save a wounded gunner from a burning gunpit, and successfully saved the gun'. Later, during an attack, 'he led two platoons of another unit over the parapet, and handed them over to their officer, who was rallying his men in the open.' On another occasion 'he fought a single howitzer with great determination for seven days under heavy shellfire, although himself wounded.'[46]

Through 1916 it was voluntary movement rather than shot, shell, accident and illness that caused the greater losses to the ranks of the North Irish Horse, though the numbers were still not large. Certainly there is no evidence of a flood of men seeking transfer to other more active units. Some men did transfer out, including at least a dozen to the Royal Flying Corps, and a few others to the Military Mounted Police.

At least eleven men were commissioned from the ranks of the North Irish Horse and left to join other regiments. David Roulston Bates, from Donoughmore in Donegal was a farmer and a North Irish Horse original from July 1908. Active in the UVF before the war, he went to France as a sergeant in February 1915 and a year later joined the Royal Irish Rifles as a second lieutenant. John McKinstry and James Dowling went to France with C Squadron in August 1914. Before the war McKinstry had managed the Ivy Weaving Company's factory at Dollingstown, Lurgan. In January 1916 he was transferred to the Gordon Highlanders as a probationary second lieutenant and in July was posted to the Royal Irish Rifles. Dowling was a Belfast timber merchant. In January 1916 he was transferred to the 28th County of London Regiment on probation and in May was posted to the Royal Irish Rifles. It seems that the challenges of command didn't suit him, and by August he was sent home and asked to resign his commission, being 'unlikely to make a suitable officer in the near future. His heart is not in his work, he lacks thoroughness, and is a poor disciplinarian.' Robert Noel Anderson, a Belfast linen merchant, embarked for France with D Squadron on 1 May 1915. In January 1916 he went on probation as a second lieutenant in the Royal Irish Rifles and a year later became a lieutenant in the 2nd Reserve Cavalry Regiment. Henry Percy Connar, a commercial traveller from Greenisland, County Antrim, went to France in May 1915 with D Squadron. A year later he was at the Officer Cadet Battalion at the Curragh, and won his commission to the Royal Flying Corps that September. After a short period with the RFC's Balloon Training Wing he transferred to the Royal Irish Fusiliers and then to the Tank Corps. Charles William Coulter, from Drumaness, County Down, was the son of a spinning mill manager and farmer. Sent to France in January 1916 with E Squadron, he was home within five months for training at officer cadet school and by November 1916 he was commissioned as a second lieutenant and posted to the Royal Welsh Fusiliers. Edward Myles Meredith, of Church Street, Antrim, was commissioned as a second lieutenant in the Royal Flying Corps. David McCausland, Donegal-born, had been living for many years in South Africa where he served in the Duke of Edinburgh's Volunteer Rifles. In 1915 he returned to Ireland, where he enlisted in the North Irish Horse. Just three months later he was commissioned as a second lieutenant in the Royal Irish Rifles. Robert James McCullough was a 20-year-old bookkeeper from Belfast. After nine months' training at Antrim he was accepted as an officer cadet. Commissioned before the year was out, he was posted to the Cheshire Regiment. Donald Graham, a medical student before the war, was posted to the Royal Army Medical Corps. Harrison Ross, from County Down, was commissioned to the Royal Irish Rifles.

The light losses amongst the two regiments in France also had an impact at home, leaving high and dry those recruits eager for the front. No more squadrons were being sent, and without significant casualties there was little need for fresh reserves. True, some vacancies were created by the sick and injured and those commissioned from the ranks or transferred to other regiments, but it was hardly enough to offer an immediate prospect of adventure for the hundreds waiting at Antrim. It is hardly surprising then that when the opportunity arose from an unexpected source, many were quick to take it.

As the fighting in France had dragged on to a bloody halt in November, other Irish regiments had fared much worse than the North Irish Horse and were in desperate need of new men to fill the gaps in their ranks. In November the reservists of the North Irish Horse were offered a ticket to France and an infantry cap badge in exchange for their saddle and spurs, the appeal probably conveyed in similar terms to that issued to the 4th Hussars at the Curragh a year earlier. 'Maj-Gen. Friend, Commanding in Ireland, had us paraded,' according to cavalry officer Edwin Alfred Godson,

> ... & said that the Infantry at the front were very hard pressed & very denuded, and as in Static Trench warfare there was no role for Cavalry, except as trench holders as infantry, he appealed to us, Officers & troopers, to transfer to the Infantry. Certainly I was of the conclusion that this war had left cavalry 'behind'.[47]

More than one hundred North Irish Horsemen answered the call. Most were volunteers from late 1915, although some had joined more recently. A handful had already seen service in France with the regiment but, having returned to Ireland to recover from illness or wounds, found themselves stuck there. Three were veterans of the fighting of August 1914 – John Connell and Thomas Maloney of C Squadron, and John Tease of A Squadron. A measure of these men's keenness to be 'in it' was the fact that, having volunteered to transfer, they lost their right to the cavalry rate of pay, meaning a shilling and twopence less per week.

The new infantrymen signed the necessary paperwork transferring them to the Royal Irish Rifles and were given new regimental numbers and a new rank – rifleman – before being sent off to exchange their cavalry kit and uniform for that of the infantry. On 7 December 1916 they embarked at Southampton for le Havre, where they were posted to the 1st Royal Irish Rifles. This battalion had been thrown into the fray more than once during the Somme fighting, and was sorely in need of new men. The former North Irish Horsemen joined their new battalion on 12 December, and were distributed among its four companies. It was a good time to adjust to the challenges of active service, for the battalion was resting at a small town called Laleu, west of Amiens and well out of harm's way. They had been there since 19 November and stayed until just after Christmas, when they were sent once more to the front, taking over a sector near the recently captured town of Combles.

In December another draft of new infantrymen was found from the ranks of the North Irish Horse reserves at Antrim, this time numbering around forty. By 9 January they were in France and headed for their new regiment, the Royal Inniskilling Fusiliers (the majority to the 10th Battalion).

The desire to see some action had no doubt been a strong factor behind the decision of these 140 Horsemen to transfer to the infantry. They would certainly get their wish, but the cost would be high. Within a year one in eight would be killed in action or die of their wounds, and many others would be seriously wounded.

Notes

1. Godson, *Private Papers: transcription of diary.*
2. NA, Kew, WO95/2914.
3. PRONI, D/1702/12/50. Balley is probably Shoeing Smith Thomas Bailey, an old North Irish Horseman from Florence Court, by then aged thirty-seven.
4. *BNL*, 12 May 1916. Spotted fever – probably trench fever, a lice-borne disease prevalent among front-line troops.
5. Letter dated 31 January 1916.
6. Letter dated 2 February 1916.
7. Letter dated 25 February 1916.
8. NA, Kew, WO95/2854.
9. Ibid.
10. Letter dated 14 March 1916.
11. Letter dated 21 October 1916.
12. NA, Kew, WO95/2445.
13. McMahon, op. cit.
14. Ibid.
15. Thompson, *Bushmills Heroes*, pp.152–3.
16. PRONI, D/1702/12/50/29.
17. *BNL*, 12 November 1914.
18. PRONI, D/1702/12/50/30.
19. PRONI, D/1702/12/50/7.
20. PRONI, D/1702/12/50/38.
21. War Office, AO 316/1916, 12 September 1916.
22. NA, Kew, WO364.
23. NA, Kew, WO95/2854.
24. PRONI, D/1702/12/50/10.
25. PRONI, D/1702/12/50/9. Augustine Birrell was Chief Secretary of Ireland. He resigned on 5 May 1916.
26. PRONI, D/1702/12/50/8.
27. Trimble, op. cit.

28. Bureau of Military History, 1913–21, Statement by Witness James Tomney, 21 October 1948, WS 169.
29. Trimble, op. cit.
30. PRONI, D/1702/12/50/11.
31. Letter provided by William Finlay's family.
32. Doherty, *The North Irish Horse*, p.35.
33. McMahon, op. cit.
34. McMahon, op. cit.
35. NA, Kew, WO95/874.
36. Corporal Joe Hoyles in Macdonald, *Somme*, p.113.
37. Mac Fhionnghaile, op. cit., p.110.
38. NA, Kew, WO95/874.
39. Ibid.
40. Ibid.
41. Ibid.
42. Rifleman Worrell, Rifle Brigade, in Macdonald, *They Called it Passchendaele*, p.77.
43. Russell, Herbie, letter to George James Dennistoun, 15 July 1918, in Mannering, Guy (ed.), *The Peaks and Passes of J.R.D.*, *pp.245–50*.
44. NA, Kew, WO339
45. De Ruvigny, *Roll of Honour*, Vol.2 p.146.
46. *LG Supplement*, 22 and 26 September 1916.
47. Godson, op. cit., additional notes, 1915.

A troop of the North of Ireland Imperial Yeomanry at annual camp at the Curragh, 1905. Men identified are Houston Graham (left, back row), Jack Adams (front row, second from left) and Lieutenant E. C. Herdman (centre, second row). *(Image courtesy: Jim Crabtree)*

A private of the North of Ireland Imperial Yeomanry, 1902-08.

Private Charles Delmege Trimble, dismounted review order, c.1908. *(Image from a collection by author R.J. Smith)*

Captain Eustace King–King, review order, c.1910. *(Image from a collection by author R.J. Smith)*

Lieutenant Samuel Barbour 'Barrie' Combe, first officer of the North Irish Horse killed in action, 30 September 1914.

Officers of C Squadron relaxing at Chateau Dhuizy in France, September 1914. Standing (left to right): Barrie Combe, Neil Graham Stewart-Richardson (?), Massereene & Ferrard. In the window, Eustace King-King (?), Richard Annesley West. Note West's 'battered slouch hat' and the German cavalry helmet (as described on p.34).

A North Irish Horse troop at Antrim, late 1914. *(Image courtesy: James M. Rankin)*

'A group of members of the North Irish Horse who are preparing for the fray at the show grounds, Londonderry. Recruited from all parts of Ulster, Belfast being well represented, they are a sturdy collection of young men, who have entered into their arduous training with great zeal and are rapidly becoming proficient in all the rudiments of musketry and horsemanship.' *(*Larne Times and Weekly Telegraph, *17 October 1914)*

Private Frank McMahon as a new recruit, late 1914.

Private Jack McGuigan, who enlisted with Frank McMahon and served with him until evacuated with trench fever at the end of 1917. *(Image courtesy: Anne Cosgrove, Newry)*

Brothers Robert, Albert and Alexander Dundee, who enlisted together on 7 September 1914. They served in France in D Squadron from May 1915. Alexander was later commissioned and awarded the Military Cross. *(Image courtesy: Mrs Dorothy Harcourt)*

A North Irish Horse private at Ballyshannon, Co. Donegal.

A North Irish Horse lance corporal.

A mounted North Irish Horse private.

Captain Neil Graham Stewart-Richardson. *(Image courtesy: Brigadier P. Stewart-Richardson OBE and Sir David Ralli Bt.)*

Lieutenant Lancelot Charles Wise, who served in France with D Squadron before transferring to the Indian cavalry. *(Image courtesy: Edinburgh University Library, from University of Edinburgh Roll of Honour 1914–1919)*

A group of North Irish Horsemen, probably at Antrim, 1915. *(Image courtesy: Public Record Office of Northern Ireland (PRONI) – Cat. No. D1977/1)*

Captain Arthur Noel Vernon Hill-Lowe, who went to France as a lieutenant with F Squadron.

Lance Corporal Hamilton Stewart (seated). On the reverse is written 'To Aunt Aggie, with Hammie's love'. Stewart, a Boer War veteran, was aged 45 when he enlisted in August 1916.

Private Ernest George Matthews. In 1914 he was commissioned and posted to the 6th Inniskilling Dragoons (Service Squadron). He was seriously wounded in an artillery bombardment during the battle of the Somme on 4 July 1916. *(Image courtesy: Shaun Matthews)*

Signallers of the 1st North Irish Horse Regiment at Pas, on the Somme front, August 1916. *(Image courtesy: PRONI – Cat. No. D1977/2)*

A group of North Irish Horsemen at rest.

Private David Hunter Bond was only 16 when he joined the Royal Inniskilling Fusiliers. After his mother claimed him back he joined the North Irish Horse. *(Image courtesy: Mrs Melva White)*

New Zealanders (from left) Gilbert Hutton Grigg, Richard Berry Kellock, Harold Plumer Kellock and John Hutton Grigg in the Royal North Devon Hussars before being commissioned and posted to the North Irish Horse. *(Image courtesy: Penny Otto and Jill McLaren)*

Second Lieutenant Gilbert Hutton Grigg.
(Image courtesy: Tessa Grigg)

Temporary grave marker for Private Frederick Thomas Cordwell, accidentally drowned while watering horses in September 1917. *(Image courtesy: Dr John Cordwell)*

Private James Lynn with his family in Randalstown in 1916. *(Image courtesy: Len Kinley)*

Corporal Frank McMahon in Egypt,
September 1917. (Inset: his sister Josie)

Private Charles Magill (right) and two other
North Irish Horsemen in Egypt, September
1917. *(Image courtesy: Paul Magill)*

Major Holt Waring, who died of wounds on 15 April
1918.

Private James Wilson, gassed on 30 August 1918. *(Image courtesy: Patrick Wilson Gore)*

Second Lieutenant James Bailey Young, who went to France as a sergeant with E Squadron, and won the Military Cross while serving with 108 Trench Mortar Battery near Hill 41 on 30 September 1918.

Private Charles Elder, the last North Irish Horseman killed in action, 7 November 1918. *(*Belfast Evening Telegraph, *2 January 1919, image courtesy: Nigel Henderson)*

North Irish Horse signaller at Vignacourt,
c. January 1919. *(Louis and Antoinette Thuillier
Collection. Courtesy: Kerry Stokes Collection,
Perth, Australia, British-19-024)*

North Irish Horse cyclist, possibly wounded,
at Vignacourt, c. January 1919. *(Louis and
Antoinette Thuillier Collection. Courtesy:
Kerry Stokes Collection, Perth, Australia,
British-40-008)*

North Irish Horse cyclist at Vignacourt,
c. January 1919. *(Louis and Antoinette Thuillier
Collection. Courtesy: Kerry Stokes Collection,
Perth, Australia, British-21-016)*

North Irish Horse cyclists, one a Lewis gunner, at Vignacourt, c. January 1919. *(Louis and Antoinette Thuillier Collection. Courtesy: Kerry Stokes Collection, Perth, Australia, British-19-028)*

North Irish Horse cyclists, one with a wound stripe, at Vignacourt, c. January 1919. *(Louis and Antoinette Thuillier Collection. Courtesy: Kerry Stokes Collection, Perth, Australia, British-19-022)*

North Irish Horse officers at Vignacourt, c. January 1919. On the right is Lieutenant Edward Arthur Atkinson. *(Louis and Antoinette Thuillier Collection. Courtesy: Kerry Stokes Collection, Perth, Australia, British-01-021)*

A Squadron football team at Vignacourt, c. January 1919. *(Louis and Antoinette Thuillier Collection. Courtesy:Kerry Stokes Collection, Perth, Australia, British-05-008)*

A Squadron at Vignacourt, c. January 1919. Front row third from left is Lieutenant Edward Arthur Atkinson, in the middle, Acting Captain Worship Booker, and third from right Lieutenant Bryant Charles Hamilton. *(Louis and Antoinette Thuillier Collection. Courtesy of the Kerry Stokes Collection, Perth, Australia, British-04-024)*

Margaret, widow of Major Holt Waring
(see Postscript).

Private Thomas Bryson and the 'unknown' North Irish Horseman, Queens Cemetery, Bucquoy, France (see Postscript). *(Image courtesy Peter Woodger)*

Chapter Five

1917: Never Yet a Chance of Killing

They are men of the North Irish Horse recently sent to us and have never yet had a chance of killing a German and they got excited and killed everyone instead of taking some prisoners as proof of success.[1]

1917 opened with a surprise withdrawal of German forces in France to heavily entrenched positions which the British came to know as the Hindenburg Line. During the year the BEF initiated four major offensives with varying success, but none resulting in a decisive breakthrough. In April they seized the Vimy Ridge at Arras and in June the Messines Ridge south of Ypres. July to November saw small gains made at an enormous cost at the Third Battle of Ypres. In November and December spectacular initial gains at Cambrai were followed by disappointment and desperate defence in the face of a determined counter-attack. The men of the North Irish Horse played a part in all these actions, but it was as infantry, at Ypres and Cambrai, that they saw the heaviest fighting and sustained their greatest losses.

Recruiting and departures

Through the year another 420 men joined the ranks of the North Irish Horse, a considerable increase on the 290 of the previous year. Perhaps only half would serve overseas, and most of these not until the closing months of 1918. Some were conscripts from other parts of the United Kingdom, like 19-year-old hammerman Thomas O'Rourke from Lanarkshire, and 27-year-old explosives worker Harry Bertram Andrews from London. Most, however, were young volunteers, less than twenty years old, from the north of Ireland, like bank clerk Albert Brice Galway from Magherafelt, and asylum attendant George Thompson from Kesh, County Fermanagh.

Older than most was 32-year-old William Coltart, the golf professional at Belfast's Cliftonville Golf Club. He would join the regiment in the field in April 1918 and serve in France and Belgium throughout the remainder of the war. Another with an unusual history was Cecil Charles Hunter Barr,

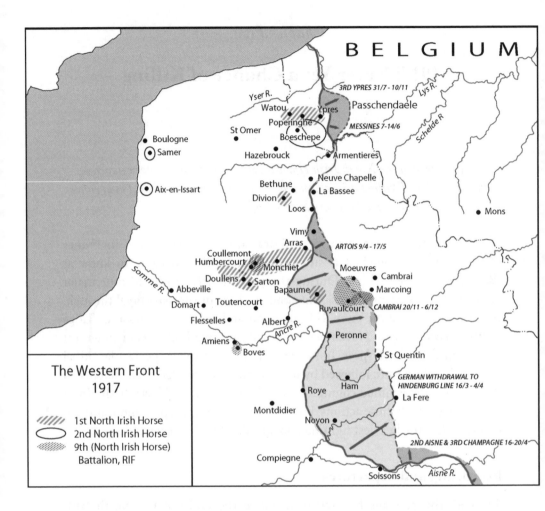

The Western Front
1917

///// 1st North Irish Horse
⬭ 2nd North Irish Horse
▓▓▓ 9th (North Irish Horse)
Battalion, RIF

who enlisted around February under the alias Charles Russell. He was English, son of a Leeds timber merchant, and had first enlisted in 1915 with the Yorkshire Regiment, though he was only sixteen. He served in France from December 1915 and during 1916 was transferred to the Royal Scots. It appears his battalion was posted to Ireland in January 1917. For some reason he deserted, but re-enlisted under his alias with the North Irish Horse. In August he transferred to the Royal Irish Rifles before being sent to France to join the 1st Battalion.

Under-age boys continued to join the regiment throughout 1917, and sometimes they were found out. They included Belfast lad Andrew Pierce, Bellaghy orphan David Brown, Dubliners Robert Graham and

Joseph McSweeney, Omagh farm labourer William James Jeffrey, Belfast apprentice fitter Robert William Brooks and Limerick farmer William Keays. Sometimes boys enlisted then went absent, were later found without their kit, admitted their age and were discharged. Was this a deliberate ploy to raise some cash by selling-off their uniform, arms and equipment? John Davidson, a 15-year-old from Shankill, enlisted with the North Irish Horse in August 1916, claiming he was a 19-year-old machinist. He deserted in September but three weeks later returned to camp dressed in plain clothes, and without his kit. He admitted his age and produced a certificate showing he had been discharged from the 4th Royal Irish Fusiliers only a week before he had joined the North Irish Horse! Albert Spence wasn't under age, but had a similar story. A 19-year-old labourer from Nevin's Row, County Down, near Lambeg, he enlisted with the 2nd Reserve Cavalry Regiment at Dublin and was posted to the North Irish Horse. He deserted a week later, being absent for a month before showing up again. It then became clear that when he enlisted he was already a deserter from the Royal Irish Rifles. The Army threw the book at him. He was charged with absenting himself without leave from the Rifles; losing by neglect his arms, equipment, clothing and regimental necessaries (twice); fraudulent enlistment; and desertion. Placed under detention for nine months, he had his pay stopped until the value of the missing items was repaid. After his release he was seldom out of trouble, but was eventually posted to the North Irish Horse in France, just as the war ended.

The numbers joining the North Irish Horse in Ireland more than matched the losses to the regiment in France during 1917. Some men left for other regiments, but the number was not large. At the end of April, ten men transferred to the Machine Gun Corps (Cavalry). Around two dozen went to the Military Mounted Police. Others, a handful, transferred to the Military Foot Police, for the most part men no longer fit for front-line service. Some men transferred to various branches of the Royal Engineers, often in recognition of their peacetime qualifications. Private John Young from Donegal was an engine fireman, so it made sense that he transfer to the Railway Operating Division. Sergeant Edward Ross had been an architecture teacher and David Bell a lithographer, so it was logical that they work for a field survey company of the Royal Engineers.

The departure of men for officer training also helped thin the ranks throughout 1917. From 1914 to 1916 only a small number had left this way, but in 1917 it became a weekly occurrence. As was usual, most men commissioned were sent to other regiments. Sixteen were posted to battalions of the Royal Irish Rifles, fifteen to other infantry regiments (mostly Irish), twelve to the cavalry, four to the artillery, three to the Army Service Corps, two to the Machine Gun Corps, and one to the Royal Flying Corps.

Officer turnover in the North Irish Horse was high during the year, and not all those sent to replace them met with the approval of the regiment's class-conscious senior officers, as one letter from Eustace Maude to his uncle Hugh de Fellenberg Montgomery makes clear:

> My dear Uncle Hugh,
> I shall be very glad when this high fever of politics is over, it will be much better for the country & much better for the NIH! However I fear there is no such luck as that happening in the near future ... I am sending out two more subalterns. I hope Cole will like them! One is very much of the 'temporary' type & I can't imagine how anyone came to recommend him.[2]

The new officers included James Graham Adam, a London-based merchant who had grown up in Portugal, who was later attached to the Portuguese Expeditionary Force as an interpreter, Alister MacLean, previously a private in the Highland Light Infantry, and William Westley Blanden, who had served at Gallipoli in the Suffolk Yeomanry. Mervyn Sinclair Hornidge, Richard Randall Webb and Geoffrey Henry Baird received their commissions together on 29 June. John Knox and William Moorhead Hunter came to the North Irish Horse in a roundabout way. Both were among the hundred or so who had transferred from the North Irish Horse to the Royal Irish Rifles and were sent to France in December 1916. After less than a month in the field they were sent to England for officer training. Both were commissioned at the end of May 1917 and posted to the North Irish Horse.

Five of the new officers joining in 1917 had come direct from the ranks of the North Irish Horse, all earning their commissions on 16 April. Robert James Downey was a North Irish Horse original from Kildartin, County Armagh. He had been in France since May 1915 with D Squadron. John Frederick Alexander Craig, from Ardstraw, County Tyrone, had been with the regiment since January 1912 and in France with F Squadron since November 1915. Arthur Ernest Dallas was an insurance clerk from Dublin and, like Craig, had come out with F Squadron. James Bailey Young and William Jones had arrived in France in January 1916 with E Squadron.

On the front

The first three months of 1917 were quiet along most of the Western Front as the snow, frost and then thaw made large-scale aggressive manoeuvres all but impossible. Elsewhere, however, big events were unfolding. On 31 January, in an attempt to starve Britain into submission, Germany declared unrestricted U-boat warfare against all ships in British waters or bound for Britain. In February the USA severed diplomatic relations with Germany as a prelude to its declaration of war in April. In Russia, rioting in Petrograd sparked the collapse of the government and the abdication of the Tsar.

For the 1st North Irish Horse Regiment, however, the long sojourn at Humbercourt continued quiet and uninterrupted, with cavalry duties for VII Corps the order of the day during January, February and most of March. Discipline was not a significant problem, though there were occasional breaches. William Warke was awarded seven days' Field Punishment No.1 for his fourth offence – using improper language to an NCO. John Riddell received the same for quitting camp and using obscene and insolent language to an NCO. Most seriously, James Wilson faced a court martial for quitting his post without orders. He was sentenced to fifty-six days' Field Punishment No.1.

Captain Murland was offered promotion to second-in-command of the 1/1st Somerset Yeomanry, but to his annoyance and disappointment his commanding officer, Lieutenant Colonel Cole, refused to release him.

On the Somme, the hundred former North Irish Horsemen serving in the 1st Royal Irish Rifles were getting their first taste of trench warfare in front of the ruins of Combles. The battalion soon moved farther south to the Quarry Farm sector in front of Bouchavesnes. This area, captured by the French in the previous September and only recently handed over to the BEF, was a dangerous part of the line, because the Germans occupied the higher ground in front of them. At the beginning of March the battalion took part in a minor attack in this sector designed to take this ground from the enemy. Within forty minutes the objectives – Pallas Trench and Fritz Trench behind it – were seized. The consolidation took longer, with artillery bombardment and counter-attack from an enemy not keen to be pushed off the ridge. For four days the Royal Irish Rifles consolidated the line in the face of heavy enemy shellfire. Twenty-seven men of the battalion were killed and many more wounded. Among the dead were four former North

Irish Horsemen. John McSparron, aged twenty-four, was from Derrychrier, County Londonderry, William Nixon, nineteen, from Enniskillen, Thomas Hall, twenty-six, from Cootehill, County Cavan, and John Nixon Gibson, twenty, from Bailieborough, Cavan. Another former North Irish Horseman, 20-year-old Robert O'Hara, had been severely wounded. He was evacuated to Salford Military Hospital in Manchester, where he clung to life for almost a month before dying on 1 April.

In the middle of March, from Arras to Soissons, the German army began to withdraw, abandoning their trenches and apparently retreating. In mockery of the tiny gains that the Allied forces had won on the Somme in months of bloody fighting, the Germans gave up 900 square miles of territory, seven times as much. In a few short weeks they fell back to new positions, carefully prepared over months, and designed to be impregnable. This the Germans called the *Siegfriedstellung*. The British called it the Hindenburg Line. It was built to last, with deep bunkers and well-constructed trenches and support lines, occupying the most advantageous territory, with row upon row of barbed wire and carefully located and fortified defensive posts. In one bold move the Germans had shortened their line by twenty-five miles, thus freeing up thirteen divisions. Behind them they left a wasteland, with forests levelled, villages destroyed and wells buried, the object being to deprive the enemy of shelter, cover and water.

Only slowly did the Allies realise what was occurring, and their advance was cautious. They were regularly held up by enemy machine-gun posts and booby traps set in dugouts and the ruined villages. The advance into new territory required efficient control over the roads and crossings, so once again the 1st North Irish Horse Regiment was detached for traffic control. They were kept at it during the last week of March and into April, with the exception of one troop detached to help the 30th Division follow the German withdrawal from the Bapaume salient south of Arras.

The German withdrawal caused a rethink of Allied plans for a spring offensive, which had included a renewal of the offensive on the Somme. The British would now conduct a subsidiary attack on the strategically important Vimy Ridge and south past Arras, while the French would attack in force along the Aisne, between Reims and Soissons. The French offensive, which began on 16 April, was the brainchild of General Robert Nivelle. Relying on the use of an overwhelming concentration of force, he promised a swift victory. Instead, the offensive was a bloody and expensive fiasco, costing the

French 130,000 casualties in five days, sparking mutiny in the ranks, and ending French offensive capability for the year. Arras and Vimy Ridge, on the other hand, were a qualified success, though the failure on the French front would increase the number of British casualties. The fighting lasted from 9 April until mid-May, the most notable success being the capture of Vimy Ridge by the Canadians on the first day. Indeed the advances made on that day were such as to encourage serious thoughts that the cavalry divisions waiting in the wings might get their chance. However, it was not to be. Stubborn German defence, especially against VII Corps, slowed the advance and prevented any offensive deployment of cavalry, with the notable exception of the capture of the high ground at Monchy-le-Preux on 11 April. Here 6 and 8 Cavalry Brigades and VI Corps Cavalry Regiment (the Northamptonshire Yeomanry) played an important role, though suffering great losses in men and horses.

The men of the North Irish Horse thrilled at the tale but were 'annoyed at being left out of the scrap'.[3] Instead, they continued their work on traffic control for VII Corps through all phases of the battle. On 24 April their headquarters moved forward to Monchiet, a village seven miles south-west of Arras, and close to the old German front line.

On 15 June the regiment marched east to billets between the villages of Blaireville and Hendecourt-lès-Ransart, part of the old German trench network but now roughly seven miles from the front line. It was a good location to learn the art of trench warfare, and that is what the regiment set out to do. However, for one man the training was too realistic. Sergeant Robert Alexander Wylie was accidentally wounded. Evacuated to the 37th Casualty Clearing Station at Avesnes-le-Comte, he died on 26 June. Wylie was a farmer, born at Garvary, County Fermanagh. He was one of the North Irish Horse originals, enlisting at Newbridge in July 1908, and had been in France with A Squadron since August 1914. Just a few months before his death he and four other Horsemen had been awarded the Long Service and Good Conduct Medal.

Not long after, orders came that the regiment was to leave VII Corps and join the recently formed XIX Corps on the Ypres front. On 16 July they reached their new billets in farmland south-west of Watou on the Belgian-French border, twelve miles west of Ypres.

Meanwhile the 2nd North Irish Horse Regiment, supporting X Corps, had seen out winter and the first month of spring at Boeschepe on the Ypres front. Every evening, bar Sunday, a party of around 100 men would take their turn at trench digging. Each night the digging party was driven by bus to an assembly point close to the front. Here they collected picks, shovels, trench formwork, wire and other paraphernalia and marched along the duckboards and through communication trenches to the assigned location, where they laboured all night before returning to their billets, filthy and exhausted, and freezing despite their exertions. Through much of this time the ground was frozen, making digging a back-breaking task, and often the digging parties faced rain, frost or snow. It was always cold. In February the thaw set in, instantly turning the roads and paths to mud and slush. The men probably didn't mind – for eighteen days the digging was suspended. It was simply too difficult to get them to the front. But then the work resumed, as did the rain and snow.

The roads leading up to the trenches were well known to the Germans and regularly shelled, as were the trenches themselves. Fortunately, they rarely did any damage to the working parties. Various training schemes and inspections were undertaken to keep the men and their officers on their toes and to relieve the monotony. X Corps Cavalry School was opened, there were musketry and signalling classes, lectures on horse management, inspections of the horses, gas masks, and kit, and medical checks for the men. Those with free time could visit the regimental canteen and recreation rooms. Occasional visitors turned up from neighbouring regiments, such as the naturalist and officer Philip Gosse:

[I sometimes visited] a very friendly squadron of yeomanry, the North Irish Horse, who were acting as Corps Cavalry, and who had a mess at Vieuxbec. I often spent the evenings with them playing a simple game they taught me called Blind Hookey or Uncle Sam. This is one of those games which appears so guileless and in which even the worst duffer at card games can join at once and be fleeced, and is, I believe, the one employed by the villain in melodramas to ruin the honest village lad.

One evening when it was decided to stop playing, one more round was proposed and agreed to, and a special prize offered. In one corner of the room stood a deal box in which the squadron fox-terrier bitch was at that very moment in the throes of labour. The prize was to be one of the puppies, the winner to make his own choice. Perhaps because I had lost consistently the whole evening, perhaps because I did not want a dog, the cards turned all in my favour. Just as the last card was played and I had been proclaimed winner, the regimental MO who was in attendance on the little bitch, informed the company that the interesting event had come to a happy conclusion, and we inspected the litter of four.

They were an odd lot of puppies, no two appearing to belong to the same breed. This curious fact the doctor explained by telling us that during the period of her courting the squadron had moved from place to place, never remaining more than one day at any.

After very carefully inspecting the litter, I chose the newborn puppy which looked to me most like a fox-terrier.[4]

In February the 2nd North Irish Horse Regiment lost serial offender Edward Menice, who transferred to the Machine Gun Corps (Heavy Branch). This would later be re-named the Tank Corps, to better reflect its real function. Menice's rebellious spirit was not dampened. In May he was reprimanded for 'failing to pay proper compliments to an officer' and in August he returned from home leave three days late. Nevertheless, he would later win promotion to corporal and serve in France for the remainder of the war as a Tank Mechanic 1st Class.

Officers continued to come and go. Colonel Goring went on leave to the UK before transferring to the Central School of Inspection, leaving Major Whitla in command. Major Foster went on leave and was then appointed Staff Captain to 70 Infantry Brigade. Major Bramston-Newman would soon leave for the reserve regiment at Antrim, a medical board finding him 'prematurely aged' as a result of illness he had contracted in the South African war. There must have been many more vacancies amongst the junior officers, for April and May saw a flood of new arrivals, fourteen in all.

April and May at Boeschepe continued with routine training and inspections. A major source of concern was the state of the horses, which by the end of winter were in very poor condition. A series of escalating inspections – by the Deputy Director Veterinary Services, Deputy Director Remounts Second Army, and even the corps commander – reached the same conclusion: the horses of the regiment were 'not 1st Class'. However, nothing could be done immediately, for another move was afoot, this time for training on the coast at Samer, a town near Boulogne. As was often the case, time away from the front was a prelude to a major offensive. This time the intention was to seize the Messines Ridge, running along the southern flank of the Ypres salient. The

Germans had occupied this ridge since early in the war, and it gave them a great tactical advantage as they looked down on the British lines.

Meticulously planned, the attack would feature the greatest use of mines undertaken in the war. Deep tunnels had been dug under the German lines all along the front, then large chambers hollowed out under their strongest defensive points. These were filled with a million pounds of explosives, to be fired simultaneously at zero hour on the morning of the attack. The attack was scheduled for 7 June, and in the days before the 2nd North Irish Horse Regiment assisted X Corps with its preparations. Three troops of the Inniskilling squadron were sent for duty with the three X Corps Divisions which would take part in the initial assault. One troop reported to the Assistant Provost Marshal, their job being to look after any prisoners. Second Lieutenant Bray went to X Corps Headquarters as an observation officer while Second Lieutenant Henry and sixteen men reported to the field engineers to clear a track for the cavalry on zero day. B Squadron was attached to the 24th Division, camped at Dikebusch Lake, which would go into action as a second wave after the initial assault. If a breakthrough occurred, it was hoped the squadron could ride through and play a more traditional cavalry role.

At 3.10am on 7 June, after a heavy evening thunderstorm, all nineteen mines were blown. It was said that the shock was felt as far away as London. The impact on the German defenders was devastating, and the advancing troops quickly overwhelmed them. The ridge and the plateau behind it were quickly captured and consolidated and German attempts to counter-attack over the next few days were repelled. It was a high point for the BEF in 1917, and together with earlier successes and the German withdrawal to the Hindenburg Line, seemed to point to future success.

The 2nd North Irish Horse Regiment was kept busy through the first day, with only two troops held in reserve, but its cavalry skills were not required for any offensive action. No casualties were sustained, though they did lose one of their former pals. Private James Talbot of Ashfield, County Cavan was one who had transferred to the 10th Royal Inniskilling Fusiliers at the beginning of the year. The 23-year-old was among the 156 men of the 36th (Ulster) Division killed during the battle.

On 8 June the various troops of the 2nd Regiment assigned across the divisions of X Corps returned to their billets at Boeschepe. Soon after they moved to nearby Kenora Camp, on the outskirts of the Belgian village of Heksken. Two large conducting parties went to Calais to collect new mounts for the regiment. Disaster came close when two 8-inch shells fell in the horse lines, but they must have been duds, for no damage was done. The officers went on staff rides and the men had occasional use of the divisional baths at nearby Westoutre. Working parties and teams of Hotchkiss gunners were sent to the trenches. Throughout July the regiment put in more training – musketry drill, aeroplane contact practice, sword exercises and range firing at the IX Corps range near Berthen – as the army prepared for a new offensive.

Mid-July 1917 found the 1st and 2nd Regiments of the North Irish Horse behind the lines on the Ypres front, as cavalry for XIX and X Corps respectively. So far it had been another fortunate year as far as casualties were concerned. Apart from Sergeant Wylie whose death was noted earlier, only two others had died, neither as a result of enemy action. Private William McKee Murphy from Ballymoney, County Antrim was on his way to join the regiment in France when he contracted pneumonia. He was hospitalised at Rouen and died there on 12 February, aged twenty-three. Private Richard Moore, also twenty-three, died in Ireland. Other casualties had occurred among those who had left the regiment. Aside from those of the Royal Irish Rifles lost in the clash at Bouchavesnes, and Private Talbot, killed at Messines, three others had lost their lives. Former North Irish Horseman Captain Charles Norman died on 12 February while serving with the Royal Horse Artillery. Lance Corporal Rowland Irvine Bradley died in the same month. He had served in France with A Squadron since August 1914 before transferring to the Royal Flying Corps' No.20 Squadron. The squadron was flying two-seater FE2d pusher biplanes. In the early morning of 20 May, Bradley and his pilot officer, Second Lieutenant Hugh Howe, took off on an offensive patrol. 'We were attacked by three Hun machines over the lines,' according to Lieutenant Howe in a letter to Bradley's father.

> We brought down one of them, and then were attacked by a fourth from the rear. We had our machine and engine damaged, compelling us to leave the fight. Not being able to reach an aerodrome in our crippled condition we had to land in a soft cornfield, but the machine not being under full control crashed, and turned over on landing, your son being smashed under the wreckage … [He] was much honoured and respected in this squadron, for he was a brave fighter and observer.[5]

This wasn't the first war tragedy suffered by the Bradley family. One brother, Albert James, was already disabled from wounds suffered serving with Princess Patricia's Canadian Light Infantry and another, Frederick, had drowned when his submarine struck a mine.

Third Ypres

The 1st North Irish Horse Regiment's move to the Ypres front in July coincided with the final preparations for what would become known as Third Ypres, a four-month slog through the Flanders mud which would gain much of the heights overlooking the Ypres salient, but at an enormous cost. Encouraged by the success of the Messines attack, the British command planned to seize all of the high ground to the east and north east of Ypres. Success would allow a general advance toward the German-occupied Belgian ports. Once again, open warfare and a big role for the cavalry was hoped for, once the line had been broken and the ridges seized. The main responsibility for the attack would fall to Gough's Fifth Army, supported by one corps of the Second Army to the right and a corps of the French First Army on the left. XIX Corp, to which the 1st North Irish Horse Regiment was now attached, was part of the Fifth Army; so they would have a part to play.

In the fortnight before the battle the regiment trained under an instructor from the Cavalry Corps. Though their billets were relatively safely located twelve miles west of Ypres, their daily activities did bring the men in harm's way. On 20 July a party came under German shellfire near Ypres, killing Lance Corporal Stewart Turner. One of his comrades, 19-year-old Private Clement Turner, was also hit by shrapnel and died later that day. Clement Turner had enlisted in November 1915, though probably under age, and was sent to France the following year. His family received letters from his officers and comrades, containing the familiar expressions of comfort:

He was the youngest in his squadron, and a good boy.

His death cast a gloom over us all. He was beloved by all, and was killed instantaneously when going to help another.

… he was such a decent chap and so bright, and he would not offend a child.

He was one of the best – a brave boy. He died a glorious death, and you ought to be proud of him.[6]

The two men lie side-by-side in Vlamertinghe New Military Cemetery, just west of Ypres.

After several delays, the Third Battle of Ypres commenced on 31 July. The 1st Regiment had already marched to a bivouac just outside Poperinghe and on the day they marched six miles along the road to Ypres, stopping at a point west of Goldfish Chateau. XIX Corps occupied a sector east of Ypres, running south from Wieltje to the Ypres-Roulers railway line. Two of its divisions, the 15th (Scottish) and 55th (West Lancashire), were to attack up the Pilckem Ridge towards Gravenstafel. Here the ground was unwooded, but pocked with shell holes, and although the water lay close to the surface, it was not the sea of mud that it would soon become. The attack would commence at 3.50am after a heavy bombardment, protected by a creeping barrage. By 5.05am the two divisions were to move through the first objective and attack the second, where they would stop and consolidate. Fresh battalions would then push through to the third objective, roughly on the line of the Langemarck–Zonnebeke road. If the attack was going well, the assault could then be pushed to the fourth objective. It was in this latter stage that the North Irish Horse would be used. The protective barrage was to be maintained in front of the third objective until 12.10pm, by which time the attacking forces should be well established. Then strong patrols of infantry and troops of the North Irish Horse would move forward – one troop under New Zealander Lieutenant Grigg assisting the 55th Division and another with the 15th Division. If the enemy's positions were not strongly held, they would seize them and move forward again, advancing beyond the fourth objective to occupy the high ground of the Passchendaele ridge, north-west of Keerselaarhoek and about Wolf Farm on the Wallemolen spur beyond the river Stroombeek.

That was the plan, and for a while the reality seemed to match it. Attacking through a heavy mist and assisted by a small number of tanks, XIX Corps reached the third objective along most of the front. Similar results were achieved by XVIII and XIV Corps to their left. However, the German defensive tactic was to defend in depth, holding the front trenches only lightly. In the early afternoon they made a heavy counter-attack. There was no chance of the British pushing on to the fourth objective and so no role for the North Irish Horse.

As the horsemen pulled back, the drizzle that had been falling for much of the day turned into heavy rain which barely ceased for days, turning the battlefield and the supply and reinforcement areas behind it into a sea of deep glutinous mud and flooded shell holes. For a time the offensive had to be brought to a halt.

By the end of that first day, despite the gains achieved, it was apparent that there would be no need for cavalry in the immediate future. The 1st North Irish Horse Regiment marched back to its billets near Watou. During August, as the battle wore on in front of them, they settled into a familiar routine of cavalry training, working parties and traffic control. The regiment sent a troop to assist the corps' assistant provost marshal; parties were sent to work under the town major of Ypres, and others to assist the 15th (Scottish) and 61st (2nd South Midland) Divisions. The most help, however, was provided to the 16th (Irish) and 36th (Ulster) Divisions. On 6 August two troops proceeded on detached duty with those divisions, and two days later another sixty men and two officers joined them.

The weather prevented any further large-scale attacks on the Ypres front until 10 August. However, enemy artillery fire kept the casualty list mounting. Among these were former North Irish Horsemen Corporal William Hanna Adams and Private William Beattie. These Belfastmen were among the forty who had transferred to the Royal Inniskilling Fusiliers at the beginning of 1917. Thirty-year-old Adams was from Strandtown, 19-year-old Beattie from Mountcollyer Street.

Following an unsuccessful assault on the Gheluvelt Plateau on 10 August, the next major action in this offensive was on 16 August, known as the Battle of Langemarck. This involved an attack by the Fifth Army along the six mile front from Langemarck south to Gheluvelt. On the front still occupied by XIX Corps, new (though tired and depleted) divisions had moved in – the 16th (Irish) and 36th (Ulster) – but this time there was no offensive role planned for cavalry units like the North Irish Horse. Instead they played a support role as runners, signallers and observers.

All along the front the attack was a bloody failure. Little ground was gained in the face of well-prepared German artillery, machine-gun fire from defensive positions including concrete pill-boxes, massed counter-attacks, and a battleground so flooded, shell-pocked and muddy that the infantry could only move forward at a crawl. The 1st Royal Irish Rifles, including many of the hundred North Irish Horsemen who had transferred in the previous December, had moved up from Ypres the evening before. At 4.45am they moved forward behind a heavy barrage:

The Battalion advanced in excellent formation and little resistance was met with as far as the Hannebeek Wood, the casualties were also slight except the Centre Company who appear to have suffered somewhat severely from Machine Guns firing from their Right front ... The Green Line was captured at about 6.20 am and an attempt was made to consolidate it, but owing to the lack of men and the heavy sniping from our left rear it was found impossible.

... We again went forward and crossed the stream which by now had been reduced to a series of small lakes. No officers could be found, and very few men, and it was reported to me that all had either been killed or wounded. I have never seen so many dead as there were in that Hanebeek Valley – both Boche and British – the majority of whom were the former.

... At about 7.50 am the enemy were seen to be working round our right flank. The position of the left was far from satisfactory; the line therefore had to fall back.[7]

When the roll-call was taken after the battalion was withdrawn from the line at the end of the day, the casualties numbered seven officers killed and three wounded, twenty-seven other ranks killed, 170 wounded, sixty-three missing, seven wounded and missing. Many of those missing were indeed dead – lost in the muddy chaos of the battlefield.

The attack by the Ulster and Irish divisions was just as great a failure. As the diary of 108 Brigade Headquarters recorded, 'no progress could be made and our attack was crushed'.[8] One battalion of the Ulster Division, the 9th Royal Irish Fusiliers, lost twenty officers and 422 others killed, wounded, captured or missing.

This day, 16 August, was the worst day yet for the North Irish Horse, or at least for those who had once served with it. Twelve men were killed in action. Two of these were officers. Second Lieutenant George Herbert Farley was a farmer from Ayr, Scotland, though Belfast-born. He had joined the North Irish Horse in September 1915 and served in France with D Squadron. After six months of officer cadet training, Farley was commissioned and posted to the 8th Royal Inniskilling Fusiliers, part of the 16th (Irish) Division. Two days before the attack he wrote the briefest of wills, which was later found with his kit:

Should I not see the end of this push I leave everything to my mother Mrs Ellie Farley, Benoni, Roy Road, Northwood, Middlesex.[9]

Second Lieutenant Wilfred Laurence Reavie, an accountant from Seagoe, Portadown, was serving with the 2nd Royal Dublin Fusiliers, also part of the 16th (Irish) Division. He had joined the North Irish Horse in September 1914 and, like Farley, had served in France with D Squadron. Despite a couple of misdemeanours he was allowed to transfer to officer cadet schools and was commissioned in April 1917. Four days after Langemarck his family received a telegram reporting that he was missing believed killed. Hope died three days later with another telegram reporting that his death had been confirmed. His captain and major also wrote letters of consolation, describing how he died 'instantaneously', shot through the head while charging a machine-gun post. 'Thank God, we have still the precious memory of our loved ones, and the assurance that death is not the end of all,' wrote Major Richard Bird.[10] Two months later Reavie's father wrote seeking any information about his death and his kit:

Dear Sirs

With reference to my son 2nd Lieut W.L. Revie, 2nd Royal Dublin Fusiliers, reported missing believed killed on 16th August & later reported killed, I should be glad to know if you have any further particulars about his death or burial. If so will you kindly send me a certificate of his death, & also the name & address of his platoon Sergt. The Captain informs us that the platoon Sergt saw my son killed. The Capt also informed us that he had sent my sons kit home on the 24th Aug, but as yet it has not arrived. Can you trace it for us? as we would like very much to have his belongings. We know of three officers who were killed on the same date as my son & their friends have received their kits fully a month ago. This makes us think it strange that our son's kit hasn't arrived home. We will feel greatly obliged if you will kindly give us all the information re my son's death at your disposal.

Yours Respectfully

John Revie[11]

Nine former North Irish Horsemen were killed in the attack by the 1st Royal Irish Rifles. Two had been with the North Irish Horse before the war began, Rifleman Ernest Augustus Stevenson of Lurgan, County Armagh, and Rifleman John Connell. Another, Rifleman Cyril (Aubrey) Morrison of Belfast, had enlisted within days of war being declared, though only aged sixteen at the time. The others were enlistees from late 1915 and 1916 –

Lance Corporal Thomas Stevenson of Newtownards, County Down, aged twenty-five; Lance Corporal William John Robinson of Broughshane, County Antrim, aged twenty; Rifleman Armour John Knox from County Tyrone, aged twenty-four; Rifleman Neason Henry Hale of Ballymoney, Antrim, aged twenty-two; Rifleman John Baxter of Donaghcloney, County Down, aged twenty-eight; and Rifleman Alexander Johnston of Camlough, County Armagh. Two were posthumously awarded medals for their bravery that day – Rifleman Johnston a Military Medal and Lance Corporal Robinson a Distinguished Conduct Medal.

> When all [Robinson's] company runners had become casualties, he acted as a runner all day, taking messages under severe conditions to advanced posts in shell holes. His successful efforts in performing this extremely dangerous and most important work contributed very greatly to the repulse of two subsequent counter-attacks.[12]

Another former North Irish Horseman killed on 16 August was Private Henry Mortimer of Portadown, who was serving in the 9th Royal Irish Fusiliers.

It is a measure of the awfulness of the fighting on 16 August that all but one of the casualties listed above have no known grave. Their bodies either disappeared into the mud of the Passchendaele ridge or were hastily buried on or near the battlefield in graves soon lost or destroyed. Only Rifleman Baxter has a known grave. He lies in the Ypres Reservoir Cemetery. The others are commemorated with tens of thousands of their fellows on the Tyne Cot Memorial, which sits atop the ridge that they were never able to reach.

Of course many more were wounded in the August fighting. North Irish Horseman Lance Corporal William Bell O'Donoghue was in the line with an officer of the regiment on 16 August when wounded in the arm and leg. '… we were having a pretty rough time,' the officer later wrote. 'O'Donoughue behaved most splendidly. I have been his troop officer for some time now, and he behaved in a "tight corner" exactly as I knew he would.'[13] Among the wounded of the 1st Royal Irish Rifles were former Horsemen William Alexander Kelly of Dromore, shot in the neck, Alexander Mitchell of Dunmurry, a head wound, and Thomas Jonas Trotter, wounded in the knee, thigh and neck. Lance Corporal David Kerr of Ballymena was badly wounded in the right arm (it had to be amputated). Former Horseman

Second Lieutenant Richard Cramp, who had once applied for a wound stripe for injuries sustained in falling off his horse, received a bullet wound in his right shoulder while attached to the 7th Royal Irish Rifles. Second Lieutenant Alexander Dundee, with the 13th Royal Irish Rifles, sustained injuries including a fractured left elbow, gunshot wounds to the back, and shell splinters in the left leg.

Third Ypres continued through September, October and into November, when the exhausted British forces finally called a halt, having deepened the Ypres salient by a mere five miles at a cost of more than 300,000 British casualties. Among them were six more former North Irish Horsemen. Rifleman John Smith of the 1st Royal Irish Rifles was killed in action on 6 September 1917. Second Lieutenant Alfred McClelland of the 1st Royal Irish Rifles died of wounds at No.2 Australian Casualty Clearing Station, Trois Arbres, Steenwerck, on 13 October. He had been with the battalion for less than a month. Lieutenant William Shields of No.45 Squadron, Royal Flying Corps, was flying his Sopwith Camel on an offensive patrol in the early morning of 5 September when he was shot down near Comines. Second Lieutenant Robert James McCullough of the 16th Cheshire Regiment was killed in action on 22 October. Second Lieutenant James Acheson MacLean of the Royal Field Artillery was killed near Wytschaete on the night of 30 September when

> a gun pit was struck by enemy fire, the charges immediately bursting into raging flames, and threatened to envelop the whole battery, with its vast stores of ammunition. Lieutenant McLean, two brother officers and a sergeant immediately rushed to the scene, their heroic and gallant attempt to isolate the fire proving fatal. Several large shells detonated causing the immediate death of all four. They were last seen, their forms silhouetted against the evening sky, combating the raging flames.[14]

During September the 1st North Irish Horse Regiment remained at its billets near Watou. Most days were occupied with squadron parades and working parties. A gas attack on 6 September took one party working at Ypres by surprise, causing ten casualties, including Private Victor Ronaldson, Herbert Miskimmin, William Gibson, William Irwin and Robert Close. The regiment came under the command of V Corps on 7 September, but little else changed. A party of two officers and fifty men was detached for signals duty for the corps. Others were sent on prisoner of war and divisional duties. On

19 September Private Frederick Thomas Cordwell drowned while watering the horses. Thirty-year-old Cordwell was from Bristol, England. He is buried at Poperinghe New Military Cemetery.

At the end of September the regiment moved from its billets near Watou to a new camp well behind the lines, just east of St Omer. It was the end of their sojourn on the Ypres front. After a week at nearby Buysscheure the regiment marched south to Molinghem and then to Divion, on the Bethune-la Bassée front.

A new role for the 2nd Regiment

In July, news came that the 2nd North Irish Horse Regiment was to be disbanded – its men to be trained as infantry and absorbed into the 9th (Service) Battalion, Royal Irish Fusiliers. There was no choice given to the men, it was a compulsory transfer, but they would retain their cavalry pay. Other cavalry units along the western front were receiving the same news, an inevitable consequence of the losses in the infantry battalions and the relative idleness of mounted units through the long stalemate. Since May 1917 the Army Council had pushed hard to reduce cavalry numbers, a view mirrored by men in the field such as the Royal Irish Fusiliers' officer Edwin Godson:

> the Cavalry are people of little account, from that day to this they might as well have been disbanded ... They have been merely an useless drain on the pocket of the nation and an additional strain on the already over taxed transport. I reckon the fodder for a regiment needs more transport daily than the rations of a whole infantry brigade.[15]

Such views had met fierce resistance from senior officers like Haig, who still believed that the moment might come when cavalry could be used in massed attacks. As a result, only six cavalry regiments were broken up. These included the 2nd North Irish Horse and both South Irish Horse regiments. (The men of the South became the 7th (South Irish Horse) Battalion, Royal Irish Regiment.) The 1st North Irish Horse survived, for the moment at least.

On 20 July the 2nd North Irish Horse Regiment left its camp for the reserve areas, finding billets two days later at Aix-en-Issart, near the coast at Abbeville. The first and saddest task for the men of the regiment was to say farewell to their horses. This process took several weeks. First, all horses were inspected and malleined (tested for glanders) by a veterinary officer from General Headquarters. Sixty-seven were found 'unsuitable for overseas work' and immediately sent away to the Mobile Veterinary Section. Orders had been received to ship the remaining riding horses to Egypt, but the remounts section in France wasn't going to let them go without picking the best for themselves. On 8 August the regiment's best horses – 131 classed as R.1 – were taken to Boulogne and replaced with 131 R.2 horses.

On 14 August a party of seventy horsemen took charge of all the regiment's riding horses, 265 in all, and led them away from camp to the railway station at Beaurainville, the first step on the long journey to Egypt. The only horses left in camp were those used for transport. Meanwhile preparations continued for the changeover to infantry. Saddlery was handed in, the men paraded in dismounted marching order, and the officers were medically tested for their fitness for infantry service. On 23 August the regiment entrained for the 36th (Ulster) Division's Base Depot at le Havre. Here they exchanged their cavalry uniform and equipment for that of the infantryman, commenced training in infantry work, and started to get used to the idea of marching, rather than riding from place to place. The men's formal transfer to the infantry took place on 28 August and the officers three days later.

With only one North Irish Horse regiment left in France, there was also less need for reserves. At home, a fine comb had been applied to the men sent home wounded, sick, or just too old, and to those who were never likely to be fit for France. On 9 July at least twenty of these men were transferred to transport work in the Home Service Labour Corps. These included nine veterans of the fighting in August and September 1914.

In France, the 1st Regiment had also been clearing its roll of surplus men, perhaps in part to make way for a draft of thirty seasoned veterans just arrived from the 3rd Hussars. On 5 September, sixty-seven other ranks 'supernumerary to establishment' were sent to le Havre to join the men of the 2nd Regiment training as infantrymen. They were chosen for the most part on a 'last in first out' basis, shipping out many of those who had arrived as reinforcements during 1916 and 1917.

Training for the new infantrymen at le Havre lasted a month, the main purpose being to sift out those who lacked the physical ability to withstand the rigours of infantry life. Often these men were too old, and sometimes too ill-disciplined. As many as three dozen failed to make the grade and were transferred to transport work in the Labour Corps in France. They included James Lynn from Drumall, Antrim. He was thirty-nine and, although useful as a groom, was beginning to suffer from severe muscle pains as a result of his service. Belfastman Johnston Robinson was a similar age. He had served in the Boer War and had cut his age by five years when he enlisted in 1914. Scotsman Joseph Humphries was at least forty-seven years old but had been in France since 1915 with F Squadron. John Crawford, a hairdresser from Kilkeel, County Down, was another Boer War veteran, now aged forty-two.

One Horseman deserted at this time. Private William Armstrong had been in the regiment since 1912 and had served in France with C Squadron since August 1914. Whether he decamped from le Havre or was at home on leave and failed to report back is unknown.

On 20 September, 495 North Irish Horsemen were pronounced fit for infantry service and transferred to the 9th (Service) Battalion, Royal Irish Fusiliers. This battalion, part of the 36th (Ulster) Division, had been formed in Belfast in September 1914. As a sop to the dismounted men of the North Irish Horse, the battalion was renamed the 9th (North Irish Horse) Battalion, Royal Irish Fusiliers.

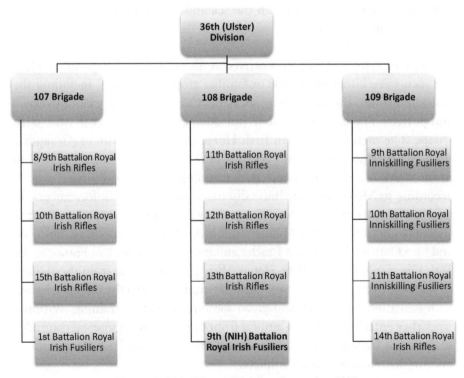

Figure 3: 36th (Ulster) Division, September 1917.

Meanwhile, the seventy North Irish Horsemen who had left camp with the horses on 14 August were making their way to Egypt under the command of Cork-born Lieutenant Thomas Henry Mowbray Leader. First stop was Marseilles, where the horses were made ready for embarkation. In all 820 horses were loaded onto the HT *Bohemian*, including the 265 of the 2nd North Irish Horse and 325 of the 2nd South Irish Horse Regiment. Along with the horses the *Bohemian* carried more than 500 military personnel. There were Indian cavalrymen returning home, Army Service Corps drivers bound for Basra, and assorted others headed for Salonika and Egypt. Those looking after the horses numbered 176, mainly men of disbanded regiments – the 2/1st Northumberland Hussars, South Irish Horse and North Irish Horse. The *Bohemian* sailed from Marseilles just after midnight on 25 August. 'We had 2 Japanese destroyers as escort for the ship,' recalled Frank McMahon,

> conditions were really tough, bad food, grooming horses and cleaning out the manure at night time. It was essential it was done at night, because the manure floated on the sea and it was a real give away for German submarines.[16]

After a short stop at Malta they arrived at Alexandria on 5 September. Here the men were kitted out in the unfamiliar tropical uniform, including the pith sun helmet, shorts and long socks instead of their heavy cloth trousers and puttees. The horses were soon unloaded and handed over to Australian troops. The men of the North Irish Horse then had the run of Alexandria until 20 September, when they boarded HMT *Sarnia* and sailed for Taranto in the south of Italy. From here they travelled by train to Florence where, according to McMahon 'the brass discussed using us as reinforcements on the Pavo' (the front on the Piave river, where British forces were assisting the Italians to hold off Austro-Hungarian forces). It came to nothing, however, and by 5 October Lieutenant Leader and his men were back in France at the 36th Division's Infantry Base Depot, their pleasant break from the routine of war now over. Here they were formally transferred to the infantry, issued with new uniform and kit and given some rudimentary training. Within a week they entrained for the Cambrai front to join their regimental comrades in their new battalion. The conversion of the 2nd North Irish Horse into an infantry battalion was now complete.

On the Hindenburg Line

The 9th (NIH) Battalion Royal Irish Fusiliers was based on a sector of the Hindenburg line in front of the city of Cambrai. They had moved here a week after the disastrous attack at Langemarck on 16 August, in sore need of rest and reinforcement. The land that greeted them was part of the sector abandoned by the Germans earlier in the year. Everything left behind had been destroyed, so as to allow no comfort or cover. 'What desolation,' wrote Lieutenant Godson as he moved in with the battalion. 'The Boches left this country in the great retreat last March and laid it waste high & low before going. No houses, no crops, no civilians, just a barren waste of rank weed & grass … [It] makes one feel very far from home.'[17]

The British front line ran in a south-easterly direction until it reached the Canal du Nord, a deep channel, but incomplete before the war began, and therefore mostly dry. Nonetheless, it was a significant barrier, its depth below ground level varying from 15 to 100 feet. To the British left, the canal ran directly north, with the Germans occupying both banks, including a heavily fortified spoil heap, thrown up during construction of the canal. To the right, the canal ran south then turned sharply to the west. The British line crossed the canal at this turning point then ran in the other direction, easterly, cutting through the remnants of a large forest – Havrincourt Wood. Most of this wood was behind the British lines, and the retreating Germans had intended to clear fell it to eliminate any cover. However, such had been the haste of their withdrawal in this sector that the task was incomplete and much cover remained. A significant feature of this part of the line was another spoil heap, known to the British as Yorkshire Bank and to the Germans as the Kalkberg (Chalk Mountain). This lay on the eastern edge of the canal at the point where it turned from south to west, in territory disputed by the British and German forces.

The German defences along this part of the Hindenburg Line were formidable, but the sector was not as well sited as it could have been, there being little opportunity to observe the British rear areas or approach routes. From the heights west of Havrincourt, the British could see as far as Cambrai. The sector itself was very quiet. Many of those opposite, such as the German 54th Infantry Division, had also been withdrawn from the fighting at Ypres. This place they called *Flandernsanatorium* – the 'Flanders convalescent home'.[18]

The 36th (Ulster) Division moved in at the end of August, the 9th Royal Irish Fusiliers taking over a section from just north of the Hermies-Havrincourt road south to the Yorkshire Bank and into Havrincourt Wood and a trench known as Hubert Avenue on Cheetham Spur. The battalion alternated in the line with the 12th Royal Irish Rifles – eight days in and eight days out. When relieved they marched three miles to the village of Ruyaulcourt, or at least what was left of it after the Germans' scorched-earth withdrawal.

Much work was done to fill the emptiness in the absence of the hospitality of French villages. Great quantities of beer were purchased and a soda water factory established (producing a drink fancifully named Boyne Water). Divisional canteens were established, adding fruit and vegetables, eggs, bread, cake and even fresh seafood to the usual rations of tobacco, biscuits, chocolate, and tinned food. There were concerts, featuring the divisional concert party *The Merry Mauves*, sporting competitions, and even agriculture on the now fallow farmland.

The first and largest draft of North Irish Horsemen to join the battalion arrived at Ruyaulcourt on 25 September. Most of the battalion was away on the front line, but those who were left greeted the new men with open arms, the regimental band 'playing them in to Ruyaulcourt where they were toasted right royally'.[19] The North Irish Horsemen spent their first days at Ruyaulcourt getting used to the new surroundings, and testing their football skills against the men of the battalion. Twice they played, and twice they lost, the score being 1–2 on each occasion. On 29 September they were able to greet the rest of the battalion when it returned from the trenches. Private John Donaldson King from Whitecross, County Armagh, wrote to his mother about his new situation:

> Just a few lines to let you know that we have joined our Battalion nearly a week ago but I had not much time to write but we are all settled now and I think we will get on all right ... The only thing we can complain of is rations – they have been very low these last few days but they are beginning to improve again but it is a queer change from our own Regiment.[20]

She would have been glad to receive the reassurance, having already lost a son in the fighting at High Wood on the Somme in July 1916.

New officers arrived at Ruyaulcourt during the next week or so – most of them from the old 2nd North Irish Horse Regiment. They included Major Whitla, Captains Uprichard, Hulse and Grant, Lieutenants Dean, Hutchinson and Whalen, and Second Lieutenant Larter. A dozen more would drift in over the following month or so. The arrival of these officers wasn't the best of news for Acting Captain Godson, who had been angling for a promotion. As he noted in his diary, '11 Officers came [with the North Irish Horse], some of them senior Captains, it would have made my adjutancy look small, very likely I would have lost it, so I need not regret not having gone to them as adjutant.'[21]

Godson need not have worried, for most of the officers of the North Irish Horse saw their transfer to the infantry as little more than a temporary arrangement. While viewing the war from the elevated heights of a cavalry mount may have been acceptable, the prospect of long marches and weeks in the mud and filth of the trenches wasn't quite what some of them had in mind when they took their commissions. So through the coming months strings were pulled and favours called in, and by the time the Battle of Cambrai began on 20 November, less than a dozen of the thirty-one North Irish Horse officers who were (or would have been) posted to the battalion were left; by the end of the year there were just five. Where did they go? Six transferred to the Tank Corps and five to the Indian Army Reserve, five faced medical boards and were declared unfit for infantry service, three were injured or hospitalised, one was allowed to resign due to his age and four transferred to other regiments. Two were severely wounded in the fighting later in 1917 and did not rejoin the battalion.

Captain Richard Filgate, then aged forty, was one of those who faced a medical hearing. A well-heeled landowner, he had been Huntsman and Deputy Master of the Louth Hounds before the war, deputing to his father-in-law Captain Filgate.[22] He had joined early in the war, served briefly with the Army Service Corps in Belfast, and was then commissioned and posted to the North Irish Horse. In July 1915 he joined C Squadron in France. However, he was badly hampered by rheumatism from an old hunting accident. The pain was manageable while he could get around on a horse, but when the regiment was converted to infantry, Filgate feared the marching would be too much to bear. A medical board classified him as permanently unfit for front-line service. He was transferred to a prisoner of war company in October 1917 but this was no more to his liking and he sought permission to resign his commission 'on the grounds of doing work of national importance'.

> I farm 1300 acres in Co Louth Ireland, all in my own hands. It is impossible to get the land worked to the best advantage in my absence, and I think that I would be doing far better work for the nation in the production of food than in my present employment.[23]

Filgate's plea was accepted.

The battalion returned to the trenches in the evening of Sunday 7 October, the North Irish Horsemen included. This was their first time in the line as infantry. The afternoon and evening were very wet and all working parties in the trenches were cancelled. New orders had come that the men were to be 'continually on the offensive while holding the line'. Despite the weather the 9th (NIH) Battalion responded with nightly patrols, inspecting enemy wire, throwing bombs into the enemy trenches, and clashing with an enemy patrol.

On 12 October the last group of North Irish Horse reinforcements, mostly the men who had taken the horses to Egypt, arrived at Ruyaulcourt. Work could now commence on fully integrating the Horsemen. After the battalion returned from the trenches, officers and men of the North Irish Horse were assigned to their new companies – A, B, C and D. The men were kept busy with working parties at Ruyaulcourt and in the line, and on construction and improvements to the village. Two more North Irish Horse officers arrived, Captain Despard and Lieutenant Vesey.

On 19 October Private John Donaldson King wrote his mother another letter:

> Just a few lines in answer to your very welcome letter and cigs ... We are having very nice weather now and a fairly good time. We got our first turn in the trenches over[,] very soft, but this is a very quiet part of the line and to tell you the truth I am far more content here than in the cavalry and I never felt in better health and you need not be afraid of me going into danger except I can't help it, and as for putting in for my commission I won't do it. I will just finish it the way I started. I am not afraid to soldier it out as a private as some of the boys are. It was easy in the North Irish Horse but it is not so easy in the infantry.[24]

The battalion was back in the line in the evening of 24 October. On 26 October a fighting patrol was sent to drive the enemy out of Wigan Copse, which they achieved with a charge which put the enemy to flight. However the clash cost one man killed and another injured. The dead man was the first North Irish Horseman to die in action since they had joined the battalion. Private Victor Nelson Bell was from Londonderry and the eldest of five brothers. He had enlisted a month after the war began, aged just seventeen, and had been in France since January 1915.

Within an hour of the clash over Wigan Copse a shell from a heavy enemy trench mortar scored a direct hit on the Lewis gun post on the right of Yorkshire Bank, killing the three men who held it. The dead men were all formerly of the 2nd North Irish Horse Regiment, and all from its Inniskilling Dragoons squadron – Private Thomas Dickinson of Galashiels in Scotland, aged twenty-eight, Private John Dunn, of Hackney, Middlesex, aged twenty-six, and Private George Christopher Reid, of Springfield, County Fermanagh, aged thirty-two. Their remains, and that of Private Bell, were brought back to Ruyaulcourt and laid to rest in the nearby Neuville-Bourjonval British Cemetery. It was a bloody introduction to life in the trenches.

For the next five days things were hotter in this sector, with machine guns and artillery active during day and night. Relief came on the evening of 1 November, the men marching back to the relative safety and comfort of Ruyaulcourt. The next day was occupied with cleaning, an inspection of clothing and equipment, and football. On Saturday 3 November C Company returned to the trenches. There was a large-scale trench raid in the offing, and it was they who were given the job. The aim was not to capture ground, but to seize enemy soldiers for intelligence and unit identification and to kill as many others as possible. It was also an opportunity to 'blood' the men of the North Irish Horse. By all accounts they were keen.

The objective was a stretch of trench running from the front line at Canal du Nord to the outskirts of German-held Havrincourt. The Ulstermen were to approach it from the south and hit it on a 200-yard front east from the canal. The artillery and trench mortars of the 12th Royal Irish Rifles would assist with a 'box barrage', designed to cut off all possible approaches by the enemy while the attack was underway.

As darkness fell, C Company in four parties entered the dry canal from their trenches on Yorkshire Bank and quietly advanced towards the German lines. They comprised four officers, sixty-seven other ranks, six stretcher-

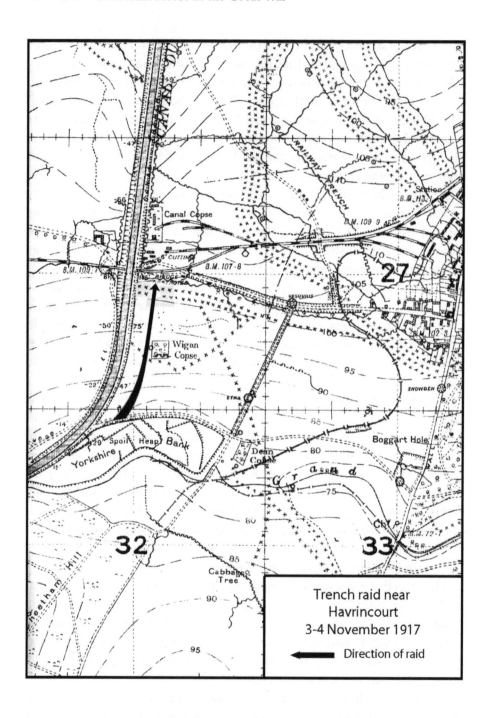

Trench raid near
Havrincourt
3-4 November 1917

◀━━━ Direction of raid

bearers and four men of the Royal Engineers. When close to the German wire the raiders left the cover of the canal and worked their way through gaps in the wire identified by earlier patrols. Only then, as they waited almost on the parapet of the German trenches, did the leading officer send up a red flare. Immediately the British artillery, trench and Stokes mortars and machine guns opened up on key points and, as a feint, on the nearby spoil heap. The Irishmen of the first and third parties leaped into the trenches and caught the enemy completely by surprise. The fight was short and bloody. According to Major General Oliver Nugent, GOC of the 36th (Ulster) Division,

> they rushed in and first met a party of 16 men coming out of their trenches. They had a lively fight with them and eventually bayonetted the whole lot. Another party of Germans were hunted out of the trenches up against their own wire and they were either bayoneted or shot. The squealing of the Germans could be heard back in our lines. Our men were rather excited and saw red and they took no prisoners. They did take some at first but got bored with them and killed them. The Germans fought quite well apparently when they were cornered.[25]

Meanwhile, the Royal Engineers were put in charge of a tunnelled dugout and blew it in after the enemy inside refused to surrender. The fourth party cleared the wire in front of them with a Bangalore torpedo and drove some enemy out of the rifle pits in the rear, sustaining two casualties. But the raid didn't go completely as planned. The second party on the right, whose job was to roll up the flank of the German trench and stop any reinforcements, found repaired wire where gaps should have been. Though held up for a while they eventually got through, having suffered heavy losses from enemy bombing.

The fight lasted twenty minutes before the Irishmen retired, amidst a heavy retaliatory bombardment on Yorkshire Bank. It seems they had had the better of it. It was estimated that some forty Germans were shot or bayoneted and more killed in the blown-in dugouts. The cost was one officer severely wounded and one other slightly wounded, one NCO killed, three other ranks missing believed killed (correctly), thirteen other ranks wounded, and one Royal Engineer severely wounded. All four of those killed were North Irish Horsemen – Sergeant Richard Irwin and Privates John Ford, John Donaldson King (whose mother would have just received his letter promising he would keep out of danger 'except I can't help it') and

Robert Heathwood. Among the wounded were Horsemen Lance Corporal Thomas Alexander Murphy and Private Thomas Charles Hawthorne.

According to Major General Nugent, the returning men were 'very pleased' with their night's work. The only dampener was the lack of prisoners. Nugent explained to his wife:

> They are men of the North Irish Horse recently sent to us and have never yet had a chance of killing a German and they got excited and killed everyone instead of taking some prisoners as proof of success and also because we want some prisoners [as] often as possible for examination.[26]

The following day the men of C Company were feted as heroes, with an inspection by their divisional commander. The post mortems would continue for weeks and from many perspectives. Medals were awarded to eight of the raiders – Military Crosses to Lieutenant Crosbie and Second Lieutenant Murphy, a Distinguished Conduct Medal to Sergeant Parmenter, and Military Medals to Henry Mackinson, George Craig, John Morrison, Thomas Chambers and Robert Averell. Lieutenant Godson, who thought the raid 'just missed being a roaring success', privately criticised his junior officers for not spotting the unbroken wire on the right.[27]

When Lieutenant Hutchinson had recovered from his own wounds, he did his best to heal those of his comrade's family. Maggie Irwin, the widow of one of those killed, received the following letters from the Lieutenant:

> Dear Mrs Irwin.
>
> I would have written to you very much sooner only I was dangerously hit myself the night your husband was killed … I do not want to stir up your sorrow afresh, but I simply must write and tell you how much I thought of him. I have been in charge of his troop since August 1916 and when we joined the Fusiliers lately, we were in the same company and on the night of the raid he was with me at the head of our party and I always felt that when he was with me I had a good pal as well as a good Serjeant, God himself only knows why I should have lived and he taken, ever since I was out of danger I have felt the loss of a good friend. Please if there is anything I can do let me know. I am still in bed and will not be up for a couple of weeks yet, I got six wounds but the dangerous one was a piece of shell that ripped up my lung.

Dear Mrs Irwin.

... You asked me about your husband's last moments. As far as I know he was unconscious when the stretcher bearers went to bring him in and I understand that he died before he was actually brought to our lines. If you know any of the Boys out there I am sure they could tell you more details, but you see I was hit practically at the same time, but being able to walk a little I got on a bit before I collapsed and was taken back by some of the men returning from the enemy lines.

I hope you will not be angry at the enclosed, which I want you to accept as a little xmas box for the little ones. It will be a sad time for you and if this little token of my sympathy will help to give pleasure to the children and through them to yourself, believe me it will be a very great pleasure indeed.[28]

Sergeant Irwin was buried at Neuville-Bourjonval British Cemetery. The family of 22-year-old Shankill man Private Robert Heathwood never quite learned the details of his fate, as his body was not recovered. He is commemorated at Thiepval Memorial. The bodies of Privates King and Ford were recovered by the Germans, as they cleared their own dead from the trenches, and laid with respect in the military cemetery in Cambrai East. Ford, a farmer from Coolbuck, County Fermanagh, left behind a young wife, Margaret, and a three-year-old child, Kathleen. Private King's mother was left mourning the loss of another son.

On the evening of 8 November the battalion returned to the line. This nine-day stint would be a quiet one, but miserable at the start due to continuous rain. The trenches, especially on Yorkshire Bank, were badly flooded and in need of repair – all available men were put to work on repairs, improvements and drainage. On 15 and 16 November unfamiliar visitors came to reconnoitre the line in the form of several 'heavy machine gun' officers. Most likely these were men of the Tank Corps preparing for the mighty tank attack to come in just a few days. The attack on the Hindenburg Line around Cambrai had been meticulously planned and would feature a relatively novel tactic for this war – surprise – through the use of massed tanks to clear a path for the infantry, and 'unregistered shooting' by the artillery. Tanks had been used since the Battle of the Somme with varying success, their mechanical unreliability and tendency to get lost balancing their undoubted shock value and ability to punch a hole through previously impenetrable wire and machine-gun posts. The big difference this time would be the number deployed – some 476, including 378 'fighting' tanks. Training, too, was much improved, with infantry and tank units working together intensively through November.

The battle was timed to commence on the morning of 20 November, along a five to six mile front from the Canal du Nord east to the Bonavis Ridge. The intention was to break through the Hindenburg lines and seize the St Quentin Canal crossings at Masnières and Marcoing, and then capture the Masnières-Beaurevoir line beyond it. The cavalry would then pour through the gap, isolate Cambrai and seize the crossings of the Sensée river to the north. Bourlon Wood, a vital ridge, would be captured. This would allow the capture of Cambrai and the St Quentin Canal north to the Sensée, and the defeat of all the German forces cut off to the west as far as the Canal du Nord.

The 36th (Ulster) Division was positioned to the left of the attack. Its job was to push the Germans out of the positions they held to the west of the Canal du Nord, sweeping north as far as the village of Moeuvres and then Inchy. The work of the first day fell to 109 Brigade; 107 and 108 Brigades, including the 9th (NIH) Battalion, were held in reserve.

Despite fears that the Germans had discovered the plan, hope ran high on the eve of the offensive. 'The setting is so different in every way,' wrote 9th (NIH) Battalion officer Lieutenant Godson.

> No preliminary bombardment & no extra firing. Hundreds of guns will open at 6.20am tomorrow which have never even registered. I doubt if the Boche has even an inkling of what is in store ... Tanks are the 'piece de resistance' 1 to every 75 yds. If they fail, all fails. The wire is unpenetrable to infantry & costs thousands of shells to cut. Tanks can Waltz through wire when they get up to it, & if so can then cross the trenches ... Infantry follow next. Then a mass of Cavalry push through.[29]

In dull mist at 6.20 on the morning of 20 November the British unleashed their artillery barrage. It was a complete surprise.

> all of a sudden the British brought down appalling drum fire on our position, forcing us to take cover in the nearest dugout. When ... the fire was lifted to the rear, we immediately occupied our positions. The sight that greeted us was completely unexpected. About twenty to thirty tanks were bearing down on us and they were only about fifty to sixty metres away.[30]

The Germans were forced back with heavy losses. Havrincourt soon fell, as did Graincourt, Ribecourt, Marcoing and much of Masnières. Only at Flesquières in the centre were the attackers thwarted. The first objective of the 36th (Ulster) Division, the spoil heap, was taken with relative ease by the 10th Inniskillings. Following this they worked their way forward along the German trenches, clearing dugouts and taking a large number of prisoners. By 10.00am they had reached the Demicourt–Flesquières road. The 9th Inniskillings resumed the advance, and then the 11th, clearing all the German trenches on the left of the canal and capturing strongpoints at Locks 7 and 6. By late afternoon they were consolidating positions well to the north of the Cambrai-Bapaume road. Their casualties had been light, but one of those killed was former North Irish Horseman Private Alexander Martin of Killycolpy, County Tyrone. He was one of the forty who had transferred to the Royal Inniskilling Fusiliers in January 1917.

Throughout this day, the 9th (NIH) Battalion was held in reserve. At 8.20am, as the Inniskillings were preparing to assault the spoil heap, the battalion moved forward to a position 500 yards east of Velu Wood. In the early afternoon they moved again, this time to the canal crossing on the Havrincourt-Hermies road, and then north to a position known as R.3. Heavy rain began to fall and the men found shelter in dugouts along Maxwell Avenue, an old British communication trench, and Derry Switch, the old front-line trench running north. Nonetheless, it was a miserable night.

The morning of 21 November brought further success. The Flesquières salient was quickly overrun and the Germans were pushed back to the Bourlon Wood and Fontaine-Notre-Dame. However, this would be the last of the dramatic advances, for while the village was taken, the defenders stubbornly held on to the wood. West of the Canal du Nord, 109 Brigade advanced further and in the afternoon attacked the village of Moeuvres. Although they were able to force their way into the southern part of the village, heavy fire from machine guns in the village and the Hindenburg trenches to the west made the position untenable and they were forced to withdraw.

The 9th (NIH) Battalion moved up to the enemy's old lines near Lock 7, where it spent the night in dugouts. Tomorrow would be their turn to join the battle, but while they were relatively fresh, their preparation had been far from ideal, as Major General Nugent confided in a letter to his wife:

It rained hard all the night of the 20th and most of yesterday there was a soft drizzle. The mud is awful and there are no roads into the recaptured area. The men have neither greatcoats nor blankets and no shelter and they have been out in the open since the 20th without a chance of sleep except what they can get lying in the mud.[31]

For the North Irish Horsemen who made up much of the 9th (NIH) Battalion, this would be their first experience as infantrymen in a real battle. While many had served as cavalry on the retreat from Mons in 1914 and had taken their turn on trench fatigues, and in recent months had occupied the trenches around Havrincourt and even participated in the trench raid, none had been involved in anything like this.

In the early hours of Tuesday 22 November 108 Brigade replaced 109 in their positions outside Moeuvres. The 9th (NIH) Battalion moved to support positions north of the Bapaume-Cambrai Road. The plan for this day and the next was that the two brigades would attack north on either side of the canal: 107 would clear the Hindenburg support trenches as far as the canal opposite Moeuvres while 108 would attack and capture Moeuvres itself. The two brigades would then push forward to capture Inchy and the ground to the east of it. Success here would make the German defence of Bourlon Wood to the right untenable, and open the possibility of further gains.

The plan had some chance of success – the troops were fresh and the Germans sorely pressed – but the odds of failure were greater. As the attackers pushed into and north of Moeuvres they would be exposed to fire on their flank from higher positions in that sector and the German supports to the north-west. Furthermore, if the attack by 107 Brigade did not keep up, the men attacking Moeuvres would be exposed to fire from their right flank.

After a forty-minute bombardment the attack commenced at 11.00am. On the right of the canal, leading companies of the 15th Royal Irish Rifles gained 500 yards of the Hindenburg support lines, but the 10th were unable to get any further. To the left, troops of the 56th (1st London) Division pushed along the enemy trenches and captured Tadpole Copse. In the centre, the 12th Royal Irish Rifles were immediately successful. They drove the German defenders out of much of the village, reaching as far as the cemetery on the western edge and the northern boundary. However, the trenches to the east of the village could not be cleared and, with the failure of 107 Brigade to keep up, the Rifles came under heavy machine-gun fire from that sector. By 3.30pm the enemy was seen massing for a counter-attack in Hobart Street, a German support trench running north to north-west of Moeuvres. An artillery barrage and reinforcements were called for, but the Rifles were driven from the village, 'apparently rather easily', was Godson's harsh assessment. The reinforcements, the 9th (NIH) Battalion, came up at 5.30pm but all they could do was help consolidate positions in the trenches immediately to the south of the village.

The 12th Royal Irish Rifles had sustained heavy casualties, including the loss of two company commanders (they would lose another the next day). One of these was 37-year-old Captain David McCausland, a former North Irish Horseman. According to the regimental diary he 'got out in front of his men and showed great courage until he was unfortunately killed'. The other, Captain William Bruce Stuart, was younger brother of North Irish Horseman Leslie Ion Stuart. He 'with his men refused to retire. He was shot in the throat but carried on giving out orders to his coy until he was again shot in the head and died.'[32]

That evening orders were received for an immediate counter-attack to take back the village. With the early onset of darkness on these late autumn days, this would be a difficult mission, but at 8.30pm three companies of the 9th (NIH) Battalion – A, B and C – made the attempt. They were driven back and took up defensive positions for the night.

The next day would be a repeat of the 22nd, with 107 Brigade attempting to roll up the Hindenburg support trenches on one side of the Canal du Nord and 108 making another attempt on Moeuvres. The difference this time would be that sixteen tanks had been provided, though none were available for the attack on Moeuvres 'where I most want them', wrote Nugent.[33]

Nugent was pessimistic about the prospects. '[T]he Germans have brought up large reinforcements and in my opinion what we don't get today we shan't get at all, unless we get Bourlon Hill. After 4 days' continuous fighting we are all rather 'out'.'[34] Nor did the weather help. The showers continued and a cold wind blew up, bringing the prospect of snow. Following a heavy bombardment of Moeuvres the attack commenced at 10.30am, the 12th Royal Irish Rifles on the left and the 9th (NIH) Battalion on the right. The Germans had anticipated the attack and commenced heavy shelling of the British trenches. Captain Godson had moved up to advanced battalion headquarters and soon found himself cut off from all communication with the rear. As the General's representative at the forward post, he took it on himself to take command. When the 12th Rifles, which was 'not in much form', fell back to their assembly trenches, Godson ordered the leading two companies of the 2nd Royal Irish Rifles to support them in a renewed attack. This did the trick, and the attack was pushed into the village.

Meanwhile a company of the 9th (NIH) Battalion made a feint attack on the strongly-wired trench running east from the village, and got in at one point, clearing it to near the canal. The other three companies had got into their sector of the village by 11.00am and held their position. An enemy counter-attack from the trenches to the west was driven off. The fighting continued through the day and despite heavy losses the enemy was gradually forced back. A third company of the 2nd Rifles was sent in to assist the 9th (NIH) Battalion, and the fourth company was sent to help those fighting on the right.

By dusk three-quarters of the village was in the hands of the Irish, but the attack by 107 Brigade on the far side of the canal had failed once again, even with the support of tanks. Exposed to enemy fire on three sides, it was agreed that the village could not be held, and the three battalions were withdrawn once again to a line along the outskirts of the village. C and D companies of the 9th (NIH) Battalion took up position in the sunken road just south of the village, while A and B companies trudged back to the trenches north of the Bapaume-Cambrai road. '[The men] are absolutely worn out from cold and lack of sleep and above all want of hot food,' wrote Nugent. 'It is really dreadful going round to see the white drawn faces and red eyes of overtired men and their clothes poor beggars. They have no time to wash nor much water to wash with.'[35]

Towards dawn on 24 November the exhausted men of the 9th (NIH) Battalion were relieved and with the other battalions of 108 Brigade, marched out to Hermies for rest and re-organisation. In the two days of fighting they had sustained more than eighty casualties. Among the officers, one was dead and six wounded (one of whom died the next day). Thirteen other ranks were dead and two more would die soon after. Sixty-seven others were wounded. Ten of the dead or dying were North Irish Horsemen. Lance Corporals Hugh Flanagan, twenty-one, of Dunluce Avenue Belast, and Frederick Scanlon, twenty-eight, of Bagnalstown, County Carlow, had been in France since arriving with F Squadron in November 1915. Private James Sleator of Keady, County Armagh, twenty-two years old, was a later reinforcement. Four of the ten had served in the 6th Inniskilling Dragoons (Service Squadron) when it was part of the 2nd North Irish Horse Regiment

– Privates William James Turkington of Killygarvin, County Tyrone, Christy McWilliams of Enniskillen, Henry Orr of Brookeborough, County Fermanagh, and Samuel Price of Belfast.

Three others were initially reported as wounded, but died soon after. Private George Galbraith of Glengormley, County Antrim, was carried off the battlefield, badly hurt. He died the next day. Private John Smyth clung to life a little longer. Evacuated to No.6 Military Hospital at Rouen, he died on 1 December. Smyth's company commander, who had served in his squadron in the North Irish Horse, wrote the familiar words of comfort to his parents John and Annie: '[He was] a fine soldier and popular among his comrades.'[36]

After being told that he was wounded, the family of Private William Petty of Agincourt Avenue, Belfast, heard nothing more of his fate, causing his father to write this heartfelt letter to Army officials in Dublin:

It is now nearly three months since my son William J Petty ... was reported wounded and I have no further official news with regard to him since yours of the (26th?). Surely something must be known about him in 3 months. I cannot think he is alive or he would have written to me or got someone to write for him. Can you give me any further (..?..) regarding him if he is alive in France. If I knew even the worst it would relieve this terrible suspense. Hoping you will be able to give me some information for which I shall feel thankful.[37]

It was not until October 1918 that Petty was officially recorded as 'presumed dead'.

Others among the wounded were Horsemen Lance Sergeant Hubert Roe and Privates Alexander Armstrong, Jeremiah Clarke, Robert John Kennedy, James Norman Fulton and John Riddell. Riddell had had the misfortune to be at home on leave when surplus men in the 1st Regiment were chosen to join the 2nd Regiment training as infantry. Riddell's name was put on the list, which brought him to Cambrai and a machine-gun bullet through his thigh.

Two Military Crosses, three Distinguished Conduct Medals and three Military Medals were later awarded to the men of the battalion for their part in the fighting at Moeuvres, Captain Despard and Lance Sergeant Hubert Roe being among the recipients.

No further attempts were made on Moeuvres and the 36th (Ulster) Division was relieved. In bitterly cold wind and snow the men, 'absolutely beat', trudged to the safety of their new camps – 108 Brigade to Beaumetz-lès-Cambrai. On 27 November the division marched farther away from the battle zone, the 9th (NIH) Battalion finding accommodation in the detraining camp on the southern edge of Rocquigny. Word now came that the division had been transferred to the XVII Corps and would move north to the Arras front, with three week's rest and recuperation promised at Ecoivres, near Mont St Éloi.

In the evening of 29 November the 9th (NIH) Battalion marched the short distance to Ytres station. After a long roundabout train journey they arrived at Beaumetz-lès-Loges, south-west of Arras, and marched to billets at nearby Simencourt. As they fell asleep, grateful for the rest, the Germans opened a massive counterstroke on the Cambrai front. The attack, accompanied by heavy artillery bombardment, fell to the north on Bourlon Wood and westward, and along the eastern battlefront and even farther to the south. While the north held, on the far south of the British line the defences broke, the Germans taking Villers-Guislain and Gonnelieu. Hundreds of guns and thousands of prisoners were taken. Divisions taken out of the line to rest were ordered back as fast as they could march. The 9th (NIH) Battalion left Simencourt and marched south, arriving at Gommecourt on the old Somme front in the evening of 30 November. Another day's march brought the battalion back to Rocquigny, the men dead beat. On 2 December they marched to Metz-en-Couture, just south of Havrincourt Wood, where they billeted for the night. The closer they got to the fighting, the more disturbing was the news. 'Terrible rumours about a reverse around Gouzecourt,' wrote Godson. 'Over 100 guns lost & thousands of prisoners, 6,000 probably. What a change from the 20th & 21st.'[38]

As the 36th (Ulster) Division marched back to the Cambrai front the line had held, more or less, but the crisis was far from over, and Bourlon Wood was now at the peak of a dangerously exposed salient. Both 108 and 109 Brigades were ordered to relieve defenders holding the line to the south of Marcoing. The 9th (NIH) Battalion moved up with the rest of 108 Brigade to support trenches, part of the old British front-line system, along Beaucamp ridge. It was freezing cold, with a bitter wind blowing. Soon after the men of the 9th (NIH) Battalion were ordered to move again, this time into the Couillet Wood south of Marcoing as reserve to 88 Brigade. The following day the rest of the division came up, ready to join the fighting, but these plans had to be quickly changed following a decision to withdraw from the Bourlon Salient, surrendering much of the ground won and held at such cost in the past fortnight. The fighting at Cambrai had left Godson pessimistic:

Certainly we are only second best in this area! our artillery negligible & what there is doesn't open promptly enough. Boche artillery very strong & able to put down a heavy barrage. German planes seem to come & go as they please, low or high. German observation balloons prominent, none of ours – no anti-aircraft guns. Result:- attacks are left to be countered by our infantry in hand to hand bombing fights. Our infantry morale having been previously knocked about by heavy accurate shell fire. The enemy infantry ... is fighting with unusual dash & tenacity.[39]

The withdrawal took place on the night of 4/5 December. At the same time, 108 Brigade moved up to what would be the new front-line position in the Couillet Valley. On the following evening 109 Brigade moved into the line on the adjacent Welsh Ridge. The line now ran east from the Canal du Nord, roughly along the old German intermediate defensive line, taking in the captured towns of Havrincourt, Flesquières and Ribecourt. South of Marcoing the line turned sharply south. This turning point in the line was at the northern end of Welsh Ridge. The densely-wooded Couillet Valley, also running from south to north, lay to the west of Welsh Ridge, and the Highland Ridge farther west. Running across the valley and ridges was the old Hindenburg trench system. Although useful for the defenders, this system was badly damaged, faced the wrong direction, and its communication lines still ran into territory held by the Germans. These had to be blocked off, but close combat with grenade and bayonet was inevitable. Second Lieutenant Lucy described the situation, close by the 9th (NIH) Battalion:

Even in darkness I could see it was a rotten, hastily dug trench with a poor parapet and no fire-bays. I took over from a sergeant, who gave me very little information beyond the general direction of the enemy. He was undisguisedly wind-up, and his men were shaken ...

I posted two platoons along the bad trench, warned the men about enemy patrols, [and] found touch with the company on the left ... I turned left to explore farther, and a sentry stopped me at a block. 'You can't go any farther, sir. There are Germans on the other side.' I turned back, found company headquarters quite near, and went down a deep dug-out to the company commander, who was sitting half asleep by a lighted candle. I told him our position appeared to be very queer, and that as far as I could make out the front line was a right angle, and that at the apex we shared the main trench with the enemy. I told him the nearest Germans must be only about twenty yards from where he was sitting, as his dug-out was close to the apex ... At the dawn 'Stand-to' I prowled round near the block. On our side of it the big trench was a shambles. Freshly killed, mutilated bodies of Irish of another regiment were laid along the fire-step, and a hand of one protruding into the trench had all the fingers neatly sheared off as if by a razor blade. Beyond our block the Germans had built their own block, and from behind it they began to fire pineapples at us. Then British shrapnel burst over us, and we found ourselves getting a dose of morning hate from our own guns.[40]

Throughout 5 and 6 December the Germans concentrated their attacks on Welsh Ridge with heavy artillery fire and hand-to-hand fighting in the old Hindenburg Line trenches. The brunt of the attack fell on 109 Brigade, particularly the 9th Inniskillings, who had to be relieved after just one day, so great were their losses. But the line held, and on 7 December the 11th Inniskillings counter-attacked, driving the Germans off the crest of the ridge. In Couillet Valley things were a little quieter for the 9th (NIH) Battalion, though still dangerous. The battalion was relieved in the evening of 8 December. They had four days' respite in brigade support, but large working parties were still required to carry wire and other supplies to the front line. At dusk on 12 December they moved back into the line, this time relieving the 2nd Royal Irish Rifles in the right sub-sector on Welsh Ridge. Then news came that the 36th (Ulster) Division would be relieved. For Major General Nugent it was none too soon:

We are really going out to rest this time, always of course if the Boche permits. We are going right back into civilisation behind the Somme battlefields into real villages and houses. It will be everything to the men to get into comfortable surroundings where there are estaminets where they can meet and talk and feel warm and we shall be able to start our Follies and cinema again. I hope nothing will intervene to prevent us moving out of this sordid waste of mud and ruins.[41]

The relief began on the night of 14 December. The turn of the 9th (NIH) Battalion came two days later, but they didn't go without a last act of defiance. At 5.00pm, as they prepared to leave, a patrol led by North Irish Horse officer George Waller Vesey stormed a German outpost in a trench running out from the British lines. Several of the enemy were shot or bayoneted, their machine gun captured, and their regiment identified. The patrol then blocked the trench, securing it from the enemy. Lieutenant Vesey was later awarded a Military Cross for his role in this action. North Irish Horsemen Sergeant George Adams Henry and Lance Corporal Alan George Clarke were awarded Military Medals.

At 9.00pm the 9th (NIH) Battalion was relieved and marched through falling snow to Metz-en-Couture. The fighting in this second phase of the Battle of Cambrai had caused them mercifully few casualties – one officer killed and two wounded, and twenty-one other ranks wounded. Among the latter were two North Irish Horseman, both of whom would die from their wounds. Lance Corporal William Thomson, a 26-year-old farmer from Ballymoney, was seriously wounded on 6 December and evacuated to the 48th Casualty Clearing Station at Ytres. He died soon after. Twenty-one year-old Patrick Sheridan of Drumullen, County Cavan, had received a gunshot wound to the chest. Soon after his father James Sheridan received the following official notification:

> Regret to report War Office wire 41581 Pte Patrick Sheridan 9th Irish Fus dangerously ill in 10 General Hospital, Rouen 18th Decr Gunshot wound chest. Regret permission to visit cannot be granted.[42]

It wasn't until 18 January that Sheridan's family was told that he was 'out of danger', but they also knew by then that his spine had been severed. When he was well enough to travel he was brought home to Ireland. He died at St Vincent's Hospital, Dublin, on 9 December 1918.

Among the non-fatal casualties of the December fighting were more North Irish Horsemen. Belfast library assistant William Brown was taken out of the line suffering from trench foot, Second Lieutenant Harold Edwin Bray had been wounded in the shoulder and foot, and Private William Warke received a head wound. Private Samuel Shiels of Crosskeys, Ballybay, was hit in the back by shrapnel and evacuated to England. Jack McGuigan, who had enlisted with Frank McMahon in 1914, was evacuated with an attack of trench fever severe enough to end his front-line service. For one, the sights and sounds of the last month's fighting had been too much to bear. Private James Magill, a railway labourer from Ballymena, was hospitalised suffering from shellshock.

On 17 December the 9th (NIH) Battalion left Metz-en-Couture and travelled through blizzards and deep snow to new billets at Coullemont, north-east of Doullens. Soon after Christmas they moved again, this time to Boves, outside Amiens.

The year ended with a new beginning for some. On 28 December up to forty men of the battalion transferred to the Tank Corps. Some twenty-four were former North Irish Horse cavalrymen and two were former Inniskilling Dragoons. This was only part of a much greater draft to the Tank Corps from assorted regiments, in part to make up the losses at Cambrai. They joined eleven North Irish Horse officers and five other ranks who had transferred to the Tank Corps during 1917. On 7 January 1918 twelve men from the 1st North Irish Horse Regiment transferred to the Tank Corps, and four others later that year.

In the Second World War the North Irish Horse would serve with distinction in North Africa and Italy as a tank regiment. These fifty-eight officers and men can therefore be seen as pioneers for the regiment. For the record, it appears that the first Horseman to join the Tank Corps was Captain Eustace Maude, who was seconded to its predecessor the Heavy Branch Machine Gun Corps on 8 December 1916. Second Lieutenant Mitchell, a veteran of August 1914, followed soon after, being commissioned from the ranks of the North Irish Horse in January 1917. The first of the other ranks to join the tanks were Wesley Freeland and Gustaf Akerlind, who had transferred in March 1917. Freeland, from Lothairn Avenue, Belfast, had worked as a compositor in a print shop before the war. Akerlind, the son of a Swedish engineer, had been working as an apprentice fitter at the Harland & Wolff shipyard in Belfast when the war began. Although he had only a year left of his five-year apprenticeship, he enlisted immediately and went to France with D Squadron in May 1915. He served in France with the Tank Corps during 1917 before transferring to Officer Cadet School. Commissioned as a second lieutenant in the Tank Corps in June 1918, he later served on the Russian front in the war against the Bolsheviks.

For the North Irish Horsemen who transferred to the Tank Corps at the end of 1917, the immediate reward was being shipped to England for a lengthy period of training. While many would return to France with the Tank Corps to participate in the final months of fighting, only two would lose their lives.

The 1st Regiment at Cambrai

What of the 1st North Irish Horse Regiment during this period? They too had expected to play a role at Cambrai. At the beginning of October the regiment had moved to Divion, on the Béthune-la Bassée front, where they spent a month training. From 12 November they rode south to Bapaume, via Estrée-Wamin, Sarton, Ribemont and Dernancourt, arriving on 19 November. The regiment was still attached to V Corps, which was to be thrown into the battle after the initial breakthrough had been made, advancing north and north-east as far as the river Sensée, pushing across the river and winning the height to its north. As it turned out, V Corps was not deployed until much later in the battle.

On the day of the attack, 20 November, all but one squadron of the 1st North Irish Horse were temporarily attached to the 40th Division of IV Corps for 'tactical duties' – advanced guard, scouting and conveying messages. For five days they stood to at Bapaume, 'ready to move at one hour's notice'. But the call never came. The 40th Division did join the fighting on 23 November, capturing much of Bourlon Wood after a hard fight, but this was no work for cavalry. Even the work of getting to the front was a trial, through heavy traffic over roads collapsing under the strain. The 40th Division dispensed with the services of the North Irish Horse on 26 November. The regiment returned to V Corps and resumed training. It was as well that they did not hear the comments of Oliver Nugent on the utility of the cavalry in this battle:

> The papers are full of what the Cavalry have done. It is a fact that the Cavalry have done absolutely nothing except block the roads and follow the Infantry ... [The Cavalry] is as much out of date in this war as a naked man with a stone axe.[43]

By now it was clear to all that cavalry would have no further role to play at Cambrai, and on 27 November the 1st North Irish Horse marched further out of the way to Sarton, near Doullens. However, it wasn't long before they were needed. V Corps had moved into the line at Cambrai at the end of November, and two troops of the North Irish Horse were soon called on to assist at corps headquarters. Then, on 9 December, five officers and 123 men were sent forward for infantry duty with the 59th (2nd North Midland) Division on the Bilhem-Chapel Wood Switch, an old German trench running

roughly north–south behind Havrincourt and west of Marcoing. They stayed
there until Christmas Eve. The regiment also sent their Hotchkiss gunners
under Lieutenant Donald Hodson to provide a permanent garrison in the
line. The 59th Division had been fighting since 29 November, helping stem
the German attack and making a safe withdrawal from the Bourlon salient.
They were exhausted and must have welcomed the help.

North Irish Horse regimental headquarters remained at Sarton until 21
December, when they moved farther west to winter quarters in the village
of Barly, north of Amiens. After Christmas the Hotchkiss gunners serving
in the line were relieved and billeted at V Corps headquarters. Three officers
and seventy-six men replaced them, this time under orders of the 63rd (Royal
Naval) Division. While they were in the line, on 30 and 31 December, the
Germans undertook a significant action on nearby Welsh Ridge. The lines
held by the 63rd Division were broken into and lost in several places, but
heavy counter-attacks managed to win back most of the ground. The action
cost the division sixty-eight officers and 1,366 other ranks killed, wounded
or missing. How the North Irish Horsemen were used in the defence is
unknown, but no casualties have been identified.

Notes

1. Letter dated 4 November 1917, in Perry (ed.), *Major General Oliver Nugent and the Ulster Division 1915–1918*, p.180.
2. Letter dated 18 June 1917, PRONI D627/430/67.
3. Howard Murland, diary 26 May 1917, in Murland, op. cit., p.188.
4. Gosse, *Memoirs of a Camp-Follower*, pp.163–4.
5. *Irish Times*, 9 June 1917.
6. Hennessy, *The Great War 1914–1918: Bank of Ireland Staff*, p.33. De Ruvigny, op. cit., Vol.4, p.217.
7. NA, Kew, WO 95/1730. Lieutenant Whitfield in Taylor, *The 1st Royal Irish Rifles in the Great War*, pp.114–15.
8. NA, Kew, WO 95/2504.
9. NA, Kew, WO 339.
10. *BNL*, 15 September 1917.
11. NA, Kew, WO 339.
12. *LG Supplement*, 26 January 1918.
13. *BNL*, 30 August 1917.
14. Major J.R. Jones, RFA, in Thompson, *Bushmills Heroes*, pp.153–4.
15. Godson, op. cit., 4 July 1917.
16. McMahon, *op cit*.
17. Godson, op. cit., 23 August 1917.

18. Sheldon, *The German Army at Cambrai*, p.6.

19. NA, Kew, WO 95/2505.

20. Metcalfe, *Blacker's Boys*, p.159.

21. Godson, op. cit., 23 September to 13 October 1917.

22. He had assumed the surname Filgate in 1917 in place of his own name – Henry – in compliance with the will of his father-in-law.

23. NA, Kew, WO 339.

24. Metcalfe, op. cit., p.160.

25. Letter dated 4 November 1917, in Perry, op. cit., pp.179–80.

26. Ibid.

27. Godson, op. cit.

28. Elliott and Stevenson, op. cit., p.15.

29. Godson, op. cit.

30. Segeant Schwarz, in Sheldon, op. cit., p.45.

31. Letter dated 22 November 1917, in Perry, op. cit., p.183.

32. NA, Kew, WO 95/2506/2. See also *BNL*, 4 January 1918.

33. Letter dated 23 November 1917, in Perry, op. cit., p.184.

34. Ibid.

35. Letter dated 25 November 1917, in Perry, op. cit., pp.186–7.

36. De Ruvigny, op. cit., Vol. III, p.253.

37. NA, Kew, WO 363.

38. Godson, op. cit.

39. Ibid.

40. Lucy, op. cit., pp.383–4.

41. Letter dated 15 December 1917, in Perry, op. cit., p.198.

42. NA, Kew, WO 363.

43. Letter dated 27 November 1917, in Perry, op. cit., p.188.

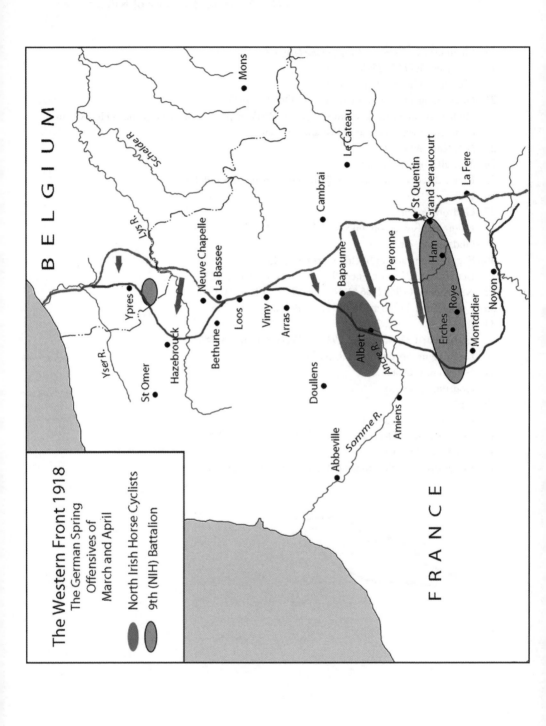

The Western Front 1918
The German Spring
Offensives of
March and April

North Irish Horse Cyclists

9th (NIH) Battalion

BELGIUM

FRANCE

Mons

Le Cateau

Cambrai

St Quentin
Grand Seraucourt

La Fere

Schelde R.

Lys R.

Neuve Chapelle

La Bassee

Bapaume

Peronne

Ham

Ypres

Hazebrouck

Bethune

Loos

Vimy

Arras

Albert

Ancre R.

Roye

Erches

Montdidier

Noyon

Yser R.

St Omer

Doullens

Somme R.

Amiens

Abbeville

Chapter Six

1918: Overwhelmed by the Hun

... surrounded and cut off ... We retired to other positions & held on for a while. Our ammunition was practically spent, the men were spent, hungry & fatigued. We lost heavily from the shell & machine Gun fire & though we tried hard to hold out we were overwhelmed by the Hun.[1]

Before the storm

The new year found the 9th (North Irish Horse) Battalion in rest billets at Boves, just outside Amiens. The 1st North Irish Horse Regiment was camped at the village of Barly, around twenty miles to the north. In Ireland, recruitment of new cavalrymen to the North Irish Horse had slowed to a trickle. With only one mounted regiment at the front few vacancies arose. However, some still came forward and were taken on; in January and February, for example, Daniel Park of Ballywatermoy, Joseph Shaw and William Clarke of Broughshane, William Reynolds and John Scott of Portglenone. Perhaps the last North Irish Horse recruit of the war – certainly one of the last – was John Cathcart of Moat Road, Ballymena, who enlisted in the first week of November 1918. Few of these 1918 recruits would see action.

Meanwhile, efforts continued to clear out those no longer fit for service. These included 59-year-old Farrier Quartermaster Sergeant James Mooney, who had stated his age as twenty-nine when he enlisted in 1911. Some, like Ezekiel Lowry and Samuel McGovern, had returned from France with wounds or injuries that left them permanently unfit for front-line service. Others were sick or suffered a physical impairment. School teacher John St Claire Clarke was discharged with defective vision. Robert Anderson was found to be asthmatic. Two men were discharged for 'feeblemindedness', one described as 'dull, stupid, lazy, unemployable; careless, indifferent and untidy and seems to have a permanent dislike of work.' Private Robert Evans of Dunmurry, County Antrim, had contracted tuberculosis while serving with A Squadron in France. He was sent home in February, discharged on a pension in March, and died on 9 November 1918, two days before the war ended. Tuberculosis was an ever-present and often fatal disease. Another who succumbed was Private Richard Elliott of Rugby Avenue, Belfast. Elliott, a bread-server, had enlisted in November 1915, but the following year was hospitalised and diagnosed with the disease, which was accepted as being a result of his military service. He was discharged and granted a full pension, but died at home on 3 March 1918.

The 1st North Irish Horse Regiment remained at Barly until mid-March. On 6 January the officers and men posted to the 59th (2nd North Midland) Division at the Bilhem-Chapel Wood Switch came out of the line and were sent for duty under the Assistant Provost Marshal of V Corps. The following day a party of Hotchkiss gunners under Lieutenant Donald O'Neill Hodson marched from V Corps Headquarters to the reserve trenches near Hermies, attached to the 17th (Northern) Division. There they stayed for twenty days before coming out for a week's rest. Some reinforcements arrived from base camp in January, among them 19-year-old Yorkshire farmer Robert Wilson and 32-year-old Monmouth mail driver Herbert Short.

After serving as commanding officer from the very beginning, Lieutenant Colonel Cole departed. Captain Thomas William Hughes, another veteran of August 1914, briefly took command. He was then replaced by Major Arthur Hamilton-Russell, who had been in France since May 1915 as commanding officer of D Squadron. On 18 February Hamilton-Russell received bad news – the 1st North Irish Horse was to be dismounted and converted to a cyclist regiment. The new regiment would be posted to V Corps, replacing the existing corps cyclist regiment which was being disbanded.

Corps cyclist regiments played a similar role to corps cavalry, though their particular advantages had long been recognised. Field service regulations of 1914 stated that cyclists

are especially suited for employment in enclosed country, where roads are good and numerous. They can traverse longer distances and move more quickly than horsemen. Cyclists ... can develop more fire in proportion to their numbers than other mounted troops, as they do not require horse holders ... In a country where the roads are good, cyclists may replace mounted patrols, and by night they are especially suited for this work.[2]

Despite the change, the new unit remained a North Irish Horse regiment. They retained their North Irish Horse cap badge and shoulder-titles, their cavalry uniform, their original squadron titles – A, D and E – and would continue drawing their reinforcements from the reserve at Antrim. But it was only a matter of weeks before they lost the most visible part of their former identity. First, fourteen Class III riding horses, ten pack horse and twenty light draught horses were transferred to the Field Remount Section. Two days later more horses were taken, this time to the 2nd Cavalry Division – 134 Class I riding horses, twelve greys and eighteen chargers. During the first fortnight of March the last of the horses were surrendered – 173 riders to the Base Remount Section at Marseilles, thirty-eight draught horses and twenty-one vehicles to Horse Transport at Abbeville (together with ten Army Service Corps drivers), and thirteen other horses to the Abbeville Veterinary Hospital.

It wasn't only horses that had to leave the regiment. A cyclist battalion was 25 per cent smaller than a corps cavalry regiment – there was no

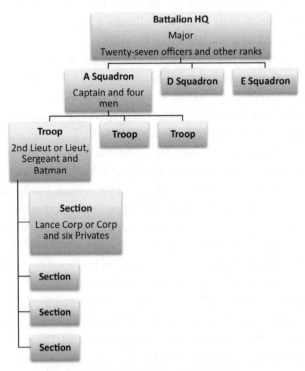

Figure 4: North Irish Horse Cyclist Regiment.

need for men to hold the horses when the unit dismounted. Each of the three cyclist squadrons comprised just four officers and ninety-four men. Command of the regiment fell to a major, rather than a lieutenant colonel, and squadrons were led by a captain rather than a major. The total strength of the regiment was therefore only 322 (see table above). On 9 March, there were 464 men in the regiment. Clearly, many officers and men were now surplus to requirements.

Within days, nine officers and sixty-three other ranks were transferred to the Machine Gun Base Depot at Camiers, and three other ranks sent to British Cavalry Base Depot at Rouen. Among these were Irish-Canadian Lieutenant Leslie Ion Stuart, a sheep farmer in Australia before the war, who had been with the regiment since joining it in the field in July 1916, Lieutenant Arthur Penrhyn Noyce, a mining engineer from Rhodesia, Squadron Quartermaster Sergeant Thomas Henry Johnston and Saddler John Rea. All were soon after posted to a hussar regiment. It appears that this was the destination of many of those who left the regiment, and it may be that those with particular skills needed by the cavalry (saddlers and shoeing smiths for example) were hand-picked. Others sent to Camiers, such as Second Lieutenant Theophilus James Forde from Hilltown, County Down, were posted to a machine-gun battalion.

Eight men were sent to cadet schools in England for officer training during March – Thomas Frederick Reid, Thomas Robert Mills, John Allen French, Samuel Brown Stevenson, Charles Warwick Clark, William Mercier, William Anderson and David Kernohan. In terms of quality it seems this was a mixed lot, despite all having lengthy experience in France. The selection was perhaps as much about shedding numbers from the roll as it was about finding new officers. Thus Shankill book-keeper Corporal John French was damned with faint praise by the officers at cadet school, being assessed as having 'very fair' education, leadership and military knowledge: 'Not good appearance but has shown much improvement & with experience should make a leader.' On the other hand E Squadron's Quartermaster Sergeant William Mercier, a bank clerk from Mountrath, Queens County, rated well: 'Good control & command & generally sound … Good type, hard worker and a leader. Should make a useful officer.' Nonetheless all eight would be commissioned in October 1918 and posted to the Royal Irish Rifles or Royal Irish Fusiliers. The timing was fortunate for these men, for they missed most, if not all, the desperate fighting of 1918. At least one, however, would see action before the war was over. William Anderson was posted to his new battalion, the 15th Royal Irish Rifles, before his official commission came through. He was killed on 20 October, three weeks before the Armistice was signed.

On 7 March an advance party from the regiment travelled to V Corps Headquarters at Villers-au-Flos to take over the equipment and stores from the old cyclist regiment. The rest of the regiment joined them a week later. Here they began the process of re-equipping as cyclists, learning new skills and training under squadron arrangements. First each man was issued with his new mount. The bicycle was made by BSA to military specifications: 24-inch frame, pump, heavy-duty tyres, lamps, leather tool-box and repair kit on the crossbar, bell, front kit carrier to hold the rider's greatcoat, rear kit carrier holding the man's pack and helmet, and attachments to secure the rifle. Training also began in use of the Lewis machine gun, the standard issue to cyclist regiments. In mid-March two officers and fifty-two other ranks from the old V Corps cyclist regiment joined the North Irish Horsemen, so despite the efforts made to reduce the numbers on the roll, it seems the regiment was still heavily over-manned.

Meanwhile, the 9th (NIH) Battalion had left their rest billets at Boves. The battalion was moving back into the line, and into unfamiliar territory, for it had been agreed that the British forces would take over from the French a new stretch running from just north of German-held St Quentin south to Barsis, five miles south of the River Oise. Battalion headquarters was at Grand Seraucourt, two and a half miles behind the line. The handover by the Frenchmen was accomplished smoothly and in good spirit, but the condition of the trenches as the weather began to warm was not as welcoming. 'All the trenches have disappeared,' complained the division's commander.

> The combined effect of frost and rain has brought them down entirely. The result is we can't use them and no more can the Germans and so all movement in the front line is being carried out in broad daylight over the top. In fact there is a sort of informal truce on which will last I daresay until one side has got its trenches habitable first and then they will snipe the others who are not ready.[3]

The 9th (NIH) Battalion moved into the line on 28/29 January. The section of the line held by the 36th (Ulster) Division ran from a point to the west of Rocourt, a suburb of St Quentin, south over the St Quentin Canal, and then turning to the east then south again, ending near Sphinx Wood and facing

German-held Itancourt. The 9th (NIH) Battalion stood at the division's extreme right.

February brought more organisational change for the BEF. The number of battalions in each infantry brigade was reduced from four to three, with many broken up. The change was dramatic – 115 battalions disappeared altogether, thirty-eight were amalgamated into nineteen, and seven became pioneers. The men who lost their battalions were sent to make up the numbers of other units, or to newly-created 'entrenching battalions'. The change was in response to a desperate lack of new men to fill the depleted ranks of the BEF in France and Belgium. The shortage was not due to any lack of men at home, where 38,000 officers and 607,000 men were waiting orders to sail. It was simply because Prime Minister Lloyd George refused to send them, in order to limit Haig's ability to undertake the sort of bloody fighting seen in the second half of 1917. Making matters worse, five British divisions had been sent to Italy to prop up that country's defences.

The re-organisation was particularly hard on the 36th (Ulster) Division, because the War Office had ordered that no regular, first-line territorial or guards battalions were to be lost. New Army formations such as the Ulster

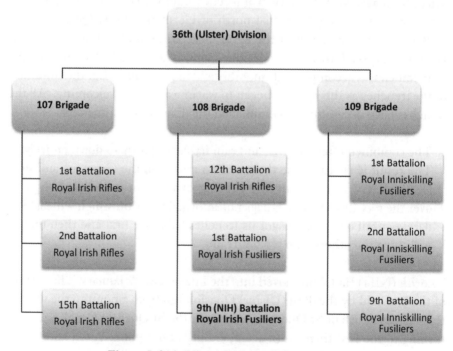

Figure 5: 36th (Ulster) Division, February 1918.

Division had to carry the losses. Of its twelve battalions, six were disbanded. Three regular battalions were brought in from other divisions, joining the two regular battalions that had come in during 1917. Only four of the twelve battalions that made up the original Ulster Division remained, one of these being the 9th (NIH) Battalion.

The change, though necessary, was not welcomed. Some mourned the dilution of their old UVF division:

> ... one of the most depressing [days] that I have ever come through. We received orders to join the 2nd Battalion Royal Irish Rifles ... We were looked upon as strangers by most of the officers who were not originally Ulster Division officers at all and who were not inclined to look at things from the Ulster point of view.[4]

... while others felt insulted by being moved to a 'political' division:

> Definitely settled that the battalion will leave that fine division, the 8th, and go to the 36th Ulster Division – the political division as we know it ... Everyone seems very sick over the move.[5]

The change marked the end of the old 36th (Ulster) Division – still northern Irish but no longer suffused with UVF sympathies. Father Gill of the 2nd Royal Irish Rifles noted that:

> A census of religions at this time showed that in the Ulster Division ... there were between 3,000 and 4,000 Catholics. When this division came from Ireland their boast was that there was not a single RC in their ranks.[6]

Given these changes and the ravages of Cambrai, how much did the 9th (NIH) Battalion still bear a North Irish Horse character? When more than 570 men from the 2nd North Irish Horse Regiment joined the battalion in September and October 1917 they made up half its strength. On the eve of Cambrai, the North Irish Horsemen could therefore truly have claimed the battalion as their own. Since then, however, casualties of battle and illness, transfers to other units such as the Tank Corps, and the arrival of 213 men from the disbanded 7th/8th Royal Irish Fusiliers, had somewhat eroded the North Irish Horse character of the battalion. Nonetheless, their numbers were still substantial. In mid-March, North Irish Horsemen still made up a third of the men of the battalion. Among the officers, however, it was a different story. Only five who had come from the 2nd North Irish Horse Regiment were left – Captain Despard, Lieutenants Vesey and Dean, and Second Lieutenants Henry and Perkins.

February also brought the adoption of a more 'elastic' defensive posture on the front line, rather than the previous determination to hold every yard no matter what the cost. This new arrangement involved three levels of defence. First was the Forward Zone – essentially the front line – held by a series of outposts, with 'redoubts' established in natural defensive positions. This zone was intended to absorb the force of an attack before the defenders withdrew to the second zone. In each brigade area the Forward Zone was manned by a single battalion, with a redoubt in each. The second line was the Battle Zone, 2,000 to 3,000 yards behind the front line. This, too, was manned by a battalion, and was to be the farthest point that any attack should reach. Behind the Battle Zone was the reserve sector, manned by a third battalion. The theory of the new defensive posture was a good one, but the situation faced by the 36th (Ulster) Division and the entire front of the Fifth Army was quite different. The Battle Zone was incomplete, there were not enough troops to man the defences, and the redoubts were too far apart. A determined and sustained attack could do a lot of damage.

For the remainder of February the 9th (NIH) Battalion engaged in training and working on cable and other trenches in the Battle Zone. On 1 March they moved into brigade support, still in the Battle Zone, at Essigny Station. Here they worked on improving the defences until the evening of 8 March, when they relieved the 1st Royal Irish Fusiliers in the Forward Zone. The week at the front was spent patrolling and wiring nightly. An enemy machine gun was captured without a fight by a small patrol in front of Sphinx Wood.

On the evening of 14 March the battalion moved into reserve at Grand Seraucourt. North Irish Horseman George Adams Henry was severely wounded this day. Henry, from Cookstown, County Tyrone, had joined the North Irish Horse in March 1912 and embarked for France in August 1914 with C Squadron. Two months earlier he had been awarded the Military Medal for bravery in the field during the fighting at Cambrai. Henry died twelve days later at the Australian General Hospital in Rouen.

The German Spring Offensive

The early morning of 21 March found the 9th (NIH) Battalion in reserve at Grand Seraucourt, a few miles behind the front line. The other North Irish Horse regiment – the V Corps Cyclists – was farther back at Villers-au-Flos, near Bapaume.

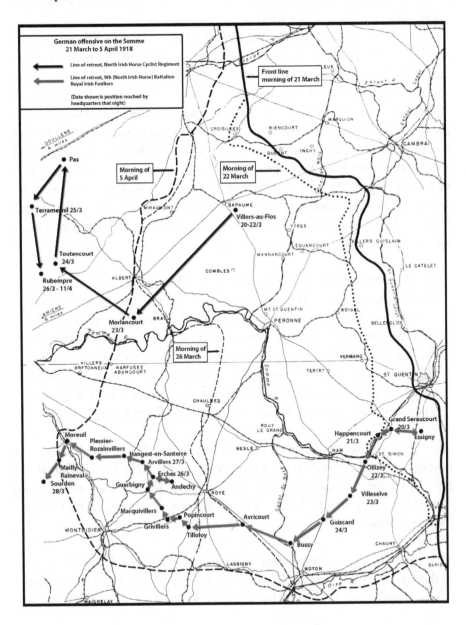

German deserters slipping into the lines held by 107 Brigade a few days before had confirmed the worst fears of some: 'massed trench mortars on the front ... great numbers of troops, particularly of artillery. St Quentin ... packed with men.'[7] '[T]he day is very near,' wrote Oliver Nugent, commanding the 36th (Ulster) Division. 'We expect to be attacked tonight or tomorrow and it is going to be a very big attack and will last for weeks. It is very grim sitting still and waiting.'[8]

The attack came on the morning of 21 March. Along a fifty-mile front from Arras to St Quentin, seventy-six battle-hardened German divisions faced twenty-six infantry and three cavalry divisions of the BEF's Third and Fifth Armies. At 4.40am a massive artillery bombardment commenced, designed to destroy not only the British front-line defences, but defensive posts to the rear, command posts, and communications. It had been meticulously prepared, and would last for five hours, sweeping back and forwards between the forward and battle zones and seeking out pre-identified targets. At 9.35 the shelling switched to the front line positions and a creeping barrage commenced. All took place in a thick fog, which hampered German observation, but helped the defenders even less. Nugent found time to pen a quick note to his wife:

The long expected has come at last ... In all my experience out here I have never known anything more terrific. It isn't a series of reports, but it is just one long roar. It seems as if there were some strange devil who watches over the Germans. This morning dawned with so thick a fog that we can't see 200 yards. All we can hear are the shells, we can see nothing and all the [telephone] lines to the front are already cut and we have to depend on runners and byke [sic] orderlies, a very slow process when as in this case the Germans are shelling all the roads.[9]

On the 36th (Ulster) Division front, most of the forward defences were quickly overrun, though it seems outposts of the 12th Royal Irish Rifles held on for longer than most. One of its officers, Second Lieutenant James Burnside, was a former North Irish Horseman, a farmer from Bellaghy, County Londonderry:

At 10-30 A.M. we were attack[ed] on the Front. S.O.S. Signals were thrown up, but got no reply from the Artillery. Owing to a heavy Fog which had settled on the Line signals could not be seen. This attack was beaten off then suddenly we were attack[ed] heavily from the Left Flank and from the back. We held the Line to 12:30 PM, during these two Hours we had very hard fighting and a great many Casualties. About 1 PM we were completely surrounded, beaten out of the Trench and by force taken prisoners.[10]

Sweeping over the first line, the German storm troops pushed on through the Forward Zone. This was the area, defended by strong redoubts and swept by machine-gun fire and artillery, that was supposed to absorb the force of the attack. But the speed and overwhelming numbers of the attacking force, combined with the fog which persisted until past midday, conspired against the defenders. Three redoubts were held by troops of the 36th (Ulster) Division in the Forward Zone – Boadicea, Race Course and Jeanne D'Arc. They were supposed to hold on for up to two days, slowing the enemy advance, but all three fell by 6.00pm. They did little to hinder the Germans, who simply raced past them into the Battle Zone, leaving others to mop up.

Soon after midday it became clear that the Germans had broken through the defences of the 14th (Light) Division on the immediate right of the 36th Ulster and had captured the town of Essigny-le-Grand on the plateau running down to Grand Seraucourt. Immediately to the west of Essigny, along the road to Grand Seraucourt, was the railway station and behind that, Station Redoubt, being held by the 1st Royal Irish Fusiliers. The 9th (NIH) Battalion had moved to a position south-east of Grand Seraucourt early in the morning, ready to move forward at short notice. At 1.10pm D Company was sent up to reinforce the 1st Royal Irish Fusiliers at Station Redoubt.

By 2.30pm, while determined attacks by the Germans from the south along the railway cutting had been repulsed for the moment, it was clear that the retreat of the division on the right had allowed the enemy to penetrate more than 3,000 yards beyond the old front line. The 36th (Ulster) Division was in grave danger of having its flank turned. The remaining three companies of the 9th (NIH) Battalion were ordered to form a defensive flank south of Essigny Station to prevent the enemy getting further around the right of the 1st Royal Irish Fusiliers via the railway cutting. The line stabilised here and remained so until dusk, but at 8.45pm orders were given that the Essigny Plateau was to be abandoned, the 36th (Ulster) Division to withdraw under cover of darkness behind the St Quentin Canal. Headquarters of the 9th (NIH) Battalion crossed the canal at Artemps to Happencourt. The bridges at the now abandoned town of Grand Seraucourt were blown in the early hours of 22 March.

Most of what happened in the confused and desperate fighting of this first day will never be known. Regimental diaries speak of battalions and companies almost 'ceasing to exist', and others speak of isolated outposts fighting bravely against overwhelming odds to the last man. Officers returning from captivity after the war were interviewed about the circumstances surrounding their capture, and invariably reported that they fought until completely surrounded and out of ammunition. The truth, of course, is not quite so cut and dried. Battalions did virtually cease to exist, but less from casualties than from surrender. The defence of the crucial Boadicea Redoubt is a case in point. The redoubt was commanded by Lord Farnham, who had earlier led F Squadron of the North Irish Horse. Cyril Falls' history of the 36th (Ulster) Division describes an 'epic' defence:

> The enemy pounded their trenches with trench mortars, attacked, was beaten off, bombarded once again, again attacked ... At half-past five ... Lord Farnham, commanding the 2nd Inniskillings, decided that further resistance was impossible. [He was] highly complimented upon their resistance by the German officers ... [It was] a rare example of that 'cold courage,' ... which has been so often displayed by soldiers of British race in all periods of the history of British arms.[11]

However, another version has the attacking Germans far from keen to attack such a strongly-held position. Instead, under a flag of truce they offered the garrison the chance to surrender.

> a few minutes later, there filed out of the redoubt a lieutenant colonel, carrying a small white dog, three captains, seven subalterns and 241 other men. Forty-one machine guns and mortars were found in the redoubt. The British lieutenant colonel asked for, and was given, a document stating that he had put up a good fight before surrendering.[12]

What is undisputable is that the day had been a spectacular success for the German forces. Almost everywhere along the fifty-mile front gains had been made only dreamed of in years of static trench warfare. The BEF's Third Army to the north had fared better, holding the attackers in many places, but German advances on either side of the Flesquières Salient at

Cambrai had left it dangerously exposed. However, the biggest danger lay on the right flank of the Fifth Army, south of St Quentin. Here the 36th (Ulster) Division, and the three divisions to its right, had been pushed out of both the Fighting Zone and much of their Battle Zone into relatively open territory with little in the way of defensive works to fall back on.

The day had also seen a dreadful loss of manpower for the 36th Ulster. The three Forward Zone battalions (a third of the division) had ceased to exist as effective fighting units. To help make up the numbers, the entrenching battalions formed from the disbanded battalions just a month before were rushed forward.

As the men of the 9th (NIH) Battalion withdrew that night, it seemed for a while that they had escaped the day's fighting relatively unscathed. Just one officer, Second Lieutenant Dalton Prenter, and four men were known to have been killed. (Two of these were probably North Irish Horsemen Private Thomas Sittlington of Larne, and Private Frank Tate of Belfast.) However, in the early hours of 22 March it became clear that matters were more serious. D Company's 16 Platoon, commanded by Second Lieutenant Perkins, and parts of two platoons of A Company were missing. The 1st Royal Irish Fusiliers was also short a platoon. All were cut off on the eastern side of the canal. With the bridges blown, they were given up as lost. No.16 Platoon had been sent the previous day to reinforce the company of the 1st Royal Irish Fusiliers holding Station Redoubt on the road from Essigny Station to Grand Seraucourt. When the decision was made to withdraw behind the St Quentin Canal, the runner sent to bring them in never made it, so they stayed put. According to Perkins:

Just before dawn I collected my men and made for the Redoubt. On the way I saw through the fog that was very dense at the time a small party coming down the Essigny–Sauracourt Road which ran through the Redoubt. On approaching I found that they were Germans, and thinking that they may have been a patrol that had got lost, shouted for them to surrender. Seeming very much surprised they started to run, so I at once ordered my men to open fire. Upon reaching the Redoubt I found it to be occupied by the enemy so I at once made off into open country with the hope of getting through, but had only gone about 500 yds when I saw a party of about fifty of our men, so made towards them, but found that they were prisoners and had a guard of six Germans. On observing who we were one of the guard came towards us and signalled for us to join them. I at once covered him with my revolver and enquired of the men as to what had happened, and I was told that during the night the Batt had retired and that the enemy were now five or six kilometres in my rear. Still thinking there was a possible chance of escape we made off again and after three hours, during which time we were avoiding numerous parties of the enemy, we next enountered Battalions of them moving up in mass formation. I then saw that escape and avoiding being taken prisoner was impossible.[13]

One of Perkins' men, North Irish Horseman Sergeant Frank McMahon, did manage to slip away and somehow made it back to the British lines.

The platoons of A Company holding the line near Station Redoubt met a similar fate. Captain and Adjutant Michael Henehan MC was at battalion headquarters at 11.00 on the night of 21 March when the order came to withdraw behind the Canal. Henehan and a runner were ordered to find the missing platoons. He did so and passed on the order to pull out. 'At about 1.30 a.m. I was returning with this Coy when we were attacked, suddenly, by a large enemy patrol, roughly about 200 strong. After a severe struggle the Coy was practically wiped out. I, with about 30 O.R. were taken prisoners.'[14]

As 22 March dawned, 108 Brigade was holding a line along the west of the St Quentin Canal, south of Happencourt. To the north 109 Brigade held on to part of the Battle Zone and did through much of the day, in the face of sustained German attacks. At 2.30 they fell back on Ricardo Redoubt, where they were overwhelmed after a brave defence, in contrast to the meek surrender of other redoubts the previous day. One of the officers who found himself cut off at Ricardo was former North Irish Horseman Second Lieutenant Samuel Simpson Hunter. Hunter, from Londonderry, was one of the hundred who joined the Royal Irish Rifles at the end of 1916. Now he was with C Company of the 1st Royal Inniskilling Fusiliers.

I took command of the remaining men in C Coy, my Coy Commander having been killed reaching the Redoubt. The enemy were following up in great numbers. He surrounded us on three sides, the North side being no good for him to attack. He then shelled us with heavies for ¾ hrs then tried to rush us from the S.E of the Redoubt, we repulsed this with bombing parties. He then changed his tactics by scouring our parapets with heavy concentrated M.G. Fire. We had considerable casualties. We had been expecting reinforcements, *none* came ... The enemy then tried to Trench Mortar us out of the place, he did very much damage ... All the officers remaining decided to have a consultation, to see if it was advisable to hold any longer. We decided to give in, all our ammunition gone, no communication, no reinforcements. We gave in at 4.30 pm 22/3/18. The last order from Brigade was 'Stick at all costs' ... When captured, the enemy were nine kilo[metre]s behind us.[15]

The 9th (NIH) Battalion remained on the St Quentin Canal at Happencourt for most of the day, until ordered to fall back in a general withdrawal to positions behind the Somme, as it ran west from the Crozat Canal and then north. In the evening the battalion fell back unmolested to Ollizey on the southern bank of the Somme near the Somme-Crozat-St Quentin junction. The 36th (Ulster) Division, with 61 Brigade attached, occupied a five-mile line from just east of Sommette-Eaucourt on the Somme to near Jussy on the Crozat Canal. Every available man had been combed out of the rear areas, headquarters and training schools to form a composite battalion to help make up the line on the division's left. Bridges along the Somme were blown (though not all) and the night passed quietly.

The following day, another that began shrouded in fog, would show just how brittle were the improvised defences along the Somme. Shortly after dawn the Germans attacked and captured the bridgehead at Ham. They crossed in force and drove south towards Aubigny and Brouchy. Worse was to come, as by late morning enemy forces were pouring across the partially destroyed railway bridge at Pithon to the east of Ham. Beyond the 36th (Ulster) Division's right flank, the 14th (Light) Division had been driven from its defensive positions around Jussy on the Crozat Canal. With the enemy now advancing west from Jussy and south from Ham and Pithon, the 36th (Ulster) Division found itself under attack from both flanks. Fighting continued through the day and despite losing ground the division held on. The 9th (NIH) Battalion gradually fell back as the pressure on the flanks of the division mounted. In the evening its headquarters evacuated Ollizey and moved three miles south-west to a farm house in front of the village of Villeselve.

During the morning of 24 March the Germans renewed their attack. The salient occupied by the 36th Ulster and other divisions collapsed, the troops falling back on Villeselve. The enemy soon had a footing in the village, but their advance was momentarily checked by a heroic cavalry charge by three troops of the 10th Hussars, the 1st Royal Dragoons and 3rd Dragoon Guards. Ordered to throw back the Germans 'using sword only', they attacked a large party of the enemy who were firing at least four machine guns from the north-east of Collezy. Charging at full gallop over 1,000 yards of open fields, they put the enemy to flight, killing or capturing over 150. Infantrymen of the 1st Royal Irish Fusiliers and 9th (NIH) Battalions followed close behind, cheering. No doubt the former cavalrymen in the 9th (NIH) felt a twinge of envy at the dashing role that might once have been theirs.

The success could only be temporary, however, and soon the retreat resumed. It may have been at this time that North Irish Horseman Private James Elliott was wounded:

> [He] was number two man feeding ammunition into a Lewis machine gun when they were ordered to retreat. The bullets were in canisters, one pair of which James had thrown across a shoulder; while bending to pick up the other pair a bullet entered his back below his ribs and cut through his lung, stopping beside his heart ... His comrade, Chuckie Clements of Limavady, hoisted James on his back carrying him a mile and a half to the field ambulance.[16]

The 36th (Ulster) Division now fell back on Berlancourt and Guiscard, the enemy continuing to press the attack through the evening and heavily shelling the villages. At 11.00pm the division came under the command of the French 62nd Division, and was ordered to withdraw to Crisolles. The 9th (NIH) Battalion remained behind, covering the withdrawal from the ridge north from Guiscard towards Berlancourt. During the night a number of casualties were sustained, including Captain George Waller Vesey, who was severely wounded. Vesey, a North Irish Horseman who had come to France with F Squadron in November 1915, was left in the care of the French when the 9th (NIH) Battalion withdrew from Guiscard the following day. Soon after they brought him to one of their hospitals, Amb. 4/51, at Ressons-sur-Matz, west of Noyon, where he died on 26 March.

Meanwhile, Frank McMahon, who had evaded capture near Essigny on the first day, was caught up in the fighting while trying to locate his battalion. Speaking good French and trained as a Hotchkiss machine gunner, he attached himself to a French machine-gun unit who were only too grateful for the assistance. Soon after, however, he received a shrapnel wound to the left arm. '[I was] told to make my way towards Paris. Everything was haywire, Armies retreating and demoralised.'[17] It would be many days before he would find his unit and medical attention.

With the exception of the 9th (NIH) Battalion, the 36th (Ulster) Division was now out of the fighting for the first time in four long days. Its commander, Major-General Nugent, understood what a disaster it had been, and that more was to come.

It is all a ghastly nightmare ... The French have been rushing up Divisions to try and stop the rot, but there is a great deal of confusion and the Germans are giving us no rest. What is left of my Division had terribly heavy fighting yesterday [24 March] and we had to fall back again ... My men have had no food, some of them for 2 and 3 days. They have had no sleep for 5 nights. They are absolutely beat ...

However, what he felt most keenly was the scorn of the French:

They hardly pretend to be civil and I can hardly wonder. We have let them in disastrously.[18]

There was little fighting on the 25th, but also little rest for the exhausted men of the 36th (Ulster) Division. After a long march they arrived at Guerbigny on the Avre river, about five miles west of Roye. Here at last they were able to steal six hours sleep, the first since the night of 20 March. For the 9th (NIH), however, not even this short rest was allowed them. Leaving the forward defensive positions around Guiscard late in the morning, they had marched through Bussy to Avricourt, then through Tilloloy, Popincourt, Grivillers, Marquivillers, Guerbigny and finally to Erches, arriving in the morning of 26 March.

While the 36th (Ulster) Division had marched west on 25 March, the Germans had broken through the French behind them. The French retired to the south-west, opening a gap to the north of Roye which the Germans immediately seized, pushing deep between the allied armies in the early morning of 26 March. Only the 36th (Ulster) and 30th Divisions stood between them and new French divisions miles to the rear. To avert disaster, the two divisions were ordered to form a new defensive line and hold on at all costs. The 36th (Ulster) Division was ordered to take up a line running north of the Avre to around Andechy. This was part of the old French front line, so fortunately there was still a good trench system in place with plenty of wire in front. The 9th (NIH) and 1st Royal Irish Fusiliers were sent to find defensive positions in front of Andechy. Unfortunately, the Germans had already reached the village. Second Lieutenant Albert Henry, who had come home from Canada on the outbreak of the war and joined the 2nd Life Guards before being commissioned and posted to the North Irish Horse, was in command of the last fifty men of B Company:

> Shortly after 9.AM on the 26th we marched out of Erches, the 1st R.Ir Fusrs in front of us, our orders being to take up a position in front of Andechy, a village about 1 mile East of Erches, to prevent enemy cavalry breaking through. Before we reached Andechy enemy in that village opened fire on the 1st R.Ir.F. M.Gs also opened fire on us from a small wood some distance to our left. We were just passing through an old trench system, the front line trench of which we ... manned by orders of Maj Brew commanding the 9th R.Ir.F. then ... Although we were told that a Battn was in position on our left we were unable to get in touch with anybody.[19]

Mixed in with the 9th (NIH) were seventy men, all that was left of the 12th Royal Irish Rifles. Even the bandsmen were included, being obliged to dump their instruments in Erches. Second Lieutenant John Pollock of 108 Trench Mortar Battery was in command:

> At about 8.30 [am] ... we were alarmed, ordered to fall in at once & march up the Erches–Andechy road, to pick out and occupy a position ... When I got clear of the village a German M.G. suddenly opened fire on us from a distance of about 500 yds. We got into open formation and continued to advance until the enemy fire became too hot. I then saw some old trenches, got the men into these, &, leaving another subaltern in command, went along these trenches until I met the 9th R. Irish Fus. I reported to the O.C. He told me that the enemy had made a slight attack but had been driven off by rifle & Lewis gun fire. I then placed my men in positions which he told me to occupy. All that day the enemy kept up rifle & M.G. fire on our line, but did not attack.[20]

The reason the 9th (NIH) had been unable to contact the units to its left was that there was no one there. The 20th Division had not been able to come up and the 30th were digging in at Bouchoir and to the north. There was a two-mile gap in the British line. The men on the ground tried to make do, but during the evening large numbers of German infantry, cavalry and transport slipped through the thinly-held flank. Soon they were in Erches, behind the line held by the 9th (NIH) Battalion. That night the battalion's commanding officer, Major Brew, together with the commanding officer of the 1st Royal Irish Fusiliers were captured, Brew being fatally wounded. Suddenly finding German troops all around them, headquarters of the 36th (Ulster) Division at Guerbigny and that of 108 Brigade were forced to beat a hasty retreat.

While headquarters escaped, there was no such luck for the men of the 9th (NIH) and 1st Royal Irish Fusiliers still holding the line. They were, however, acutely aware of the danger they were in. The sound of gunfire and sight of enemy Very lights behind them, and the ominous failure to return of runners, stretcher-bearers, ration and ammunition parties told its own story. Nevertheless, they stayed put. According to Second Lieutenant Bremner:

> That night ... it was very obvious that the Germans had worked round us to our left rear & that our position was very dangerous .... A limited supply of ammunition was I believe ... obtained from the 109th Brigade which carried us through the succeeding days' fighting.
>
> I had a consultation with 2/Lt J Scott on whom the command of the Battalion had devolved, as to the advisability of retiring from the salient. He told me that a message had been received, I think from Division, to that effect, but that instructions would be sent later as to the method of carrying it out. These orders were never received. The German Very lights on the night of the 26th March again showed us how dangerous our position was. I again conferred with 2/Lt J Scott. This time on the advisability of getting out of the salient on our own initiative as I had concluded that we were practically cut off & out of touch with our Brigade Hdqtrs. He decided to confer with the C.O. of the 1st Bn R.I.F Major Clement and the decision come to was to hang on.[21]

During the morning the Germans attacked the lines held by the 9th (NIH) and the 1st Royal Irish Fusiliers, and 109 Brigade to their right, as well as the French forces to their right on the other side of the Avre. Around midday the French began to withdraw, forcing the 1st, 2nd and 9th Royal Inniskilling Fusiliers of 109 Brigade to pull out as well. The 9th (NIH) and the 1st Royal Irish Fusiliers were left high and dry. The day's story is told by Second Lieutenants Henry, Slatter and Bremner, all of the 9th (NIH) Battalion.

[Henry] When it became daylight on the morning of the 27th we could see that the enemy had advanced past our left flank and had got batteries into position to our left rear firing away from us. I was also informed that morning that during the previous night the Battn on the right of the 1st R.I.F had retired. The position then was that we were surrounded … We maintained our positions that morning, during which time our Lewis Guns fired on Enemy artillery passing round our left flank.

[Slatter] At daybreak I observed large masses of the enemy & much transport going down the road leading westwards to Erches. The enemy was out of effective rifle range. I was unable to prevent his advance. No orderlies sent for rations, water, or ammunition had return[ed] … since previous day. During morning of 27th March, the enemy began to attack from both flanks & left rear …

By midday it became clear that their position was untenable.

[Slatter] after holding him until mid-day, acting in co-operation with the officer temporarily in charge of 9th R.I.F I withdrew across the Erches-Andechy road. No orders being received & Major Brew not having returned we attempted to withdraw south-westwards. We discovered that the only trench leading W. led on to the road running W. from Andechy. Down this the enemy was moved [sic] large masses of troops & cavalry & with our small force it would have been impossible to break through. To withdraw further would have necessitated leaving [the] trench & coming under fire from rifles, machine guns & field guns firing at point-blank range. It was impossible to return to the vacant position as the enemy now held these & was pushing further. Without food & with very little ammunition it was not possible to wait until night-fall. Unable to oppose the enemy advance longer we were compelled to surrender to vastly superior enemy forces.

[Henry] About 2 p.m. the enemy attacked the 1st R.Ir.F. driving them out of the trenches with bombs, about this time also he opened fire on us from a battery of field guns at close range. About 3 p.m. I was ordered by 2nd Lt Scott, actg adjt, to take my Coy and take up position in a trench in rear of the 1st R.Ir.F's position. This I did, having several casualties from enemy M.G.s in getting there. By the time we had reached this trench all the 1st R.Ir.F in front of our position had been captured. The trench we were in was a deep communication trench with no fire-steps, therefore undefendable. There were four other officers with me at this time, and from our position we could see that enemy infantry were in possession of a ridge about two miles in rear of us. We therefore had a consultation, in which senior N.C.O.s were included, and in view of the fact that the men were all exhausted, having had neither food nor water since the morning of the 26th, and that only a few had any ammunition, we decided that it was impossible to extricate ourselves from our position, and that to avoid unnecessary casualties it would be better to surrender to the enemy, which we did at about 3.30 P.M.

[Bremner] we were surrounded and cut off. The whole of that day we played havoc with the German Troops & Transport which were advancing on both sides of us. Near dusk they brought up Batteries (?) of Field Guns & blew us out of our positions. We retired to other positions & held on for a while. Our ammunition was practically spent, the men were spent, hungry & fatigued. We lost heavily from the shell & machine gun fire & though we tried hard to hold out we were overwhelmed by the Hun.[22]

All the men of the 9th (NIH) who had held the line in front of Andechy were forced to surrender. The diary of 108 Brigade reported that only 200 men of the battalion – those who had been held in reserve – were left. Only one officer and nineteen men of the 1st Royal Irish Fusiliers got away. The 200 9th (NIH) reserves joined the Royal Irish Rifles battalions of 107 Brigade and fell back to a ridge south-east of the village of Arvillers, where they remained for the night.

On the evening of 27 March the remnants of the 36th (Ulster) Division were relieved by French troops. The remains of the 9th (NIH) Battalion, under Captains Despard, Crosbie and Dean, and Second Lieutenant Davidson, marched during 28 March to Sourdon, west of Montdidier, where they remained for the night. They were just thirteen miles from Amiens. By 29 March the division was moving further back into reserve. The 9th (NIH) marched via Ailly-sur-Noye and Jumel to Taisnil. At Taisnil the roll was taken, and it made dreadful reading – two officers killed in action, six wounded, fourteen missing and one missing believed wounded; and among the other ranks, fifteen killed in action, seventy-one wounded, 431 missing, and one missing believed wounded. Weeks later, when the roll was finally signed off, the numbers had changed little. Twenty-four of the missing had rejoined, three others were found to be wounded and one was sick. However, four others had been added to the missing and wounded lists.

In the chaos of retreat, it was impossible to know what had happened to many of the missing officers and men, and it was only years later that more accurate numbers could be compiled. We now know that five officers of the battalion were killed in action or died of wounds from the beginning of the German offensive until the end of March. Another five were wounded and fifteen captured. At least thirty other ranks of the battalion were killed in action and no fewer than eleven more would die from their wounds in coming weeks, six while prisoners of war. At least 137 others were wounded, and 319 were prisoners of war.

What of the North Irish Horsemen in the battalion? Before the German offensive they numbered about 336 of the battalion's effective strength of 1,058. Only about 170 answered the roll call unwounded when it was taken at Taisnil on 29 March. Almost half their strength was gone. Some fourteen of the forty-six in the battalion who were killed or died of wounds were North Irish Horsemen. The loss of Captain Vesey and Privates Sittlington and Tate has already been described. Private James Frazer Johnston of Blacklion, County Cavan, had died of wounds in the arms of his pal Herbert Brownlee during the Battalion's march from Guiscard to Erches. The Germans buried him with dozens of other British casualties south of the town of Roye. For six former Horsemen who lost their lives during the retreat, their dates of death and burial places were forgotten – Private Thomas Cartmill from Newry, Private Arthur Sidney Crawford from Dublin, Private Mark Lee from Irvinestown, County Fermanagh, Private Thomas Lyons from Belfast, Private John Moon from Muff, County Donegal, and Private John Forbes, from Moneydollog, County Antrim. Reports sent to Forbes's family suggest he was killed on the second day of the battle 'while attempting to rescue a wounded comrade from German hands'.[23]

Four of the fourteen North Irish Horse fatalities died while prisoners of war. Private William Patrick Stuart, a house-painter and decorator from Belfast, had suffered head wounds and was captured, dying within days. Private William Biggart from Ballymoney had suffered stomach and thigh wounds and died while a prisoner on 3 April. Private George Morrison of Coleraine died of wounds on 22 April. Twenty-one-year old Private Thompson Harpur of Londonderry lingered until 18 May before succumbing to his wounds. One of the first to enlist with the North Irish Horse when the war began, he had been in France for almost three years.

At least thirty-eight of the Battalion's North Irish Horsemen were wounded. Percy Reid's mild shrapnel wound and Samuel William Montgomery's bullet wound to his chest would heal, and both men would be back to re-join the fighting in 1918 and sustain further injury. For others, their fighting days were over. Corporal Frank McMahon, who had walked for days with a shrapnel wound to his arm and no medical attention, finally made it to safety. He was sent to Deauville then Harfleur, 'where I was convalescent and marked B.3, got a job as a clerk to the Commandant of a British staging camp for Americans'.[24] Here he saw out the war.

Of the 431 other ranks initially listed as missing from the battalion when the roll was taken at Taisnil, 142 were North Irish Horsemen. Crawford, Sittlington, Tate and Lee were dead, but no one knew their fate at the time. Nine others made their way back to the battalion soon after. Some others would drift back in the coming weeks, or be located in hospitals. William Gordon and William Brown were soon found to be wounded, not missing. Robert John Hull's father George received a letter from the Army informing him that his son was missing. He was pleased to be able to write back with the news that Robert had written him three letters, proving that he was in fact safe, and with the battalion. George Mark, a vanman from Ballymena, was located in hospital with a face wound. Most of the North Irish Horsemen listed as missing were prisoners of war – some 111 of them. For the families of the missing it would be a long and anxious wait for some intimation that their boy was alive.

Seven former North Irish Horsemen serving in other regiments also lost their lives as a result of the German offensive in March. Scottish-born Lance Corporal William Govan was serving with the Military Mounted Police when he died of wounds on 22 March. Under-aged deserter from the Royal Scots, Rifleman Cecil Charles Barr (see previous chapter), was with the 1st Royal Irish Rifles when he was killed on 24 March during the fighting between Cugny and Villeselve. Rifleman Thomas Johnston of Ballynamaddy, County Antrim, was with the 2nd Royal Irish Rifles during the same day's fighting, and was one of the near 100 killed when the battalion was cut off and made a determined but hopeless last stand. Nearby on the same day the 23rd Entrenching Battalion had fought a determined withdrawal from the west of Ham, during which former North Irish Horseman, 21-year-old linen apprentice Second Lieutenant Robert Victor Lyons, was killed. Two days later Second Lieutenant Archibald Moore of the 22nd Entrenching Battalion was killed in action as he led his platoon in a counter-attack on a captured village five miles west of Nesle. Corporal Hubert Roe, from Bradford, was wounded while serving with the 1st Royal Irish Fusiliers and died soon after. Lance Corporal Robert Hanna was one of the many of the 1st Royal Inniskilling Fusiliers captured during the German offensive. Hanna had originally joined the North Irish Horse in January 1912 and had served in France with C Squadron in the early fighting of August 1914. He died of wounds on 20 April 1918 and was buried in the German extension to the communal cemetery at la Capelle-en-Thiérache.

No longer of much use as a fighting force, the 36th (Ulster) Division was taken out of the line for rest and re-organisation. On 30 March the depleted 9th (NIH) Battalion marched north to Sauleux, just outside Amiens, where they boarded trains for Gamaches, then Eu on the French coast near Abbeville. From Eu they marched to billets at St Quentin-la-Motte.

Much later, some of those involved in the retreat had their service recognised, but this had been no glorious victory, so the awards were few and far between – one Distinguished Service Order, two Distinguished Conduct Medals, four Military Crosses, one Bar to a Military Cross, seven Military Medals and one Mention in Despatches. The North Irish Horsemen in the battalion won their share. Captain Despard was awarded a Distinguished Service Order:

> During five days of retirement, while as second in command of the battalion, he throughout displayed very high qualities as a leader. While in command of the rearguard the gallantry and determination with which he disputed the ground was largely responsible for the safe withdrawal of the rest of the main body.[25]

Acting Captain Herbert Shelton Dean won a Military Cross:

> When all the troops on his left had retired, this officer held his position with great determination, subsequently falling back and protecting the left flank.[26]

Military Medals went to Sergeant George Nesbitt, a veteran of August 1914, wounded during the retreat, and Privates William Adamson, Thomas Alexander McClelland and Robert Tughan.

The German offensive continued for another week, finally petering out on 5 April. The attacking troops were exhausted and they had outdistanced their supply lines and heavy artillery. By contrast, the Allies had managed to stabilise their defences, bringing up fresh reserves to relieve the sorely pressed divisions that had retreated over so many miles. The offensive was, in terms of ground gained, a spectacular success. Nothing like it had been seen since 1914. The Germans had taken back all the ground they had surrendered when they withdrew to the Hindenburg Line in 1917, all the ground lost at Cambrai, and every inch won by the BEF at such cost on the Somme from July to November 1916. Even more, they had captured miles of territory that had been in British and French hands throughout the war. Their front now ran west from la Fère, along the Oise through Chauny and Noyon, and farther still past Montdidier, curving north past Villers Bretonneux to the Ancre. Farther on, more modest gains had been made, running north as far as Vimy. However, the offensive had failed to deliver the decisive blow that its planners had hoped for. At enormous cost in men and material they had simply created a huge salient which could not long be defended. Further German offensives would come in the following months, but with the reserves held back in England now flowing freely to France and Belgium and thousands of American troops arriving, the moment of crisis had almost passed.

The North Irish Horse Cyclist Regiment had also played a part in meeting the German offensive from 21 March, though not to the extent of the 9th (NIH) Battalion. When the offensive began, the cyclists were at V Corps Headquarters at Villers-au-Flos, south-east of Bapaume. V Corps was part of the BEF's Third Army, commanded by General Sir Julian Byng. The corps held the Flesquières Salient, the section of the front fought over during the Battle of Cambrai.

The salient was well defended, the British holding strong positions with relatively large numbers of men and artillery, in contrast to the thin defences of the Fifth Army to the south. The Germans understood this, and therefore planned not to attack the salient head on, but to take on weaker points on either side, encircling it in a pincer movement. Nonetheless, the men in the salient were kept busy during the first day, with subsidiary attacks and heavy artillery bombardment, particularly with mustard gas, which caused casualties numbering in the thousands. Little ground was lost in the Flesquières Salient itself, but the enemy made significant progress on its flanks during that first day. It was clear by evening that V Corps was in a very dangerous position, so in the early hours of 22 March a limited withdrawal was made from the tip of the salient.

Throughout the 21st the North Irish Horse Cyclist Regiment remained at Villers-au-Flos with V Corps Headquarters, ready to move at short notice. Their role would be crucial in a fast-changing situation where the need to keep in touch with the corps' fighting units was vital. The ever present danger was that units would be left 'in the air' by the withdrawal of those on their flanks, or that they would fail to 'keep in touch', leaving dangerous gaps. The cyclists of the North Irish Horse were therefore kept busy as 'runners' – gathering information and conveying orders.

On 22 March the squadrons were moved forward, closer to the action, with individual parties detailed to the various divisional headquarters. Other detachments were put at the disposal of the Assistant Provost Marshal for traffic duties.

On 23 March V Corps began a full withdrawal from the salient, and only just in time, for the Germans continued to make progress on either flank. By dawn on 24 March the job was part done, with all the ground won in the fighting at Cambrai a few months ago given up and the men marching across the featureless land cleared by the Germans in their withdrawal to the Hindenburg line a year before. But the line was still well ahead of where ideally it should have been; a dangerous salient had been formed around Bertincourt by the pressure of the German advance, and a wide gap had formed between V Corps and VII Corps to the south – very few troops stood in the two miles between le Mesnil and Sailly Saillisel. The *Official History* eloquently describes the position:

> Tired is not strong enough an expression to describe the state of the troops, most of whom were still suffering from gas shelling in the Flesquières Salient ... No words also could convey any picture of the confusion of the night of the 23rd/24th March: troops wandering about to find their brigades and battalions, in an area without landmarks, ... dumps burning and exploding; gaps in the line; the Germans attacking almost behind the V. Corps front; the atmosphere charged with uncertainty, and full of the wildest reports and rumours.[27]

During the day V Corps Headquarters had moved back to Meaulte, just south of Albert, for Villers-au-Flos would soon be in German hands. Headquarters of the North Irish Horse Cyclist Regiment went with them, finding billets at nearby Morlancourt, but many of the men remained in action throughout the day, carrying on their vital assignments attached to divisions and on traffic control. Three of the regiment were wounded on this day, two North Irish Horsemen and one of the Army Cyclist Corps' men attached to the regiment. The Horsemen were Privates James Edward Rainey and James Laughlin, both from A Squadron. Rainey was later discharged as a result of his wounds. Laughlin, from Belfast, was awarded a Military Medal for the role he played, specifically 'a gallant act in the face of the enemy under heavy fire'.[28]

The following day was one of continuing crisis on the V Corps front, with the Germans driving a deep wedge through the gap that had formed between V and VII Corps. But the risk of encirclement that had dogged the corps since the opening of the offensive had gone, and signs began to emerge that the German infantry was outrunning its artillery support. By the end of the day V Corps had fallen back to a line running through the old Somme battlegrounds of 1916 – le Sars, Martinpuich, High Wood, Bazentin and Mametz Wood. Farther north, Bapaume had been abandoned. The line was more secure than it had been on the previous day, but it was not strongly held, and the men were exhausted. The North Irish Horse cyclists' regimental headquarters again followed V Corps headquarters in a further withdrawal, moving during the evening to Toutencourt, west of Albert. Six more men were wounded in action this day, three from A Squadron, two from E Squadron, and one from the Army Cyclist Corps. The names of three are known: Lance Corporal Samuel Charles McNabb from Ballymacrea, County Antrim, Lance Corporal Victor Eccleston Cassidy from Shankill, and Private Samuel Matchett.

Throughout 25 March V Corps continued to come under sustained attack from the German infantry, and continued to fall back across the old Somme battleground. By the end of the day they had reached the banks of the Ancre, the starting point for the Battle of the Somme on 1 July 1916. Following a decision that the strongest defensive position would be the high ground on the west of the river, the remnants of V Corps crossed over during the night and took up positions on familiar group running from Albert north to Hamel. In this sector at least, the Germans would get no farther. During this day the North Irish Horse cyclists had marched nine miles north to Pas before being ordered to return part of the way to Terramesnil where they remained for the night. Why this move took place is unclear. V Corps Headquarters remained at Toutencourt throughout the 25th and 26th. Perhaps the initial move was to help plug a gap in the defences between V and IV Corps, which did not materialise.

The line on the Ancre held on 26 March, despite several determined German efforts. The North Irish Horse cyclists moved their headquarters six miles south to Rubempre, just west of Toutencourt. The regiment suffered its first fatalities of the retreat on this day when two men were killed whilst on a reconnaissance mission. Private Reginald George Armstrong, a Dubliner educated at St Andrew's College, had enlisted on his eighteenth birthday at the end of 1915. Private John James Durneen was an apprentice draper from Clogher, County Tyrone. He had enlisted at much the same time as Armstrong and was much the same age. They are buried together in Toutencourt Communal Cemetery.

German attempts to break through across and around the Ancre continued on 27 March, but with little success. Behind the British front, traffic congestion remained a problem, with relieved and retiring troops blocking the passage forward of reinforcements, artillery and supplies. The North Irish Horse cyclists were employed at key points directing traffic, while others were occupied on Lewis-gun training. Close to the front Lance Corporal Thomas John McCormick was killed. McCormick, from Castlederg, County Tyrone, was a 1912 enlistee who had gone to France with A Squadron in August 1914.

From here on, as the German advance slowed and the line stabilised, life for the North Irish Horsemen returned to something approaching normality. While regimental headquarters remained at Rubempre, the men were employed closer to the lines as corps guides, on traffic control and as runners to V Corps heavy artillery. More casualties were sustained, though none fatal – three men of the Army Cyclist Corps and one from D Squadron, perhaps the latter being Samuel Gordon from Kilkeel, wounded in the hand around this time.

With the German assault halted it was time to hand around the plaudits, and those under the immediate gaze of corps headquarters were well placed to claim their share. Two members of A Squadron were awarded the Military Medal, James Laughlin (mentioned earlier) and Sergeant William Scott, while Squadron Sergeant Major James Harvey King was Mentioned in Despatches. V Corps routine orders of 7 April included the following note of praise from its commander Lieutenant General Fanshawe:

The Corps Commander wishes to express his pleasure at the efficient manner in which the traffic has been controlled by the North Irish Horse (especially the Corps Traffic Detachment) under the difficult conditions of a retreat. He attributes the comparatively light losses in guns and transport suffered by the V Corps very largely to their self sacrificing devotion to duty.[29]

The 9th (North Irish Horse) Battalion moves to Ypres

While the North Irish Horse cyclists would see no more fighting until August, the 9th (NIH) Battalion would have no such luck. As devastating as the retreat from St Quentin had been, more was to come. April had begun well, with the battalion resting on the coast at the resort town of Ault, where they were able to fit in some swimming between cleaning up and training parades. Oliver Nugent wrote home:

I am in a most delightful old 13th Century house in the village of Gamaches, a few miles from the sea. The [36th] Division is now collected around the area and I hope we may be given time to reorganise and get some men and specialists trained.

... I don't know where our reserves and reinforcements are to come from as the Irish regiments are exhausted and there are no reserves left in Ireland.[30]

Nugent was right about the Irish reserves. Without enforcement of conscription in Ireland there were few to draw on. The division would have to be rebuilt with Englishmen, together with the Irishmen left over from the short-lived entrenching battalions.

On 3 and 4 April the division marched to Eu and entrained for Flanders, well away from the scene of the recent fighting and hopeful of a chance to rest and rebuild. The 9th (NIH) Battalion found billets at Herzeele before moving into reserve at Siege Camp, just north-west of Ypres. 'The only communications are duckboard tracks laid over the surface of the mud,' wrote Oliver Nugent. '... the country to the front and rear is an indescribable waste of mud, shellholes and water, bleak and desolate beyond words.'[31]

Far from moving to a quiet sector, the 9th (NIH) Battalion found itself once again at the sharp end of a German offensive. The attack began on 9 April to the north of Givenchy against the BEF's First Army and the weakly-held Portuguese lines. A dramatic advance was made, only slowed in the end by desperate fighting by reinforcements rushed in to plug the gap. It appears that one of these reinforcements was Private William Morrow of the North Irish Horse Cyclist Regiment. Morrow must have been posted to another regiment at the time, for he was miles away from his unit at Rubempre. Whatever the reason, it was an unlucky one for him, for he was killed in action that day.

On 10 April, as the now undefendable Armentières was evacuated, the German attack extended farther north to the Messines Ridge and Wytschaete. The 36th (Ulster) Division sent one of its brigades, 108, to assist. They moved into defensive positions around Kemmel, the 9th (NIH) Battalion at Lindenhoek Corner. The fighting during the day in this sector had been severe, but although the enemy had gained a foothold on the Messines ridge, the line had held. Nevertheless, the prospect for the coming days was less hopeful, as the line was held only thinly by a mixture of units new to the area, all of which had seen severe fighting and losses during March.

If the British defenders had hoped for a pause on 11 April they were to be disappointed. Along the line north from Givenchy to the Ypres-Comines Canal, the Germans attacked in force. In the southern sector they made further significant gains against the XI and XV Corps, so much so that by evening there seemed a real risk that Hazebrouck was in danger and a wedge might be driven between the First and Second Armies. To the north the enemy made progress south of the river Douve, and attacked heavily to the river's north.

It was to this latter sector that 108 Brigade was sent. The 9th (NIH) Battalion took up positions running north from the Wulverghem–Messines Road and the Douve. Battalion headquarters moved to Stinking Farm on the banks of the river. To their right was Hill 63, a strategically important point at the southern edge of the Messines Ridge. The 1st Royal Irish Fusiliers moved to close support of the line running along the ridge from Messines north to Wytschaete; the 12th Royal Irish Rifles in support on the Wulverghem–Spanbroekmolen ridge. At around 3.30pm the enemy attacked the ridge onto which the 1st Royal Irish Fusiliers had been sent, between Pick House and 4 Huns Farm. At first they gained a footing, but a gallant counter-attack by the Fusiliers and South African units drove them out again with heavy casualties. A further attack preceded by heavy bombardment began at 7.30pm, but again the defenders held on. An hour later, the 9th (NIH) Battalion, to the south, reported it was coming under machine-gun fire from its flank – Hill 63 – which was now in enemy hands. Due to the loss of the Hill 63 a small withdrawal was made during the evening to the Wulverghem-Spanbroekmolen ridge, pivoting on Wytschaete to the north. However, in this sector the day was judged a success, with the corps commander sending the following message to the men fighting here:

> Although some of the troops have been recently engaged in defeating the enemy elsewhere and have been made up with drafts from our fine reserves all units are continuing the process of wearing down the enemy by sticking it out and killing Huns with magnificent courage and determination.[32]

The message was direct, but neatly summed up the strategy – absorb the blows, exhaust the enemy.

The diary of 108 Brigade reported one officer wounded, sixteen other ranks killed, 116 wounded and ninety-nine missing on this day. Whilst the 1st Royal Irish Fusiliers carried the bulk of these casualties, two men of the 9th (NIH) Battalion had died of wounds, one being North Irish Horseman Private William John McAuley from Randalstown, County Antrim. McAuley died at the No.10 Casualty Clearing Station, where he had been taken with severe wounds to his right thigh and buttock.

On 12 April there were further dangerous advances by the Germans towards Hazebrouck. South of the Douve, they made small advances towards Neuve-Église, a high point west of Hill 63. To the east and north-east of Ypres, the high ground captured with so much blood during Third Ypres less than a year ago was now dangerously exposed by the German advances to the south, so from the evening of 11 April the British and Belgian troops holding this sector began a withdrawal to a shorter line, essentially giving up all their gains of 1917.

In the sector occupied by 108 Brigade, no ground was lost on 12 April, despite severe fighting late in the day. The 1st Royal Irish Fusiliers, so weakened by the recent fighting, was formed into a company and attached to the 9th (NIH) Battalion, not itself in prime condition. At 6.40pm the Germans mounted a major assault on the ridge held by 108 Brigade along the Messines-Wulverghem road and south of it to the Douve. It was touch and go for a while, with troops of the 9th (NIH) Battalion giving way on the left, but the situation was restored by a counter-attack led by Lieutenant Colonel Kelly, commanding officer of the battalion, and former North Irish

Horse officer Major Holt Waring, now with the 12th Royal Irish Rifles. According to an officer who saw the action:

> The Hun broke us at one point & Holt got out over the top, calling the boys by their Christian names & in about 2 seconds he had them rallied & going up the hill cheering like mad & simply hunted the Hun like sheep. Holt was about 20 yards in front of the lot, stick in one hand & revolver in the other. It was a glorious charge, & simply saved the situation.[33]

By 8.25pm the line was restored and the situation quiet. The fight had been successful but costly. The brigade had lost five officers killed, six wounded and one missing, and three other ranks killed, 109 wounded and 145 missing. Among the many casualties in the 9th (NIH) were Second Lieutenant David Joseph Miller (killed) and Captain Herbert Shelton Dean (wounded), leaving just one North Irish Horse officer in the battalion. Miller, from Banbridge, County Down, had been an apprentice linen designer before the war, and was known as a first-class marksman. He had served in France with E Squadron before being commissioned and posted to the Royal Irish Fusiliers. Dean recovered and served out the war with the North Irish Horse reserve at Antrim.

The 13th was a relatively quiet day on the front occupied by 108 Brigade. Attacks during the day were repelled by Lewis-guns, rifle-fire and grenades. Farther to the south, however, the high ground of Neuve-Église was lost by late evening, opening the way for the Germans to attack all the high ground running from Mont de Cats through Mont Noir, Mont Rouge and Mont Kemmel. At midnight the 9th (NIH) and 1st Royal Irish Fusiliers were relieved and made their way back to the rear of Mont Kemmel for rest and re-organisation. At best they could only make up a two-company battalion. The 12th Royal Irish Rifles remained in the line. Barely rested, near midday the two battalions were ordered forward again – the 1st were sent to the Beehive Dugouts in support of the 12th Royal Irish Rifles north of Wulverghem, while the 9th (NIH) were sent to the Kemmel defences.

Early in the morning of 15 April a heavy bombardment of artillery and trench mortars was opened on the sector held by the 12th Royal Irish Rifles, followed by a strong infantry attack. The line held by the battalion broke, and a new line was established a few hundred yards back in an old communication trench, Kingsway. A counter-attack by the battalion and 1st Royal Irish Fusiliers failed to win back the lost ground. Major Holt Waring was mortally wounded.

The 9th (NIH) Battalion was rushed forward from the Kemmel defences to the Regent Street trench, just behind Kingsway. Two platoons under Captain Crosbie were then sent forward to re-establish the line from Kingsway Trench to the original line on its left. This was carried out successfully, but later in the afternoon the platoons were partly surrounded and had to beat a hasty retreat, suffering heavy casualties. A number of men of the battalion were captured during this day's action. One, Private John Bell, from Loughbrickland, County Down, was either captured wounded and died soon after, or his body was found by the Germans on the battlefield and buried where he lay, next to the road from Messines to Wulverghem.

By day's end the BEF had lost another large chunk of ground, including Bailleul to the south, and in 108 Brigade's sector a further strategic withdrawal was carried out during the night.

The loss of Holt Waring was a blow for the brigade and, of course, for family at home. Waring had commanded the North Irish Horse's C Squadron until August 1916, when he transferred to the Royal Irish Rifles. Soon after his death the battalion's chaplain, Andrew Gibson, wrote to Margaret, his widow:

Dear Mrs Waring

It is with profound sorrow I write to tell you of the death in action of your husband, one of the bravest men I have ever met. Throughout the Regiment to-day wherever one goes, whether amongst officers or men, there is the same voice heard of admiration for his splendid heroism & deep sorrow that we have lost him ... What he did for us I could not put into words, but during the bitter fighting in which we had been engaged since we came into this area about a week ago, he has been the very soul of our resistance, the leader of our active opposition. On Monday morning the 15th inst our sector was attacked after a heavy artillery bombardment. He was in the line organizing, encouraging and visiting the various positions. His presence was everywhere most helpful and his cheery words stiffened the courage of all. This he kept doing until he was hit. At first he thought he could walk back to Headquarters to report but becoming faint he was put on a stretcher and died before he reached the aid post. One piece had penetrated a little above the heart & apparently it was this wound which caused his death. He was brought back to where there is a Military Cemetry [sic] & I went there and made arrangements for his burial & found a Padre of his own faith who kind[ly] undertook to conduct the funeral service and some of our own men dug his grave. I hope this is a little comfort to know that his body was reverently and affectionately laid to rest ... I join with you & your sorrow tho' I know that outsiders like me can only stand outside the door of your home of grief while you meet your sorrow alone within. But while the struggle is going on I hope it is something to know there are other eyes with tears in them and other hearts feeling the pain and the loss. We are passing through a hard time but please God we shall win through in the end. Everywhere there are homes with the dark cloud of sorrow resting on them & hearts that are breaking with that great company of the sorrowful we must try to be brave and patient to help them in their need & for the sake of those who have died so nobly. They would not wish us to grieve over much ... Many are treading in His steps to-day & your brave husband is one of the most shining examples. [34]

Royal Irish Fusiliers officer Joseph Lennon wrote to his cousin on 21 April:

We had a most awful time this last month, we have had the hardest fighting ever we've had to do yet. Our division, the Red Hand, has had a most trying time but all came out colours flying & all ranks did splendid work. I am very sorry to tell you the sad news Major Waring was killed. I was with him a few hours before he met his death & I am very pleased to tell you he died a most gallant death, leading his men over the top with a stick in his hand & calling them all by their names, Tom, Jack, & Harry. I was fighting a few yards on his right. We lost some splendid fellows, but Major Waring was an excellent & gallant soldier ... The men would follow him to Hell, they simply loved him & he loved them. I have heard the men speak of him as if they had lost a father. [35]

Howard Murland, a friend of Holt Waring, wrote despairingly in his diary:

Poor Holt Waring has been killed, having survived for so long. All the old families are being wiped out in this bloody war, all my friends. [36]

In the early hours of 16 April 108 Brigade was withdrawn into reserve positions at Clydesdale Camp, north of Mont Kemmel. Even here there was little safety, the camp being heavily shelled the next day, forcing brigade headquarters to relocate and the men to seek shelter in the nearby ditches.

On the following evening orders were received that the brigade should assemble 400 men to go forward and report for duty on the western slopes of Mount Kemmel. A composite battalion formed from the 9th (NIH), 1st Royal Irish Fusiliers and a Lewis-gun detachment of the 12th Royal Irish Rifles marched wearily south towards their rendezvous. On the way they were caught in a storm of enemy shelling. The result was dreadful. Almost a quarter of their number were killed or wounded – ninety-seven officers and men. Those left gave what help they could to the wounded and proceeded to their destination, where they remained through the day before being relieved by French troops moving in to take over the Kemmel defences. The action at Mont Kemmel had cost the composite battalion one officer and eleven men killed, fifty-five wounded and thirty missing. Eventually thirty-eight were listed as dead. None has a known resting place, such was the ferocity of the artillery bombardment that had torn through the battalion.

Thirty-one of the dead were from the 9th (NIH) Battalion. The background of these men tells something about the changing nature of the battalion. Twelve were English, mainly from London, but eleven were North Irish Horsemen – it seems the cavalrymen still made up a considerable number of the battalion, despite the recent losses.

Among them was Charles Beauclerk Despard, the battalion's last remaining captain, and its last remaining North Irish Horse officer. The 37-year-old had been working as a rancher in Canada when the war began. No stranger to military service, Despard had served in the 74th Imperial Yeomanry in the Boer War, being Mentioned in Despatches for gallantry. He had quickly returned to Ireland, was immediately commissioned as a lieutenant and was posted to the 9th Royal Munster Fusiliers. Despard had other ideas, however, and had already joined the 6th Inniskilling Dragoons (Service Squadron) and kitted himself out with the uniform and equipment of a cavalry officer. The authorities allowed him to stay. Despard went to France with the Inniskillings in October 1915 and remained with them when they joined the 2nd North Irish Horse Regiment. Soon after his death Despard's widow received letters from his commanding officer and the chaplain, telling her that 'he was going to relieve other troops when a shell fell beside him wounding him severely in the thigh, he was taken at once to a dressing post, but died just after being admitted'. Captain Despard was buried in a cemetery near Kemmel, the location of which was lost in subsequent fighting.[37]

The other ranks were Private Frederick St George Cooke, a grocer from Lisburn, County Antrim, who left a widow, Jane, and three sons to mourn him. Private Allan Davey from Carrickfergus, County Antrim, also left a widow, as did Private William George Leinster from Drummullen, Farnham. The others were Privates Joseph Arthur Bowden from Cootehill, County Cavan, Robert McConnell, from Cloughfin, County Antrim, Robert Park, from Magherafelt, County Londonderry, William Lindsay and William Thomas Elliott, both from Letterbreen, County Fermanagh, William McGahey from Blacklion, County Cavan, and Lance Corporal Randal Edmund McManus from Dungannon, County Tyrone.

During the night of 18/19 April what was left of 108 Brigade marched away from the Kemmel front to re-join the 36th (Ulster) Division, which was holding a section of the line north-east of Ypres. The badly mauled 9th (NIH) Battalion reached Siege Camp at 5.30am, where they had their first real rest in many days.

On the front, the fighting had died down since 18 April, and French troops had taken over the line running from Bailleul to Spanbroekmolen. The German attack resumed on 25 April, the object being to seize Mont Kemmel and drive through to Poperinghe, cutting off the Ypres salient. It began in spectacular fashion, with the French thrown off Mont Kemmel and the surrounding defences within an hour. Mounting losses and exhaustion, however, soon slowed the offensive. Nonetheless, enemy success along the Ypres-Comines Canal on 26 April convinced the British command that another withdrawal along the salient, to the outskirts of Ypres, was necessary. On the night of 26/27 April 107 and 109 Brigades withdrew to the canal north of Ypres. Farther back, the 1st Royal Irish Fusiliers were sent to man a reserve outpost line south of Elverdinghe while, 1,200 yards behind them, the 9th (NIH) and 12th Royal Irish Rifles moved to another fall-back position, or 'line of resistance'.

The German offensive around Ypres was finally called off on 29 April, but for the men of the Allied armies still manning the line and reserve defences, the following month was a tense one. The 9th (NIH) Battalion remained in reserve, holding and strengthening the new trenches and outposts. Such was their depleted state that only a skeleton force could be mustered to man the reserve trenches at night. On 23 May they moved from support positions on the canal to relieve the 12th Royal Irish Rifles in the right sub-sector. This period in the lines was relatively quiet. Fighting patrols were sent out towards likely enemy posts – Von Hugel Farm, Cheddar Villa, Jasper Farm, Rat Farm – but failed to find any enemy. It seemed that truly the 'Boche [was] out of wind'.[38]

Notes

1. Second Lieutenant Thomas Bremner, WO339.
2. War Office, *Field Service Regulations: Part I*, pp.15, 110–11.
3. Letter dated 20 January 1918, in Perry, op. cit., p.201.
4. Lieutenant T. H. Witherow, in Taylor, *The 2nd Royal Irish Rifles in the Great War*, p.112.
5. Lieutenant Whitfield in Taylor, *The 1st Royal Irish Rifles in the Great War*, p.123.
6. Father Gill in Taylor, *The 2nd Royal Irish Rifles in the Great War*, p.114.
7. Falls, *The History of the 36th (Ulster) Division*, p.192.
8. Letter dated 20 March 1918, in Perry, op. cit., p.210.
9. Letter dated 21 March 1918, in Perry, op. cit., pp.210–11.
10. NA, Kew, WO339.
11. Falls, op. cit., p.201.
12. Middlebrook, *The Kaiser's Battle*, pp.267–8.
13. NA, Kew, WO339.
14. Ibid.
15. Ibid.
16. Mac Fhionnghaile, op. cit., pp.110–11.
17. McMahon, op. cit.
18. Letter dated 25 March 1918, in Perry, op. cit., pp.215–16.
19. NA, Kew, WO339.
20. Ibid.
21. Ibid.
22. Ibid.
23. *Ballymena Observer*, 3 May 1918, from website *Ballymena 1914–1918: carved in stone …
but not forgotten.*
24. McMahon, op. cit.
25. *LG Supplement*, 16 September 1918
26. Ibid.
27. *Official History of the Great War: Military Operations, France and Belgium, 1918, Vol. I*,
pp.380–1.
28. *BET*, 9 May 1918.
29. NA, Kew, WO95/761.
30. Letter dated 1 April 1918, in Perry, op. cit., p.221.
31. Letters dated 7 and 9 April 1918, in Perry, op. cit., pp.223, 225.
32. NA, Kew, WO95/2504.
33. Letter written to a Mrs Hanson of Larne by her son, from Combe/Waring collection.
34. From Combe/Waring collection.
35. Ibid.
36. Murland, op. cit., p.282.
37. *Inst in the Great War: The Fallen of RBAI*, www.instgreatwar.com/index.htm. NA,
Kew, WO339. Some of the other men killed in the bombardment may also have been
buried here, their location similarly lost.
38. Godson, op. cit., 30 April 1918.

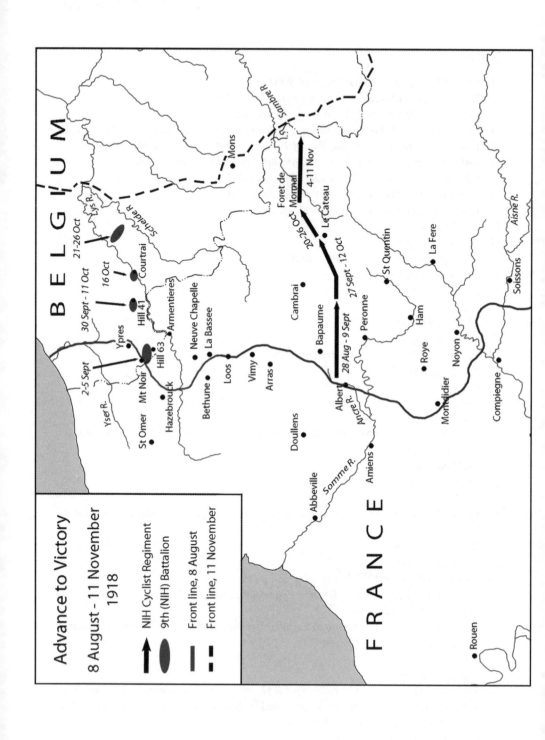

Advance to Victory

**8 August - 11 November
1918**

NIH Cyclist Regiment

9th (NIH) Battalion

Front line, 8 August

Front line, 11 November

Chapter Seven

1918: Gallant to a Degree

I am deeply grateful for the magnificent assistance rendered to this Division by the squadron of V Corps Cyclists, North Irish Horse, during the past sixteen days. They have been gallant to a degree, unflagging in energy, and although placed under different Brigadiers almost daily, have never failed to supply me with early and accurate information.[1]

Rebuilding the regiments

As the German offensives petered out, the North Irish Horse regiments were able to recuperate and start rebuilding. For the North Irish Horse cyclists, relief had come early. By 12 April the danger on the Amiens front was over, the Germans having shifted their attention to the north. That day the V Corps Cyclists marched out of Rubempre to new billets six miles to the west in the town of Naours, clearing the way for a large body of French troops moving in to shore up the defences north of the Somme.

The cyclists remained at Naours, in relative peace, for almost four months. April and May were spent with training and lectures in dismounted action, scouting, map reading, musketry, bombing, use of the Lewis gun and the box-respirator, and tactical schemes with the 12th Machine Gun Squadron. A collection was taken up to buy food and comfort parcels for the men of the 9th (NIH) Battalion captured during the March offensive. Three officers and ninety-seven men were sent on a working party to Varennes, near the new front line. A corps theatre opened at Naours with live performances and films on show. During June and July the regiment was occupied on traffic duty, as corps guides, runners and orderlies at corps headquarters, with ammunition columns, and on signals and bridge guard duties.

Officer turnover in the regiment was high during this period, nine men leaving from April to July, mostly to the Royal Field Artillery. Four of these were the seemingly inseparable New Zealand twins Gilbert and John Grigg and their cousins Harold and Richard Kellock. All left to undergo periods of probation in artillery brigades. In July Captain Murland, whose transfer had been resisted a year before, was posted to the Royal Garrison Artillery for duty with the horse lines. Another to leave was A Squadron's George Bramato Brown, a linen manufacturer from Helen's Bay, County Down. Brown had applied for transfer to the Royal Naval Volunteer Reserve, citing his experience cruising and racing yachts and motor-boats:

> I was part owner of the 8 metre yacht 'Cobweb' for 4 years ... As well as racing I did a lot of cruising in her in the Irish Sea and along the west coast of Scotland ... in 1915 another amateur and myself took a 40ft racing motor boat from Belfast Lough to Oban and back & I have had a lot of experience with motor engines. I owned my first Car, a racing 'Calthorpe' in 1910.[2]

Some of the other ranks moved on too. Richard Torrance, Edward Hall and David Wilson transferred to the Military Mounted Police in June. Boer War veteran Samuel Doak was transferred to the Labour Corps, the fate of many who were too old or no longer fit enough to serve in a combat role. Private Hiram Robinson, a farmer from Fivemiletown who had first served in France with A Squadron in August 1914, left for a more prestigious post. In May he joined the British Section of the Supreme War Council at Versailles.

However, despite these changes, the North Irish Horse Cyclist Regiment was not dramatically different from what it had been at the beginning of the war (apart of course from the absence of horses). It was still very much a North Irish regiment. The relatively few casualties meant that many of the men were the same, and replacements for the sick, wounded or killed still came from the reserve squadrons at Antrim. The senior officers, too, were still largely of the 'gay careless foxhunters of the north' mould, rather than the urban professional type promoted from the ranks in many other regiments. Major the Hon Arthur Hamilton-Russell was still in command, though he would soon be relieved. A, D and E Squadrons were commanded by Captain James Cunningham Gordon Kirkpatrick, Acting Captain Hugh Edmund Langton Montgomery and Captain Ian Archibald Finlay respectively. Kirkpatrick, now aged twenty-seven, had applied for a commission in the North Irish Horse immediately after the war broke out. By 15 August 1914 he was a second lieutenant and by January 1916 promoted in the field to captain. Following a fall from his horse in September 1916, he was twice classed by a medical board as unfit for further active service in France, but twice returned there, most recently when he rejoined the North Irish Horse Cyclists on 21 July 1918. Finlay, described in an earlier chapter, was a 40-year-old Scottish cavalryman, an officer veteran of the Boer War who had been with E Squadron since its arrival in France at the beginning of January 1916. Montgomery, twenty-two, was the son of Hugh Maude de Fellenberg Montgomery and Mary Montgomery (née Massingberd). He was studying at Christ Church, Oxford, in 1915 when he sought an appointment in the Lincolnshire Regiment, but soon after transferred to the North Irish Horse.

Among the subalterns were Edward Arthur Atkinson, Geoffrey Ruthven Austin, James O'Neill and Herbert Gavin Elliot. Atkinson, from Waringstown, County Down, was educated at St Columba's College, Dublin, the son of the Archdeacon of Dromore. He had been working as a rancher in Saskatchewan, Canada, on the outbreak of the war, and joined the 9th Canadian Mounted Rifles. Once in England he gained a commission in the North Irish Horse, joining the 1st Regiment in the field in April 1917. Austin, the son of a clergyman, was also in Canada when war was declared. He joined Lord Strathcona's Horse, later winning a commission and being posted to the North Irish Horse. O'Neill, from Collingstown, County Westmeath, joined the regiment as an officer in January 1917. Elliot, a Shanghai tea merchant, had returned home and quickly won a commission in the North Irish Horse, his experience as a trooper in the Shanghai Light Horse no doubt smoothing the way.

Throughout 1918 the other ranks of the North Irish Horse continued to be a good source of officers. More North Irish Horsemen were commissioned from the ranks in 1918 than in any other year of the war – at least sixty-nine. Most came from the North Irish Horse Cyclist Regiment or the reserve regiment at Antrim. Those serving in the 9th (NIH) Battalion had much less chance – just seven of the sixty-nine came from that regiment. Some forty of the new officers were posted to Irish regiments, sixteen to various English infantry regiments, five to the Reserve Regiment of Cavalry, and five to the Machine Gun Corps. One of those commissioned was Warrant Officer William Moore, who had been the first man to sign up with the North Irish Horse in July 1908. He was posted to the Army Service Corps.

The number of North Irish Horsemen commissioned over the whole period of the war was remarkably high – some 152 became officers. Most were commissioned in 1917 and 1918, with the Army in need of experienced men to replace those lost in the attrition of the Somme, Ypres, and the German Spring Offensive. While just thirty North Irish Horsemen were commissioned in the first three years of the war, the numbers for 1917 and 1918 were fifty-three and sixty-nine respectively. Most were drawn from the initial rush of recruits, those who joined the ranks from August 1914 to the end of 1915. Of the 1,093 men who enlisted during this period, 125 would be made officers – more than one-in-ten. Particularly striking are the numbers for the August to December 1914 enlistees. More than one-in-six had become officers by the end of the war. The odds were much less favourable for the men who had joined before the war, at around one-in-twenty. Most likely this reflects the rural background of these men, they not being seen as having the necessary leadership skills, education or 'class' to make a good officer, compared to the better educated professional urban class of men who rushed to the recruiting offices after the war began. As far as I can establish, all North Irish Horsemen commissioned from the ranks were Protestant.

If August 1918 had found the North Irish Horse Cyclist Regiment still recognisable from the squadrons that had left Antrim in 1914 and 1915, the same could not be said for the 9th (NIH) Battalion. The fighting since November 1917 had cut a wide swathe through the North Irish Horse officers and men who had marched in to their new battalion at Ruyaulcourt in September that year. Of the thirty-five officers on the battalion's books at the end of July 1918, none had served with the North Irish Horse when it was a cavalry regiment. It was a similar story among the men. Before the March 1918 offensive a third of the battalion had once been North Irish Horse cavalrymen. Up to half were lost in that fighting, and more around Mont Kemmel in April. In the following months the battalion's losses were made-up by reinforcements from home – some Irish, some combed from other units, many of them English. The only 'new' North Irish Horse cavalrymen were those returning to the battalion from hospital or leave. By the beginning of August, around 120–150 of the 970 men in the battalion were North Irish Horsemen. Though much diminished, it was still a sizeable core.

While the German offensive on the Ypres salient had ended in April, it had been another month before the survivors in the 9th (NIH) Battalion could breathe easy. On 29 May they were relieved, making their way to Hospital Farm Camp, south-west of Elverdinghe. Here they remained in divisional reserve for three days, cleaning up and bathing, with some fatigues sent to work on the reserve trenches and others training. Soon after they marched farther back to a camp near Proven. The new divisional commander, Major

General Clifford Coffin, inspected the battalion and handed out medal ribbons on 9 June. Among those recognised with the Military Medal were North Irish Horsemen Private Samuel Wasson from Strabane and Private William McCarley from Ballymena.

Unknown to the battalion's North Irish Horsemen, this week also saw the death of one of their former comrades, in tragic circumstances. Private James Magill of Ballymena, who had suffered shellshock at Cambrai, was one of the many made prisoner on the first day of the German attack in March. On 6 June he was being held in a camp at Ham, close to where he had been captured. That night he was killed by a bomb dropped during a French air raid. Magill was one of more than twenty British soldiers killed in the raid. In a cruel twist, a month later his mother Catherine received a much delayed letter from him, reassuring her that he was well.

In the following month two more North Irish Horsemen died while prisoners of war – Private George William Stronge of Boho, County Fermanagh, and Private John Nicholl of Clones, County Monaghan. Life for prisoners of the Germans could indeed be harsh. Henry Emerson of Fivemiletown was one of the men of the 9th (NIH) Battalion captured in March:

I was taken to St. Quentin on the 30th March ... we were put in what had been a cottage or cow-house ... There were no beds or blankets given us, and our clothes were never off us. It was very cold weather, and there was no heating apparatus, not even a roof on the buildings.

The food here was a small loaf of black bread to four men per day; ... soup, very thin, once a day, preserved turnips seemed to be in it; coffee made of burnt barley; tea in the evenings, only it was not tea; no meat, no fats. There was only a small quantity of each kind of food, and all the men got very low on this diet ...

The work I had to do here was burying the dead. I spent the whole of the three weeks at this. The guard indulged in plenty of abuse and knocked us about, but I do not know any case of any man being badly injured ... We were in big rooms with the roofs all shattered, and not wired round. The latrines were old places dug out in the yard. It was very filthy and dirty, and there was no payment for work.[3]

Letters written home to friends and family tried to make light of the difficulties. This from Sergeant Wille Lockhart to his mother at Jerretspass, Newry:

Dear Mother,

    ... I am keeping quite well so I am sure this is the best news I can give you. I hope you are keeping well yourself, Charles, Rowland, Maggie and the little girl. I will be glad when I get a letter of course, they are delayed a lot here, then write as plain as you can as everything is looked at. The Sergts do not work unless they like, so when the parcels arrive, we should not grumble under the circumstances ...

With Love, Willie[4]

From 6 July the 36th (Ulster) Division began taking over the front line. They faced south towards the German salient made by the recent offensive, but for once the British held the high ground, with Mont des Cats and Mont Noir at their backs. The 9th (NIH) Battalion occupied the reserve lines around Piebrouck, on the forward slopes of Mont des Cats, before moving to the Croix de Poperinghe–Hoogenacker sector in front of Mont Noir.

On the night of 18/19 July they relieved the 12th Royal Irish Rifles in the Meulehouck sector. Here a major raid was planned on the German lines for the early hours of 22 July, the object being a strong point called Shoddy Farm. Captain Murphy led the raid with the assistance of four other officers, including the newly arrived Second Lieutenant Francis John Elliott McFarland. McFarland, a civil engineer from Howth, County Dublin, had joined E Squadron of the North Irish Horse in France at the end of 1916. He had later seen service in Palestine, where he earned a Military Cross. McFarland wasn't supposed to be with the raiding party, but according to one of the raiders 'when we were going out Mr McFarland came after us, & said he wanted to go, ... he went without Shell helmet or revolver'.[5] By 12.27 the raiding party had got quietly into position, but fifteen minutes later it was spotted by the enemy, who sent up SOS flares:

His barrage came down in No Man's Land and M.Gs opened from the road running N.E. from La Bourse and the house at [Wirral Farm]. On barrage starting the raiding party at once opened L.G. fire and moved forward: at the same time our barrage was phoned for and came down at 12.50 a.m. Throughout the raid there was very heavy fighting, the enemy garrison being estimated at about 70–100 men with 5 M.Gs. One prisoner and 2 M.Gs were captured, the second M.G. was lost owing to bearer becoming a casualty. Enemy casualties estimated about 30. Our casualties were 2 Officers and 4 O.Rs missing and 11 wounded.[6]

Second Lieutenant McFarland was one of the missing. Patrols sent out for two nights found no trace of him, so it was thought he might have been captured. It wasn't until the following year that he was officially accepted as being dead. Another North Irish Horseman was among the five killed that night – Private William Frederick Christy Arthur, a 20-year-old farmer's son of Douglas Bridge, County Tyrone. Sergeant John Lockhart was one of seven men awarded a medal for the action, in his case for the role he played leading a bombing party.

On the night of 23/24 July 108 Brigade was relieved, the 9th (NIH) Battalion resting for a fortnight behind Mont des Cats. On the night of 2 August C Company and a platoon of D Company went out on a working party. By the end of the night two had been killed and four wounded, presumably by enemy artillery. The two killed were North Irish Horsemen, Private Samuel William Speers of Crossmaglen, County Armagh, and Private John Edward Riddell of Portrush, County Antrim. Riddell had only recently returned to the battalion, having been wounded at Cambrai. Both were buried in the nearby cemetery at Bertenacre.

Advance to Victory

By 8 August the Allied armies were ready to return to the offensive. The 9th (NIH) Battalion made ready to return to the front line, and miles to the south the North Irish Horse Cyclist Regiment rode forward to their old billets at Rubempre.

The Battle of Amiens began on 8 August with a meticulously prepared surprise attack, supported by artillery and massed tanks and assisted by a heavy fog, on a wide front north and south of Amiens. It was the British Fourth Army – largely Canadians and Australians – and the French First Army that led the attack, and it was a complete success. On this day alone more than 12,000 Germans surrendered, leading German commander Ludendorff to describe it as the 'Black Day' of the German Army. Within days the Germans had been pushed back many miles, and their confidence shattered.

Neither the North Irish Horse Cyclists nor the 9th (NIH) Battalion were involved in the battle, but a number of former Horsemen were. One, fatally wounded, was Private William Waller, then attached to the 9th (Queen's Royal) Lancers. Possibly wounded during a charge on a group of German machine guns between Méharicourt and Fouquescourt on 9 August,

Waller died soon after. Another former North Irish Horseman serving in the 9th Lancers, Canadian-born Lieutenant Samuel Gardner Brockwell, was captured during the same action. Private Ernest Wilson was one of the North Irish Horsemen who had transferred to the Tank Corps at the end of 1917. On 9 August thirteen of the new Mark V* tanks of the 15th Tank Battalion were assigned to support the 2nd Australian Division in the attack near Vauvillers. Although eleven were hit and one broke down, the Australians were able to reach their objective. Wilson's tank was one of those hit and the crew were badly gassed. Having got the crew out, Wilson took up a position with a machine gun, firing on the enemy until the others became unconscious, this action earning him a Military Medal.

The North Irish Horse cyclists watched the Fourth Army's advance to the south with mounting excitement and prepared for the moment that their turn would come. From 14 to 16 August on the front occupied by V and IV Corps, the Germans pulled back from a six-mile bulge in the line north-west of the Ancre, giving up Serre and Beaumont Hamel. Men of the North Irish Horse joined the pursuit, putting into practice their advance guard training. On 16 August they lost one man on the west bank of the Ancre, north of Hamel. Private Wesley McClelland, from Cookstown, County Tyrone, had been with the regiment in France since August 1914.

On 16 August news came of the role the regiment would play in the next phase of the advance. The cyclists would be the vanguard to V Corps, a similar role to the old cavalry advance guard, riding ahead of the advancing troops, seeking out enemy concentrations and strong points, and keeping touch with the enemy as he withdrew. A Squadron under Captain Kirkpatrick was allotted to the 21st Division, D Squadron under Captain Montgomery to the 17th (Northern) Division, and E Squadron under Captain Finlay to the 38th (Welsh) Division.

The attack was to begin on 21 August. V Corps' 21st Division would attack north of the Ancre, with its 1st and 2nd Lincolns in front. To assist them, two officers and sixty-seven other ranks of the North Irish Horse cyclists were attached, taking with them all nine of the regiment's Lewis guns.

The eve of the battle found the 2nd Lincolns, with their North Irish Horse Lewis gunners, positioned east and south-east of Beaumont Hamel. That evening the Germans opened an intensive mustard gas bombardment on the reserve positions. The 2nd Lincolns, mostly young men new to the front, were caught in the narrow ravine and sustained many gas casualties, among them being four North Irish Horsemen. At zero hour a Stokes mortar barrage and hurricane bombardment by light guns commenced. Beaucourt was secured by 10.00am and many enemy captured. Further progress was made during the day, with the 2nd Lincolns advancing along the river until close to Grandcourt. Meanwhile, the 1st Lincolnshire Regiment and their North Irish Horse Lewis gunners advanced on a narrow front as far as the Puisieux Road, running north from the Ancre at the Bois d'Hollande, before being held up by German machine-gun fire from the ridge further east. Two companies of the 2nd Lincolns were now ordered to advance through the 1st Lincolns, take the ridge, and continue forward. They reached a sunken road close to Miraumont, where machine-gun, rifle and trench-mortar fire from all sides, including the yet to be captured Grandcourt behind them, caused them to halt and dig in. The day had been a considerable success, though the crossings along the Ancre were not yet consolidated. Throughout the day the North Irish Horse Lewis gunners were made good use of, though at a cost. Three men of A Squadron were killed; D Squadron lost Second Lieutenant O'Neill and one other wounded, and E Squadron three wounded. Those killed were Privates Thomas Bryson, John Martin Roberts and Robert Ross. Ross, from Belfast, was probably killed during the assault on Beaucourt, for he was buried in the nearby Beaucourt Cemetery. Bryson and Roberts were pre-war Horsemen who had served together in France since August 1914. Bryson, aged twenty-eight, was from Carrigallen, County Leitrim, and Roberts, thirty, from Stillorgan, County Dublin. Both were killed north of the Bois d'Hollande on the slope running up from the Puisieux Road, so were probably with the final push by the 2nd Lincolns. They were buried where they fell.

The next day, 22 August, passed relatively quietly, with preparations to resume the advance the following day. Dawn found various platoons of the 1st and 2nd Lincolns and the 12/13th Northumberland Fusiliers, with the North Irish Horse Lewis gunners, holding the sunken road captured the previous day. At 5.00am the enemy attacked the left flank held by a company of Northumberland Fusiliers, forcing them back, and at the same time made their way forward on the right along the Ancre valley. Lewis-gun fire on the latter group ended the danger there. The danger on the left, however, was only eased when men of the Northumberland Fusiliers and a detachment of North Irish Horsemen under Lieutenant Atkinson with three Lewis guns were brought into action under heavy fire, 'nullifying the attempts of the enemy, and enabling the battalion to hold its position'.[7]

Further attacks were made by the Germans later in the day, at one point getting within thirty yards of the sunken road, but all were dispersed. Atkinson's North Irish Horse detachment was withdrawn. Months later he was awarded the Military Cross for his part in this action.

The following day was one of spectacular success across most of the Third and Fourth Army front, with much ground won and many prisoners captured. V Corps' advance was more limited, and the old battlefields of the Somme remained in German hands for another day. However, the moment was near, and there would soon be a need for quick intelligence and forward patrols as V Corps' infantry battalions pushed the enemy back. The North Irish Horse's E Squadron joined the 38th (Welsh) Division; D Squadron the 17th (Northern) Division; and A Squadron the 21st Division. The regiment's Lewis gunners were ordered back to their squadrons. Headquarters of the regiment moved closer to the action – from Rubempre to Toutencourt, and then to Beaussart. The three squadrons would spend the rest of the war operating as divisional, rather than corps cyclists – the conditions of war having returned to the sort of mobility not seen since 1914, when the horsemen had first ridden as divisional cavalry.

On 24 August V Corps pushed across the Ancre and chased the Germans from much of the old Somme killing grounds north-east of Albert, thanks to a cleverly executed night attack. Before midnight, troops of the 21st Division's 64 Brigade had attacked and eventually seized the spur running to the south of Miraumont, holding it throughout the day despite for a while being almost completely surrounded. The 38th (Welsh) Division crossed the Ancre immediately to the north of Albert from 1.00am, and were joined by the 17th Division to their north. Together they achieved the sort of success that had been planned for 1 July 1916, capturing Thiepval, la Boisselle, Ovillers and pushing on towards Pozières and Contalmaison.

The North Irish Horsemen attached to each of the three divisions played their part during the day, though individual battalion diaries are mostly silent. The diary of the 2nd Lincolnshire Regiment, however, noted that at 2.00pm battalion headquarters, B and C Companies and a detachment of the North Irish Horse crossed the Ancre to the south and moved to position in Boom Valley, east of Grandcourt. Five hours later they moved farther forward to old trenches near the Miraumont Road.

Further advances were made the following day, V Corps capturing Contalmaison, Pozières, Bazentin-le-Petit, Martinpuich, Courcelette and le

Sars. On the left the 21st Division advanced as far as le Barque, the North Irish Horse detachment attached to headquarters of the 2nd Lincolns advancing during the day from positions north of Courcelette to east of le Sars. Here the advance had been so rapid that for a moment a gap of almost 1,000 yards formed to the right. It was plugged just in time by 110 Brigade, assisted by the 2nd Lincolns headquarters, C Company and the North Irish Horsemen.

Following a heavy downpour on the night of 25/26 August, the pattern of early morning attacks continued. The 21st Division on the left advanced on the Ligny-Thilloy-Sars Road, but made little progress and sustained heavy casualties. One of these was A Squadron's Private Adam Gordon Kelly from Keady, County Armagh. Kelly, twenty-eight, a pre-war enlistee with the North Irish Horse, was buried south of the Butte de Warlencourt. In the centre the 17th (Northern) Division, with a troop of D Squadron attached to each brigade, made substantial progress, capturing and advancing beyond Eaucourt l'Abbaye and High Wood. The 38th (Welsh) Division, supported by E Squadron, were ordered to take Bazentin-le-Grand and advance on Longueval, a task they achieved, though again with considerable losses. Three North Irish Horsemen were among the dead in this sector. Private Frederick Livingstone from Cavan was buried just south of Mametz Wood on the slope rising east to Montauban. Privates George Gill, aged twenty-four, and John McVea, twenty-three, were both from Belfast. Gill was buried just to the south of Bazentin-le-Grand. McVea's body was either buried, then lost, or never found.

Also assisting the 38th (Welsh) Division that day were dismounted patrols of the 6th Dragoon Guards (Carabiniers). Ordered to clear the village of Longueval, they met strong opposition and were driven back, sustaining many casualties. One of those badly wounded was a former North Irish Horseman attached to the Carabiniers, Alfred Henry Huggins of Fortlongfield, County Cavan. The 21-year-old was evacuated to the 38th Casualty Station at Fienvillers, where he died on 30 August.

For the next four days British forces advanced in fits and starts. No dramatic breakthroughs were made and the troops were growing tired. The Germans fell back gradually, leaving behind enough machine-gun posts and artillery to cover their retreat. Still, however, the ground won was remarkable when compared with the dreadful bloody slogs of 1916 and 1917. Morale was high. The diary of the 2nd Lincolns noted that the men are now prepared for any exceptional strain which they may be called upon to undergo. Every man is satisfied that it requires several Boches to equal one of ours.[8]

It was confidence bought at a heavy cost. In the eleven days of fighting the North Irish Horse Cyclists had lost more than 10 per cent of their strength, with seven killed and twenty-seven wounded. The wounded included Second Lieutenant Albert Henry Cleaver of A Squadron (gassed) and Second Lieutenant James O'Neill. Among the other ranks wounded were James McAteer from Ballymena (wounded in the shoulder by a German machine gunner on 24 August); Herbert Short from Monmouth (wounded in the back on 26 August); Robert Wilson from Fulford, York (wounded in the neck, arm and shoulder on 29 August); James Wilson from Dunadry and Samuel Crawford from Broughshane, County Antrim (both gassed); and Thomas Montgomery of Clonavon, Ballymena.

The British assault continued for the first three days of September, winning back more of the ground lost in March. On 1 September the 38th (Welsh) Division captured Morval and pushed on towards Sailly Saillisel, although their left flank was driven back by a determined counter-attack when the 17th (Northern) Division failed to capture le Transloy. E Squadron was held in 38th (Welsh) Division reserve just south of Lesboeufs. Beaulencourt was attacked by troops of the 21st Division, with A Squadron assisting in the capture of the village. D Squadron, now commanded by Acting Captain George Talbot Plum, carried out patrol work for the 17th (Northern) Division. Plum was new to France, but had been given command of the squadron from Hugh Montgomery when he arrived on 29 August. E Squadron, too, had had a change in command. On 30 August Captain Finlay was hospitalised with tonsillitis and soon after transferred to a cavalry regiment. His place was taken, briefly, by Lieutenant Donald O'Neill Hodson, and after that by Captain John Grant.

On 2 September little progress was made by the 38th (Welsh) Division as it cleared German resistance out of Sailly Saillisel and waited for the capture of le Transloy on its left. Sailly Saillisel had earlier been reported clear, but this was not the case, as troops of the 2nd Royal Welsh Fusiliers discovered. Three patrols of North Irish Horse cyclists (E Squadron) were sent to reconnoitre the ruined village and report back on the positions held by the enemy. Their mission successfully accomplished they pulled back to a quarry behind the village while the Welshmen fought their way through. In contrast to the previous day, the 17th (Northern) Division in the centre met with great success, seizing le Transloy and pushing on to capture Rocquigny. Meanwhile, to their north, A Squadron patrols had found the ridges east of Beaulencourt to be held strongly by the enemy. Nonetheless, the 21st Division was able to win further ground during the day.

During the night of 2/3 September the Germans quietly withdrew from their positions to the more defendable Canal du Nord, so quietly that it was well into the morning before the British realised they had gone. The North Irish Horsemen of E Squadron had taken up defensive positions in North Copse, west of Sailly Saillisel, to stop any enemy advance up the valley, and it was not until 10.55am that reports came in that le Mesnil-en-Arrouaise, well to the east, was clear. The squadron then joined the pursuit to the Canal, attached to the 38th (Welsh) Division. By evening they were camped just west of Etricourt on the Canal du Nord. D Squadron was similarly employed with the 17th (Northern) Division. Two troops were attached to 50 Brigade, which was ordered to continue the advance, the cyclists scouting in front. By 3.30pm they had reached the high ground overlooking the Canal du Nord between Ytres and Etricourt, where they found the enemy well entrenched on the far side. D Squadron's role in the day's action won praise from the division's commander:

> During the advance from Rocquigny to the Canal-du-Nord, sections patrolled ahead of the Infantry and sent back most useful reports as to the position of the enemy. One patrol on arrival at Etricourt dismounted and came into action against an enemy Machine Gun nest on the East bank of the Canal-du-Nord and compelled it to withdraw.[9]

A Squadron, meanwhile, had spent the day well behind the lines, south of le Barque. The narrowing of the V Corps front during the advance had squeezed out its division, the 21st, which was sent back for a much-needed rest.

Despite being close to the action, the North Irish Horse cyclists saw no fatalities from enemy action during these first days of September. However, there were losses elsewhere, one being arguably the Horse's most famous. Major Richard Annesley West had been with the North Irish Horse from the beginning, when he enlisted as a private in frustration that his commission had not come through fast enough. He saw action in the retreat from Mons and in June 1915 transferred to the 1st/1st North Somerset Yeomanry, serving with that unit as a captain and temporary major and winning a Distinguished Service Order. In December 1917 he transferred to the Tank Corps. During the August offensive the courage and leadership he showed in command of a company of Whippet tanks in the fighting east of Villers-Bretonneux, eschewing the armour for a horse, earned him another award, this time the Military Cross:

> He had two horses shot under him during the day, and he and his orderly killed five of the enemy and took seven prisoners. He rendered great services to the cavalry by his personal reconnaissances, and later in the day, under heavy machine-gun fire, he rallied the crews of disabled Tanks and withdrew them with great skill.[10]

By 21 August West's Tank Corps battalion had moved north to the Third Army's VI Corps front, their objective being to support the infantry advance to the railway in the vicinity of Courcelles. A thick fog had descended before dawn, and many of the attackers lost their direction. West, now commanding the regiment, moved forward with the attack to help maintain cohesion, at first mounted and then on foot after his horse was shot. The attack was a success and West was awarded a Bar to his DSO.

On 2 September VI Corps attacked Vaulx Vraucourt over ground difficult for tanks and infantrymen alike. The Whippets were initially held back for use later in the day, so West rode forward to follow the progress of the infantry.

> [He] arrived at the front line when the enemy were in process of delivering a local counter-attack. The infantry battalion had suffered heavy officer casualties, and its flanks were exposed. Realising that there was a danger of the battalion giving way, he at once rode out in front of them under extremely heavy machine-gun and rifle fire and rallied the men. In spite of the fact that the enemy were close upon him he took charge of the situation and detailed non-commissioned officers to replace officer casualties. He then rode up and down in front of them in face of certain death, encouraging the men and calling to them, 'Stick it men; show them fight; and for God's sake put up a good fight.' He fell riddled by machine-gun bullets.[11]

The counter-attack was repelled, though whether the danger justified West's suicidal heroics is open to speculation. Nonetheless, for his 'most conspicuous bravery, leadership and self-sacrifice' in the fighting at Courcelles and Vaulx-Vraucourt, Lieutenant Colonel West was awarded the Victoria Cross, Britain's highest military honour. He is the only North Irish Horseman to have received that award.

On the same day that West fell, Private Alexander Blair, a North Irish Horse cyclist, died miles behind the lines. Blair was under age when he enlisted in 1916 and had suffered the humiliation of his mother claiming him back. However, he waited his chance and enlisted again. Robert Thompson's *Ballymoney Heroes* includes Blair's sister Jeannie's vivid memories of his last leave:

Alex was allowed home from France on compassionate leave [following the death of his brother], and one of her memories is of seeing the sun glinting on the buttons of Alex's uniform as the funeral moved up the hill away from the house ... Alex had to return to his unit immediately the funeral was over and he left for the last time that evening. Jeannie ... can still remember Alex's last words to her as he left the house. Toys were few in those days and he promised to bring her a wee circus the next time he was home. [A short time later he died.] A report in the Constitution of 5th October 1918 tells of him being in hospital suffering from shell-shock.[12]

Private Blair is buried at Varennes Military Cemetery.

The German Army had intended to hold the line at the Canal du Nord, but in this they would be severely disappointed. On 4 September the 38th (Welsh) Division forced a crossing at Manancourt and after a hard fight consolidated on the far-side ridge. E Squadron of the North Irish Horse, after initially being used as runners between battalions, was detailed to carry ammunition for the attacking troops and assist in holding the positions won. To the north, where the canal runs through a long tunnel, the 17th (Northern) Division, made light work of the crossing. D Squadron was attached to this division and was employed on reconnaissance, patrols being sent out to Ytres and Etricourt prior to their capture.

On 5 September, a very wet day, the 7th Lincolnshire Regiment and 7th Border Regiment of the 17th (Northern) Division attacked and seized further ground, getting close to the outskirts of Equancourt, but the town itself remained in enemy hands. D Squadron was employed in keeping the 7th Lincolns in touch with its brigade, and on patrol work. E Squadron, working with the 38th (Welsh) Division, was held up by machine-gun fire from the ridge running south from Equancourt to Nurlu. The division was relieved at the end of the day by the 21st Division, E Squadron riding back to divisional headquarters.

On 6 September it was discovered that the enemy had again abandoned its positions, so over two days the two V Corps divisions were able to advance with little resistance over thousands of yards, occupying Equancourt, Fins, Sorel le Grand, Dessart Wood and Heudicourt. A and D Squadrons were used throughout for reconnaissance and as patrols and runners, providing most useful intelligence and winning praise from the commander of the 17th (Northern) Division:

> When all the forward telephone wires were cut and the Power Buzzer [was] out of action, the [D Squadron] Cyclists riding down the Fins-Gouzeaucourt Road maintained communication from the forward Battns to the Dessart Wood Report Centre.[13]

Further progress was made on 8 and 9 September, though in the face of stiffer opposition and worsening weather, and then for a short while the BEF drew breath. Practically all the ground lost during the German March offensive had been retaken, and now, once again, they faced the Hindenburg Line defences.

For days the line on the V Corps front remained fairly static. A Squadron continued its work as runners and reconnaissance for the three brigades of the 21st Division until 16 September, when it moved back to the east of Heudicourt for a short rest. Soon after, three men were awarded the Military Medal: Corporal Johnston Armstrong of Kesh, County Fermanagh, Corporal Joseph Smith Bailey of Castleblayney, County Monaghan, and Private Hubert Kearon of Dublin. Armstrong and Bailey were veterans, in France with the squadron since August 1914. By contrast, Kearon was just eighteen and had enlisted less than a year before.

D Squadron rested at Lechelle, following the relief of the 17th (Northern) by the 38th (Welsh) Division on the night of 11/12 September, and received letters of praise from the commanders of 50 Infantry Brigade and 17th (Northern) Division:

The patrolling done by the Cyclists and the information which they obtained, has proved invaluable and largely contributed to the success of the operations.[14]

... The Cyclists were of the greatest use, their keenness was most marked, and they carried out the tasks allotted to them in a most competent manner.[15]

E Squadron was kept busy as the 38th (Welsh) Division moved back into the line. On 12 September it moved to 114 Brigade Headquarters where its men were employed as runners, ammunition and ration carriers, and keeping touch between battalions. On 16 September the squadron moved back to divisional headquarters at Etricourt where they received lavish praise from the divisional commander.

I am deeply grateful for the magnificent assistance rendered to this Division by the squadron of V Corps Cyclists, North Irish Horse, during the past sixteen days. They have been gallant to a degree, unflagging in energy, and although placed under different Brigadiers almost daily, have never failed to supply me with early and accurate information.

I desire especially to place on record my appreciation of the manner in which this sqn, on the 4th inst, took forward ammunition to the troops of the 114th Bde through a very heavy HE and gas barrage, across the Canal du Nord.

I shall be very happy to forward any recommendations for immediate awards that the Squadron Commander may see fit to submit.[16]

E Squadron's commander took him at his word, and as a result five men were awarded the Military Medal: Sergeant Thomas Jamison from Antrim, Sergeant William Brown from Cootehill, County Cavan, Corporal Robert Cooke Blair from Belfast, Acting Corporal William Stevenson from Ballymena, and Lance Corporal David Connolly from Belfast. Their officer commanding, Donald O'Neill Hodson, would later be awarded the Military Cross for the role he played in the fighting.

On coming under heavy fire from a party of the enemy in concealed positions, he at once attacked them, capturing eighteen, and killing the remainder. Later, during an attack, he organised three Lewis-gun teams to protect the flank, and thus caused a flanking movement by the enemy to be repulsed.[17]

New officers arrived during this brief period of rest, some new to the regiment, others old faces. Second Lieutenant Worship Booker, who had been in France with C Squadron in 1914, returned and joined A Squadron after a long period recovering from a severely broken leg. Second Lieutenant William Westley Blanden, late of the Suffolk Yeomanry, joined D Squadron. During September command of the regiment passed from Major Hamilton-Russell to Major Arthur Edward Phillips. Phillips, an Englishman, had no previous association with the regiment, having served through the war as a captain then major in the Royal West Kent Regiment. His arrival was just one sign that even this North Irish Horse regiment was losing its north of Ireland character. Another was the arrival on 18 September of a new draft of fifty-six men from Boulogne. Most, probably all, were English. They had been serving at home with various other regiments until compulsorily transferred to the North Irish Horse and shipped to France. They included, for example, 28-year-old London dock labourer Archibald James Moss, originally with the 4th Buffs, 19-year-old clerk Garnett Wesley Cornwell from Rowley, Staffordshire and 19-year-old Albert Garnett, both of whom had served with the Derbyshire Yeomanry.

While most of the attention during August and early September was on the dramatic advance on the Amiens–Arras front, life around Ypres had also been eventful. On the night of 8 August 108 Brigade ended its fortnight's rest and marched to a section of the line on the forward slope of Mont Noir, facing south to German-held Bailleul. The 9th (NIH) Battalion relieved the 2nd Royal Inniskilling Fusiliers on the right, on high ground known as Meulehouck.

The battalion found an active front. Enemy artillery fire was heavy and clear weather meant much aircraft activity. The men watched dogfights, saw an enemy balloon brought down in flames, and ducked for cover when a German airplane strafed their trenches. Offensive patrols were sent out each night. Two on the night of 9 August were spotted and fired on, one of the two wounded being North Irish Horseman Percy Reid. On the night of 11 August a large patrol attempted a raid on Shoddy Farm. They got to within thirty yards of the farmhouse but then realised it was too heavily manned to attempt an assault. Matters got worse when the party was attacked from behind by a German patrol. Grenades were thrown by the Germans and hand-to-hand fighting ensued. Eventually the raiders made it to safety. Their leader was missing, two other ranks were dead and two wounded. North Irish Horseman Lance Corporal James Taggart was one of the wounded (the second time for him in four months), this time in the right knee, and severely enough to end his active service. The two who died in the raid were also North Irish Horsemen. Private William Brown, wounded in the March offensive, had only recently returned to the battalion. His comrades brought him, badly-wounded, to safety, but he died soon after. The other casualty was 33-year-old upholsterer Private Andrew Pepper from Bloomfield, Belfast. His body was not recovered.

On the night of 16 August the battalion was relieved and moved to support positions at Mont Noir. Soon after an attack by the 15th Royal Irish Rifles advanced the line a quarter of a mile, capturing Mural and Wirral Farms. Second Lieutenant John Knox, who had served with the North Irish Horse until commissioned, was awarded a Bar to his Military Cross for the way he handled his platoon in the attack.

> Having reached his final objective, he found the platoon on his right held up. He at once led an attack on the point and captured it, taking a machine gun and six prisoners. Then he worked along fences, clearing out three enemy posts, and established touch with the division on the right.[18]

The 9th (NIH) and 1st Royal Irish Fusiliers were now ordered to prepare for an attack on their front. At 8.30pm on 23 August they moved into position and gaps were cut in the wire.

> Our front was very quiet. The morning opened dull and rain fell. Three of our planes flew over the line and one enemy. At 7 a.m the Coys. were in position ... Our barrage opened with m.g fire and trench mortars. After one minute the artillery barrage started and the Coys moved forward to the attack. After a few minutes the enemy put up lights which were replied to by artillery fire. This fell first upon the 1st Royal Irish Fus. front but then worked across our own ... Some of our own 18 pdr. shells fell very short ... Our smoke barrage was not very heavy especially on the right. The enemy seemed to be taken by

surprise and were more inclined to run than fight. The objectives were reached without much opposition … At 8 a.m. the whole objective was taken and consolidation was carried on until 10 a.m … There was slight enemy shelling throughout the day on front line area and on the Meulehouck.[19]

A counter-attack in the early evening was repelled by artillery and machine-gun fire. The attack had been a complete success, breaking the German defensive positions and exposing Bailleul. Among the awards given were Military Medals to Private Joseph Coulter of Fivemiletown, formerly of the 6th Inniskilling Dragoons (Service Squadron) and 2nd North Irish Horse Regiment, and Private Joshua Paul of Maghera, County Londonderry.

A fortnight of rest and training was now planned, and on the night of 29/30 August the battalion was relieved and marched to billets in corps reserve near the village of St Sylvestre-Cappel. However, hope of a quiet time evaporated when news came that the Germans were pulling back along a wide front. From the canal south of Ypres down to the la Bassée Canal the enemy had penetrated far to the west in April – they were now giving it all up.

The 9th (NIH) Battalion, with 108 Brigade, was ordered forward to Mont des Cats, then for two days moved forward in close support of 109 Brigade. There was no panic in the enemy withdrawal and while the advancing troops found the defenders few in number, their resistance, particularly through well-sited machine-gun posts, ensured a cautious and methodical pursuit. At the end of 1 September 108 Brigade was ordered to relieve 109 and continue the pursuit. Overnight, the 12th Royal Irish Rifles and 1st Royal Irish Fusiliers moved forward, the 9th (NIH) held in reserve. The first object for the brigade was Neuve-Église, which was captured after stiff resistance and house-to-house fighting. In the evening and throughout the next day the two battalions pushed on further. By late afternoon they were approaching the northern and western slopes of Hill 63 and other landmarks of the bitter fighting of April. The 9th (NIH) Battalion, having moved forward to Neuve-Église, was now ordered to take over the whole 108 Brigade front from the 1st Royal Irish Fusiliers and 12th Royal Irish Rifles. During the evening they moved into position, the line running south from St Quentin Cabaret and then turning south-west to l'Alouette.

On 4 September the battalion attacked along the Douve River, while the 29th Division attacked Hill 63 on their right flank. At first all went well. On the left, a platoon of D Company moved forward, keeping to the right of the Wulverghem-Messines Road. The other three platoons, however, lost direction and wandered to the right, eventually reaching Winter Trench near Stinking Farm. To their right, two platoons of C Company kept direction and also reached Winter Trench, keeping to the right of the wayward platoons of D Company. The other two platoons of C Company were sent left to fill the gap and assist the platoon of D Company along the road to Fort Lindsay and Hanbury Support Trench. A Company reached its objectives to the right, and B Company was held in support at South Midland Farm on the Wulverghem-Messines Road.

By late morning, however, 88 Brigade on the forward slopes of Hill 63 began to pull back from its outpost line. The enemy quickly followed up, exposing the forward troops of the 9th (NIH) Battalion to heavy fire and forcing them to withdraw. Three platoons of B Company were sent to cover the retiring troops and a new line was established along a hedge running south from the road in front of South Midland and la Plus Douve farms, but not before around twenty men of the battalion were cut off and forced to surrender. A dangerous gap existed on the right flank, where touch could not be established with 88 Brigade. One company of the 1st Royal Irish Fusiliers was sent forward to assist. In the meantime German troops had crept forward along the valley of the Douve and along the Northern slopes of Hill 63. They launched an attack on the battalion's right flank, but were repelled by machine-gun and rifle fire. The rest of the day and that night passed relatively quietly, although patrols were sent out by both sides and the Germans engaged in fairly heavy shelling with high explosives and gas. Heavy rain added to the men's discomfort.

One man of the battalion recognised for his actions on this day was North Irish Horseman Lance Corporal James Gracey.

> After his section commander had been wounded he took command and led a charge on two enemy machine-gun positions, inflicting heavy casualties on the enemy. Subsequently, though wounded himself, he assisted the stretcher-bearers in bringing in the wounded under heavy machine-gun fire.[20]

The following morning the 9th (NIH) Battalion was ordered to re-take the ground held briefly the day before – from Boyle's Farm to Stinking Farm north of the Douve. Two platoons each from B and C Companies moved off at 5.00am under a light barrage but soon got into trouble. No ground was gained. Patrols sent out later in the day met stiff resistance.

During the night 108 Brigade was relieved, the 9th (NIH) handing over their positions to the 2nd Royal Irish Rifles. The long march back to billets at Cyprian Farm near Keerseborm on the western edge of Ravelsberg Ridge was made all the more difficult by a heavy enemy gas bombardment.

The battalion's losses since 31 August had been four officers wounded, twenty-five other ranks killed, five died of wounds, ninety-three wounded and twenty made prisoner. They had taken back much of the ground lost during the fighting in April. Among those killed in action were three North Irish Horsemen, Privates George Mark, Samuel Pinkerton and William Fairbairn Timbey, all of whom died on 4 September. Mark, twenty-two, a vanman from Ballymena, had returned to the battalion after being wounded in the face in March. Timbey, also twenty-two, was from Belfast. Pinkerton, thirty-one, from Londonderry, was one of those who served with the 6th Inniskilling Dragoons (Service Squadron) when it joined the 2nd North Irish Horse Regiment. Another Horseman, Private James Kelly, a linen apprentice from Belfast, had had his leg badly broken by a bullet or shell, and though evacuated to the 62nd Casualty Clearing Station at Arneke, died on 5 September. Among the many wounded were North Irish Horsemen Private John Campbell, a farm labourer from Carnmoney, County Antrim, wounded in the left leg and right knee, Sergeant Robert Alexander Williamson of Dungannon, wounded in the knee, and Private Robert Kennedy of Ballymena, hit by a shell fragment in the right shoulder. Their active service was over.

For nearly two weeks the 9th (NIH) Battalion rested well back from the fighting. On 8 September the brigade moved even farther back, near Mont des Cats, the 9th (NIH) billeted in Berthen, Sutton Farm and Cato Copse. A week of training and inspections ensued, with church parades each Sunday – on 15 September the battalion diary mentioned something once unthinkable in a battalion of the 36th (Ulster) Division, a service for Roman Catholics.

On 16 September the 9th (NIH) Battalion moved forward to divisional support, finding billets in the ruins of the old lunatic asylum outside Bailleul. They would not, however, return to the front line in this sector. A new offensive was being planned along the entire British line, from Ypres to St Quentin. The 9th (NIH) Battalion would play their part, but farther north.

Meanwhile, well to the south, preparations were underway for the next offensive on the front occupied by V Corps and its North Irish Horse cyclists. D and E Squadrons rested behind the lines and trained in the skills needed for open warfare – bombing, use of the Lewis gun, and map reading. A Squadron saw more action, assisting 64 Brigade (21st Division) in an offensive on the high ground and old British trench system in front of Gouzeaucourt and Villers-Guislain on 18 September. The operation involved all the divisions of V Corps apart from the 33rd Division, which had just joined the corps from the Ypres front. The day saw much hard fighting in heavy rain, with several counter-attacks beaten off, but most objectives were taken, large hauls of war material captured, as well as many hundreds of prisoners. Following the capture of Chapel Hill and the railway line beyond it, 64 Brigade had passed through 62 and continued the advance, soon taking Beet Trench on the outskirts of Villers-Guislain. A Squadron moved forward with the brigade's advanced headquarters to Chapel Hill. In the early afternoon a troop of the squadron was sent forward to find out if the village was still held by the enemy. They reported that it appeared to be held in strength, with enemy machine-guns positioned in the south-west corner of the village. Squadron patrols were also sent to gain touch with 51 Brigade in Gauche Wood on the line running west of Villers-Guislain and to the south of Gouzeaucourt. On 19 September the new lines were consolidated. A Squadron cycled back to Equancourt, leaving one troop at 64 Brigade headquarters. For the next week they practised bombing, Lewis gunnery and map reading. A draft of forty-eight reinforcements arrived at regimental headquarters.

Along the British front, from Arras to the north of St Quentin, the BEF had won back almost all the ground lost at the beginning of the year. The Germans now stood with their backs to the Hindenburg Line. It was still a formidable defensive barrier, but the British reserves were now deep and the men full of confidence, whereas the Germans had little more to give, and knew that the war was lost. The Allies determined on a massive final push on all fronts to end the war before winter. On 26 September the French and Americans would attack between the Meuse and Reims; then the British Third Army and the right of the First Army would attack in the Cambrai sector; the attack would then broaden to Flanders with the British Second Army and the Belgians; and finally there would be a joint British-French assault in the St Quentin Canal sector.

V Corps, on the extreme right of the Third Army, played little role in the first two days of the offensive on this front, the main effort being on breaking the Hindenburg defences in front of Cambrai. But in preparation for the coming advance, the North Irish Horse cyclist squadrons were ordered to divisions – this time A Squadron was attached to the 38th (Welsh) Division, D Squadron to the 21st, and E Squadron to the 33rd.

The attack of 27 September by the Third Army was a spectacular success. In two days the BEF pushed across the Canal du Nord, captured all of the towns, villages, woods and trenches that had seen such bitter fighting during the Battle of Cambrai, and reached the St Quentin Canal in front of Cambrai itself. The following day on the V Corps front, patrols of the 1st Lincolnshire Regiment found the Germans had evacuated Gouzeaucourt. The town was taken, but the enemy had had plenty of time to make good his defences to the east of the village, as the British would learn the next day.

A curious distraction occurred at this time with the return of an old face to the North Irish Horse Cyclist Regiment. Major Neil Graham Stewart-Richardson had last seen active service with the regiment in 1914. Sent home ill, he had remained at Antrim before being attached to Allenby's force in Egypt. Here he won praise (a DSO and Mention in Despatches) for his command of the 1st/4th Royal Scots Fusiliers in the advance from Gaza and the capture of Jerusalem. However, after his unit moved to France he fell foul of his commanding officer and was recommended for demotion due to a lack of 'organising power' and inability to instil 'a proper standard of discipline' in his battalion. Stewart-Richardson avoided the humiliation when he was injured and returned to England to recuperate. Here he was posted to a course in command at senior officers' school, but an administrative error saw him instead sent to France to rejoin the North Irish Horse. This was a surprise to the regiment, for it had no vacancies, and he was soon moved sideways, posted to the Assistant Provost Marshal of V Corps. To some extent, Major Stewart-Richardson's difficulties epitomise the change wrought by the war on the BEF from 1914 to 1918. The man whose good-natured jibe sparked Crozier's 'gay careless foxhunters of the North' epithet had fought with courage and distinction, but had struggled to adapt to a war based more on organisation than gallantry.

On 29 September V Corps was ordered to attack Villers-Guislain and Gonnelieu, positions well sited and strongly defended by the enemy. A patrol by the North Irish Horse's D Squadron east of Gouzeaucourt reported as much. The 21st and 33rd Divisions were in the line at the time, and their attacks, commencing at 3.30am, were repelled. During the following night it was noticed that the enemy was unusually quiet. Patrols pushed out in the early morning found that they had gone. The Germans had withdrawn two miles to the western bank of the St Quentin Canal, destroying all crossing points. The canal here was wide and deep – it was a strong barrier, and behind it ran the Hindenburg defences. Through the day the 33rd and 21st Divisions pushed forward to the canal, aided by patrols of E and D Squadron cyclists.

For two days the divisions of V Corps examined the new barrier they faced and contemplated how a successful crossing might be made. Enemy machine gunners and snipers were active throughout. D Squadron, based just north of Gouzeaucourt, sent out patrols to reconnoitre the crossings of the Canal at Banteux-Bantauzelle on the corps' left flank. It found that Bantouzelle on the east of the Canal was occupied by the enemy but Banteux to the west was clear, that the bridges were burning, and the canal well covered by enemy machine guns. E Squadron, on the right flank, was attached to 100 Brigade of the 33rd Division. A patrol under Second Lieutenant Downey examined the canal north of Ossus in preparation for a small raid which, however, was called off. On 3 October they moved to the rear but were heavily shelled with a gas barrage, fifteen men reported as gassed. A Squadron remained in reserve, camped between Equancourt and Fins, attached to the 38th (Welsh) Division. One troop was attached to divisional headquarters, the officers employed on reconnaissance work, while each brigade was sent two sections of cyclists to work as runners and despatch riders.

Immediately to the right of V Corps the Fourth Army's attack on the Hindenburg defences had been held up, partly due to the inexperience of the American troops being used. A resumption of that attack was planned for 3 October, the 38th (Welsh) Division being lent to XIII Corps to support those troops. This time the enemy was thrown back. The 38th (Welsh) Division followed on, through Epéhy and Lempire to Bony on the canal itself. A Squadron of the North Irish Horse followed close behind them, headquarters finding billets at Epéhy on 5 and 6 October.

The Fourth Army's success had made the German positions on the canal in front of V Corps untenable. During the night of 4 October they quietly pulled back, abandoning the carefully prepared Hindenburg defences and saving V Corps the trouble of a bloody crossing. The retirement was discovered early on 5 October and it was evident that the withdrawal had been hasty, patrols finding 'fires still smouldering, & remains of food not quite cold'.[21] Makeshift crossings were constructed and soon the men of the 21st and 33rd Divisions were again pushing forward, patrols of the North Irish Horse seeking touch with the enemy. Three miles on they found them, on a line running south from Bonne-Enfance Farm to Aubencheul-aux-Bois. Enemy resistance again stiffened and only limited progress was made on 6 October. D Squadron crossed the canal near Bantouzelle and sent out three patrols: Second Lieutenant Blanden's party to Bonne-Enfance Farm; Sergeant Rainey's to Gratte-Panche Farm; and Second Lieutenant Austin's to Montecouvez Farm. While the first two were found clear of the enemy, Montecouvez was strongly held (though soon captured). Gratte-Panche Farm became squadron headquarters. E Squadron went forward with the 33rd Division, patrolling to Aubencheul-aux-Bois and Mortho Wood. At both points they were held up by enemy machine guns. That night the 38th (Welsh) Division moved into the line from the south-west, relieving the 33rd Division, which moved into corps reserve. E Squadron went with them, though not very far, spending the next three days in an old Hindenburg Line support trench south of Bois Mallard.

During 7 October, plans were made for an assault the following day; this would be a long day for V Corps. In this sector they faced the last German trench system – the Beaurevoir Line, and behind it the heavily defended village of Villers-Outreaux. These defences were to be overcome in a 'preliminary' operation beginning at 1.00am prior to the main attack in daylight on Walincourt. The commanding officer of the 2nd Royal Welsh Fusiliers was not entirely exaggerating when he briefed his officers that behind these lines 'the enemy … had no other defensive position except a line many miles back, which was only in course of preparation, and that if we could push him out of here the War was as good as won'.[22]

The night before the attack heavy rain fell, hampering preparations and soaking the men. Nevertheless the 21st and 38th (Welsh) Divisions of V Corps swept over the Beaurevoir Line and captured Villers-Outreaux and Malincourt. By day's end the line had advanced some 5,000 yards and 873 of the enemy were captured. It had not, however, been a walkover, with the night attack on Villers-Outreaux facing heavy resistance until a bold frontal attack on the village by the 2nd Royal Welsh Fusiliers broke through.

During the day D Squadron had moved forward with the 21st Division to the newly captured Ardissart Farm, close behind Angle Wood. Here they were transferred to the 17th (Northern) Division, which was to relieve the 21st in the evening. (The 33rd Division relieved the 38th (Welsh) at the same time.) During the night D Squadron patrols under Second Lieutenant Austin and Lieutenant Montgomery scouted thousands of yards ahead of the front line, to Wallincourt, Selvigny and Caullery, and found that the Germans had gone. With the Beaurevoir Line lost the enemy was pulling back almost ten miles to the Selle river, leaving the barest of defensive posts to slow the British advance.

The advance by V Corps was aided by a new tactic, with no prior artillery barrage and the use of a powerful composite advance guard including a field artillery brigade, a company of Royal Engineers, a company of machine gunners and a squadron of North Irish Horse cyclists. As the enemy retired, touch was maintained by the cyclists. The infantry and artillery were brought into play when resistance stiffened. Using this tactic the 33rd Division sent E Squadron of the North Irish Horse forward with its 19 Brigade as advance guard. One troop under Second Lieutenant Downey was attached to the 1st Queen's (Royal West Surrey) Regiment, another under Lieutenant Hodson to the Cameronians (Scottish Rifles), and the third with brigade headquarters for use as runners. Advance guard for the 17th (Northern) Division was its 51 Brigade, with D Squadron of the North Irish Horse employed in the same way as E Squadron. Meanwhile, A Squadron remained in reserve with the 38th (Welsh) Division, finding billets in Villers-Outreaux and being employed on communication between its battalions and brigades. For the next two days the 17th (Northern) Division and 33rd Division pursued the Germans to the Selle, occupying village after village on the way – Walincourt, Selvigny, Caullery, Clary, Montigny, Tronquoy, Bertry, Troisvilles, Inchy. These bore little damage from the war, bar some looting and damage to roads to slow the advance, and were still occupied by French civilians. An artillery officer of the 17th (Northern) Division describes his entry into Selvigny:

> Hundreds of old men and old women, young women and children, were flocking into the street; tricolours, come from heaven knows where, were hanging from the windows of nearly every house; all were chattering, laughing, occasionally cheering ... Bunches of flowers were produced and given to everyone, our men grinning and making friends in a way particularly their own.[23]

The men of D and E Squadrons shared in the celebrations as they moved on towards the high ground west of the Selle.

On the second day 50 Brigade had passed through 51 to take over the advance guard, and 98 Brigade took over from 19, but D and E Squadrons remained in front. German resistance stiffened. As troops of 50 Brigade moved out of Inchy they came under fire from close range on their left – a couple of enemy field guns and a nest of machine guns east of Clermont Wood. After British artillery fire forced the field guns to withdraw, the North Irish Horse cyclists and a company of the 7th East Yorkshire Regiment cleared the machine-gun nests.[24]

As the divisions of V Corps reached the Selle, north from le Cateau to Neuvilly, heavy machine-gun and artillery fire from the east of the valley made it clear that the enemy planned to make another stand. V Corps troops tried to secure the ground on the eastern side of the river on 11 and 12 October, but enemy counter-attacks drove them back. On 12 October, E Squadron of the North Irish Horse (33rd Division) marched back from Troisvilles to Hurtevent Farms behind Clary for a short rest. Five days later they moved up to Bertry. A Squadron, still attached to the 38th (Welsh) Division, moved up to Clary on 11 October, then two days later to Bertry, and on the 16th to le Fayt, three miles behind the front line, as preparations were finalised to force the Selle defences, the men being employed as despatch riders for brigade headquarters. A Squadron gained a new officer commanding at this time – Acting Captain Worship Booker replacing Captain Kirkpatrick, who was put in command of D Squadron, replacing Acting Captain Plum. D Squadron, attached to the 17th (Northern) Division, moved back to rest billets at Inchy on 11 October. A few men were employed as brigade and battalion runners and the rest stood to in case there was a breakthrough. On 14 October they moved farther back to Montigny.

A well-organised attack on Sunday 20 October finally carried the Selle and the high ground beyond it, with the 17th (Northern) and 38th (Welsh) gaining all their objectives. Zero hour had been set for 2.00am. On the right 113 and 114 Brigades of the 38th (Welsh) Division attacked, with a troop of North Irish Horse cyclists attached to each brigade for 'exploitation and communication'.[25] Three were wounded in the fighting. The 17th (Northern) Division on the left was equally successful, capturing Neuvilly by 5.00am and Amerval by midday. D Squadron, attached to the division's 52 Brigade, was in reserve, ready to move at short notice.

The First, Third and Fourth Armies prepared for a fresh attack on 23 October, the Germans now having no prepared line of defence. On V Corps front the attack was to be made by the 33rd Division on the right and 21st on the left. A Squadron moved back to le Fayt with the 38th (Welsh) Division, D Squadron transferred to the 21st Division and moved to Neuvilly, and E Squadron moved up with the 33rd Division.

Once again the attack was successful, V Corps advancing as much as six and a half miles in two days and reaching the outskirts of Englefontaine and the edge of the massive Forêt de Mormal. E Squadron advanced with the 33rd Division, moving to Hernies Mill near Bois-de-Vendegies. That night they sent out patrols to locate the divisional troops in front and the following day advanced with the brigade to Paul Jacques Farm, then to Wagnonville. A patrol under Second Lieutenant Austin was sent out to reconnoitre Englefontaine. They rode right through the village and located the enemy on the far side. Later two Lewis-gun teams were sent to occupy posts on the east side of village. In fact, Englefontaine proved to be more heavily occupied that the E Squadron patrols had reported, and it was not until a sustained attack was mounted in the early morning of 26 October that it was cleared.

On 25 October E Squadron headquarters was forced out of Wagnonville by heavy enemy shelling, moving to Poix-du-Nord. Two troops of D Squadron had also moved there and been attached to 62 and 64 Brigades. Squadron headquarters and No.1 Troop moved to Vendegies and were attached to 110 Brigade. None of the cyclists, however, were needed that day. A Squadron moved forward with the 38th (Welsh) Division to Forest, and the next day to Poix-du-Nord. As they rode the long straight road through Montay, those who had been been with the squadron in August 1914 may have recognised the ground where they had first entered the war, for le Cateau was in the vicinity.

In just over a month the Germans had been driven from all their carefully prepared defensive positions. V Corps had advanced roughly twenty-five miles, a gain only dreamed of for most of the war. Casualties among the attacking troops had been high, the British Army losing more than 120,000 killed, wounded or missing in October alone. The North Irish Horse took its share of these. Some thirty-four men of the regiment had been wounded or gassed, though only one fatally. Private John Evans, probably wounded on 22 October as the squadron came under enemy shellfire moving to assembly positions late at night, died three days later. Aged twenty-five, he was one of the September draft from England. Others wounded included Jack Reid of Searce near Newry, David Johnston of Ballymena, Sloan Bolton of Maghera, County Londonderry, John Martin of Lurgan and Clifford Arnold of Belfast.

The balance of October and first days of November were quiet for the North Irish Horse cyclists as static warfare returned for a short time. A Squadron remained at Poix-du-Nord under orders of 115 Brigade, then rode back to Forest for a rest. D Squadron was stood to at Poix-du-Nord for a couple of days and then put to work salvaging on the old battlefield. E Squadron marched back to Troisvillers when the 33rd Division was relieved. Major Phillips went home on leave, two new officers arrived from Antrim, two men were sent to officer cadet school, and £30 was raised for packages to send to the 9th (NIH) Battalion prisoners of war. The new officers were 43-year-old Ceylon tea planter Geoffrey Henry Baird, and 24-year-old Magherafelt bank clerk William Moorhead Hunter. Only Hunter had seen active service, and that less than a month with the Royal Irish Rifles in the winter of 1916–17.

The Spanish flu, which had been sweeping through all the armies in France, caught up with the North Irish Horse cyclists at this time, fatally for some. Private Herbert Brennan of regimental headquarters was evacuated to hospital on 1 November and died two days later. Private Charles Woodside of D Squadron was admitted to hospital on the same day and died a week later.

November saw what would be the final push of the war. On the front occupied by V Corps zero hour was set for the morning of the 4th. The corps was to attack east through the Forêt de Mormal. This would be a new type of fighting, and not easy. Mormal, a forest of beech and oak, ran three to four miles across, cut through by numerous woodland tracks and streams. While the Germans had felled acres of the forest, much remained, and between the jumping-off line and the forest was a confusion of orchards and wired hedges. Three of the attacking brigades were given units of North Irish Horse cyclists from A and D Squadrons – 113 and 114 Brigades of the 38th (Welsh) Division, and 50 Brigade of the 17th (Northern) Division.

Morning fog greatly helped the attacking troops and by early next day much of the forest was in British hands. All the objectives had been reached and in some cases patrols pushed out well beyond. The North Irish Horse cyclists were kept busy, their Lewis gunners for example sent to help form a defensive flank for the 17th (Northern) Division when its advance outstripped the division on the right. Inevitably, some casualties were sustained; as many as ten North Irish Horsemen being gassed or hit by bullet or shell. Second Lieutenant Baird was struck by a shell fragment which passed through his left forearm. He was evacuated to England, having been in France for less than a week. Private John Cully was less fortunate. A pre-war Horseman from Glenanne, County Armagh, Cully was fatally wounded.

On 5 November, in cold and heavy rain which would continue for days, the 33rd and 21st Divisions passed through the 38th and 17th to continue the advance, encountering only light resistance until they reached the Sambre, which was forded at several points under cover of darkness. A Squadron assisted the 33rd Division through the day, and their headquarters moved forward to a divisional report centre at les Grandes Patures deep in the forest. D Squadron had patrolled well ahead of the advancing infantry in the morning, reaching Berlaimont on the Sambre at 9.00am. Here they engaged the enemy for more than an hour until the leading companies of the 21st and 33rd Divisions reached them. E Squadron was employed through the day too, half the squadron with each of the attacking divisions.

On 6 November further progress was made on V Corps' front, though slowed by the continuing German rearguard action, terrible weather, and the difficulty of bringing up artillery and supplies over the boggy roads and destroyed river crossings. The North Irish Horse continued its patrol and communication work, with headquarters of A and D Squadrons moving up to Sarabas and Berlaimont, while E Squadron re-united and moved back to Englefontaine for the night.

The success of the 33rd and 21st Divisions over the past two days won them no relief – the momentum had to be maintained for another day and it was impossible to bring the fresh divisions up in time. Despite cold and a heavy mist, which made it difficult to keep direction and maintain touch with flanking battalions, further progress was made on 7 November, with Eucelin and Pot de Vin taken by the 33rd Division. It was a hard fight, as described in the diary of the 5th/6th Cameronians, part of 19 Brigade:

[The] men were suffering from the heavy rain and continual exposure in the open without any opportunity of drying themselves. Until our men reached Eucelin no opposition was encountered but once there heavy shell fire was opened. The enemy had left small parties in the village who were quickly overcome. Progress, however, was impeded by heavy machine gun fire mainly from the left flank and edge of Limont Fontaine ... Numerous Machine Guns defended the N.W. edge of Bois du Temple and the enemy was still able to harass the village of Eucelin and its approaches by heavy bursts of artillery and trench mortar fire.[26]

A Squadron spent the day working as advance guard to 19 Brigade. When they reached the woods to the east of Pot de Vin they came under heavy machine-gun fire. In the ensuing fight, 23-year-old Private Charles Elder of Belfast was killed. Private Elder would be the last North Irish Horseman killed in action in the Great War. He was buried close to where he fell, just north of Pot de Vin.

On the 21st Division front D Squadron cyclists were acting as advance guard. As they reached the outskirts of Limont-Fontaine, they were held up by heavy enemy rifle and machine-gun fire. The advance was halted until a full-scale assault could be mounted on this village and Eclaibes. In preparation, the North Irish Horse cyclists were sent out to pinpoint the enemy machine-gun nests. The subsequent attack was a success and the villages were cleared.

Late in the evening the exhausted divisions were relieved by the 17th (Northern) and 38th (Welsh) Divisions. In three days they had advanced as much as nine miles. A Squadron spent the following day resting at Sarabas, while D Squadron moved back from Bachant to Berlaimont. Meanwhile E Squadron, attached to 51 Brigade of the 17th (Northern) Division, moved forward, two sections sent as runners for the brigade's two advanced battalions. On 8 November they moved to near Limont-Fontaine to support the day's attack on the German positions on the Mauberge-Avesnes road. Throughout the day the enemy rearguard held up strongly from well-covered positions in the woods and orchards ahead of the advancing troops. However, after dark two patrols from E Squadron were sent forward, returning with reports that that the enemy had departed, the village of Beaufort being completely clear. The 17th (Northern) Division rushed forward, securing the ground before dawn.

Dawn of 9 November revealed that the German rearguard had been covering a major withdrawal. The ground ahead was clear for miles. Patrols of cyclists and cavalry were sent east to regain touch with the enemy. E Squadron was sent to reconnoitre the village of Damousies, two miles east of Beaufort. They found it abandoned, save one German who was glad enough to be taken prisoner.

> The villagers told them that all night the Germans had been marching past, and the last of them had gone before sunrise ... the bridge over the river was intact and the villagers of Obrechies, on the farther side, were flying little tricolours from their houses and gave another enthusiastic welcome to our men as they rode in.[27]

E Squadron established a report centre at Damousies to receive intelligence from cavalry patrols and take them back to brigade headquarters at Beaufort. In the evening they took over the outposts established during the day by the cavalrymen until relieved by the infantry. They then returned to billets at Beaufort.

News of the German retreat had cut short the rest break of A and D Squadrons. During the day they rushed up to carry out forward patrol work. A Squadron joined 113 Brigade of the 38th (Welsh) Division at Dimchaux, while D Squadron moved up to Beaufort. On 10 November, A Squadron moved to Hestrud, on the Belgian border, and Eccles, forming an outpost line from Hestrud north towards Cousolre. D Squadron established outposts for the 21st Division at Obrechies, Choicies and Quivelon. E Squadron rested at Beaufort.

Miles away on the French coast, at a military hospital in le Treport, two North Irish Horsemen passed away. They were Lance Corporal Robert Henry Hill, aged twenty-one from Londonderry, and Trooper William Hillocks, aged twenty-five, from Derriaghy, County Antrim. Hill had enlisted at the beginning of September 1914 and went to France in May 1915 with D Squadron. He died as a result of injuries sustained on 1 November, probably at Poix-du-Nord. Hillocks, who had enlisted in mid-1917, had probably fallen ill while at the British Cavalry Base Depot at Rouen.

On the Ypres front through September and October the 9th (NIH) Battalion had also seen plenty of action. As the battalion rested at the Bailleul asylum in the middle of September, a major new offensive was being planned, this time the focus being to the north and east of Ypres, the goal being to win back the old Passchendaele Line abandoned in April. The 36th (Ulster) Division was transferred to II Corps. This meant a move north to Watou, four miles west of Poperinghe, where they found billets in Borden and Endersley Camps. The attack in this sector was scheduled to begin on 28 September. II Corps occupied the trenches directly east of Ypres, with its 9th (Scottish) and 29th Divisions to commence the attack. Although the enemy lines were not as heavily defended as they had once been, the German defenders retained many advantages, including their pill-boxes, dugouts, and superior observation. Nor had the landscape changed – it was still a shell-torn, muddy wilderness, littered with wire and abandoned war material.

The 36th (Ulster) Division was in reserve on the first day, ordered to move forward quickly to follow up the hoped for advance. On the day of the attack, the 9th (NIH) Battalion moved by rail to Siege Camp near Vlamertinghe, and then marched to Ypres, finding accommodation at Salvation Corner just north of the town. The news they received through the day couldn't have been better. In the face of all previous experience, and despite heavy rain for most of the day, the attack by II Corps and the troops to their left and right was an outstanding success. By dusk the enemy had been driven off the entire Ypres ridge, and places such as Frezenberg, Westhoek, Polygon Wood, Zonnebeke, Hooge and Sanctuary Wood were in British and Belgian hands once more.

On the following morning, after a night of freezing, torrential rain, 109 Brigade of the 36th (Ulster) Division joined the attack, capturing Terhand, the southern outskirts of Dadizeele, and reaching Vijfwegen. Already the battlefront had moved beyond the shell-blasted landscape into something closer to open countryside, with hedges, farm buildings and villages facing the advancing troops. Once again the day's advance by much of II Corps, and the Belgians to their north, had been spectacular; to their right less so, but farther south the Germans pulled out of Wytschaete and Messines, abandoning their last foothold on the ridge.

Early in the morning of 30 September 108 Brigade took over from 109; the 9th (NIH) Battalion replacing the 1st Royal Inniskilling Fusiliers. The battalion's orders were to advance, with the 12th Royal Irish Rifles on their left, first to Vijfwegen, then to Mooreseele. However standing near Vijfwegen was a small rise, Hill 41, which had been well fortified by the Germans and afforded a wide field of fire on any troops attempting to move past it. Furthermore, the Germans had recovered from the initial shock of the last two days, while the British troops were tired, wet and hungry, and had outrun their artillery. The day became a battle for possession of Hill 41 and the farmhouses and pill-boxes on and around it. The commanding officer of the 9th (NIH) Battalion ordered his battalion to advance over ground to the south of Hill 41, while protecting his exposed right flank:

> sent [a] message to 12th R.I.R. that I could not keep up with their advance which was unopposed to Dadizeele. 'B' & 'C' Coys came under machine Gun fire almost at once after moving through the R. Innis. Fusrs, but 'A' Coy on the left met with no opposition until they reached the east side of Methuen Wood when they came under M.G. fire from houses [to the south-east] about 9.30 am.
>
> … I decided to push forward my reserve [D] Company to Vijfwegen so as to keep touch with the 12th R.I.R. who were now well in advance

of my left & then by pushing south to … help the other companies to advance.

At 9.30am as D Company advanced along the Terhand-Vijfwegen Road it came under machine gun fire from Leadhall Copse and the cluster of houses to the south that had held up A Company. A and D Companies attacked and cleared these enemy posts as far as the railway line running south from Vijfwegen, with only slight casualties. To the south, B Company cleared the enemy from Walpole Copse, Turnbull Farm, Goldsmith Farm and Pawn Farm, they too reaching the railway line. The division to the right was still well back, so it was impossible for the battalion's right to push on further.

At 11.am. I now found my left held up by a strong point & pill Box & by the enemy in Sandsfield Farm & another farm [nearby]. I arranged a joint attack on these two so as to assist the 12th R.I.R. who reported that they were attacking on my left.

By 12.30 pm. The strong point was captured with 12 prisoners & 2 Machine Guns, an officer & 20 Other Ranks being killed. The remainder of the garrison which numbered nearly 100 were pursued up the hill for 300 or 400 yards but our men had to return to the strong point owing to heavy M.G. fire from [the] flanks … The attack on Sandsfield House failed owing to enemy counter-attack which was launched from Carton House. The enemy crept down hedges between Denbenham House & Sandfield Farm & took our attack in flank just as they reached the farms.

At 1.30 pm. A second attack was attempted but could not progress owing to heavy crossfire from the south & from Cheviot Corner.

4 pm. During the whole day the M.G. fire kept increasing & was by now very heavy & all movement was very difficult. The shellfire was becoming very heavy especially about Leadhall Copse.

The 29th Division were not coming up, & my front was already very extended, 2,500 yards. I had lost five officers & about 100 O.Rs so I decided not to attack further but reorganise the companies until the right began to come up.[28]

Many acts of valour had been seen during the day's fighting, including two North Irish Horsemen. Second Lieutenant Simon Logan won a Military Cross for his conduct

> while leading his platoon in an attack on an enemy strong-point, which was captured, and a number of the enemy killed or taken prisoner. Later, when his company commander was mortally wounded and lying in the open, he went out under withering fire and brought him in.[29]

James Bailey Young, commissioned from the ranks of the North Irish Horse in April 1917, was serving in 108 Brigade's Light Trench Mortar Battery.

> He brought his trench mortar into action in the open under heavy machine-gun fire 250 yards from a farm. When his base plate broke, he stood up and held the mortar until all his ammunition was fired, putting a machine gun out of action. He then used his team as infantry and joined in the attack protecting a flank. He was eventually wounded, after much good work.[30]

At 4.00pm the 12th Royal Irish Rifles attacked Hill 41 from the north under cover of a smoke and high explosive barrage. They succeeded in clearing a wood then capturing Twigg Farm near the top of the hill, claiming thirty-one prisoners and eighty killed. However, a strong counter-attack drove them back to their starting point.

The 9th (NIH) Battalion remained in position through 1 October, playing a support role for the troops attacking Hill 41. At 9.15pm they were relieved and withdrew to the vicinity of Terhand, sustaining sixteen casualties in the process. Here they gained rest and food, checked and replaced missing equipment, and counted the cost of the fighting. They had lost eight officers and 139 men in the struggle for Hill 41 – twenty-nine were killed in action, seven more had or would soon die of their wounds, and more than 100 were wounded. Some of these casualties, of course, were North Irish Horsemen. Private William James Abercrombie, aged twenty-five, was from Blacklion, County Cavan, and Private Joseph Coulter, twenty-four, from Fivemiletown, County Tyrone. Private Frank Best, twenty-two, from Richhill, County Armagh, died of wounds of 3 October, and Lance Corporal Alexander Erskine, from Shankill, Belfast, died a week later.

Two former North Irish Horsemen serving in other battalions of the 36th (Ulster) Division had also lost their lives. Private William Henry Dundas, 27, a farmer from Drumcrow, County Fermanagh, had been in France with C Squadron of the Horse since the beginning. Dundas transferred to the 1st Royal Irish Fusiliers at the beginning of 1918 and had just returned from leave when he joined his battalion's attack on Hill 41. Corporal Charles Edward Houston of Belfast was serving in the 2nd Royal Inniskilling Fusiliers when he was killed during a German counter-attack on the line occupied by his battalion on 2 October.

On the night of 4 October the 9th (NIH) Battalion returned to Hill 41. Only thirteen officers and 390 other ranks could be mustered, such had been the damage inflicted in recent weeks, though a similar story could be told all along the front. After two fairly quiet days, patrols pushed forward on the night of 6 October and occupied Mansard Farm and strategic points around it. Only Goldflake Farm on the southern part of Hill 41 remained to be taken. Second Lieutenant Bryson, older brother of North Irish Horseman Thomas Bryson, who had recently been killed north of the Ancre, took out a patrol to test the defences around Goldflake. The patrol met strong resistance from a well-manned garrison and Bryson was hit by shellfire, his body recovered from the field a week later.

From 7 to 9 October preparations were made for another attempt to drive the enemy off Hill 41. The artillery was finally arriving in large numbers, and each night the wire behind the front line was cut to assist the passage of advancing troops.

At dawn [on the 11th] a party of thirty O.Rs under 2/Lieut Darling MC formed up in Twig Farm. At 10.00 under cover of a barrage and smoke screen, they rushed Goldflake Fm, capturing 14 prisoners, 3 M.G & killing about 10 of the enemy. A position about 100 yards S.W of the farm was consolidated. The hostile barrage was extremely heavy … Our casualties were 1 killed & 2 wounded.

The enemy was not done, however, and just before 6.00pm an intense artillery barrage preceded a powerful counter-attack on Goldflake, Mansard and Twigg Farms.

The garrison in Goldflake Fm withdrew after inflicting very heavy casualties on the enemy who were caught in fours on the road. The garrison of Mansard Fm was surrounded & fought their way back. The enemy succeeded in reaching Twig Fm but was held up by a small party which still held out in front of the farm. The enemy was finally cleared from Twig Fm by a counter attack. Mansard & Goldflake Fms remained in his hands ... Our casualties during the day were 2 officers & 25 O.Rs.[31]

That night the 9th (NIH) Battalion was relieved. Among their casualties had been two North Irish Horsemen. Lance Corporal Joseph Deery, twenty-four, from Castlederg, County Tyrone, and Private Robert John Hull, an engine driver from Lambeg, County Antrim. In 1916 a kick from a horse had fractured Hull's skull, and in March 1918 he had been briefly posted as missing. This time ill fate made no mistake. He was buried near where he fell in front of Twigg Farm. Luckier was Private Samuel William Montgomery from Ballymena. He had survived a chest wound the previous March and this time was hit by a piece of shrapnel in the left shoulder, sending him home wounded but alive.

The offensive in Flanders resumed on 14 October. Hill 41 was overrun quickly and within two days the British were at or within sight of the Lys River. One of those killed during the advance was former Horseman Lance Corporal William Reid of Portstewart, County Londonderry. Reid was one of the hundred men who had transferred to the 1st Royal Irish Rifles at the end of 1916. On 14 October the battalion had attacked towards Gulleghem, east of Moorseele, 'without Artillery Support, and was held up by 3 belts of barbed wire and heavy machine gun opposition'.[32] Reid was buried on the eastern edge of Moorseele. South-east of Ypres the 7th (South Irish Horse) Battalion, Royal Irish Regiment, joined the attack of the 30th Division towards Wervicq. One of its officers, former North Irish Horseman Raymond Green from Sydney, Australia, won a Military Cross for skillful and courageous leadership against enemy machine-gun posts, during which numerous prisoners were captured. Soon after he sent his mother a small package:

I am sending along an Iron Cross which I had given to me in a little scrapping a few weeks ago, I only hope it reaches you OK as I really value it – it is what we all class as the best souvenir of all. I hope you are all well and that I am soon back home again – we have been having fairly hard times lately but the news is great.[33]

Meanwhile the 9th (NIH) Battalion moved forward with 108 Brigade, passing over Hill 41 to spend the night of 14 October near the newly-won town of Kezelberg. The following day they continued east, resting at Copper Corner on the outskirts of Moorseele. On 16 October 108 Brigade advanced to Courtrai on the Lys. All bridges here had been blown, so under cover of a smokescreen a small party of 9th (NIH) infantrymen was ferried across the river, protecting a party of Royal Engineers while they built a pontoon. One of the infantrymen was North Irish Horseman Lance Corporal Robert Armstrong, in command of a Lewis gun section. 'By getting his gun into position on the other side of the canal he was able to cover the remainder of the party. He personally fired the gun and put out of action two enemy machine guns.' Once the bridge was in place Second Lieutenant Steele led his platoon across and rushed an enemy machine-gun post, capturing it with a team of six men. Soon after, however, the bridge was destroyed by shellfire, preventing another party under North Irish Horseman Second Lieutenant Logan from crossing. Undeterred, Logan commandeered a pontoon boat and made the crossing under heavy fire.

The Royal Engineers were unable to rebuild the pontoon, leaving the bridgehead party, about sixty men, stranded. For four hours they held out. When the enemy were seen massing for a counter-attack Lance Corporal Armstrong 'crossed a main street to get into a position from which he could fire and disperse the enemy, inflicting many casualties'. [34] Finally, it was decided to abandon the bridgehead and under cover of darkness the men were brought back in a pontoon boat. That evening the battalion was relieved, marching to rest billets at Drie Masten. The day's losses amounted to one killed and twenty-five wounded. Among the awards later given for the day's fighting, Second Lieutenant Logan won a Bar to his Military Cross, and Lance Corporal Armstrong a Distinguished Conduct Medal.

Three days of relative peace followed, with cleaning-up, re-organisation, inspections and a church parade. The 36th (Ulster) Division was now moved north, taking from the Belgian Army a section on the Lys north from Bavichove to the point at which the Roulers Canal joins the river. On 20 October the 9th (NIH) Battalion marched north to Lendelede, where they took advantage of the town's excellent German-built baths before moving east through Hustle to the river.

Throughout this day 107 and 109 Brigades of the 36th (Ulster) Division had forced their way across the Lys and were now pushing forward against stiff resistance. Two former Horsemen serving in other battalions of the 36th

(Ulster) Division had lost their lives, and one would die soon after. Private Robert Richmond of Killeshandra, County Cavan, was killed during the 9th Royal Inniskilling Fusiliers' advance near Spriete. Second Lieutenant William Anderson, twenty-three, of Greenisland, County Antrim, died as the 15th Royal Irish Rifles pushed across the Deerlyck-Waereghem road towards the Gaverbeek, after taking charge of his company when the company commander had been hit. Second Lieutenant John Knox, also with the 15th Royal Irish Rifles, was badly wounded and died three days later.

During the night of 20/21 October 108 Brigade relieved 109, their orders being to continue the advance. In front were the 1st Royal Irish Fusiliers and 12th Royal Irish Rifles. For three days the 9th (NIH) Battalion was held in reserve, the advance being slowed by a lack of French success on the left and delays in bringing artillery over the Lys. On 23 October the 1st Royal Irish Fusiliers entered the village of Heirweg, but were driven out by a strong counter-attack. Former Horsemen Second Lieutenant James Denny of Belfast and Private William John Wallace were killed in the fighting. Both were buried south of the village.

On 24 October the 1st Royal Irish Fusiliers were relieved by the 12th Royal Irish Rifles, the 9th (NIH) moving up into support close behind the Heirweg positions. The following day in fine weather a further advance was attempted by these two battalions, moving south-east past Heirweg towards Bergstraat. By now the 9th (NIH) could only muster twelve officers and 276 other ranks. Although an advance of 1,000 yards was made, the ground was heavily defended with multiple machine-gun posts causing severe casualties and necessitating much hand-to-hand fighting. By the afternoon the intensity of the fire from the flanks and from another rise named Hill 41 forced a partial withdrawal. The battalion's casualties had been high, with close to fifty killed or wounded. Among the dead were North Irish Horsemen Privates Michael McVeigh from Londonderry and George Moorhead Shannon from Belfast. At dusk the 9th (NIH) Battalion took over the right sector from the 12th Royal Irish Rifles, consolidating the position the following day.

Elsewhere in France and Belgium men who had once served with the North Irish Horse were also dying. On 28 September, in the Ypres sector, Royal Field Artillery officer Lieutenant Harold Kellock was wounded in the back. He died at Boulogne a week later. (His brother, Lieutenant William Kellock, had been wounded at Flers a month earlier.) Private John Scott of Ballymena, serving in the 19th Hussars, was killed in action on 8 October, aged twenty-one. Tom Savage of Larne, who had written home in August 1914 that he would soon be able to 'swank French', was killed in action while serving as an officer in the Rifle Brigade, exactly a month before the war ended. Second Lieutenant Harold Percival Nixon of Belfast, serving in the Wiltshire Regiment, was killed in action near the Belgian town of Warcoing.

Further afield, too, the last months of the war saw the death or wounding of other former North Irish Horsemen. Farthest from home was Lieutenant Robert Campbell Russell of Whitehead, County Antrim. Russell was serving in the Mesopotamian theatre with the Dunsterforce Expedition. According to his commanding officer,

> I had given him a special job to cover the retirement of another unit in case they were forced back. He did this so well that the unit had practically no casualties in the retirement. He was one of the last to leave the position, and was hit in the body just before coming away. He was carried in by one of our men ... and these two were the actual last to leave. I saw him in the ambulance on his way to the Russian hospital train, and had a word or two with him. He died the same evening in the British hospital in town.[35]

Hundreds of miles to the north Second Lieutenant Thomas Whiteside of Moy, County Tyrone, was preparing to fight the Bolsheviks. Whiteside had served in France with the North Irish Horse from 1915. In 1918 he was commissioned, posted to the Machine Gun Corps, and sent to Murmansk with the Syren Force, part of Britain's North Russian Expeditionary Force. This officer would be wounded in the fighting around the Russian village of Kodish in February 1919. Four former Horsemen died while serving with the Egyptian Expeditionary Force. Private Robert McCready of Belfast, then serving with the Nottinghamshire Yeomanry, died in Egypt on 6 August. Two months later Privates Charles McDaniel and Matthew Haggan died of illness while serving with the Staffordshire Yeomanry in Palestine. Farther south, Private George Killough of the Royal Irish Regiment died of pneumonia. On 10 October Private Samuel Shiels, with 770 others, boarded the mail ship RMS *Leinster* as it sailed from Kingstown, County Dublin for Holyhead. Shiels was returning to the 9th (NIH) Battalion after recovering from a hernia. An hour later the *Leinster* was hit by two torpedoes fired by a German U-boat. The vessel sank and more than 500 people, including Private Shiels, lost their lives. Shiels's body was recovered and he was laid to rest in Ballybay First Presbyterian Churchyard.

The end

On 27 October the 9th (NIH) Battalion was relieved by the 4th Royal Sussex Regiment, and marched to billets at Hustle. They didn't know it at the time, but their war was over. After a welcome night's rest the men woke in good spirits, helped by the kindly attention and home cooking of the civilian population. The following day they marched via Bissinghem to Lauwe, near the town of Menin, where they stayed for the night. On Sunday the Lauwe church held a service for Roman Catholics and the usual inspections and re-organisation were carried out, followed by lectures by company commanders on 'the course of the war'. On Monday evening a dance was held in the school room, with the local population invited.

The first day of November took on almost a holiday atmosphere. It was clear that the war was nearly won. The weather continued fine and the battalion enjoyed a trip to the baths. The civilian population put on a dance for the men and the battalion's officers held a dinner, hosting senior officers from the brigade. The brigade marched the short distance to Mouscron on 2 November, the 9th (NIH) Battalion billeted at nearby Luingne. Here another civilian concert was given and 'the massed drums of the 1st and 9th Battns played selections in the Grand Place, Muscron, where a large & interested gathering gave them a rousing reception.'[36]

The fighting in France and Belgium officially ended at 11.00am on 11 November 1918. GHQ issued the following message that morning:

> Hostilities will cease at 11.00 hours to-day, November 11th. Troops will stand fast on the line reached at that hour, which will be reported by wire to Advanced G.H.Q. Defensive precautions will be maintained. There will be no intercourse of any description with the enemy until receipt of instructions from G.H.Q.[37]

The 9th (NIH) Battalion, now in billets at Mouscron, had received intimation of the news the previous night:

> ... great jubilations ensued. Fife & Drum Bands played in the streets and flares and rockets of all description illuminated the sky.[38]

The day itself dawned fine. News of the Armistice was confirmed and spread throughout the town, the population enthusiastically applauding the battalion as their deliverers.

Miles to the south, but also on the French-Belgian border, the three squadrons of the North Irish Horse Cyclist Regiment were manning outpost lines when the news came. They were little more than a twenty miles from Mons, where the war had begun for the BEF four years before, and had recently passed over the ground where the regiment had first seen action.

In general the British troops received news of the Armistice with little by way of celebration. The diary of the 7th (South Irish Horse) Battalion, for example, noted 'very little excitement amongst the Troops when the news was made known'.[39] Writing in India at the time, former North Irish Horseman Robert Sterling noted with disgust that

when the welcome news reached us, I naturally anticipated celebrations of some sort, but no! The news seemed to be received with indifference & one would have imagined India had had nothing to do with the war at all. In the Wheeler Club, more interest appeared to be taken in the Meerut Races than in the cessation of hostilities! The war hadn't bothered them much evidently![40]

In the week following the Armistice the North Irish Horse cyclists moved to nearby Dimechaux and Choicies to establish examining posts on roads leading in the direction of the enemy and prevent the movement of civilians and fraternisation between the opposing forces. Signs of peace began to emerge. On 13 November the regimental order book noted that boot blackening and button polish were now available in the regimental canteen. Then came a notice that all tents and anti-aircraft Lewis-gun mountings were to be handed in. The first of many post-war plaudits came with the award of a Military Medal to Squadron Sergeant Major Boyd. On 19 November the three squadrons rode to regimental headquarters at Berlaimont, and the following day through the Forêt de Mormal to Poix-du-Nord. For the remainder of the month the men were kept busy with salvage work each morning and recreation in the afternoons. A regimental sports' committee was formed and a corps boxing tournament announced.

At the beginning of December the regiment marched back to more familiar territory – the village of Vignacourt, near Amiens. Here war-time discipline was further relaxed – reveille was put back thirty minutes to 7.00 am and the only duties through the day were occasional fatigues, physical training and route marches. There was plenty of time for leisure activities, and many took advantage of the services offered by the local photographers,

Louis and Antoinette Thuillier, whose glass-plate negatives were printed onto postcards and sent home. Thousands of these negatives were recently discovered at the farm where the photographs had been taken, among them more than a dozen showing men of the North Irish Horse Cyclist Regiment.

Two large drafts of reinforcements arrived on 22 November and 10 December. These were mostly Irishmen who had enlisted during 1917 and had been waiting at Antrim to join the regiment in France – men like Albert Brice Galway, bank clerk from Magherafelt, Alfie Spence, labourer from Lambeg, and George Thompson, asylum attendant from Kesh. While there would be little glory in store for them, their arrival did clear the way for others in the regiment to go home. The first of these left the regiment on 12 December. Those lucky enough to be classed as 'key workers' – men with skills in high demand and vital for Britain's economic recovery – were the first allowed home.

The 9th (NIH) Battalion spent November at Mouscron. While training, route marches and parades continued, more time was allowed for recreation. Inter-company football matches were held and the battalion took on others in the brigade, fighting out a 2–2 draw with the 12th Royal Irish Rifles, and defeating the 1st Royal Irish Rifles by 6 tries to 1 at rugby.

On Sunday 17 November a special thanksgiving service was held by the Second Army at nearby Roubaix. Four officers and sixty-five other ranks from the battalion attended. A brigade thanksgiving was held the next day at St Joseph's College in Mouscron, and the following day a battalion parade and march past.

Efforts were made to look to the men's future, with a school established at the Convent School. Unfortunately, it seems the men had a different view, and none turned up on its opening day. The relaxed atmosphere continued through December, with many sporting competitions held between the three battalions of 108 Brigade. The battalion took part in divisional parades and inspections on the airfield of nearby Halluin on 6 and 16 December, and on 7 December six officers and 150 other ranks marched to Roubaix, where His Majesty the King was paying a visit.

By now, however, the men's minds were turning to home – not just to the call of friends and family, but the fear that the best jobs would soon be taken. On 12 December the first man, a coal miner, was sent home for demobilisation. Four more followed the next day.

Although the fighting had ended on 11 November, the losses continued. The day after the Armistice Private John Johnston of the North Irish Horse Cyclist Regiment died in France. On 14 November in a military hospital at Rouen, Private James Adair died of pneumonia. On 30 November, 20-year-old Private William Mills of Castleblayney, County Monaghan, died at home. Four days later, Private Robert William Kerr, a prisoner of war since the previous March, died in Hamburg. On 7 December Private Brownlow Thompson died of pneumonia in London's Queen Alexandra's Military Hospital. Thompson, from Eglish, County Armagh, had been on leave from the 108th Trench Mortar Battery when he contracted the disease. The last North Irish Horseman to die in 1918 was Private Patrick Sheridan, wounded at Cambrai in 1917, who breathed his last in Dublin's St Vincent's Hospital on 9 December.

Notes

1. Major General Thomas Astley, letter dated 8 September 1918, in Doherty, *op cit*, p.30.
2. NA, Kew, WO339.
3. NA, Kew, WO161/100.
4. Transcript courtesy of Olive Nelson, William Lockhart's granddaughter. Rowland and Charles were his brothers and 'Maggie and little girl' Charles's wife and daughter.
5. Letter from Private William Taylor in McFarland service file, NA, Kew, WO339.
6. NA, Kew, WO95/2504.
7. *LG Supplement*, 1 February 1919. NA, Kew, WO 95/2154 2nd Lincolnshire Regiment diary,.
8. NA, Kew, WO95/2154.
9. NA Kew, WO95/761.
10. *LG Supplement*, 7 November 1918.
11. *LG Supplement*, 30 October 1918.
12. Thompson, *Ballymoney Heroes*, pp.353–4. According to another record he died of wounds.
13. NA, Kew, WO95/761.
14. Ibid.
15. Ibid.
16. Doherty, op. cit., p.30.
17. *LG Supplement*, 11 January 1919.
18. *LG Supplement*, 7 November 1918.
19. NA, Kew, WO95/2505.
20. *LG Supplement*, 5 December 1918.
21. NA, Kew, WO95/2422, 1st Scottish Rifles (The Cameronians) diary.
22. Dunn, *The War the Infantry Knew*, p.550.
23. Atteridge, *History of the 17th (Northern) Division*, pp.424–5.
24. Ibid., p.428.

25. Depree, *A History of the 38th (Welsh) and 33rd Divisions*, p.487.
26. NA, Kew, WO95/2422, 5th/6th Scottish Rifles (The Cameronians) diary.
27. Atteridge, op. cit., pp.467–8.
28. NA, Kew, WO95/2505.
29. *LG Supplement*, 1 February 1919.
30. Ibid.
31. NA, Kew, WO95/2505.
32. NA, Kew, WO95/2502/3.
33. Transcript of letter provided by Green's daughter, Joan Collings.
34. *LG Supplement*, 2 December 1919.
35. *BNL*, 11 December 1918.
36. NA, Kew, WO95/2505.
37. *Official History of the Great War 1914–1918: Military Operations France & Belgium, 1918, Vol. V,* p.552.
38. NA, Kew, WO95/2505.
39. NA, Kew, WO95/2330.
40. Sterling, diary 1919–21, PRONI, T3240/1.

Chapter Eight

1919 and Beyond:
The Promise of a Nation's Gratitude

To the men who returned strong and virile the future opens up bright with hope; the maimed have the promise of a nation's gratitude, which must find fruition; [and] the cenotaph bears silent witness to the thousands who paid the supreme sacrifice.[1]

The fighting may have ended on 11 November 1918, but many frustrating weeks would pass before the men of the North Irish Horse could return to Ireland.

Among the first home were those who had been held as prisoners of war. Thousands returned to Ireland during December and January, including the scores of North Irish Horsemen captured in the German offensives of March and April 1918. Among the returned prisoners was Farrier Sergeant Alexander Kennedy of Waringstown, held captive since August 1914.

Meanwhile the North Irish Horse Cyclist Regiment remained at Vignacourt. During January a winter holiday mood persisted. The regimental order book includes, for example, an order that 'no snowballs are to be thrown at the drivers of passing vehicles'.[2] Despite the relaxed atmosphere the regiment was still 'in the field', so breaches of discipline could be harshly punished. Albert Spence received seven days' Field Punishment No.2 for 'hesitating to obey an order'. Ballymena horse trainer James McAteer got twenty-one days for being drunk and refusing an order.

The process of demobilisation continued. In January 1919 the commanding officer, Major Phillips, three other officers and 150 men left for home. Captain Grant took command and Lieutenant Austin was appointed Adjutant. Two more officers and 106 men left in February.

Awards for gallantry and other good service in the latter part of 1918 were handed out in the months following the Armistice. Major Phillips received a Distinguished Service Order; Military Crosses went to Worship Booker, Hugh Montgomery, Donald O'Neill Hodson and Edward Arthur

Atkinson. SSM Humphrey Boyd added a Bar to his Military Medal. Ten men were awarded the Military Medal: RSM John Wright from Belfast; SSM Robert James Carmichael from Silloth; SSM Frank Harding from Lisburn; Sergeants William Glendining from Lisbellaw, William McMurray from Lurgan and Samuel Rainey from Lisburn; Lance Sergeant John Clancey from Moy; Corporal William James Johnston from Kilcock; Acting Corporal Robert Cromes Stewart from Seaford; and Private Joseph Close from Banbridge. Sergeant Rainey also collected a Meritorious Service Medal. Six were Mentioned in Despatches: Captains Herbert Gavin Elliot, John Grant and James Kirkpatrick; Corporal William McCalmont; Lance Corporal Robert Dougall; and Private Abraham Scott.

By 19 March all that was left of the North Irish Horse at Vignacourt was a cadre of three officers, five NCOs and twenty-seven rank and file, together with perhaps two dozen men who had arrived late in 1918, these being retained for transfer to the Army of Occupation on the Rhine.[3] On 7 June Acting Captain Austin and the men assigned to the Army of Occupation were posted to the IV Corps Cyclist Battalion and left for Rolsdorf, near Cologne, where they would remain until sent home in November. On 11 June those left at Vignacourt, an officer and seven men, left for le Havre where they embarked for home. The regimental depot at Antrim was closed and the remaining men moved to the Curragh, where they took part in the national victory celebrations on 19 July.

At Luingne the 9th (NIH) Battalion had waited just as long to receive orders for home. By now, perhaps just one-in-ten of its number had served as cavalrymen in the North Irish Horse. The atmosphere was relaxed, with censorship of letters ended and the only concerns in the battalion diary being that the men had to bathe in cold water due to shortages of heating fuel. During January competitions were held between brigades, battalions and companies in rugby, football, tug-of-war, and cross-country running. The men were able to use the baths at Mouscron, whist drives were held, and the battalion concert troupe, 'The Sandbags', performed for the officers and men. A more exotic entertainment came when the battalion watched a game of basketball between two American teams in Mouscron Square. On 28 January the battalion marched to Herseaux aviation ground to receive its 'colours', a silk Union Jack, from the corps commander.

Training and fatigues continued, but the work was varied and not as hard as in wartime. There were parades in the town square and route marches through the surrounding countryside, ceremonial drill, a practice fire alarm and training in the use of the fire pump at the Mouscron Fire Station, kit and billet inspections, Lewis-gun instruction and physical training. Lectures were given in subjects as varied as 'demobilisation', 'platoon drill' and 'venereal disease'.

By the end of February eight officers and 402 men had left for home, as had most of the horses and transport, and the battalion school had closed its doors. The last draft left on 8 March. Most of those remaining were destined for the Army of Occupation on the Rhine and would soon join the 5th Royal Irish Regiment, then based at Nettersheim, south of Cologne. In all, sixty-nine other ranks from the 9th (NIH) Battalion transferred, just six of these being former North Irish Horsemen – Lance Corporal Percy Reid and Privates David Chambers, Thomas Charles Hawthorne, John Lorimer, Samuel Miller and William Nelson.

On 9 June 1919 the battalion's last three officers and twenty-three other ranks left Mouscron for dispersal camp. Among them, one officer and five other ranks were detailed with the prestigious task of transporting and handing over the battalion's colours to the authorities at Armagh Cathedral.

During 1919 and the years following, more North Irish Horsemen died as a result of their war service. Captain Robert Livsey Yates, one of the regiment's original officers in 1908, died on 4 January 1919. He had resigned his commission in October 1917 and the authorities eventually agreed that the tuberculosis which had caused his death was a result of his service. Lieutenant Thomas Humphrey Hesketh died at the end of January from scarlet fever and pneumonia. He had served as an officer in the 2nd North Irish Horse Regiment during 1916 and 1917 before transferring to the 21st (Empress of India's) Lancers. Lieutenant Leslie Ernest McNeill of Stranocum, County Antrim, died on 25 March from influenza. McNeill had been one of the 'gentleman recruits' who sailed for France with C Squadron in August 1914 before being commissioned in the 4th (Royal Irish) Dragoon Guards. Private James Montgomery died at home in Belfast on 17 June. On the anniversary of the signing of the Armistice, Robert William Nesbitt died in Belfast from the effects of gas poisoning contracted while serving in France or Belgium. Major Eustace Anthony Maude's death on 9 October 1919 was unrelated to the war – he disappeared while sailing his 8-ton yawl *Fiona* along the English coast – but as a serving officer he still qualified for commemoration by the War Graves Commission.

The last North Irish Horseman officially acknowledged to have died as a result of the war was Lance Corporal Percy Reid of Newtownbreda, County Down. Reid enlisted in the North Irish Horse on 4 January 1916, aged eighteen. An orphan, he had been living with his aunt Harriet Mercer and working as a linen trade apprentice. In November 1916 he went to France as a reinforcement for the regiment and was twice wounded while serving with the 9th (NIH) Battalion. After the Armistice he elected to remain in the service and in February 1919 was posted to the 5th Royal Irish Regiment on the Rhine. Reid returned home in September 1919 and was discharged a month later. By then he was suffering from pulmonary tuberculosis contracted in the latter part of his military service. Percy Reid died at home on 24 May 1921.

The strong, the maimed and the glorious dead

On Saturday 9 August a victory parade was held in Belfast to celebrate the signing of the peace treaty at Versailles (delayed for some weeks so as not to clash with the Orange Day marches). For almost three hours, 36,000 men and women marched down the Antrim Road, passing in front of City Hall where Field Marshal French took the salute, past a temporary cenotaph on Donegall Square North piled high with floral wreaths and bearing in raised gilt letters the inscription 'The glorious dead; in memory of our gallant comrades', then on to Ormeau Park where refreshments had been laid on.

The 9th (NIH) Battalion, Royal Irish Fusiliers, took its place in the march with the battalions of the 36th (Ulster) Division, while squadrons of the North Irish Horse and Inniskilling Dragoons marched with the many other regiments. Bringing up the rear of the procession were more than 700 wounded men, in most cases carried by a fleet of motor vehicles, some so badly incapacitated that they could only lie on stretchers, but all, so the newspapers reported, 'cheerful and hopeful'.

Thus, according to the *Belfast News-Letter*, ended 'the last official act of the Great War'.

To the men who returned strong and virile the future opens up bright with hope; the maimed have the promise of a nation's gratitude, which must find fruition; [and] the cenotaph bears silent witness to the thousands who paid the supreme sacrifice. [4]

For many of the 'strong', the 'maimed', and even the 'glorious dead', the future would not be so clear.

Among the strong, many were able to resume their lives where they had left off, though against a backdrop of the partition of Ireland and the violent struggle that followed in the north and south. Those from the country, like Johnny Heenan of Barbican Farm, Newcastle, returned to farming, while others found work where they could in the cities and towns of Ulster. Being an ex-serviceman could be useful in seeking work, particularly for government jobs. James Elliott wrote to the authorities seeking a copy of his military record 'As I have in for a job as rural district postman, and an ex service man is the only man that will get the job'.[5] Many found employment in the Royal Irish Constabulary, including Sampson Trotter from Kesh, County Fermanagh, and Charles Magill of Cairncastle, County Antrim.

All had their stories of the war, and what they chose to share was passed down as family tradition. Often it was the day-to-day experiences rather than the tales of battle that they recalled. Private John Nesbitt Kerr of Newry told his son that it was so cold at the front that 'when your hair was washed it would turn to icicles before you could put a comb through it'. Robert Noel Anderson spoke of his lasting sorrow at having to leave his horse Heidi in France when he returned to Ireland.

Most of those who had come from far afield, from Canada, South Africa, Argentina, Australia and New Zealand, returned home with their medals and memories – Raymond Green returned to Sydney (having first cleaned up at a military equestrian competition on Paris Plage, le Touquet, winning six of the eight events on his horse Billy). Edward Arthur Atkinson returned to Saskatchewan, Bryant Charles Hamilton to Adelaide, Samuel Brockwell to Buenos Aires, Benjamin Johnston to Alberta, Herbert Elliot to Shanghai, and the Grigg twins to Canterbury, New Zealand.

Others joined the Irish diaspora. Leslie Ion Stuart left to work on his uncle's sheep station in New South Wales. David Hunter Bond of Drumskinney, County Tyrone, went to Western Australia. William Buchanan went to Canada, then the USA, before returning to farm his uncle's property at Bridgetown, County Donegal. William Coltart built a successful career as the professional at a succession of golf clubs in the USA. Closer to home, Willie McStay moved back to Glasgow and captained the Celtic football club, winning four league titles and three Scottish cups in a long playing career. Three North Irish Horse pals, William Holmes, George Ferris and Arthur McGookin, sailed together for New Zealand in 1921. William Maguire, a

Boer War veteran, left for Western Australia in 1922, where he worked as a farmer, prospector and house painter. Frank McMahon, too, eventually left for Australia, after experiencing the economic and political difficulties at home:

> I was demobilized in 1919, returned to Ireland. There wasn't any jobs I could do offering, [so] I went off to Liverpool, but the unemployment was worse than in Ireland ... I had sat for an examination as a Railway clerk in Ireland but had heard no word, [so] I took a job as a barman in Liverpool and after a time I received a telegram informing me I had passed my examination ... I returned to Ireland and was posted to a job as the Locomotive Superintendent clerk.[6]

In Ireland, McMahon's military abilities found an outlet with the outbreak of the civil war and in the cross-border fighting around Newry. He aligned himself with the pro-Treaty forces, as did many Irish soldiers who had returned from the war. However, by the end of 1922 he was forced to leave Ireland. Staying at first with family in Manchester, McMahon recalled the stories Australian soldiers had told him about their country.

> During my time in France, I had met many Australians, and liked them. The Australian and Irish soldiers got on well together, they seemed to have much in common, disregard for unnecessary discipline and a devil may care way about them ... the Irish regiments were always pleased if the Australians were near them in the trenches.[7]

He raised the funds for a passage and left for Australia, arriving in Melbourne in January 1923. Here, and later in Sydney, he made a new life, marrying an Australian girl with whom he had three children. When the Second World War began he joined the Australian Army and served much of the war as a regimental sergeant major at a prisoner of war camp in Hay, New South Wales.

Almost as numerous as the 'strong' were the 'maimed' – the men damaged by the war in body or mind. They weren't left entirely to fend for themselves, but as the country did its best to forget the privations and misery of the war, the wounded often served as an unwanted reminder of that past.

All were entitled to appear before a medical board and make a case for a pension, based on their degree of impairment. Owen Short from County

Wicklow, for example, had spent the last years of the war in hospitals in Glasgow, Dumfries, and the convalescent camp at Ballykinlar. By 1920 he was suffering from

> headaches, sleeplessness, nervousness. States that he has lost confidence in himself. Does not have war dreams. States that his memory is bad. Knee jerks slightly exaggerated. No tremor of hands. Slight tremor of tongue. States that he has been twelve months in hospital suffering from Shell Shock.

The board rated his degree of disability at 30 per cent.[8]

Others sought special consideration. Worship Booker, for example, wrote to the War Office in June 1919:

> When in France in 1915 I met with an accident which resulted in me been [sic] sent home to England ... I was marked unfit for active service for over twelve months and although when I once declared myself fit and the Medical Board passed me fit my own Regimental Doctor would not pass me fit when my order came for overseas. I again at a medical board declared myself fit and went overseas in 1918 and took command of a Sqn of NIH and gained the MC altho my ankle troubled me as it does now.
>
> Could not some little gratuity be given me to repay me for this accident and after affects. I always did my little best for my country, was the first volunteer from my county in France, therefore I think I deserve a little consideration.[9]

Whether physical or psychological, the damage caused by the war stayed with the men for many years, if not a lifetime. Charles Magill's daughter Kathleen remembered:

> He told me he was caught in an explosion and buried alive, but managed to claw his way out of the earth. For years [after the war] he never wore a turtle-neck sweater or shirt, because he felt like he was suffocating. At Marne my dad said his leg was badly injured by shrapnel ... All his life, my father suffered tremendous leg pain, I think in his left leg from the shrapnel fragments. On damp and cold days, he often limped.[10]

William Rooney from Bryansford was twice wounded. The second time a bullet lodged so close to his spine that doctors thought it too dangerous to operate. He carried the bullet with him, and the agony it caused, until 1938 when a surgeon successfully removed it.[11]

Among the 'glorious dead' were 211 men of the North Irish Horse. Nearly two-thirds lie in identified graves in more than ninety cemeteries across the world, mostly in France, Belgium, the United Kingdom and Ireland. Two are in cemeteries in Germany, four in the Middle East and one in Pakistan. Only in four cemeteries are they concentrated in numbers greater than four. Seven men lie in Belgium's Dadizeele New British Cemetery and six in Harelbeke New British Cemetery, victims of the final offensive of the war. Five lie in Neuville Bourjonval British Cemetery, killed in the trench warfare leading up to the Battle of Cambrai, and five in St Sever Cemetery Extension, a large site filled by the military hospitals in and around Rouen.

The bodies of seventy-six North Irish Horsemen were never found, their burial places were lost, forgotten or abandoned, or the wooden cross placed over their grave and bearing their name was destroyed in later fighting. The Imperial War Graves Commission had determined that each of the 'lost, the unknown, but not forgotten dead' must also be commemorated by name, and as a result vast memorials to the missing dot the former battlefields of Belgium and France. Here are listed the names of the missing North Irish Horsemen, at Tyne Cot, Pozières, Cambrai, Ploegsteert, Ypres (Menin Gate), Thiepval, la Ferté-sous-Jouarre, Vis-en-Artois, le Touret, Loos and in the Ham British Cemetery. The names of others are inscribed on memorials at Brookwood in England and Baku in Azerbaijan.

In the years after the war, thousands of British servicemen volunteered to join labour companies to painstakingly search the old battlefields for grave sites, exhume the bodies and remove them for reburial at permanent military cemeteries. Every effort was made to identify those they found. Sometimes the grave was marked with a cross bearing the man's name and unit but, if not, the remains were searched for identity discs, paybooks or anything else that could identify the man or his regiment. In other cases, smaller cemeteries and those poorly located were closed and the bodies removed to new locations.

By the time the searches by the Graves Concentration Units were ended in September 1921, 204,650 bodies had been taken from the battlefield and laid to rest in permanent military cemeteries. Even so, another 38,000 bodies were found in the next three years, often by farmers returning to their land,

and in the mid-1920s between twenty and thirty were still being found each week. Among those re-interred were forty-one North Irish Horsemen. The number is most likely higher, but some would be among those whose bodies could not be identified and whose gravestones bear the simple inscription:

A SOLDIER
OF THE GREAT WAR

KNOWN UNTO GOD

Among the North Irish Horsemen re-interred were thirteen whose original burial places track the German retreat across Belgium through September and October 1918. They now lie in the Dadizeele New British Cemetery and Harlebeke New British Cemetery. On the Somme the bodies of six North Irish Horse cyclists killed during the offensive of August 1918 were located and brought to the Ancre British Cemetery, Flatiron Copse Cemetery, Queens Cemetery and Ovillers Military Cemetery. On the Ypres front, the bodies of Major Holt Waring and Private John Bell were moved to the Wulverghem-Lindenhoek Road Military Cemetery. The body of the last North Irish Horseman killed in action, Private Charles Elder, was moved to Dourlers Communal Cemetery Extension. In Germany the many who had died as prisoners of war were moved to a small number of larger cemeteries. They included Lieutenant James Dennistoun, moved from the Ohrdruf Prisoner of War Cemetery to the Niederzwehren Cemetery in Cassel, Hessen. The remains of prisoner of war Private George Johnston, removed from Forbach Military Cemetery in Lorraine, were carried many miles west for reburial in the Perreuse Chateau Franco–British National Cemetery, near Paris.

Old Comrades

The North Irish Horse ceased to exist as a fighting unit soon after its return to Ireland. Its men were discharged and most of its officers were asked to resign their commissions, their services being no longer required. Nonetheless the regiment retained its place in the Army List, shown as a militia unit after 1921.

The first Old Comrades' dinner was held on Wednesday 27 February 1924 at Thompson's Restaurant in Belfast. Some ninety officers and men attended, and between speeches, toasts and entertainment, a sum of £500 was raised to erect a memorial to the regiment's fallen. Just over a year later the memorial was unveiled – a large stained-glass window in the east wall of the Belfast City Hall. The window depicts a youthful warrior in golden armour holding a sword and helmet. Above him is the badge of St George, the Patron Saint of cavalry, and below the regiment's battle honours – Retreat from Mons, Marne 1914, Aisne 1914, Armentières 1914, Somme 1916–18, Albert 1916, Messines 1917, Ypres 1917, Pilckem, St Quentin, Bapaume 1918, Hindenburg Line, Epehy, St Quentin Canal, Cambrai 1918, Selle, Sambre, France and Flanders 1914–18. Two large bronze tablets placed on either side of the window list the names of the fallen.[12]

The second Old Comrades' dinner was as well attended as the first. In proposing the toast to the regiment, Lord Massereene, who had commanded C Squadron in France in 1914, declared that they were 'some of the happiest moments of his life … He never had a better lot of men than in the squadron he commanded'. He also noted that he had recently asked Lord Derby if the regiment might be revived, but was told 'there was no hope'.[13]

Three years later similar sentiments were expressed at the reunion dinner where 'old comrades in arms spent a pleasant evening exchanging stories of the days when a good horse and a good fellow were always welcomed to the regiment'. One speaker reflected on the 'great pity that in Ulster there were no volunteer regiments of Yeomanry, [but] even if the North Irish Horse were turned into a tank unit they would still give a splendid account of themselves.'[14]

In the middle years of the 1930s the North Irish Horse became the subject of some good-natured jests and gained the title 'the one-man regiment'. The regiment had been 'disembodied' since 1920, existing in name only, with no rank and file and an ever-shrinking list of officers. By 1930 the Army List showed just four – Honorary Colonel the Earl of Shaftesbury, Honorary Chaplain the Reverend Walter Auchinleck Stack (who had held the position since 1904), Major Sir Ronald Deane Ross and Captain Thomas William Hughes. After Hughes retired in 1934, Major Ross was the last remaining combat officer. The 'one-man regiment' title was coined, and it stuck. When retailer Moss Bros produced *An Illustrated Army List*, a gentle parody of the official list of officers, it included an entry for the North Irish Horse mocking in poetry and picture its status as a regiment without officers or men.

Have ye ivver heard the story of that famous Oirish Rigimint,
The loikes of it was never seen from Larne to Donegal,
And they look so foine in green and whoite, though faith Oi'll give ye just
a hint
There's not a Captain in it nor a Corporal at all:

There's a Colonel and, begorra, there's an honorary Chaplain, too,
That's there to tache the bhoys to be a credit to the corps,
And if they had some shquadrons, sure 'tis foine they'd look and iligint
With their green plumes all a-wavin' and the Colonel to the fore.

They never sound reveillé, faith, they haven't any thrumpeterr,
And there's divil a liftinint or a sargint in the force,
But when the bugle blows for the bhoys to go to war,
They'll be ridin' off to glory on the North Oirish Horse.

Moss Bros *Illustrated Army List*.

On 14 July 1936 in the House of Commons Harold Balfour asked a series of questions about the regiment, including: what were the duties of the honorary chaplain, how many church parades had been held during the past two years, and 'whether the attendance had been voluntary or compulsory'. To general merriment, the Secretary of State for War (Duff Cooper) responded that

> the North Irish Horse … has been left in what I can perhaps best describe as a state of suspended animation. All the other ranks of this unit having completed their engagements, and recruiting for it being suspended, the strength at present consists of one officer only. In these circumstances my hon. and gallant friend's questions do not arise.

Mr Cooper went on to say that while the regiment 'may not fulfil any important purpose it certainly does not do any harm'.[15]

Two years later, when Major Ross reached the fifty-year age limit and retired, the North Irish Horse ceased to exist. The *Daily Express* reported its passing with a blank section purporting to be a photograph of the regiment's last roll call.

However, in less than a year, in the face of the growing danger of a new war with Germany and Britain's belated decision to re-arm, it was decided that the North Irish Horse would be reconstituted as a light tank unit of the Royal Armoured Corps. In the coming war it would play an important role as an armoured regiment in the North African and Italian campaigns.

Today the North Irish Horse survives as B (North Irish Horse) Squadron of the Scottish and North Irish Yeomanry, and 40 (North Irish Horse) Signal Squadron of the 32nd Signal Regiment. The former squadron has recently returned to the regiment's roots as a cavalry unit, though now equipped with R-WMIK Land Rovers. Men of the squadrons have seen service in places such as Afghanistan, the Balkans and Iraq.

THE ODD SPOT

BRITAIN'S one-man regiment, the North Irish Horse, disappears today.

Major Sir Ronald Ross, Conservative M.P. for Londonderry, the only serving officer, has reached the age limit, and his retirement is announced in last night's London Gazette.

Since the war all the rank and file of the regiment have ended their engagements, and all the other officers have reached the age limit.

Picture of the last roll-call of the North Irish Horse

The Daily Express, 13 July 1938.

Notes

1. *BNL*, 11 August 1919.
2. *North Irish Horse Order Book*, 31 January 1919.
3. The officers were Captain Grant, Lieutenant Downey and Lieutenant Austin. The NCOs included Sergeant Alexander Chesnut, SSM Frank Harding, WO Frank Mells and Corporal Joseph Stafford.
4. *BNL*, 11 August 1919.
5. NA, Kew, WO363.
6. McMahon, op. cit.
7. Ibid.
8. NA, Kew, WO364.
9. NA, Kew, WO339.
10. Magill, *The Magills of the Meetinghouse*, p.36.
11. *Mourne Observer*, 1 July 1966.
12. A matching window for the regiment's fallen of the Second World War has since been erected.
13. *BNL*, 1 May 1925.
14. *BNL*, 10 November 1928.
15. *The Times*, 15 July 1936.

Postscript

The wives, mothers, sisters, daughters and sweethearts of the men of the North Irish Horse are largely absent from the records of the Great War. Yet they had to bear an equal share of the consequences of the fighting. Below are the stories of two women from very different backgrounds, both of whom lost a loved one to the war.

Margaret Waring

Margaret Waring lost her husband Holt during the fighting on the Ypres front in April 1918. On 22 November 1918 she wrote to his sister:

Dearest Esther

So many thanks for your long letter. I was delighted to get it, & to know you are thriving again. A box of eggs was posted yesterday. I hope you got them. Would you mind returning the box? I was away for a couple of nights with Mabel Annesley, & did so enjoy it, & now am back in harness again, very much so. It seems to be one wild rush from morning till night, what with the War Pensions (?) & now <u>politics</u> on the top of everything. How I do hate it, but we're being worried up by Women's Unionist Ass[ocia]tion & I suppose must take an interest in these matters. I find it very hard to come down to the same old party politics, & small minded ideas that always go with an election, after all these wonderful deeds that we've been watching in France. Somehow now the War is over I feel that Holt has come 'home' just as surely as the others, I can't just tell you why, but as long as the War went on I felt that his thoughts & ideas were only partly mine & the rest belonged to his men & his country. But now we are just *one* again, & so it will be always he & I together till the end of the chapter. It is *lovely* weather here, which is a help.

Margaret Waring remained at her husband's family home, Waringstown House, and was active in the local community and in Unionist politics for many years. She died fifty years after the death of her husband, on 9 May 1968.

Amelia Nixon (formerly Roberts)

In an article to mark the fiftieth anniversary of the Battle of the Somme, the *Mourne Observer* interviewed some locals who had fought there. One, Johnny Heenan of the North Irish Horse, recalled seeing the mother of one of his pals after the war 'wearing the medals of her … sons, laying a wreath at an armistice service'.

The mother was Amelia Nixon. On 27 July 1916 one of her 5 sons, Gunner William Henry Roberts of the Royal Field Artillery, died of wounds on the Somme. Just eighteen months later another son, Stoker 1st Class Eddie Roberts, drowned when HMS *Racoon* struck rocks in a blizzard off Donegal and sank with all hands. In August 1918 she lost a third son, John Martin (Jack) Roberts, who had been in France and Belgium with A Squadron of the North Irish Horse since the beginning. The three brothers were honoured by name on the Downpatrick War Memorial.

Amelia Nixon never knew the location of Jack's last resting place, for there is no record of his body being recovered from the battlefield. He was probably one of the thousands whose remains were found after the war but could not be identified.

In 1919, men of 117 Labour Company, searching the old Somme battlefields for the bodies of British servicemen, came across an unmarked grave on a gentle slope west of the ruins of the village of Miraumont. They dug up his body and, searching it for any clue to his identity, found a cap badge bearing the crowned harp of the North Irish Horse. A little further up the slope they found another grave, this time marked with a cross which told them that this man was Private Thomas Bryson of the North Irish Horse, killed in action on 21 August 1918. The bodies of the two Horsemen were taken to nearby Bucquoy, where they were laid to rest, side by side, in the Queens Cemetery. The gravestone of the unknown North Irish Horseman is marked with the regimental badge, a cross, and the simple inscription 'A soldier of the Great War. North Irish Horse. Known unto God.'

By tracking the movements of the North Irish Horse squadrons during the war and the records of all the men whose burial place is unknown, it can now be concluded that this unknown North Irish Horsemen is almost certainly Amelia Nixon's son, Private John Martin Roberts.

Appendices

Appendix I   Timeline
Appendix II   Monthly recruitment: August 1914 to December 1916
Appendix III   Casualties
Appendix IV   Awards and decorations

North Irish Horse Timeline 1908 to 1919

North Irish Horse		General events	
1907–1913			
Jly 1908	North of Ireland Imperial Yeomanry disbanded and re-formed as the North Irish Horse.		
1909	First annual camp at Dundrum Bay, Co. Down.		
1910	Annual camp at Bellarena, Co. Londonderry.		
1911	Annual camp at Newbridge, Co. Kildare.		
		11 Apr 1912	Third Home Rule Bill introduced.
1912	Annual camp at Dundrum, Co. Down.		
		28 Sept 1912	Signing of the Ulster Covenant.
		13 Jan 1913	Ulster Volunteer Force formally established.
1913	Annual camp at Bundoran, Co. Donegal.		
1914			
		20 Mar	The Curragh incident.
		24 Apr	Larne gun running.
		25 May	Home Rule Bill approved by the House of Commons.
Jun–Jly	Annual camp at Dundrum, Co. Down.		
		4 Aug	Britain declares war on Germany.
5 Aug	NIH mobilised.		

North Irish Horse		General events	
	1914		
		7–16 Aug	British Expeditionary Force lands in France.
		14–30 Aug	Battles of the Frontiers.
17 Aug	A Squadron sails from Dublin for le Havre and assigned as GHQ cavalry.		
20–21 Aug	C Squadron sails from Belfast for le Havre and assigned as 5th Division cavalry.		
22 Aug	A Squadron arrives at le Cateau.		
		23 Aug	Battle of Mons.
24 Aug	Two troops of A Squadron (Cole) assigned to the 4th Division, two troops (Herdman) to GHQ.	23 Aug to 5 Sept	'Retreat from Mons' takes BEF south to within a short distance of Paris.
25 Aug to 5 Sept	Herdman's troops withdraw with GHQ to St Quentin, Noyon, Compiegne, Dammartin and Melun.		
25 Aug	C Squadron arrives at St Quentin.		
26 Aug	Cole's troops in fighting at le Cateau, attached to 3rd Division, then rearguard on the retreat.	26 Aug	Battle of le Cateau.
28 Aug	Cole's troops reach Crisolles and rejoin 4th Division.		
28–30 Aug	C Squadron joins retreat and locates its Division near Pontoise.		
1 Sept	First NIH fatality.		
	C Squadron in rearguard action at Crépy-en-Valois.	1 Sept	Clash at Néry.
2 Sept	Cole's troops reach Dammartin, C Squadron at Vinantes.		
3 Sept	Cole's troops and C Squadron withdraw over the Marne.		

North Irish Horse		General events	
4 Sept	Cole's troops at Jossigny, C Squadron at Tournan, the furthest extent of their retreat.		
		5 Sept	Furthest extent of German advance.
		5–10 Sept	Battle of the Marne. German retreat begins.
6–12 Sept	C Squadron advance guard to 5th Division on advance to the Marne and then to the Aisne.		
6–8 Sept	Cole's troops of A Squadon advance guard to 4th Division.		
9 Sept	A Squadron reunited at GHQ.		
12 Sept	C Squadron reaches the Aisne.	12–15 Sept	Battle of the Aisne.
		18 Sept	Home Rule Bill becomes law, but postponed for duration of the war.
30 Sept	First NIH officer casualty.	22 Sept to Nov	The 'race to the sea'.
8–13 Oct	A and C Squadrons move to St Omer with GHQ.	3–19 Oct	BEF moves from the Aisne to Flanders.
		19 Oct to 22 Nov	First Battle of Ypres.

1915			
Jan – Dec	A Squadron on the Ypres front as GHQ cavalry.		
Jan to Apr	C Squadron on the Ypres front as Corps HQ cavalry.		
		10–13 Mar	Battle of Neuve Chapelle.
14 Apr	C Squadron transfers to 3rd Division. They remain with this division on the Ypres front for the remainder of the year.		
		22 Apr to 25 May	Second Battle of Ypres, commencing with first use of gas, by the Germans.
		25 Apr	Allied forces land in the Dardanelles.

North Irish Horse	General events
1915	

	North Irish Horse		General events
1 May	D Squadron sails from Southampton for le Havre as cavalry to the 51st Division. They move to the la Bassée front.		
		9 May to 18 Jun	Allied spring offensive.
Jly	Contingent of NIH leaves for Egypt and Dardanelles as military mounted police.		
28 Jly	D Squadron moves to the Somme front.		
		6 Aug	Landing at Suvla and beginning of Battle of Sari Bair (Dardanelles).
20 Aug	First 'time expired' man leaves the regiment.		
		25 Sept to 6 Nov	Allied autumn offensive.
6 Oct	6th Inniskilling Dragoons (Service Squadron) arrives at le Havre with 36th (Ulster) Division.		
Nov	Largest ever monthly intake of recruits for NIH.		
16 Nov	F Squadron sails from Southampton for le Havre as cavalry to the 33rd Division. The squadron is sent to the la Bassée front.		
		19 Dec	Haig succeeds French as Commander in Chief.
		19 Dec to 8 Jan	Evacuation of Gallipoli Peninsula.

1916	

	North Irish Horse	General events
4 Jan	A Squadron leaves GHQ and becomes cavalry to the 55th Division.	
11 Jan	E Squadron sails from Southampton for le Havre as cavalry to the 34th Division. The squadron is sent to the Ypres front.	

North Irish Horse		General events	
		27 Jan	Military Service Act passed, imposing conscription on single men aged 18–41.
Feb	A Squadron moves to the Arras front.		
		21 Feb to 31 Aug	Battle of Verdun – German offensive.
		24 Apr to 1 May	Irish Rebellion.
May	C and F Squadrons move to the Somme front and are attached to 49th (West Riding) Division.		
10 May	A, D and E Squadrons form the 1st North Irish Horse Regiment, attached to VII Corps. They concentrate at Grouches.		
21 May	F Squadron transfers to 32nd Division.		
25 May	F Squadron renamed B Squadron.	25 May	Second Military Service Act passed, extending compulsion to married men and preventing 'time expired' men from leaving.
1 Jun	C Squadron transfers to 36th (Ulster) Division.		
21 Jun	B and C Squadrons and 6th Inniskilling Dragoons (Service Squadron) form 2nd North Irish Horse Regiment, attached to X Corps. They concentrate at Toutencourt.		
23 Jun	1st Regiment moves to Pas.		
5 Jly	Two troops of Inniskilling Dragoons Squadron, 2nd Regiment, caught in a German artillery barrage in Aveluy Wood.	1 Jly to 18 Nov	Battle of the Somme.
9–24 Jly	2nd Regiment clearing Somme battlefield of bodies and equipment.		
2 Aug	2nd Regiment moves to Flesselles.		
10 Sep	1st Regiment moves to Humbercourt, where they remain until April 1917.		

North Irish Horse		General events	
1916			
		24 Oct to 18 Dec	Battle of Verdun – French counter-offensive.
26 Oct	2nd Regiment begins move north to the Ypres front.		
18 Nov	2nd Regiment arrives at Boeschepe, where it remains until May 1917.		
7 Dec	One hundred North Irish Horsemen at Antrim transfer to the RIR and embark for France.		
1917			
9 Jan	Forty North Irish Horsemen at Antrim transfer to the Inniskillings and embark for France.		
4–8 Mar	The hundred former NIH in RIR in local attack near Bouchavesnes.		
		16 Mar to 4 Apr	Germans withdraw to the Hindenburg Line.
		6 Apr	USA declared war on Germany.
		9 Apr to 17 May	French and British Artois and Champagne offensives.
7 Jun	2nd Regiment held ready to exploit breakthrough at Messines.	7–14 Jun	Battle of Messines.
mid-Jun	Orders that 2nd Regiment be disbanded. Other ranks to be compulsorily transferred to infantry.		
13–16 Jly	1st Regiment moves to the Ypres sector and attached to XIX Corps.		
22 Jly to 23 Aug	2nd Regiment moves to Aix-en-Issart and begin 'dismounting' process.	28 Jly	Tank Corps formed from Heavy Branch, Machine Gun Corps.
		31 Jly to 10 Nov	Third Battle of Ypres.
31 Jly	1st Regiment held ready to exploit XIX Corps success at Third Ypres.		

North Irish Horse		General events
14 Aug to 5 Oct	One officer and 70 men convey 2nd Regiment's horses to Egypt.	
16 Aug	Thirteen former NIH killed at Langemarck (Third Ypres).	
		20 Aug to 15 Dec Battle of Verdun – Second French offensive.
23 Aug	2nd Regiment moves to 36 Infantry Base Depot at le Havre.	
5 Sept	67 other ranks supernumerary to 1st Regiment transferred to 36 Infantry Base Depot.	
6 Sept	Ten men of 1st Regiment casualties in gas attack at Ypres.	
7 Sept	1st Regiment transfers to V Corps.	
20–25 Sept	495 2nd Regiment other ranks transfer to the RIrF - 304 sent to 9 RIrF. The remainder sent in following weeks. Battalion re-named 9th (NIH) Battalion Royal Irish Fusiliers.	
1–11 Oct	1st Regiment moves to la Bassée front.	
12 Oct	72 other ranks (Egypt group) join 9th (NIH) Battalion at Ruyaulcourt.	
3 Nov	9th (NIH) Battalion in major trench raid near Havrincourt.	
12–20 Nov	1st Regiment moves south to Bapaume.	
		20 Nov to 6 Dec Battle of Cambrai.
22–23 Nov	9th (NIH) in attack on Moeuvres (Cambrai).	
1–23 Dec	1st Regiment moves to Sarton, then to winter quarters at Barly.	

North Irish Horse		General events	
1917			
4–8 Dec	9th (NIH) in defensive battle south of Marcoing (Cambrai).		
9–24 Dec	1st Regiment in the line west of Marcoing.		
17–28 Dec	9th (NIH) moves to winter quarters near Amiens.		
28 Dec	26 former NIH cavalrymen transfer from 9th (NIH) Battalion to Tank Corps.		
1918			
7 Jan	Twelve men of the 1st Regiment transfer to the Tank Corps.		
7–19 Jan	9th (NIH) Battalion moves to St Quentin front.		
		Feb	BEF restructure reduces size of divisions from twelve to nine battalions.
18 Feb	Orders received that 1st Regiment to be dismounted and become a cyclist regiment.		
14 Mar	1st Regiment travels to Villers-au-Flos and becomes the NIH Cyclist Regiment, attached to V Corps.		
21–30 Mar	9th (NIH) Battalion in fighting retreat with heavy losses from St Quentin to near Amiens.	21 Mar to 5 Apr	German spring offensive (Operation MICHAEL).
23–26 Mar	NIH Cyclists retreat from Villers-au-Flos to Rubempre.		
4 Apr	9th (NIH) Battalion moves to Ypres front.		
10–15 Apr	9th (NIH) Battalion in heavy fighting around Kemmel and Messines Ridge.	9–29 Apr	German Lys Offensive.

North Irish Horse		General events	
		10 Apr	Third Military Service Act raises age limit to 50, and extends conscription to Ireland (though never implemented).
18 Apr	Eleven former NIH cavalrymen among the dead in an artillery barrage on the 9th (NIH) Battalion near Kemmel Hill.		
		27 May to 6 Jun	German Aisne offensive.
		9–13 Jun	German Noyon-Montdidier offensive.
6 Jly	9th (NIH) Battalion moves back into the line in the Kemmel sector.		
		15 Jly to 7 Aug	German Marne offensive.
		8 Aug to 11 Nov	Allied 'Advance to Victory'.
21 Aug to 3 Sept	NIH Cyclists advance guard to V Corps, advancing from the Ancre to the Canal du Nord.	8 Aug to 3 Sept	Amiens offensive.
24 Aug	9th (NIH) Battalion in successful attack on German positions near Mont Noir.		
31 Aug to 5 Sept	9th (NIH) Battalion joins pursuit following German withdrawal, moving from Mont des Cats to Douve river valley, where severe fighting takes place.		
2 Sept	A/Lt Col Richard Annesley West killed in action with the Tank Corps, earning him a VC.		
4–9 Sept	NIH Cyclists with V Corps advance towards Hindenburg Line.		
		12 Sept to 4 Nov	Breaking the Hindenburg Line offensive.

North Irish Horse		General events	
1918			
29 Sept to 6 Oct	NIH Cyclists with V Corps advance to St Quentin Canal and close to Villers-Outreaux.	28 Sept to 19 Oct	Allied offensive in Flanders.
30 Sept to 11 Oct	9th (NIH) Battalion with 36th (Ulster) Division in severe fighting to capture Hill 41.		
8–10 Oct	NIH cyclists with V Corps overrun Beaurevoir Line and reach the Selle at Neuvilly.		
14–16 Oct	9th (NIH) Battalion with 36th (Ulster) Division advance to the Lys and force crossing at Courtrai.		
20–25 Oct	NIH Cyclists with V Corps cross the Selle and advance to Forêt de Mormal.		
21–26 Oct	9th (NIH) Battalion with 36th (Ulster) Division advance south-east from the Lys.		
27 Oct	9th (NIH) Battalion relieved and marches to rest billets.		
4–10 Nov	NIH Cyclists with V Corps push through Forêt de Mormal and advance several miles beyond.		
7 Nov	Last North Irish Horseman killed in action.		
		11 Nov	Armistice. Hostilities cease.
7–10 Dec	NIH Cyclists move to billets at Vignacourt, near Amiens.		

North Irish Horse		General events	
	1919		
28 Jan	9th (NIH) Battalion receives its 'colours'.		
Mar to May	9th (NIH) Battalion men remaining in the army transfer to the 5th Royal Irish Regiment and move to Cologne, Germany.		
Jun	NIH headquarters at Antrim closes.		
7 Jun	Men of the NIH Cyclist Regiment remaining in the army transfer to IV Cyclist Battalion and move to Rolsdorf, Germany.		
9 Jun	9th (NIH) Battalion cadre leaves Mouscron for home.		
11 Jun	NIH Cyclist Regiment cadre leaves Vignacourt for home.		
		28 Jun	Treaty of Versailles signed.
		9 Aug	Victory parade in Belfast.

Appendix II

Monthly Recruitment:
August 1914 to December 1916

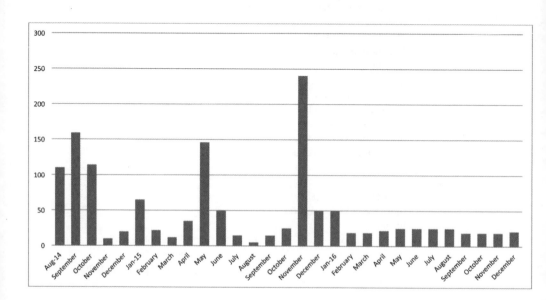

Appendix III

North Irish Horse Casualties 1914 to 1921

Date	Name and rank	Unit in which last serving	How died	Where buried/ commemorated
1914				
1 September	Driver Matthew Callanan	ASC, attached NIH	Accidentally killed	la Ferté-sous-Jouarre Memorial, Seine-et-Marne, France
15 September	Private William H. Moore	NIH	KIA	la Ferté-sous-Jouarre Memorial, Seine-et-Marne, France
15 September[1]	Private Henry St. George Layard Scott	NIH	KIA	la Ferté-sous-Jouarre Memorial, Seine-et-Marne, France
30 September	Lieutenant Samuel Barbour Combe	NIH	DoW	le Touret Memorial, Pas-de-Calais, France
23 October	Corporal Edmond Buchanan	NIH	Died	Epsom Cemetery, Surrey, England
1915				
2 March	Private William Irwin	NIH	Disease	Longuenesse (St Omer) Souvenir Cemetery, Pas-de-Calais, France
17 March	Corporal David William Ritchie	NIH	Died	Longuenesse (St Omer) Souvenir Cemetery, Pas-de-Calais, France
22–26 April	Lance Corporal William Thomas Graham	Canadian Expeditionary Force	KIA	Ypres (Menin Gate) Memorial, Ieper, West Vlaanderen, Belgium
24 May	Private George Harper	NIH	Spinal meningitis	Netley Military Cemetery, Hampshire, England
25 September	Second Lieutenant Robert Hutchinson Andrews	RIR	KIA	Bois Grenier Communal Cemetery, Nord, France

Date	Name and rank	Unit in which last serving	How died	Where buried/ commemorated
13 November	Private Townley Sherwood Gillespie	NIH	Died	Belfast City Cemetery, Northern Ireland
1916				
27 April	Private James McArow	NIH	Spotted fever	Doullens Communal Cemetery Extension No.1, Somme, France
23 June	Private William James Finlay	NIH	KIA	Foncquevillers Military Cemetery, Pas-de-Calais, France
30 June	Second Lieutenant Johnston Shaw Kirker Hunter	RFA	KIA	St Vaast Post Military Cemetery, Richebourg-l'Avoue, Pas-de-Calais, France
3 July	Private Alexander Watt	6th Inniskilling Dragoons (Service Squadron)	KIA	Thiepval Memorial, Somme, France
28 July	Private Thomas Wright	NIH	DoW	Étaples Military Cemetery, Pas-de-Calais, France
9 August	Lieutenant James Robert Dennistoun	RFC	DoW, prisoner of war	Niederzwehren Cemetery, Hessen, Germany
3 October	Lieutenant James Kenneth MacGregor Greer	Irish Guards	DoW	St Sever Cemetery, Rouen, Seine-Maritime, France
27 October	Private Albert Milton Boyle	NIH	Tuberculosis	Drumcree Church of Ireland Churchyard, County Armagh, Northern Ireland
24 December	Private John McClelland Cromie Darragh	6th Inniskilling Dragoons	Died	St Riquier British Cemetery, Somme, France
1917				
12 February	Captain Charles Norman	Reserve Regiment of Cavalry	Accidental injuries	Puchevillers British Cemetery, Somme, France
12 February	Private William McKee Murphy	NIH	Pneumonia	St Sever Cemetery Extension, Seine-Maritime, France

Date	Name and rank	Unit in which last serving	How died	Where buried/ commemorated
6 March	Lance Corporal John McSparron	RIR	KIA	Fins New British Cemetery, Sorel-le-Grand, Somme, France
6 March	Rifleman William Nixon	RIR	KIA	Fins New British Cemetery, Sorel-le-Grand, Somme, France
7 March	Rifleman Thomas Hall	RIR	KIA	Sailly-Saillisel British Cemetery, Somme, France
7 March	Rifleman John Nixon Gibson	RIR	KIA	Thiepval Memorial, Somme, France
1 April	Rifleman Robert O'Hara	RIR	DoW	Hamilton (Bent) Cemetery, Lanarkshire, Scotland
2 May	Lieutenant Lancelot Charles Wise	3rd Lancers (Skinner's Horse)	Illness	Rawalpindi War Cemetery, Pakistan
6 May	Private Richard Moore	NIH	Accident	Annahilt Presbyterian Churchyard, County Down, Northern Ireland
20 May	Lance Corporal Rowland Irvine Bradley	RFC	KIA	Hazebrouck Communal Cemetery, Nord, France
7 June	Private James Talbot	Inniskillings	KIA	Ypres (Menin Gate) Memorial, Ieper, West-Vlanderen, Belgium
26 June	Sergeant Robert Alexander Wylie	NIH	DoW	Avesnes-le-Comte Communal Cemetery Extension, Pas-de-Calais, France
20 July	Private Clement Douglas Turner	NIH	DoW	Vlamertinghe New Military Cemetery, Ieper, West-Vlaanderen, Belgium
20 July	Lance Corporal Stewart Lyttle Turner	NIH	KIA	Vlamertinghe New Military Cemetery, Ieper, West-Vlaanderen, Belgium

Date	Name and rank	Unit in which last serving	How died	Where buried/ commemorated
31 July	Second Lieutenant Samuel McCullagh Linden	RGA	KIA	Ypres (Menin Gate) Memorial, Ieper, West-Vlaanderen, Belgium
8 August	Corporal William Hanna Adams	Inniskillings	KIA	Ypres (Menin Gate) Memorial, Ieper, West-Vlaanderen, Belgium
9 August	Private Samuel Robinson	NIH	Died	Mendinghem Military Cemetery, Poperinge, West-Vlaanderen, Belgium
16 August	Rifleman Neason Henry Hale	RIR	KIA	Tyne Cot Memorial, Zonnebeke, West-Vlanderen, Belgium
16 August	Second Lieutenant George Herbert Farley	Inniskillings	KIA	Tyne Cot Memorial, Zonnebeke, West-Vlanderen, Belgium
16 August	Second Lieutenant Wilfred Laurance Reavie	Royal Dublin Fusiliers	KIA	Tyne Cot Memorial, Zonnebeke, West-Vlanderen, Belgium
16 August	Lance Corporal Thomas Stevenson	RIR	KIA	Tyne Cot Memorial, Zonnebeke, West-Vlanderen, Belgium
16 August	Rifleman Ernest Augustus Stevenson	RIR	KIA	Tyne Cot Memorial, Zonnebeke, West-Vlanderen, Belgium
16 August	Rifleman John Connell	RIR	KIA	Tyne Cot Memorial, Zonnebeke, West-Vlanderen, Belgium
16 August	Rifleman Alexander Johnston	RIR	KIA	Tyne Cot Memorial, Zonnebeke, West-Vlanderen, Belgium
16 August	Rifleman Armour John Knox	RIR	KIA	Tyne Cot Memorial, Zonnebeke, West-Vlanderen, Belgium
16 August	Rifleman Cyril Aubrey Morrison	RIR	KIA	Tyne Cot Memorial, Zonnebeke, West-Vlanderen, Belgium
16 August	Private Henry Mortimer	RIrF	KIA	Tyne Cot Memorial, Zonnebeke, West-Vlanderen, Belgium

Date	Name and rank	Unit in which last serving	How died	Where buried/ commemorated
16 August	Lance Corporal William John Robinson	RIR	KIA	Tyne Cot Memorial, Zonnebeke, West-Vlanderen, Belgium
16 August	Rifleman John Baxter	RIR	KIA	Ypres Reservoir Cemetery, Ieper, West-Vlanderen, Belgium
16 August	Private William Beattie	Inniskillings	DoW	Lijssenthoek Military Cemetery, Poperinge, West-Vlaanderen, Belgium
5 September	Lieutenant William Shields	RFC	KIA	Voormezeele Enclosures No.1 and No.2, Ieper, West-Vlaanderen, Belgium
6 September	Rifleman John Smith	RIR	KIA	Ploegsteert Memorial, Comines-Warneton, Hainaut, Belgium
19 September	Private Frederick Thomas Cordwell	NIH	Accidentally drowned	Poperinghe New Military Cemetery, Poperinge, West-Vlaanderen, Belgium
30 September	Second Lieutenant James Acheson MacLean	RFA	KIA	Kemmel Chateau Military Cemetery, Heuvelland, West-Vlaanderen, Belgium
9 October	Private Thomas Alexander McReynolds	Royal Warwickshire Regiment	KIA	Tyne Cot Memorial, Zonnebeke, West-Vlaanderen, Belgium
13 October	Second Lieutenant Alfred McClelland	RIR	DoW	Trois Arbres Cemetery, Steenwerck, Nord, France
22 October	Second Lieutenant Robert James McCullough	Cheshire Regiment	KIA	Tyne Cot Memorial, Zonnebeke, West-Vlanderen, Belgium
26 October	Private Victor Nelson Bell	9th (NIH) Battalion RIrF	KIA	Neuville-Bourjonval British Cemetery, Pas-de-Calais, France
26 October	Private Thomas Dickinson	9th (NIH) Battalion RIrF	KIA	Neuville-Bourjonval British Cemetery, Pas-de-Calais, France

Date	Name and rank	Unit in which last serving	How died	Where buried/ commemorated
26 October	Private John Dunn	9th (NIH) Battalion RIrF	KIA	Neuville-Bourjonval British Cemetery, Pas–de–Calais, France
26 October	Private George Christopher Reid	9th (NIH) Battalion RIrF	KIA	Neuville-Bourjonval British Cemetery, Pas–de–Calais, France
3 November	Sergeant Richard Irwin	9th (NIH) Battalion RIrF	KIA	Neuville-Bourjonval British Cemetery, Pas–de–Calais, France
3 November	Private John Ford	9th (NIH) Battalion RIrF	KIA	Cambrai East Military Cemetery, Nord, France
3 November	Private John Donaldson King	9th (NIH) Battalion RIrF	KIA	Cambrai East Military Cemetery, Nord, France
3 November	Private Robert Heathwood	9th (NIH) Battalion RIrF	KIA	Thiepval Memorial, Somme, France
20 November	Private Alexander Martin	Inniskillings	KIA	Cambrai Memorial, Louverval, Nord, France
22 November	Captain David McCausland	RIR	KIA	Cambrai Memorial, Louverval, Nord, France
22 November	Lance Corporal Hugh Flanagan	9th (NIH) Battalion RIrF	KIA	Cambrai Memorial, Louverval, Nord, France
22 November	Private William Petty	9th (NIH) Battalion RIrF	KIA	Cambrai Memorial, Louverval, Nord, France
23 November	Lance Corporal Fred Scanlon	9th (NIH) Battalion RIrF	KIA	Cambrai Memorial, Louverval, Nord, France
23 November	Private Christopher McWilliams	9th (NIH) Battalion RIrF	KIA	Cambrai Memorial, Louverval, Nord, France
23 November	Private James Sleator	9th (NIH) Battalion RIrF	KIA	Cambrai Memorial, Louverval, Nord, France
23 November	Private Henry Orr	9th (NIH) Battalion RIrF	KIA	Cambrai Memorial, Louverval, Nord, France

Date	Name and rank	Unit in which last serving	How died	Where buried/ commemorated
23 November	Private Samuel Price	9th (NIH) Battalion RIrF	KIA	Cambrai Memorial, Louverval, Nord, France
23 November	Private William James Turkington	9th (NIH) Battalion RIrF	KIA	Cambrai Memorial, Louverval, Nord, France
24 November	Private George Galbraith	9th (NIH) Battalion RIrF	DoW	Grevillers British Cemetery, Pas-de-Calais, France
25 November	Private Thomas Kearney	RIRegt	KIA	Croisilles British Cemetery, Pas-de-Calais, France
1 December	Private John Smyth	9th (NIH) Battalion RIrF	DoW	St Sever Cemetery Extension, Rouen, Seine-Maritime, France
6 December	Private William Thomson	9th (NIH) Battalion RIrF	DoW	Rocquigny-Equancourt Road British Cemetery, Manancourt, Somme, France
12 December	Private George Turkington Murray	RIRegt	KIA	Templeux-le-Guerard British Cemetery, Somme, France

		1918		
11 February	Private John Johnston	9th (NIH) Battalion RIrF	DoW	Grand-Seraucourt British Cemetery, Aisne, France
24 February	Private Samuel Devine	9th (NIH) Battalion RIrF	Died	Gloucester Old Cemetery, Gloucestershire, England
3 March	Private Richard Elliott	NIH	Tuberculosis	Brookwood (United Kingdom 1914–1918) Memorial, Surrey, England
21 March	Private Thomas Sittlington	9th (NIH) Battalion RIrF	KIA	Pozières Memorial, Somme, France
21 March	Private Frank Tate	9th (NIH) Battalion RIrF	KIA	Noyon New British Cemetery, Oise, France
22 March	Lance Corporal William Govan	MMP	DoW	Pozières Memorial, Somme, France

Date	Name and rank	Unit in which last serving	How died	Where buried/ commemorated
24 March	Second Lieutenant Robert Victor Lyons	RIR	KIA	Pozières Memorial, Somme, France
24 March	Rifleman Cecil Charles Hunter Barr (alias Charles Russell)	RIR	KIA	Pozières Memorial, Somme, France
24 March	Rifleman Thomas Johnston	RIR	KIA	Pozières Memorial, Somme, France
25 March	Private James Frazer Johnston	9th (NIH) Battalion RIrF	DoW	Roye New British Cemetery, Somme, France
26 March	Captain George Waller Vesey	9th (NIH) Battalion RIrF	DoW	Vignemont French National Cemetery, Oise, France
26 March	Second Lieutenant Archibald Moore	RIR	KIA	Pozières Memorial, Somme, France
26 March	Lance Sergeant George Adams Henry	9th (NIH) Battalion RIrF	DoW	St Sever Cemetery Extension, Rouen, Seine-Maritime, France
26 March	Private Reginald George Armstrong	NIH Cyclist Regiment	KIA	Toutencourt Communal Cemetery, Somme, France
26 March	Private John James Durneen	NIH Cyclist Regiment	KIA	Toutencourt Communal Cemetery, Somme, France
27 March	Corporal Thomas John McCormick	NIH Cyclist Regiment	KIA	Senlis Communal Cemetery Extension, Somme, France
21–28 March	Private Thomas Cartmill	9th (NIH) Battalion RIrF	KIA	Pozières Memorial, Somme, France
21–28 March	Private Arthur Sidney Crawford	9th (NIH) Battalion RIrF	KIA	Pozières Memorial, Somme, France
21–28 March	Private John Forbes	9th (NIH) Battalion RIrF	KIA	Pozières Memorial, Somme, France
21–28 March	Private Mark Lee	9th (NIH) Battalion RIrF	KIA	Pozières Memorial, Somme, France

Date	Name and rank	Unit in which last serving	How died	Where buried/ commemorated
21–28 March	Private Thomas Lyons	9th (NIH) Battalion RIrF	KIA	Pozières Memorial, Somme, France
21–28 March	Private John Moon	9th (NIH) Battalion RIF	KIA	Pozières Memorial, Somme, France
30 March	Private William Patrick Stuart	9th (NIH) Battalion RIrF	DoW, prisoner of war	Ham British Cemetery, Muille-Villette, Somme, France (Villers St Christophe Churchyard Memorial)
3 April	Private William Biggart	9th (NIH) Battalion RIrF	DoW, prisoner of war	Pozières Memorial, Somme, France
8 April	Corporal Hubert Roe	RIrF	DoW	Wimereux Communal Cemetery, Pas-de-Calais, France
9 April	Private William Alexander Morrow	NIH Cyclist Regiment	KIA	Hinges Military Cemetery, Pas-de-Calais, France
11 April	Private William John McAuley	9th (NIH) Battalion RIrF	DoW	Lijssenthoek Military Cemetery, Poperinge, West-Vlaanderen, Belgium
12 April	Second Lieutenant David Joseph Miller	9th (NIH) Battalion RIrF	KIA	Tyne Cot Memorial, Zonnebeke, West-Vlaanderen, Belgium
13 April	Second Lieutenant Edward Myles Meredith	RAF	Flying accident	Haringhe (Bandaghem) Military Cemetery, Poperinge, West-Vlaanderen, Belgium
13 April	Private William John Donnelly	Tank Corps	KIA	Loos Memorial, Pas-de-Calais, France
14 April	Private Robert Irwin	9th (NIH) Battalion RIrF	KIA	Tyne Cot Memorial, Zonnebeke, West-Vlaanderen, Belgium
15 April	Major Holt Waring	RIR	DoW	Wulverghem-Lindenhoek Road Military Cemetery, Heuvelland, West-Vlaanderen, Belgium
18 April	Captain Charles Beauclerk Despard	9th (NIH) Battalion RIrF	KIA	Tyne Cot Memorial, Zonnebeke, West-Vlaanderen, Belgium

Date	Name and rank	Unit in which last serving	How died	Where buried/ commemorated
18 April	Private Robert Park	9th (NIH) Battalion RIrF	KIA	Tyne Cot Memorial, Zonnebeke, West-Vlaanderen, Belgium
18 April	Private Joseph Arthur Bowden	9th (NIH) Battalion RIrF	KIA	Tyne Cot Memorial, Zonnebeke, West-Vlaanderen, Belgium
18 April	Private Frederick St. George Cooke	9th (NIH) Battalion RIrF	KIA	Tyne Cot Memorial, Zonnebeke, West-Vlaanderen, Belgium
18 April	Private Allen Davey	9th (NIH) Battalion RIrF	KIA	Tyne Cot Memorial, Zonnebeke, West-Vlaanderen, Belgium
18 April	Private William Thomas Elliott	9th (NIH) Battalion RIrF	KIA	Tyne Cot Memorial, Zonnebeke, West-Vlaanderen, Belgium
18 April	Private William George Leinster	9th (NIH) Battalion RIrF	KIA	Tyne Cot Memorial, Zonnebeke, West-Vlaanderen, Belgium
18 April	Private William Lindsay	9th (NIH) Battalion RIrF	KIA	Tyne Cot Memorial, Zonnebeke, West-Vlaanderen, Belgium
18 April	Private Robert McConnell	9th (NIH) Battalion RIrF	KIA	Tyne Cot Memorial, Zonnebeke, West-Vlaanderen, Belgium
18 April	Private William McGahey	9th (NIH) Battalion RIrF	KIA	Tyne Cot Memorial, Zonnebeke, West-Vlaanderen, Belgium
18 April	Lance Corporal Randal Edmund McManus	9th (NIH) Battalion RIrF	KIA	Tyne Cot Memorial, Zonnebeke, West-Vlaanderen, Belgium
19 April	Private John A. Bell	9th (NIH) Battalion RIrF	KIA	Wulverghem-Lindenhoek Road Military Cemetery, Heuvelland, West-Vlaanderen, Belgium
20 April	Lance Corporal Robert J. Hanna	Inniskillings	DoW, prisoner of war	la Capelle-en-Thierache Communal Cemetery, Aisne, France
22 April	Captain Samuel Treherne Bassett Saunderson	RAF	Flying accident	Shawbury, St Mary's Churchyard, Shropshire, England
22 April	Private George Morrison	9th (NIH) Battalion RIrF	DoW, prisoner of war	Hautmont Communal Cemetery, Nord, France

Date	Name and rank	Unit in which last serving	How died	Where buried/ commemorated
11 May	Lance Corporal William Leckey	RIR	KIA	Gwalia Cemetery, Ieper, West-Vlanderen, Belgium
18 May	Private Thompson Harpur	9th (NIH) Battalion RIrF	DoW, prisoner of war	Avesnes-sur-Helpe Communal Cemetery, Nord, France
25 May	Private Francis James Morrison	9th (NIH) Battalion RIrF	DoW	Gwalia Cemetery, Ieper, West-Vlanderen, Belgium
6 June	Private James Magill	9th (NIH) Battalion RIrF	DoW, prisoner of war	Ham British Cemetery, Muille-Villette, Somme, France
8 July	Private George William Stronge	9th (NIH) Battalion RIrF	Died, prisoner of war	Hautmont Communal Cemetery, Nord, France
22 July	Private William Frederick Christy Arthur	9th (NIH) Battalion RIrF	KIA	Bailleul Communal Cemetery Extension, Nord, France
22 July	Private John Nicholl	9th (NIH) Battalion RIrF	Died, prisoner of war	Hautmont Communal Cemetery, Nord, France
22 July	Second Lieutenant Francis John Elliott McFarland	9th (NIH) Battalion RIrF	KIA	Tyne Cot Memorial, Zonnebeke, West-Vlaanderen, Belgium
3 August	Private John Edward Riddell	9th (NIH) Battalion RIrF	KIA	Bertenacre Military Cemetery, Fletre, Nord, France
3 August	Private Samuel William Speers	9th (NIH) Battalion RIrF	DoW	Bertenacre Military Cemetery, Fletre, Nord, France
6 August	Private Robert McCready	Nottinghamshire Yeomanry (Sherwood Rangers)	Died	Alexandria (Hadra) War Memorial Cemetery, Egypt
11 or 12 August	Private William Brown	9th (NIH) Battalion RIrF	DoW	Mont Noir Military Cemetery, St Jans Cappel, Nord, France
12 August	Private Andrew Pepper	9th (NIH) Battalion RIrF	KIA	Ploegsteert Memorial, Comines-Warneton, Hainaut, Belgium

Date	Name and rank	Unit in which last serving	How died	Where buried/ commemorated
16 August	Private Wesley McClelland	NIH Cyclist Regiment	KIA	Ancre British Cemetery, Beaumont-Hamel, Somme, France
16 August	Private William Waller	9th Lancers (Queen's Royal)	DoW	St Sever Cemetery Extension, Rouen, Seine-Maritime, France
21 August	Captain Edwin Sinton	RE	KIA	Villers Station Cemetery, Villers-au-Bois, Pas-de-Calais, France
21 August	Private Thomas Bryson	NIH Cyclist Regiment	KIA	Queens Cemetery, Bucquoy, Pas-de-Calais, France
21 August	Private John Roberts	NIH Cyclist Regiment	KIA	Vis-en-Artois Memorial, Pas-de-Calais, France
21 August	Private Robert Ross	NIH Cyclist Regiment	KIA	Ancre British Cemetery, Beaumont-Hamel, Somme, France
26 August	Private George Gill	NIH Cyclist Regiment	KIA	Flatiron Copse Cemetery, Mametz, Somme, France
26 August	Private Frederick Livingstone	NIH Cyclist Regiment	KIA	Flatiron Copse Cemetery, Mametz, Somme, France
26 August	Private Adam Gordon Kelly	NIH Cyclist Regiment	KIA	Ovillers Military Cemetery, Somme, France
26 August	Private John McVea	NIH Cyclist Regiment	KIA	Vis-en-Artois Memorial, Pas-de-Calais, France
26 August	Sergeant William Garnett Wolsley Irwin	9th (NIH) Battalion RIrF	DoW	Arneke British Cemetery, Nord, France
30 August	Trooper Alfred Henry Huggins	6th Dragoon Guards (Carabiniers)	DoW	Fienvillers British Cemetery, Somme, France
31 August	Lieutenant Robert Campbell Russell	North Staffordshire Regiment	DoW	Baku Memorial, Azerbaijan
31 August	Private Robert George Donaldson Montgomery	Inniskillings	DoW	Bertenacre Military Cemetery, Fletre, Nord, France

Date	Name and rank	Unit in which last serving	How died	Where buried/ commemorated
2 September	Acting Lieutenant Colonel Richard Annesley West	Tank Corps	KIA	Mory Abbey Military Cemetery, Pas-de-Calais, France
2 September	Private Alexander Blair	NIH Cyclist Regiment	Died	Varennes Military Cemetery, Somme, France
4 September	Private George Mark	9th (NIH) Battalion RIrF	KIA	Ploegsteert Memorial, Comines-Warneton, Hainaut, Belgium
4 September	Private Samuel Pinkerton	9th (NIH) Battalion RIrF	KIA	Ploegsteert Memorial, Comines-Warneton, Hainaut, Belgium
4 September	Private William Fairbairn Timbey	9th (NIH) Battalion RIrF	KIA	Ploegsteert Memorial, Comines-Warneton, Hainaut, Belgium
5 September	Private James Kelly	9th (NIH) Battalion RIrF	DoW	Arneke British Cemetery, Nord, France
7 September	Rifleman Thomas McCready Henderson	RIR	KIA	Kandahar Farm Cemetery, Heuvelland, West-Vlanderen, Belgium
14 September	Rifleman Thomas McKillop	RIR	KIA	Ploegsteert Memorial, Comines-Warneton, Hainaut, Belgium
30 September	Private William James Abercrombie	9th (NIH) Battalion RIrF	KIA	Dadizeele New British Cemetery, Moorslede, West-Vlanderen, Belgium
1 October	Private William Henry Dundas	9th (NIH) Battalion RIrF	KIA	Tyne Cot Memorial, Zonnebeke, West-Vlanderen, Belgium
1 or 7 October	Private Joseph Coulter	9th (NIH) Battalion RIrF	KIA	Dadizeele New British Cemetery, Moorslede, West-Vlanderen, Belgium
2 October	Corporal Charles Edward Houston	Inniskillings	KIA	Dadizeele New British Cemetery, Moorslede, West-Vlanderen, Belgium

Date	Name and rank	Unit in which last serving	How died	Where buried/ commemorated
3 October	Private Frank James Best	9th (NIH) Battalion RIrF	DoW	Dadizeele New British Cemetery, Moorslede, West-Vlaanderen, Belgium
6 October	Lieutenant Harold Plumer Kellock	RFA	DoW	Terlincthun British Cemetery, Wimille, Pas-de-Calais, France
8 October	Private John Scott	19th Hussars (Queen Alexandra's Own Royal)	KIA	Busigny Communal Cemetery Extension, Nord, France
10 October	Lance Corporal Alexander Erskine	9th (NIH) Battalion RIrF	DoW	Lijssenthoek Military Cemetery, Poperinge, West-Vlaanderen, Belgium
10 October	Private Samuel Shiels	9th (NIH) Battalion RIrF	Drowned at sea	Ballybay First Presbyterian Churchyard, County Monaghan, Ireland
11 October	Second Lieutenant Thomas John Savage	Rifle Brigade	KIA	St Aubert British Cemetery, Nord, France
11 October	Lance Corporal Joseph Deery	9th (NIH) Battalion RIrF	KIA	Dadizeele New British Cemetery, Moorslede, West-Vlaanderen, Belgium
11 October	Private Robert John Hull	9th (NIH) Battalion RIrF	KIA	Dadizeele New British Cemetery, Moorslede, West-Vlaanderen, Belgium
13 October	Private George Johnston	9th (NIH) Battalion RIrF	Died, prisoner of war	Perreuse Chateau Franco British National Cemetery, Seine-et-Marne, France
14 October	Lance Corporal William James Reid	RIR	KIA	Dadizeele New British Cemetery, Moorslede, West-Vlaanderen, Belgium
15 October	Private Charles Henry McDaniel	Staffordshire Yeomanry	Illness	Damascus Commonwealth War Cemetery, Syria
17 October	Private Matthew Haggan	Staffordshire Yeomanry	Illness	Beirut War Cemetery, Lebanon

Date	Name and rank	Unit in which last serving	How died	Where buried/ commemorated
20 October	Second Lieutenant William Anderson	RIR	KIA	Harlebeke New British Cemetery, West-Vlaanderen, Belgium
20 October	Private Robert Richmond	Inniskillings	KIA	Harlebeke New British Cemetery, West-Vlaanderen, Belgium
23 October	Second Lieutenant James Denny	RIrF	KIA	Harlebeke New British Cemetery, West-Vlaanderen, Belgium
23 October	Private William John Wallace	9th (NIH) Battalion RIrF	KIA	Harlebeke New British Cemetery, West-Vlaanderen, Belgium
23 October	Second Lieutenant John Knox	RIR	DoW	Terlincthun British Cemetery, Wimille, Pas-de-Calais, France
24 October	Private George Killough	RIRegt	Pneumonia	Deir-el-Belah War Cemetery, Israel and Palestine
25 October	Private John Evans	NIH Cyclist Regiment	DoW	Awoingt British Cemetery, Nord, France
25 October	Private Michael McVeigh	9th (NIH) Battalion RIrF	KIA	Harlebeke New British Cemetery, West-Vlaanderen, Belgium
25 October	Private George Moorhead Shannon	9th (NIH) Battalion RIrF	KIA	Harlebeke New British Cemetery, West-Vlaanderen, Belgium
26 October	Second Lieutenant Harold Percival Nixon	Wiltshire Regiment	KIA	Warcoing Churchyard, Pecq, Hainaut, Belgium
26 October	Lance Corporal Harold Irvine	6th Dragoon Guards (Carabiniers)	Pneumonia	Breandrum Cemetery, Fermanagh, Northern Ireland
3 November	Private Herbert Brennan	NIH Cyclist Regiment	Pneumonia	Awoingt British Cemetery, Nord, France

Date	Name and rank	Unit in which last serving	How died	Where buried/ commemorated
3 November	Private William McCormick	9th (NIH) Battalion RIrF	DoW	Kezelberg Military Cemetery, Wevelgem, West-Vlaanderen, Belgium
4 November	Private John Cully	NIH Cyclist Regiment	DoW	Forest Communal Cemetery, Nord, France
7 November	Private Charles Elder	NIH Cyclist Regiment	KIA	Dourlers Communal Cemetery Extension, Nord, France
8 November	Private Charles Richard Woodside	NIH Cyclist Regiment	Pneumonia	Rocquigny-Equancourt Road British Cemetery, Manancourt, Somme, France
9 November	Private Robert Evans	NIH Cyclist Regiment	Tuberculosis	Derriaghy Christ Church Churchyard, County Antrim, Northern Ireland
10 November	Lance Corporal Robert Henry Hill	NIH Cyclist Regiment	Injuries	Mont Huon Military Cemetery, le Treport, Seine-Maritime, France
10 November	Private William Hillocks	NIH Cyclist Regiment	Illness	Mont Huon Military Cemetery, le Treport, Seine-Maritime, France
12 November	Private John Johnston	NIH Cyclist Regiment	Died	Caudry British Cemetery, Nord, France
14 November	Private James Adair	NIH Cyclist Regiment	Pneumonia	St. Sever Cemetery Extension, Rouen, Seine-Maritime, France
30 November	Private William Mills	NIH Cyclist Regiment	Died	Ballybay First Presbyterian Churchyard, County Monaghan, Ireland
4 December	Private Robert William Kerr	9th (NIH) Battalion RIrF	Heart disease/ inflammation of lungs, prisoner of war	Hamburg Cemetery, Germany

Date	Name and rank	Unit in which last serving	How died	Where buried/ commemorated
7 December	Private Brownlow Thompson	9th (NIH) Battalion RIrF	Pneumonia	Eglish (Drumsallen) Church of Ireland Churchyard, County Armagh, Northern Ireland
9 December	Private Patrick Sheridan	9th (NIH) Battalion RIrF	DoW	Drumcor Catholic Churchyard, County Cavan, Ireland
1919				
4 January	Captain Robert Livsey Yates	NIH	Tuberculosis	Brookwood (United Kingdom 1914–1918) Memorial, Surrey, England
28 January	Lieutenant Thomas Humphrey Hesketh	21st Lancers (Empress of India's)	Scarlet fever, pneumonia	Cathcart Cemetery, Renfrewshire, Scotland
19 February	Private Frederick McConnell	NIH	Illness	Manorcunningham (Errity) Presbyterian Churchyard, County Donegal, Ireland
25 March	Lieutenant Leslie Ernest McNeill	4th Dragoon Guards (Royal Irish)	Influenza	Sanderstead (All Saints) Churchyard, Surrey, England
17 June	Private James Montgomery	NIH	Died	Belfast (Dundonald) Cemetery, Northern Ireland
9 October	Major Eustace Anthony Whaley Maude	Tank Corps	Drowned at sea	Brookwood (United Kingdom 1914–1918) Memorial, Surrey, England
11 November	Sapper Robert William Nesbitt	RE	Died from the effects of gas	Belfast City Cemetery, Northern Ireland
1921				
24 May	Lance Corporal Percy Reid	ASC	Tuberculosis	Brookwood (United Kingdom 1914–1918) Memorial, Surrey, England

Note

1. CWGC records Scott's date of death as 8 October 1914.

Appendix IV

North Irish Horse Awards and Decorations
1914 to 1919

Award	Name and rank (when award given)	Regiment (when award given)	LG Supplement date[1]
Victoria Cross	A/Lieutenant Colonel Richard Annesley West	Tank Corps	30 October 1918
Order of the British Empire (Officer of the Military Division)	Major Valentine George Whitla	3rd (King's Own) Hussars	3 June 1919
Order of the British Empire (Member of the Military Division)	Captain Thomas Aston	NIH	3 June 1919
The Most Distinguished Order of St Michael and St George	Major Viscount John Henry Michael Cole	NIH	14 January 1916
Bar to Distinguished Service Order	A/Lieutenant Colonel Richard Annesley West	Tank Corps	7 November 1918
Distinguished Service Order	Captain Charles Beauclerk Despard	9th (NIH) Battalion, RIrF	16 September 1918
	Major (A/Lieut Col) Arthur Kenlis Maxwell, Lord Farnham	Inniskillings	3 June 1918
	Major Arthur Edward Phillips	Royal West Kent Regiment	1 January 1919
	A/Lieutenant Colonel Neil Graham Stewart-Richardson	Royal Scots Fusiliers	11 April 1918
	Captain Richard Annesley West	North Somerset Yeomanry	1 January 1918
Bar to Military Cross	Second Lieutenant John Knox	RIR	7 November 1918
	Lieutenant Simon Logan	9th (NIH) Battalion, RIrF	8 March 1919

Award	Name and rank (when award given)	Regiment (when award given)	LG Supplement date[1]
Military Cross	Captain John Valentine Adair	12th Lancers	8 March & 4 October 1919
	Lieutenant Edward Arthur Atkinson	NIH Cyclist Regiment	1 February 1919
	A/Captain Worship Booker	NIH Cyclist Regiment	3 June 1919
	Lieutenant Charles William Coulter	Royal Welsh Fusiliers	11 January 1919
	A/Captain Herbert Shelton Dean	9th (NIH) Battalion RIrF	16 September 1918
	Captain Charles Beauclerk Despard	9th (NIH) Battalion RIrF	4 February & 5 July 1918
	Second Lieutenant Alexander Dundee	RIR	24 July 1917
	Second Lieutenant Raymond Green	RIRegt	30 July 1919
	Lieutenant James Kenneth MacGregor Greer	Irish Guards	LG ref not located – believed to be 11 January 1916
	Second Lieutenant William Lyttle Harcourt	RIR	16 September 1918
	Lieutenant Donald O'Neill Hodson	NIH Cyclist Regiment	11 January 1919
	Second Lieutenant John Knox	RIR	18 February 1918
	Second Lieutenant Simon Logan	9th (NIH) Battalion, RIrF	1 February 1919
	Second Lieutenant Francis John Elliott McFarland	RIrF	26 July 1918
	Lieutenant John McKinstry	RIR	30 July 1919
	Second Lieutenant James Acheson MacLean	RFA	26 September 1916
	Second Lieutenant Robert Arthur Arland Macready	Leinster Regiment	3 March 1917
	Lieutenant Hugh Edmund Langton Montgomery	NIH Cyclist Regiment	3 June 1919

Award	Name and rank (when award given)	Regiment (when award given)	LG Supplement date[1]
	Captain Ronald Deane Ross	NIH	1 January 1918
	A/Captain Edwin Sinton	RFA	16 September 1918
	Captain Richard Reginald Smart	NIH	3 June 1919
	Second Lieutenant James Noel Greer Stewart	RIR	15 October 1918
	Lieutenant Alexander Frederick Traill	RA	22 September 1916
	Lieutenant George Waller Vesey	9th (NIH) Battalion RIrF	16 August 1918
	Sergeant Major Thomas Henry Waldren 42666	Inniskillings	3 June 1918
	A/Major Richard Annesley West	Tank Corps	7 November 1918
	Second Lieutenant James Bailey Young	9th (NIH) Battalion, RIrF	1 February 1919
Distinguished Conduct Medal	Lance Corporal Robert Armstrong 41695	9th (NIH) Battalion, RIrF	2 December 1919
	A/Lance Corporal James Gracey 41572	9th (NIH) Battalion, RIrF	5 December 1918
	A/Sergeant John Lockhart 41148	9th (NIH) Battalion, RIrF	1 January & 3 September 1919
	Lance Corporal William John Robinson 40839	RIR	22 October 1917 & 26 January 1918
	Corporal Hubert Roe 41147	9th (NIH) Battalion, RIrF	28 March 1918
Bar to Military Medal	Squadron Sergeant Major Humphrey Boyd H/71014	NIH Cyclist Regiment	23 July 1919
	Private Edward W McKeown D/21257	6th Inniskilling Dragoons	11 December 1918
Military Medal	Private William Adamson 41271	9th (NIH) Battalion, RIrF	29 August 1918
	Corporal Johnston Armstrong H/71111	NIH Cyclist Regiment	11 February 1919
	Private Robert Averell 41534	9th (NIH) Battalion, RIrF	23 February 1918

Award	Name and rank (when award given)	Regiment (when award given)	LG Supplement date[1]
	Corporal Joseph Bailey H/71168	NIH Cyclist Regiment	11 February 1919
	Corporal Robert Cooke Blair H/71512	NIH Cyclist Regiment	11 February 1919
	Squadron Sergeant-Major Humphrey Boyd H/71014	NIH Cyclist Regiment	13 March 1919
	Sergeant William Brown H/71707	NIH Cyclist Regiment	11 February 1919
	Squadron Sergeant-Major Robert James Carmichael H/71419	NIH Cyclist Regiment	20 August 1919
	Private Thomas Clyde Chambers 41256	9th (NIH) Battalion, RIrF	23 February 1918
	Lance Sergeant John W. Clancey H/71683	NIH Cyclist Regiment	20 August 1919
	Lance Corporal Alan George Hart Clarke 41483	9th (NIH) Battalion, RIrF	19 March 1918
	Private Joseph Close H/71273	NIH Cyclist Regiment	20 August 1919
	Lance Corporal David Connolly H/71603	NIH Cyclist Regiment	11 February 1919
	Private Alfred Connor 40639	Inniskillings	4 October 1917 (BNL)
	Private Joseph Coulter 41530	9th (NIH) Battalion, RIrF	24 January 1919
	Sergeant William H. Glendinning H/71157	NIH Cyclist Regiment	20 August 1919
	Squadron Sergeant Major Frank Raymond Harding H/71109	NIH Cyclist Regiment	20 August 1919
	Lance Sergeant George Adams Henry 41401	9th (NIH) Battalion, RIrF	19 March 1918
	Sergeant Thomas Jamison H/71660	NIH Cyclist Regiment	11 February 1919
	Lance Corporal Francis Jennings 41338	9th (NIH) Battalion, RIrF	20 August 1919

Award	Name and rank (when award given)	Regiment (when award given)	LG Supplement date[1]
	Rifleman Alexander Johnston 40880	RIR	2 November 1917
	Corporal William James Johnston H/71404	NIH Cyclist Regiment	20 August 1919
	Private Hubert Kearon H/71983	NIH Cyclist Regiment	11 February 1919
	Private James Laughlin H/71529	NIH Cyclist Regiment	12 June 1918
	Private William McCarley 41329	9th (NIH) Battalion, RIrF	7 October 1918
	Private Thomas Alexander McClelland 41307	9th (NIH) Battalion, RIrF	29 August 1918
	Private Edward W McKeown D/21257	6th Inniskilling Dragoons	25 April 1918
	Sergeant William McMurray H/71279	NIH Cyclist Regiment	20 August 1919
	Private John Morrison 41327	9th (NIH) Battalion, RIrF	23 February 1918
	Sergeant George Nesbitt 41198	9th (NIH) Battalion, RIrF	29 August 1918
	Private Joshua Paul 41355	9th (NIH) Battalion, RIrF	24 January 1919
	Sergeant Samuel Rainey H/71343	NIH Cyclist Regiment	20 August 1919
	Sergeant William Scott H/71023	NIH Cyclist Regiment	12 June 1918
	A/Corporal William Stevenson H/71654	NIH Cyclist Regiment	11 February 1919
	A/Corporal Robert Cromes Stewart H/71511	NIH Cyclist Regiment	20 August 1919
	Private Robert Tughan 41280	9th (NIH) Battalion, RIrF	29 August 1918
	Private Samuel Wasson 41414	9th (NIH) Battalion, RIrF	7 October 1918
	Private William Watt 1001	NIH	19 November 1917
	Corporal Richard Randall Webb 28295	RE	11 October 1916
	Private Ernest Wilson 304882	Tank Corps	13 March 1919

Award	Name and rank (when award given)	Regiment (when award given)	LG Supplement date[1]
	Regimental Sergeant-Major John Wright H/71197	NIH Cyclist Regiment	20 August 1919
Mentioned in Despatches	Lieutenant James Graham Adam	NIH	5 July 1919
	Second Lieutenant Henry Tottenham Armstrong	RIrF	Medal Index Card
	Second Lieutenant Gustaf William Akerlind	Tank Corps	Medal Index Card
	Squadron Sergeant-Major Thomas Alfred Barns 3657	NIH	15 June 1916
	A/Sergeant Worship Booker	NIH	22 June 1915
	A/Captain James Arthur Coey	RIR	20 May 1918
	Major Viscount John Henry Michael Cole	NIH	1 January 1916
	Air Mechanic Second Class Fred G Davin	RFC	15 May 1917
	Captain Charles Beauclerk Despard	9th (NIH) Battalion, RIrF	30 April 1919
	Lance Corporal Robert J Dougall H/71222	NIH Cyclist Regiment	5 July 1919
	Squadron Sergeant-Major Robert James Downey 41	NIH	15 May 1917
	Lieutenant Walter Alexander Edmenson	RFA	4 January 1917
	A/Captain Herbert Gavin Elliot	NIH Cyclist Regiment	5 July 1919
	Major Arthur Kenlis Maxwell, Lord Farnham	Inniskillings	11 December 1917
	A/Lieutenant-Colonel Arthur Kenlis Maxwell, Lord Farnham	Inniskillings	20 May 1918
	Sergeant Samuel Gibson	MMP	Medal Index Card
	Brevet Colonel Walter Goring	3rd (King's Own) Hussars	25 January 1917
	Major Donald S. Graham	RAMC	Medal Index Card

Award	Name and rank (when award given)	Regiment (when award given)	LG Supplement date[1]
	Capt John Grant	NIH Cyclist Regiment	5 July 1919
	Second Lieutenant James Kenneth MacGregor Greer	3rd Dragoon Guards	1 January 1916
	Major the Hon Arthur Hamilton–Russell	NIH	15 May 1917
	Captain Thomas William Gillilan Johnston Hughes	NIH	15 May 1917
	Major David Alfred William Ker	NIH	5 July 1919
	Squadron Sergeant-Major James Harvey King H/71022	NIH Cyclist Regiment	20 May 1918
	Captain James Cunningham Gordon Kirkpatrick	NIH Cyclist Regiment	5 July 1919
	Corporal William G McCalmont H/71624	NIH Cyclist Regiment	5 July 1919
	Private Richard McIlwaine 788	NIH	17 February 1915
	Major Algernon William John Clotworthy, Viscount Massereene & Ferrard	NIH	19 October 1914
	Major Algernon William John Clotworthy, Viscount Massereene & Ferrard	NIH	17 February 1915
	Captain Walter Ashley Montgomery	NIH	11 December 1917
	Captain Warren Murland	NIH	15 May 1917
	Second Lieutenant Arthur Charles Nugent	5th Lancers	22 February 1916 (BNL)
	A/Sergeant William Henry Phayre 1471	MMP	16 January 1918
	Major Arthur Edward Phillips	Royal West Kent Regiment	Medal Index Card
	Quartermaster and Hon Lieutenant John Edward Pittaway	NIH	27 February 1917 (BNL)

Award	Name and rank (when award given)	Regiment (when award given)	LG Supplement date[1]
	Private Abraham Scott H/71462	NIH Cyclist Regiment	5 July 1919
	Squadron Sergeant-Major William A Sewell 993	NIH	22 June 1915
	Captain Frederick Rutherford Skillen	Liverpool Regiment	8 July 1919
	Lieutenant Richard Reginald Smart	NIH	20 May 1918
	A/Lieutenant-Colonel Neil Graham Stewart-Richardson	NIH	7 October 1918
	Major Holt Waring	NIH	15 June 1916
	Major Holt Waring	NIH	15 May 1917
	Major Holt Waring	RIR	20 May 1918
	Lieutenant Richard Annesley West	NIH	19 October 1914
	Captain Richard Annesley West	North Somerset Yeomanry	11 December 1917
	A/Lieutenant-Colonel Richard Annesley West	Tank Corps	20 December 1918
	Major Valentine George Whitla	3rd (King's Own) Hussars	Medal Index Card
	Corporal John Wright 1008	NIH	17 February 1915
Meritorious Service Medal	Corporal Frederick D.W Ferguson H/71099	NIH	17 June 1918
	Saddler Corporal Robert J Hassard H/71294	NIH	17 June 1918
	Sergeant Samuel Rainey H/71343	NIH	18 January 1919
	Regimental Sergeant-Major William A Sewell 993	NIH	1 January 1918
	Sergeant William Stevenson 1198	NIH	4 June 1917
	Battery Sergeant-Major John Percy Ward 88382	RFA	4 June 1917
Special Reserve Long Service and Good Conduct Medal	Sergeant Thomas Henry Metcalfe 244	NIH	24 January 1916 (BNL)

Award	Name and rank (when award given)	Regiment (when award given)	LG Supplement date[1]
	Sergeant Robert Alexander Wylie 70	NIH	13 April 1917 (BNL)
	Corporal Samuel J Wylie 74	NIH	13 April 1917 (BNL)
	Squadron Sergeant-Major Charles Delmege Trimble 97	NIH	13 April 1917 (BNL)
	Squadron Quartermaster-Sergeant James Malcolm Wherry 558	NIH	13 April 1917 (BNL)
	Sergeant David Matchett 742	NIH	13 April 1917 (BNL)
Ordre du Mérite Agricole (France)	Lieutenant-Colonel Viscount John Henry Michael Cole	NIH	7 October 1919
Croix de Guerre (France)	Major Ronald Deane Ross	NIH	19 June 1919
Croix de Guerre (Belgium)	Sergeant John Lockhart 41148	9th (NIH) Battalion, RIrF	4 September 1919
	Major Adrian Hulse	Inniskillings	4 September 1919
Military Order of Aviz, Chevalier (Portugal)	Lieutenant James Graham Adam	NIH	24 October 1919
Médaille Militaire (France)	Private Francis James Colquhoun 590	NIH	5 November 1914 (AO.466/1914)
	Private James McArow 164	NIH	5 November 1914 (AO.466/1914)
Gallantry certificate	Private Charles Bell 71621	NIH	3 August 1917 (BNL)

Note

1. The date of Gazettal could occur many months after the award was won. Where no Gazettal has been located the alternative source and date is noted.

Bibliography

Books and Other Printed Material

Aldrich, Mildred, *A Hilltop on the Marne: being letters written June 3–September 8, 1914*, Houghton Mifflin, Boston, 1916.

Atteridge, A. Hilliard, *History of the 17th (Northern) Division*, Robert Maclehose, Glasgow, 1929, reprint by The Naval & Military Press, East Sussex.

Baring, Maurice, *R.F.C. H.Q. 1914 – 1918*, G.Bell & Sons, London, 1920.

Becke, Major E. F., *Order of Battle*, HMSO, London, 1945.

Bowman, Timothy, *The Irish Regiments in the Great War: Discipline and morale*, Manchester University Press, Manchester, 2003.

—— 'The North Began ... but when? The formation of the Ulster Volunteer Force', in *History Ireland*, Vol. 21 No.2, March/April 2013.

Burke, Tom, *The 16th (Irish) and 36th (Ulster) Divisions at The Battle of Wijtschate – Messines Ridge, 7 June 1917: A battlefield tour guide*, The Royal Dublin Fusiliers Association, Dublin, 2007.

Burrowes, Brigadier General, *The 1st Battalion: The Faugh-a-Ballaghs in the Great War*, Gale & Polden, Aldershot.

Coleman, Frederic, *From Mons to Ypres with French: A personal narrative*, Williams Briggs, Toronto, 1916.

The Committee of the Irish National War Memorial, *Ireland's Memorial Records 1914–1918*, Dublin: Maunsel & Roberts, 1923 (via Ancestry.com).

Crozier, Brigadier General, *A Brass Hat in No Man's Land*, Jonathan Cape, London, 1930.

Davies, Travis Philip (ed.), *1914 to 1919: A Medical Officer's Diary and Narrative of the First World War, by Travis Hampson MC*, published online 2001.

Depree, Major General H. D., *A History of the 38th (Welsh) and 33rd Divisions: In the Last Five Weeks of the Great War*, reprint by The Naval & Military Press in association with the Royal Artillery Museum.

Doherty, Richard, *The North Irish Horse: A Hundred Years of Service*, Spellmount, Staplehurst, 2002.

Dorman, Captain Edward Mungo, 'The North Irish Horse', in *The Army Review*, Vol. III, 192, October 1912.

Dunn, Captain James Churchill, *The War the Infantry Knew, 1914–1919: A Chronicle of Service in France and Belgium*, P. S King, 1938 (1994 Abacus ed.).

Elliott, Leslie & Stevenson, David; Hudson, Mark (ed.), *The Story of a Banner: Waringstown during World War 1*, The Waringstown Somme Heritage Association.

Falls, Cyril, *The History of the 36th (Ulster) Division*, McCaw, Stevenson & Orr, 1922, reprint by The Naval & Military Press, East Sussex.

French, Field Marshal Viscount, *1914*, Constable and Company, London, 1919.

Gibson, Major Edwin, & Ward, G. Kingsley, *Courage Remembered*, HMSO, London, 1989.

Gleichen, Brigadier General Count, *The Doings of the 15th Infantry Brigade: August 1914 to March 1915*, William Blackwood & Sons, Edinburgh and London, 1917.

Gosse, Philip, *Memoirs of a Camp-Follower*, Longmans, Green & Co., London, 1934, reprint by The Naval & Military Press, East Sussex.

Grayson, Richard S, *Belfast Boys: How Unionists and Nationalists Fought and Died Together in the First World War*, Continuum UK, London, 2009.

Gudmundsson, Bruce I., *The British Army on the Western Front 1916*, Osprey Publishing, Oxford, 2007.

Harris, Henry, *The Irish Regiments in the First World War*, The Mercier Press, Cork, 1968.

Harvey, Colonel J. R. and Cape, Lieutenant Colonel H. A., *The History of the 5th (Royal Irish) Regiment of Dragoons [and] The 5th Royal Irish Lancers*, Gale & Polden, Aldershot, 1923.

Hennessy, Thomas F., *The Great War 1914–1918: Bank of Ireland Staff, Service Record*, Alex Thom & Co, Dublin, 1920.

Henshaw, Trevor, *The Sky Their Battlefield: Air Fighting and the Complete List of Allied Air Casualties from Enemy Action in the First War*, Grub Street, London, 1995.

Hobson, Chris (ed.), *Airmen Died in the Great War 1914–1918*, J. B. Hayward & Son, Suffolk, 1995.

Hodges, Paul, '"They don't like it up 'em!": Bayonet Fetishization in the British Army during the First World War', in *Journal of War and Culture Studies*, Vol.1 No.2, 2008.

Holmes, Richard, *Riding the Retreat: Mons to the Marne – 1914 Revisited*, Jonathan Cape, 1995 (2007 Pimlico ed.)

Home, Brigadier General Sir Archibald, *The Diary of a World War I Cavalry Officer*, D. J. Costello Publishers, Kent, 1985.

Hutchinson, Lieutenant Colonel Graham Seton, *The Thirty-Third Division in France and Flanders*, reprint by The Naval & Military Press, East Sussex.

James, Brigadier E. A., *British Regiments, 1914–1918*, The Naval & Military Press, East Sussex, 1978 (1998 ed).

Jeffery, Keith, *Ireland and the Great War*, CUP, Cambridge, 2000.

Kenyon, David, *Horsemen in No Man's Land: British Cavalry & Trench Warfare 1914–1918*, Pen & Sword Military, Barnsley, 2011.

Livesey, Anthony, *The Viking Atlas of World War I*, Viking, London, 1994.

Lucy, John F, *There's a Devil in the Drum*, 1938, reprint by The Naval & Military Press, East Sussex.

McCarthy, Chris, *The Somme: The Day-by-Day Account*, Arms & Armour Press, 1983 (1998, Brockhampton Press ed.).

MacDonagh, Michael, *The Irish at the Front*, Hodder and Stoughton, London, 1916.

Macdonald, Lyn, *1914*, Michael Joseph, London, 1987.

—— *1915: The Death of Innocence*, Headline Book Publishing, 1993.

—— *Somme*, Michael Joseph, London, 1983.

—— *They Called it Passchendaele*, Michael Joseph, London, 1978.

—— *To the Last Man: Spring 1918*, Viking, London, 1998.

Mac Fhionnghaile, Niall, *Donegal, Ireland and the First World War*, An Crann, Leitirceannain, 1987.

Magill, Paul, *The Magills of the Meetinghouse, Cairncastle*, Shanway Press, 2010.

Mannering, Guy (ed.), *The Peaks and Passes of J.R.D.: from the note-books, diaries and letters from life of James Robert Dennistoun*, JRD Publication, Geraldine, 1999.

Metcalfe, Nick, *Blacker's Boys: 9th (Service) Battalion, Princess Victoria's (Royal Irish Fusiliers) (County Armagh) & 9th (North Irish Horse) Battalion, Princess Victoria's (Royal Irish Fusiliers), 1914–1919*, Writersworld, Woodstock, 2012.

Middlebrook, Martin, *The First Day on the Somme: 1 July 1916*, Allen Lane, London, 1971.

—— *The Kaiser's Battle, 21 March 1918: The First Day of the German Spring Offensive*, Allen Lane, 1978 (1983, Penguin Books ed.).

The Monthly Army List, HMSO, London, various months, 1903 to 1919.

Munby, Lieutenant Colonel J. E., *A History of the 38th (Welsh) Division*, Hugh Rees, London, 1920, reprint by The Naval & Military Press, East Sussex.

Murland, Jerry, *Departed Warriors: The story of a family in war*, Matador, Leicester, 2008.

Nicholls, Jonathan, *Cheerful Sacrifice: The Battle of Arras, 1917*, 1990 (2013 Pen & Sword edition).

Orr, Philip, *The Road to the Somme: Men of the Ulster Division Tell Their Story*, The Blackstaff Press, Belfast, 1987.

Perry, Nicholas (ed.), *Major General Oliver Nugent and the Ulster Division 1915–1918*, Sutton Publishing for the Army Records Society, 2007.

Presbyterian Church of Ireland, *Roll of Honour 1914–1919*, The Presbyterian Historical Society of Ireland, Church House, Belfast, reprint by The Naval & Military Press, East Sussex.

De Ruvigny, Marquis, *De Ruvigny's Roll of Honour, 1914–18*, 1922, reprint by The Naval & Military Press, East Sussex.

Sheffield, Gary & Bourne, John (eds), *Douglas Haig: War Diaries and Letters, 1914–1918*, Weidenfeld & Nicolson, London, 2005.

Sheldon, Jack, *The German Army at Cambrai*, Pen & Sword, 2009.

Sinn Fein Rebellion Handbook: Easter 1916, Weekly Irish Times, Dublin, 1917.

Summers, Julie, *Remembered: The History of the Commonwealth War Graves Commission*, Merrell Publishers, London, 2007.

Takle, Patrick, *Battleground Europe: The Affair at Néry*, Pen & Sword, Barnsley, 2007.

Taylor, James W, *The 1st Royal Irish Rifles in the Great War*, Four Courts Press, Dublin, 2002.

—— *The 2nd Royal Irish Rifles in the Great War*, Four Courts Press, Dublin, 2005.

Terraine, John, *Mons: The Retreat to Victory*, Pen & Sword, Barnsley, 1960 (2010 ed.).

Thompson, Robert (comp. & ed.), *Bushmills Heroes, 1914–1918*, Robert Thompson, Bushmills, 1995 (2008 ed.).

—— *Ballymoney Heroes, 1914–1918*, Robert Thompson, Bushmills, 1999.

—— *Coleraine Heroes, 1914–1918*, Robert Thompson, Bushmills, 2004.

—— *Inishowen Heroes, 1914–1918*, Robert Thompson, Bushmills, 2007.

Townshend, Charles, *Easter 1916: The Irish Rebellion*, Allen Lane, London, 2005.

Trimble, Charles D., *Memories of The North Irish Horse*, Armagh, 2002.

Tuchman, Barbara W., *The Guns of August*, Presidio Press, New York, 1962 (2010 ed.).

Vere-Laurie, Florence (ed.), *Letters of Lt-Col George Brenton Laurie*, Gale & Polden, Aldershot, 1921.

War Office, *Army Orders*, HMSO, London, 1908–19.

—— *Field Service Regulations: Part I, Operations*, HMSO, London, 1909 (reprinted with amendments 1912).

—— *Field Service Regulations: Part II, Organization and Administration*, HMSO, London, 1909 (reprinted with amendments 1914).

—— *The King's Regulations and Orders for the Army*, HMSO, London, 1912 (reprinted with amendments 1914).

—— *Manual of Military Law*, HMSO, London, 1907.

—— *Soldiers Died in the Great War, 1914–1919*, HMSO, London, 1921.

Watson, Captain W. H. L., *Adventures of a Despatch Rider*, William Blackwood & Sons, Edinburgh and London, 1915.

—— *Tales of a Gaspipe Officer*, in Blackwoods Magazine, Leonard Scott Publication, New York, 1915–17.

Westlake, Ray, *British Battalions in France and Belgium 1914*, Leo Cooper, London, 1997.

Cd Roms

The National Archives British Trench Map Atlas: The Western Front 1914–18, The Naval & Military Press, East Sussex, 2008.

Official History of the Great War 1914 – 1918: Military Operations France & Belgium, The Naval & Military Press, East Sussex, 2010.

The Silver War Badge, The Naval & Military Press, East Sussex, 2013

Manuscripts, Diaries, Letters and Other Unpublished Material

National Archives, Kew
Air Ministry
Department of the Master-General of Personnel: Officers' Service Records. AIR76

War Office
First World War and Army of Occupation Diaries. WO95.

Service Medal and Award Rolls Index, First World War (Medal Index Cards – via Ancestry. com). WO372

Service Medal and Award Rolls, First World War. WO329

Officers' Services, First World War, Long Number Papers. WO339

Miscellaneous Unregistered Papers, First World War (prisoner of war interview reports). WO161/100

Soldiers' Documents, First World War 'Burnt Documents' (via Ancestry.com). WO363

Soldiers' Documents from Pension Claims, First World War (via Ancestry.com). WO364

Embarkation returns, at home for abroad – July to September 1917. WO25/3558

Public Records Office of Northern Ireland

Cole, Lord J.H.M., letters, 1914–17. D1702/12/50

Maude, Eustace H., letter to Hugh de Fellenberg Montgomery, Fivemiletown, Co. Tyrone, 18 June 1917. D627/430/67

Sterling, Captain Robert, diary 1919–21. T3240/1

Copeland Trimble, W., letter to Carson, 20 January 1915. D1507/A/11/5

The Ulster Covenant. www.proni.gov.uk

Other

Combe, Lieutenant Samuel Barbour and Waring, Captain Holt, collection comprising letters, photographs and press clippings, from the author's collection.

Geographical Section, General Staff, *Ordnance Survey maps of France and Belgium, 1:100,000.*

Godson, Captain Edwin Alfred, *Private Papers*, including transcription of diary, Imperial War Museum, London, Cat. No. 10995.

McMahon, Francis Joseph, *Round the World on a Bob a Day*, handwritten manuscript, c.1970.

North Irish Horse Order Book, transcription for 1918 provided by Bracken Anderson

Wise, Lieutenant Lancelot, letters to his family, 1914–16, made available by Lance and Peter Wise.

Newspapers and Magazines

The Ballymena Observer
The Belfast Evening Telegraph
The Belfast News-Letter
History Ireland
The Irish Times
The Lurgan Mail
The Times

Internet Sources

Ancestry. www.ancestry.com

Ballymena 1914–1918: carved in stone … but not forgotten. www.freewebs.com/snake43

Bureau of Military History, 1913–21, Statement by witnesses. www.bureauofmilitaryhistory.ie

Commonwealth War Graves Commission. www.cwgc.org

Eddies Extracts. http://freepages.genealogy.rootsweb.ancestry.com/~econnolly/index.html

Firstworldwar.com: A multimedia history of world war one. www.firstworldwar.com

Great War Forum. www.1914-1918.invisionzone.com/forums/

Imperial War Museum. www.iwm.org.uk

Inst in the Great War: The Fallen of RBAI. www.instgreatwar.com/index.htm

International Committee of the Red Cross: Prisoners of the First World War. http://grandeguerre.icrc.org/

Letters from the Front: My Grandfather's Letters 1914–1919. www.johnadams.org.uk/letters/

Library and Archives Canada: Soldiers of the First World War. www.bac-lac.gc.ca/eng/discover/military-heritage/first-world-war

London Gazette. www.london-gazette.co.uk

National Archives. www.nationalarchives.gov.uk/records/our-online-records.htm

National Archives of Ireland: Census 1901/1911. www.census.nationalarchives.ie

North Irish Horse and Steeds of Steel. www.northirishhorse.net

North Irish Horse in the Great War. www.northirishhorse.com.au

Northern Bank – War Memorials/Roll of Honour. www.northernbankwarmemorials.blogspot.com.au

Public Record Office of Northern Ireland. www.proni.gov.uk

The Great War 1914–1918: A Guide to WW1 Battlefields and History of the First World War. www.greatwar.co.uk/

The Long, Long Trail: The British Army in the Great War of 1914–1918. www.1914-1918.net

The South Irish Horse. www.southirishhorse.com

Belfast Presbyterians in the Great War. www.greatwarbelfastpresbyterian.com

Index

Abercrombie, William James, 258, 309
Acheson, Willie, 5, 13, 15, 45, 69
Adair, James, 267, 312
Adair, John Valentine, 76, 86, 87, 315
Adam, James Graham, 142, 319, 322
Adams, John, 17
Adams, William Hanna, 152, 300
Adamson, William, 208, 316
Age of recruits, 55–6, 64, 99
Akerlind, Gustaf, 180, 319
Alexander, John, 111
Allen, James, 55, 69
Allenby, General Edmund, 21, 45, 246
Anderson, Robert, 185
Anderson, Robert Noel, 7, 135, 273
Anderson, William, 188–9, 262, 311
Andrews, Harry Bertram, 139
Andrews, Robert Hutchinson, 18, 82, 94, 297
Annesley, Richard Arthur, 107
Armstrong, Alexander, 175
Armstrong, Henry Tottenham, 319
Armstrong, James Robert, 67
Armstrong, Johnston, 238, 316
Armstrong, Reginald George, 212, 304
Armstrong, Robert, 261, 316
Armstrong, William, 159
Arnold, Clifford, 251
Arras and Vimy Ridge offensive, 144–5
Arthur, William Frederick, 229, 307
Ashcroft, Hugh, 17, 48
Aston, Thomas, 314
Atkinson, Edward, 225, 231–2, 269–70, 273, 315
Auber, Joseph, 129–30
Aulich, Mildred, 29

Austin, Geoffrey, 225, 248–9, 251, 269, 270, 281n
Australian Imperial Force, 128, 160, 229–30, 274
Averell, Robert, 17, 168, 316
Awards and decorations, 9, 44–5, 71–2, 102, 133–4, 145, 155, 168, 175, 179, 192, 208, 211–12, 227–30, 232, 236–40, 243, 246, 258, 260–1, 265, 269–70, 314–22

Bailey, Joseph Smith, 238, 317
Bailey (Balley), Thomas, 101, 137n
Baird, Geoffrey Henry, 142, 252–3
Baring, Maurice, 29
Barns, Thomas, 17, 319
Barr, Cecil Charles, 139–40, 207, 304
Barrett, Samuel, 66
Bates, David Roulston, 134
Baxter, John, 155, 301
Beattie, William, 152, 301
Belgian Army, 45, 71, 215, 245, 256, 261
Bell, Charles, 322
Bell, David, 141
Bell, John, 217, 277, 306
Bell, Victor Nelson, 165, 301
Bennett, Hugh, 13
Beresford, Ernest Philip, 97
Best, Frank James, 258, 310
Biggart, William, 206, 305
Blair, Alexander, 237, 309
Blair, Robert Cooke, 239, 317
Blanden, William Westley, 142, 240, 248
Bolton, Sloan, 251
Bond, David Hunter, 100, 273
Booker, Worship, 16, 72, 94, 240, 250, 269, 275, 315, 319

Boston, John, 90
Bowden, Joseph Arthur, 220, 306
Bower, Stanley, 66
Boyd, Humphrey, 20, 265, 270, 316, 317
Boyd, James, 17
Boyle, Albert Milton, 70, 131, 298
Bracken, William 17, 47
Bradley, Rowland Irvine, 149, 299
Bramston-Newman, Richard, 53, 89, 124, 147
Bray, Harold Edwin, 148, 179
Bremner, Stuart Bruce, 97
Bremner, Thomas, 203, 205
Brennan, Herbert, 252, 311
Brew, John George, 202–204
Brewer, Cecil, 75
Brewer, Frank, 75
British Army:
    British Expeditionary Force, xix–xxi, 2, 15, 18, 19, 24–6, 29–33, 36, 38, 47–8, 82, 122–3, 139, 190, 217, 245–6
    GHQ, xvi, 19–21, 23, 25–6, 28–30, 36, 44–7, 69, 100, 264
    Armies:
        First, 213–14, 245, 250
        Second, 150, 214, 245, 266
        Third, 86, 194, 196, 209, 232, 236, 245–6, 250
        Fourth, 229–30, 232, 247, 250
        Fifth, 150, 152, 192, 194, 197, 209
    Corps:
        I, 21, 24, 37
        II, 21–2, 24, 31, 37, 39, 45, 255–6
        III, 45–6, 122
        IV, 78, 181, 212, 230, 270
        V, 104, 156, 181–2, 186, 189, 193, 209–13, 223, 230, 232, 235, 238–9, 245–53
        VI, 145, 236
        VII, 119–20, 122, 143, 145, 210–11
        VIII, 122
        IX, 149
        X, 119, 121–3, 127–8, 145–6, 148–9
        XI, 214

        XIII, 122, 247
        XIV, 151
        XV, 122, 214
        XVII, 176
        XVIII, 151
        XIX, 145, 149–52
    Infantry Divisions:
        1st, 26
        2nd, 26
        3rd, 21–3, 26, 72, 81, 103
        4th, 20–1, 24, 26, 29–33, 36, 46
        5th, 19, 22, 24, 26–31, 33, 36
        6th, 46
        7th, 45
        9th (Scottish), 255
        14th (Light), 195, 199
        15th (Scottish), 151–2
        16th (Irish), 50, 77, 152–4
        17th (Northern), 186, 230, 232–5, 237–8, 248–50, 252–4
        20th (Light), 202
        21st, 77, 230, 232–5, 238, 245–8, 250–1, 253–5
        24th, 104, 148
        29th, 242, 255, 257
        30th, 144, 201–202, 260
        32nd, 77, 110, 121–3, 125
        33rd, 69, 245–53
        34th, 68, 107–108, 126
        36th (Ulster), 50–2, 89, 104, 121–4, 132, 148, 152–3, 158–60, 162, 167, 170–1, 175–6, 178, 189–92, 194–7, 199–201, 203, 205, 208, 213–14, 218, 220, 228, 244, 255–6, 259, 261–2, 272
        37th, 120
        38th (Welsh), 230, 232–5, 237–9, 246–55
        40th, 181
        46th (North Midland), 117, 120, 122
        48th (South Midland), 128
        49th (West Riding), 104, 110, 121
        51st (Highland), 58, 76–7, 105
        54th (East Anglian), 90

55th (West Lancashire), 100, 151
56th (1st London), 120, 122, 172
59th (2nd North Midland), 117, 181–2, 186
61st (2nd South Midland), 152
63rd (Royal Naval), 182
Infantry Brigades:
  9 Brigade, 103
  14 Brigade, 126
  15 Brigade, 22, 27, 29, 33, 36
  19 Brigade, 249, 250, 253, 254
  50 Brigade, 235, 238–9, 250, 252
  51 Brigade, 245, 250, 254
  52 Brigade, 250
  61 Brigade, 199
  62 Brigade, 245, 251
  64 Brigade, 232, 245, 251
  70 Brigade, 147
  88 Brigade, 176, 243
  97 Brigade, 125
  98 Brigade, 250
  100 Brigade, 247
  107 Brigade, 159, 170, 172–4, 190, 194, 205, 220, 261
  108 Brigade, 153, 159, 170, 172–4, 176–7, 190, 198, 203, 205, 214–18, 220, 229, 240, 242, 244, 256, 258, 261–2, 264, 266
  109 Brigade, 159, 170, 171–2, 176–8, 190, 198, 203, 220, 242, 256, 261–2
  110 Brigade, 233, 251
  113 Brigade, 250, 252, 255
  114 Brigade, 239, 250, 252
  115 Brigade, 252
Infantry Battalions:
  Argyll & Sutherland Highlanders, 86
  Border Regiment, 237
  Cameron Highlanders, 23
  Camerionans (Scottish Rifles), 249, 253
  East Yorkshire Regiment, 250
  Hampshire Regiment, 24
  Irish Guards, 106, 133
  Leinster Regiment, 71, 94
  Lincolnshire Regiment, 225, 230–3, 237–8, 246

London Regiment, 83
Norfolk Regiment, 27
Northumberland Fusiliers, 231
Queens (Royal West Surrey) Regiment, 249
Rifle Brigade, 126, 263
Royal Dublin Fusiliers, 154
Royal Inniskilling Fusiliers:
  1st Battalion, 190, 198–9, 203, 208, 256
  2nd Battalion, 21–3, 190, 196, 203, 240, 259
  8th Battalion, 153
  9th Battalion, 159, 171, 178, 190, 203, 262
  10th Battalion, 123, 137, 148, 159, 171
  11th Battalion, 159, 171, 178
Royal Irish Fusiliers:
  1st Royal Irish Fusiliers, 159, 190, 192, 195, 197, 200, 202–205, 208, 214–16, 219–20, 241–3, 259, 262, 264
  7/8th Royal Irish Fusiliers, 191
  9th Royal Irish Fusiliers (NIH), see North Irish Horse
  9th Royal Irish Fusiliers (Service), 153, 155, 157, 159
Royal Irish Regiment:
  1st Battalion, 263
  5th Battalion, 271, 272
  7th Battalion (SIH), 157, 260, 265
Royal Irish Rifles, 71, 134–5, 142, 205
  1st Battalion, 48, 82, 136, 140, 143–4, 152–6, 190, 207, 260, 266
  2nd Battalion, 34, 174, 178, 190–1, 207, 244
  7th Battalion, 156
  8/9th Battalion, 159
  10th Battalion, 159, 172
  11th Battalion, 159
  12th Battalion, 159, 162, 165, 172–3, 190, 194, 202, 214, 216, 219–20, 228, 242, 256–8, 262, 266
  13th Battalion, 156, 159

14th Battalion, 159
15th Battalion, 159, 172, 188, 190,
    241, 262
Royal Scots Fusiliers, 140, 246
Royal Sussex Regiment, 264
Royal Welsh Fusiliers, 234, 248
Suffolk Regiment, 28
Wiltshire Regiment, 263
Army Service Corps, 15, 19, 25–6, 38,
    94, 142, 187, 225
Cavalry Corps, 45
Cavalry Divisions, 21, 45–6, 103, 108,
    187
Cavalry Brigades, 26, 145
Cavalry Regiments:
    3rd Dragoon Guards, 133, 200
    4th Dragoon Guards, 20, 271
    6th Dragoon Guards, 233
    1st Dragoons, 200
    6th (Inniskilling) Dragoons, 132, 272
        Service Squadron, 51–2, 54, 57, 67,
        83, 94, 119, 121–2, 124–5, 128–9,
        132, 148, 165, 174, 180, 219, 242,
        244
    3rd Hussars, 158
    4th Hussars, 136
    10th Hussars, 200
    15th Hussars, 72–3
    19th Hussars, 262
    5th Lancers, 33
    9th Lancers, 20, 229–30
    21st Lancers, 271
    Reserve Cavalry, 129, 135, 141, 225
Entrenching battalions, 190, 197,
    207–208, 213
Indian Army, 132, 163
    3rd Lancers (Skinner's Horse), 104,
    107
Labour Corps, 158, 224, 283
Machine Gun Corps, 141–2, 147, 180,
    188, 225, 263
Military Police, 81, 90, 134, 141, 207, 224
Royal Artillery, 22, 26, 35, 64, 94, 134,
    149, 156, 223–4, 262, 283

Royal Engineers, 19, 26, 30, 43, 75, 84,
    141, 167, 249, 261
Royal Flying Corps, 29, 132, 135, 149,
    156
Tank Corps, 147, 151, 163, 169–70,
    173–4, 180, 229–30, 236
Trench Mortar Battery, 202, 258, 267
Yeomanry and other non-regular units:
    King Edward's Horse, 10n, 68, 89
    London Scottish, xvi
    North of Ireland Imperial Yeomanry,
    1–3, 18
    North Irish Horse see entry under 'N'
    Northamptonshire Yeomanry, 145
    Northumberland Hussars, 160
    Nottinghamshire Yeomanry, 263
    Oxfordshire Hussars, xvi
    South of Ireland Imperial Yeomanry,
    1–2
    South Irish Horse, xvi, 2–3, 15, 18,
    76–7, 92–3, 157, 160, 260, 265
    Staffordshire Yeomanry, 263
    Yorkshire Hussars, 103
Brockwell, Samuel Gardner, 230, 273
Brooks, Robert William, 141
Brown, David, 140
Brown, George Bramato, 224
Brown, William, 124, 179, 207, 241, 307
Brown, William, 239, 317
Brownlee, Herbert, 206
Brunsdon, Sydney, 110
Bryson, Joseph, 259
Bryson, Thomas, 231, 259, 283, 308
Buchanan, Edmond, 47, 297
Buchanan, James, 47
Buchanan, William, 273
Burnside, James, 194–5

Callanan, Matthew, 25–6, 59n, 297
Cambrai, Battle of, 169–79, 181–2
Campbell, John, 244
Canadian Expeditionary Force, 74, 77, 225,
    229
Carmichael, Robert James, 270, 317

Carson, Edward, 49, 50–2, 115

Cartmill, Thomas, 206, 304

Cassidy, Victor Eccleston, 211

Casualties, 19, 31, 41, 47, 63, 70, 73–4, 82, 123, 131, 143–5, 149, 153, 156, 167, 174–5, 179, 205–208, 215–16, 219–20, 234, 244, 251–2, 258, 297–313

Cathcart, John, 185

Cavalry, utility of, 119, 136, 157, 181

Chamberlayne, Athelstan, 124

Chambers, David, 271

Chambers, Thomas, 168, 317

Chesnut, Alexander, 281n

Clancey, John, 270, 317

Clark, Charles Warwick, 188

Clarke, Alan George, 179, 317

Clarke, Jeremiah, 175

Clarke, John St Claire, 100, 185

Clarke, William, 185

Cleaver, Albert Henry, 234

Cleland, William, 87

Clements, James (Chuckie), 200

Close, Joseph, 270, 317

Close, Robert, 156

Coburn, James, 47–8, 69

Coey, James Arthur, 42, 94, 319

Coffin, Clifford, 227

Cole, John Henry Michael, Lord, 11, 13, 15, 17, 20–4, 26, 29–33, 36–7, 45, 69–70, 76, 79–81, 90–1, 100–103, 110, 113, 115–16, 119, 123, 142–3, 186, 314, 319, 322

Colquhoun, Francis James, 17, 38, 44–5, 114, 322

Coltart, William, 139, 273

Combe, Samuel Barbour, xvi, 6, 8–9, 16, 26–7, 30–2, 36, 41–4, 297

Concerts, 58, 69, 71, 88, 93, 97, 162, 264, 270

Connar, Henry Percy, 135

Connell, John, 136, 154, 300

Connolly, David, 239, 317

Connor, Alfred, 317

Conscription, 112–13, 139, 213

Cooke, Frederick St G., 219–20, 306

Cooke, William, 124

Copeland, William, 114

Cordwell, Frederick Thomas, 157, 301

Cornwell, Garnett Wesley, 240

Corry, Robert, 90

Cosgrove, Samuel, 74–5

Cotter, Maurice Edward, 53

Coulter, Charles William, 135, 315

Coulter, Joseph, 242, 258, 309, 317

Courts Martial, see Discipline

Crabbe, Arthur Bingham, 119

Craig, Henry Ernest, 91

Craig, George, 168

Craig, James, 55–6

Craig, John Frederick, 89, 142

Craig, William, 71

Cramp, Richard, 156

Cramsie, James Randal, 94

Crawford, Arthur Sidney, 206–207, 304

Crawford, John, 53–4, 159

Crawford, Samuel, 234

Crosbie, Thomas Edward, 168, 205, 217

Crozier, Frank, 15–16, 246

Cully, John, 253, 312

Cunningham, Fred, 69

Curragh, The, 1–2, 4, 7, 9, 13, 129, 135–6, 270

Dallas, Arthur Ernest, 142

Darling, Norman ffolliott, 18, 42–3, 94, 107

Darragh, John McClelland, 131–2, 298

Darragh, Matthew, 132

Davey, Allan, 220, 306

Davidson, Albert, 205

Davidson, John, 141

Davin, Fred, 319

Dean, Herbert Shelton, 129–30, 163, 192, 205, 208, 216, 315

Deery, Joseph, 260, 310

Dennistoun, James Robert, 89, 131–3, 277, 298

Denny, James, 262, 311

Desertion, 15, 140–1, 159

Despard, Charles Beauclerk, 164, 175, 192, 205, 208, 219, 305, 314–15, 319
Devine, Samuel, 303
Dickinson, Thomas, 165, 301
Dickson, James, 17
Discipline, 4–5, 15, 39, 47–8, 55, 57, 66–7, 69, 71, 93, 101, 109, 110–11, 129, 141, 143, 269
Doak, Samuel, 110–11, 224
Donaldson, John, 54
Donnelly, William John, 305
Dorman, Edward Mungo, 3–5
Dougall, Robert, 270, 319
Douglas, John Henry, 75
Dowling, James, 18, 134
Downes, Leonard, 125
Downey, Robert James, 142, 247, 249, 281n, 319
Dundas, William Henry, 259, 309
Dundee, Albert, 57
Dundee, Alexander, 57, 156, 315
Dundee, Robert, 57
Dunn, John, 165, 302
Durneen, John James, 212, 304

Earnshaw, Frederick, 64
Easter Rebellion, 115–17
Edmenson, Walter Alexander, 94, 319
Elder, Charles, 254, 277, 312
Elliot, Herbert Gavin, 97, 225, 270, 273, 319
Elliott, James, 19, 126, 200, 273
Elliott, Richard, 186, 303
Elliott, William Thomas, 220, 306
Ellison, Private, 35
Emerson, Henry, 227
Erskine, Alexander, 258, 310
Espey, Wingfield, 28
Evans, John, 251, 311
Evans, Robert, 124, 185–6, 312
Ewart, George, 17, 48

Farley, George Herbert, 153–4, 300
Farnham, Arthur Kenlis Maxwell, Lord, 6, 8–9, 10n, 58, 89, 196, 314, 319

Ferguson, Frederick, 321
Ferris, George, 273
Filgate, Richard Alexander, see Henry
Finlay, Ian Archibald, 107–108, 224–5, 230, 234
Finlay, William James, 120–1, 298
Flanagan, Hugh, 174, 302
Forbes, John, 124, 206, 304
Ford, John, 167, 169, 302
Forde, Theophilus James, 188
Freeland, Wesley, 180
French Army, 19, 25, 29, 31, 40, 45, 86, 122, 144–5, 150, 200–201, 203, 229
French, Sir John, xvi, 18–19, 21, 25–6, 29, 45, 47, 69, 272
French, John Allen, 188
Fulton, James Norman, 175

Galbraith, George, 175, 303
Gallipoli, 80, 90, 142
Galway, Albert Brice, 139, 266
Garnett, Albert, 240
Gas, 73, 82, 91, 110, 156, 209–10, 230–1, 234, 239, 243, 244, 247, 251–2, 270
George V, His Majesty King, 48, 80, 266
Gibson, Andrew, 217–18
Gibson, John Nixon, 144, 299
Gibson, Samuel, 319
Gibson, William, 156
Gill, George, 233, 308
Gill, Father Henry, 191
Gillespie, John, 17
Gillespie, Townley Sherwood, 298
Gilligan, John Vanner, 16, 46, 60n
Gilliland, Ernest, 20
Gleichen, Br. Gen. Edward, Count, 22, 27, 33, 36
Glendining, William, 270, 317
Glyn, John Paul, 97
Godson, Edwin Alfred, 136, 157, 161, 163, 168, 170, 173–4, 176–7
Goggin, James, 18
Gordon, Samuel, 120–1, 212
Gordon, William, 207
Gore–Browne, Brevet Major Eric, 83

Goring, Walter, 124, 147, 319
Gorrie, Thomas Robert, 99
Gosse, Philip, 146–7
Gourley, Joseph, 125
Govan, William, 207, 303
Gracey, James, 243, 316
Graham, Donald, 135, 319
Graham, Robert, 140
Graham, William Thomas, 74, 297
Grant, John, 8, 16, 31, 46, 81–2, 163, 234, 269, 270, 281n, 320
Green, Raymond, 260, 273, 315
Greer, James Kenneth, 13, 16, 42–3, 131, 133–4, 298, 315, 320
Grigg, Gilbert Hutton, 107–108, 151, 223–4, 273
Grigg, John Hutton, 107–108, 151, 223–4, 273

Haggan, Matthew, 263, 310
Haig, Field Marshall Sir Douglas, 24, 157, 190
Hale, Neason Henry, 155, 300
Hall, Edward, 224
Hall, Thomas, 144, 299
Hall, William, 47
Hamill, Vincent Joseph, 100
Hamilton, Bryant Charles, 273
Hamilton–Russell, Arthur, 76, 83, 86–7, 186, 224, 240, 320
Hampson, Travis, 19, 25
Hancock, Bernard, 129
Hanna, Robert, 208, 306
Harcourt, William Lyttle, 315
Harding, Frank, 270, 281n, 317
Harper, George, 73, 297
Harpur, Thompson, 206–207, 307
Harrison, Stuart, 56
Harvey, Nathaniel, 105
Hassard, Robert, 321
Hawthorne, Thomas Charles, 168, 271
Heathwood, Robert, 168–9, 302
Heenan, John, 273, 283
Henderson, John, 17, 47, 114–15
Henderson, Thomas McCready, 309

Henehan, Michael, 198
Henry, Albert William, 148, 192, 202–205
Henry, George Adams, 179, 192, 304, 317
Henry, Richard Alexander, 104, 130, 163–4, 183n
Herdman, Emerson Crawford, 8, 15, 17, 20, 26, 30, 37, 39–40, 106, 119
Herron, Robert, 81
Hesketh, Thomas Humphrey, 129–30, 271, 313
Hickman, Br. Gen. Thomas Edgecumbe, 52, 112
Hicks, George, 17, 38
Hill, Robert Henry, 255, 312
Hill-Lowe, Arthur Noel, 89, 110
Hillocks, William, 255, 312
Hindenburg Line, 139, 144, 161, 169–73, 177–8, 238, 245–8, 278
Hodson, Donald O'Neill, 182, 186, 234, 239–40, 249, 269, 315
Holland, Philip, 18
Holmes, William, 273
Home Rule, 7–9, 50, 116
Hornidge, Mervyn Sinclair, 142
Hotchkiss machine-gun, 105, 110, 130, 149, 182, 186, 200
Houston, Charles Edward, 259, 309
Howe, Hugh, 149
Huggins, Alfred Henry, 233, 308
Hughes, Thomas William Gillilan, 7, 15, 22–3, 186, 278, 320
Hull, Robert John, 111, 207, 260, 310
Hulse, Adrian, 163, 322
Humphries, Joseph, 56, 159
Hunter, Johnston Shaw, 94, 131–2, 298
Hunter, Samuel Simpson, 198
Hunter, William Moorhead, 142, 252
Hutchinson, William Henry, 129–30, 163, 168–9

Irish Volunteers, 50
Irvine, Harold, 311
Irwin, Richard, 35–6, 49, 167–9, 302
Irwin, Robert, 305
Irwin, William, 70, 297

Irwin, William, 156
Irwin, William Garnett, 308

Jackson, William, 71
Jamison, Thomas, 239, 317
Jeffrey, William James, 141
Jennings, Francis, 317
Jocelyn, Visc. Robert, 6, 8–10, 15, 25, 47, 64
Joffre, Gen. Joseph, 25, 31
Johnston, Alexander, 155, 300, 318
Johnston, Benjamin, 273
Johnston, David, 251
Johnston, George, 277, 310
Johnston, James Frazer, 206, 304
Johnston, John, 303
Johnston, John, 267, 312
Johnston, Thomas, 207, 304
Johnston, Thomas Henry, 188
Johnston, William James, 270, 318
Jones, William, 142
Joyce, Thomas Victor, 94

Kearney, Thomas, 303
Kearon, Hubert, 238, 318
Keays, William, 141
Kellock, Harold Plumer, 107–108, 223–4, 262, 310
Kellock, Richard Berry, 107–108, 223–4, 262
Kelly, Adam Gordon, 233, 308
Kelly, James, 244, 309
Kelly, Lt. Col. Philip Edward, 215
Kelly, William Alexander, 155
Kennedy, Alexander, 28, 269
Kennedy, Robert John, 175, 244
Ker, David Alfred William, 15, 17, 320
Kernohan, David, 188
Kerr, David, 155
Kerr, John, 48
Kerr, John Nesbitt, 273
Kerr, Robert William, 267, 312
Kidd, Frank, 49
Killough, George, 263, 311
Kilpatrick, William, 39
King, James Harvey, 212, 320

King, John Donaldson, 162, 164, 167, 169, 302
King-King, Eustace, 16, 60n, 73, 78–9
Kinnear, Robert, 47, 69, 111
Kirkbride, Clarence Donovan, 129–30
Kirkpatrick, James Cunningham, 74, 76, 86, 87, 105, 224, 230, 250, 270, 320
Knox, Armour John, 155, 300
Knox, John, 142, 241, 262, 311, 314–15
Knox, Richard, 89
Kyle, Private, 22

Larter, Charles Brunskill, 163
Laughlin, James, 211, 212, 318
Laurie, Lt. Col. George Brenton, 48–9
Le Cateau, Battle of, 21–2
Leader, Thomas Henry, 89, 104, 160
Leckey, William, 307
Lee, Mark, 206–207, 304
Leinster, William George, 220, 306
Lennon, Joseph, 218
Lewis gun, 133, 165, 189, 200, 202, 204, 212, 216, 219, 223, 230–2, 240, 245, 251–2, 261, 271
Linden, Samuel McCullough, 99, 300
Lindsay, Andrew, 17
Lindsay, Fred, 32, 35, 73
Lindsay, William, 220, 306
Linton, Wallace, 64
Livingstone, Frederick, 233, 308
Livingstone, William, 17, 47
Lockhart, John, 229, 316, 322
Lockhart, William, 9, 227–8
Logan, Simon, 258, 261, 314, 315
Loos, Battle of, 82
Lorimer, John, 271
Lowry, Ezekiel, 185
Lucy, John, 34–5, 177–8
Lynn, James, 64, 158–9
Lyons, Robert Victor, 207, 304
Lyons, Thomas, 206, 305

McArow, James, 17, 23, 44, 103, 114, 298, 322
McAteer, James, 234, 269

McAuley, William John, 215, 305
McCalmont, William, 270, 320
McCarley, William, 227, 318
McCartan, Dr Patrick, 116–17
McCartney, Walter James, 14, 58n
McCausland, David, 135, 173, 302
McClelland, Alfred, 156, 301
McClelland, Thomas Alexander, 208, 318
McClelland, Wesley, 230, 308
McConnell, Frederick, 313
McConnell, Robert, 220, 306
McCormick, Fred, 93
McCormick, Thomas John, 212, 304
McCormick, William, 312
McCready, Robert, 263, 307
McCullagh, Henry, 69
McCullough, Robert James, 135, 156, 301
McDaniel, Charles Henry, 263, 310
MacDonald, Frank, 93
McFarland, Francis John, 99, 228–9, 307,
    315
McFarland, William, 100
McFerran, William James, 18, 28, 48, 71
McGahey, William, 220, 306
McGivern, George, 87
McGookin, Arthur, 273
McGovern, Samuel, 183
McGuigan, Jack, 53–4, 67, 93, 111, 121,
    179
McIlroy, William, 125
McIlwaine, Richard, 43, 71–2, 320
McKeown, Edward, 316, 318
McKernon, Edward, 73
McKillop, Thomas, 309
Mackinson, Henry, 168
McKinstry, John, 18, 134, 315
McLanahan, William, xvi, 32, 59n
MacLean, Alister, 142
MacLean, James A., 94, 110, 134, 156, 301,
    315
McMahon, Arthur, 15
McMahon, Francis, 53–5, 65, 67, 89,
    109–10, 121–2, 124–5, 160, 179, 198,
    200–201, 207, 274

McManus, David, 57
McManus, Hubert, 57
McManus, Randal Edmund, 57, 220, 306
McMurray, William, 65, 270, 318
McNabb, Samuel Charles, 211
McNeill, Leslie Ernest, 13, 16, 42, 133,
    271, 313
MacReady, Robert Arthur, 94, 315
McReynolds, Thomas Alexander, 301
McSparron, John, 144, 299
McStay, William, 99–100, 273
McSweeney, Joseph, 141
McVea, John, 233, 308
McVeigh, Michael, 262, 311
McWilliams, Christopher, 175, 302
Magill, Charles, 273, 275
Magill, James, 124, 179, 227, 307
Maguire, William, 273–4
Maloney, Thomas, 136
Mark, George, 207, 244, 309
Martin, Alexander, 171, 302
Martin, John, 250
Martin, William, 15
Massereene & Ferrard, A.W.J.C.
    Skeffington, Visc., 6, 8, 10n, 11, 13, 14,
    16–17, 24, 32–3, 36, 41, 44, 48–9, 71, 73,
    86, 113, 278, 320
Matchett, David, 322
Matchett, Samuel, 211
Matthews, Ernest George, 93–4, 124–5
Maude, Eustace Addison, 9, 55, 89, 119
Maude, Eustace Anthony, 9, 142, 180, 271,
    313
Mells, Frank, 281n
Menice, Edward, 18, 39, 129, 147
Mercer, Harry, 65
Mercier, William, 188
Meredith, Edward Myles, 64, 135, 305
Messines, Battle of, 147–8
Metcalfe, Thomas Henry, 321
Miller, David Joseph, 216, 305
Miller, Samuel, 271
Mills, Thomas Robert, 188
Mills, William, 267, 312

Miskimmin, Herbert, 156
Mitchell, Alexander, 155
Mitchell, John Samuel, 180
Moir, Stewart Harris, 28, 47
Moisley, William, 18, 80
Mons, Battle of, 19–20
Montgomery, Hugh de Fellenberg, 142, 225
Montgomery, Hugh Edmund, 224–5, 230, 234, 249, 269, 315
Montgomery, James, 271, 313
Montgomery, Robert George, 308
Montgomery, Samuel William, 207, 260
Montgomery, Thomas, 234
Montgomery, Walter Ashley, 68, 320
Moon, John, 206, 305
Mooney, James, 56, 185
Moore, Archibald, 208, 304
Moore, Joseph, 39
Moore, Richard, 149, 299
Moore, William, 17, 225
Moore, William, xvi, 38–9, 297
Moore, William Henry, 66
Morrison, Cyril (Aubrey), 154, 300
Morrison, Francis James, 307
Morrison, George, 206, 306
Morrison, John, 168, 318
Morrow, William, 214, 305
Mortimer, Henry, 155, 300
Morton, William, 20, 22, 24–5, 49
Moss, Andrew, 87
Moss, Archibald James, 240
Mountford, John, 48
Murland, Howard, 9, 218
Murland, Warren, 7, 9, 76, 105, 143, 224, 320
Murphy, John Joseph, 168, 228
Murphy, Thomas Alexander, 168
Murphy, William McKee, 149, 298
Murray, George Turkington, 303

Nationalists/ Nationalism, 50, 52, 115–16
Nelson, William, 271
Nesbitt, George, 17, 208, 318
Nesbitt, Robert William, 271, 313
Newell, Harry, 24, 36, 71, 82–3

Nicholl, John, 125, 227, 307
Nixon, Amelia (formerly Roberts), 283
Nixon, Harold Percival, 263, 311
Nixon, William, 144, 299
Norman, Charles, 149, 298
North Irish Horse:
  formation of, 1–2
  headquarters in Ireland, 2, 11, 13, 52–3, 106
  reorganisation to corps cavalry, 119–20
  transfer of men to other units, 90, 134, 135–7, 141, 180, 187–8, 224, 270, 271
  uniform, 3
  A Squadron, 11–15, 17–26, 29–33, 35–40, 44–9, 58, 69–71, 81, 90–1, 100–103, 111–14, 119–20, 145, 149, 186–7, 211–12, 224, 230–5, 238, 240, 245–7, 249–55, 283
  B Squadron (later named F), 117, 119
  C Squadron, 11–12, 14–18, 24, 26–36, 38–44, 46–9, 53, 58, 70–3, 81–3, 91–2, 103–104, 113, 119, 121–2, 124, 126, 128–9, 134, 136, 159, 163, 192, 208, 240, 259, 271
  D Squadron, 58, 73, 74–9, 83–8, 92–3, 104–105, 110–11, 113, 115, 119–20, 135, 142, 153–4, 180, 186–7, 212, 224, 230–5, 237–40, 245–55
  E Squadron, 68–9, 107–108, 111, 119–20, 135, 142, 187, 188, 211, 216, 224–5, 228, 230–5, 237–9, 245–55
  F Squadron (later named B), 69, 88–90, 93, 108–10, 117, 119, 121–2, 124, 126, 128–30, 132, 142, 148, 159, 174, 196, 200
  G Squadron, 119
  H Squadron, 119
  1st Regiment, 119–24, 143, 144–5, 149, 150–2, 156–7, 158, 180–2, 186–9
  2nd Regiment 119, 121–31, 146–9, 157–65, 191–2, 271
  9th (NIH) Battalion, Royal Irish Fusiliers, 159, 161, 164, 185, 189–92, 193, 223, 225, 226–9, 240–1, 264, 266, 270–2

in Battle of Cambrai, 170–9
in retreat from St Quentin, 195–208
in German Ypres offensive, 213–20
in Advance to Victory, 241–4, 255–62
Cyclist Regiment, 186–9, 223–6, 265–6, 269–70
in German Spring offensive, 209–13
in Advance to Victory, 229–40, 245–55
Noyce, Arthur Penrhyn, 97, 188
Nugent, Arthur Charles, 58, 320
Nugent, Maj. Gen. Oliver, 167, 168, 171–4, 178, 181, 189, 194, 201, 213

Occupation of recruits, 17–18, 56–7, 65, 69, 89, 99
O'Donoghue, William Bell, 155
Officers commissioned from the ranks, 93–4, 134–5, 141–2, 188–9, 225–6
O'Hara, Robert, 144, 299
O'Neill, James, 225, 231, 234
O'Rourke, Thomas, 139
Orr, Henry, 175, 302
O'Sullivan, Private, 109–110

Park, Daniel, 185
Park, Robert, 220, 306
Parmenter, W.R., 168
Patterson, James, 111
Patterson, Robert, 66
Paul, Joshua, 242, 318
Pepper, Andrew, 241, 307
Perkins, Charles James, 163, 192, 197–8
Petty, William, 175, 302
Phayre, William Henry, 320
Phillips, Arthur Edward, 240, 252, 269, 314, 320
Pierce, Andrew, 140
Pinkerton, Samuel, 244, 309
Pittaway, John Edward, 68, 320
Plum, George Talbot, 234, 250
Pollock, John, 202
Prenter, Dalton, 197
Price, Samuel, 175, 303
Punishment, see Discipline

Quinn, Sergeant, 125

Rainey, James Edward, 211
Rainey, Samuel, 248, 270, 318, 321
Ramsey, James, 126
Rea, John, 188
Reavie, Wilfred Laurence, 154, 300
Recruiting, 3–4, 13, 49–55, 58, 63–4, 97, 99, 139, 185, 296
Redmond, John Edward, 51, 116
Reid, George Christopher, 165, 302
Reid, Jack, 251
Reid, Percy, 207, 240, 271–2, 313
Reid, Thomas Frederick, 188
Reid, William James, 260, 310
Reinforcements, 58, 67–8, 88, 97, 124, 129, 131, 158, 186–7, 213, 226, 245, 266
Religion, 7, 17, 53–4, 57, 64, 67, 99, 112–13, 191, 226, 244
Reynolds, William, 185
Richardson, Gordon, 17, 112
Richmond, Robert, 262, 311
Riddell, John Edward, 143, 175, 229, 307
Ritchie, David William, 70, 297
Roberts, John Martin, 231, 283, 308
Robinson, Hiram, 20, 49, 224
Robinson, Johnston, 159
Robinson, Samuel, 300
Robinson, William John, 155, 301, 316
Rodgers, James, 58n
Roe, Hubert, 175, 208, 305, 316
Ronaldson, Victor, 64, 156
Rooney, William, 103, 276
Ross, Edward, 141
Ross, Harrison, 135
Ross, Robert, 231, 308
Ross, Ronald Deane, 8, 15, 17, 35, 82, 278, 280, 316, 322
Roulston, William, 73
Royal Irish Constabulary, 8, 116, 273
Russell, Charles, 140, 304
Russell, Herbie, 132
Russell, Robert Campbell, 94, 263, 308

Sands, John, 39
Saunderson, Samuel Treherne, 306
Savage, Tom, 17, 262–3, 310
Scammell, Francis William, 54
Scanlon, Frederick, 64, 174, 302
Scott, Abraham, 270, 321
Scott, Henry St G., xvi, 38–9, 60n, 297
Scott, John, 185
Scott, John, 262, 310
Scott, John Eric, 203–204
Scott, William, 212, 318
Seawright, Thomas, 17
Service, David, 17
Sewell, William, 72, 321
Seymour, Thomas, 125
Shannon, George Moorhead, 124, 262, 311
Shaw, Joseph, 185
Sheridan, Patrick, 179, 267, 313
Sherston, Thomas Peter, 88
Shields, William, 94, 156, 301
Shiels, Samuel, 179, 263, 310
Short, Herbert, 186, 234
Short, Owen, 274–5
Sinton, Edwin, 93–4, 308, 316
Sittlington, Thomas, 197, 207, 303
Skillen, Frederick Rutherford, 93, 321
Slatter, Thomas, 203–204
Sleator, James, 174, 302
Smart, Richard Reginald, 130, 316, 321
Smith, Andrew, 22
Smith, John, 156, 301
Smith–Dorrien, Lt. Gen. Horace, 21, 23,
    31, 45–6
Smyth, John, 175, 303
Smyth, William Bates, 97
Smyth, William Stewart, 65
Somme, Battle of the, 122–8
Speers, Samuel William, 229, 307
Spence, Albert, 141, 266, 269
Sport/sportsmen, 6, 18, 65, 70, 74, 79,
    85–6, 87–8, 97, 99–100, 105–106, 130,
    139, 162, 266, 270, 273
Spring Offensive of 1918, 193–220
Sproule, Timothy, 39
Stack, Walter Auchinleck, 278

Stafford, Joseph, 281n
Sterling, Robert, 17, 33–4, 36, 46, 48, 71,
    92, 265
Stevenson, Ernest Augustus, 154, 300
Stevenson, Samuel Brown, 188
Stevenson, Thomas, 155, 300
Stevenson, William, 239, 321
Stevenson, William, 317
Stewart, Hamilton, 99
Stewart, James Noel, 316
Stewart, Robert Cromes, 270, 318
Stewart–Richardson, Neil Graham, 8, 16,
    33, 35, 40–2, 47, 58n, 119, 246, 314, 321
Stronge, George William, 227, 307
Stuart, Leslie Ion, 97, 173, 188, 273
Stuart, William Bruce, 173
Stuart, William Patrick, 206, 305

Taggart, James, 241
Talbot, James, 148, 299
Tate, Frank, 197, 207, 303
Tease, John, 136
Thomson, William, 179, 303
Thompson, Brownlow, 267, 313
Thompson, George, 139, 266
Timbey, William Fairbairn, 244, 309
Tomney, James, 116
Torrance, Richard, 224
Traill, Alexander Frederick, 94, 134, 316
Training, 4–7, 65, 67–8, 129
Trench raids, 165–9, 228–9, 240–1
Trimble, Charles, 5–6, 14, 56, 61n, 75, 117,
    322
Trimble, William Copeland, 7, 51–2, 61n,
    129
Trotter, Sampson, 273
Trotter, Thomas Jonas, 155
Tughan, Robert, 208, 318
Turkington, William James, 175, 303
Turner, Clement, 150–1, 299
Turner, Stewart, 150–1, 299

Uhlans, 27–30, 32–7, 39
Ulster Volunteer Force, 7–9, 13, 14, 47,
    50–1, 54, 115, 121, 134, 191

Under age recruits, 47, 56–7, 66, 100, 140–1, 237

Unionists/ Unionism, 7–9, 50–1, 112–13, 282–3

Uprichard, Forster Green, 6–7, 103, 104, 128, 163

Vesey, George, 89, 164, 179, 192, 200, 304, 316

Waldren, Thomas Henry, 316

Wallace, Donald (Dan), 17, 45, 60n

Wallace, William John, 262, 311

Waller, William, 229–30, 308

Ward, John Percy, 64, 321

Waring, Holt, 6, 8–9, 16, 73, 76–7, 91–2, 103, 124, 129, 216–18, 277, 282–3, 305, 321

Waring, Ruric, 16, 50, 58n

Waring, Margaret, 217, 282–3

Warke, William, 57–8, 143, 179

Wasson, Samuel, 227, 318

Watson, Frederick, 27, 32, 38

Watson, Robert, 18, 35

Watt, Alexander, 124, 298

Watt, George, 124

Watt, William, 318

Webb, Richard Randall, 142, 318

Weiner, Bernard, 57

West, Richard Annesley, 13–14, 16, 27–8, 34, 39, 40–1, 44, 70, 73, 235–7, 309, 314, 316, 321

Whalen, Frederick Joseph, 129–30, 163

Wherry, James Malcolm, 322

White, James, 33

White, William, 33

Whiteside, John, 9, 17

Whiteside, Thomas, 263

Whitla, Valentine George, 124, 147, 163, 314, 321

Wilkinson, Hugh, 89

Williamson, Robert Alexander, 244

Williamson, Thomas, 126

Wilson, David, 224

Wilson, Ernest, 230, 318

Wilson, James, 143, 234

Wilson, Robert, 186, 234

Wilton, Thomas, 90

Wise, Lancelot Charles, 68, 74, 75–8, 83–8, 92–3, 104–107, 299

Woodside, Charles, 252, 312

Wray, James, 17, 39

Wright, John, 18, 71, 270, 319, 321

Wright, Thomas, 123, 128, 298

Wylie, Robert Alexander, 17, 145, 299, 322

Wylie, Samuel, 17, 322

Yates, Robert Livsey, 8, 271, 313

Young, James Bailey, 142, 258, 316

Young, John, 141

Ypres, battles, 46–7, 73–4, 150–7